THE SCIENTIFIC EVALUATION OF FREUD'S THEORIES AND THERAPY

THE SCIENTIFIC EVALUATION OF FREUD'S THEORIES AND THERAPY

A BOOK OF READINGS

EDITED BY
SEYMOUR FISHER
AND
ROGER P. GREENBERG

Basic Books, Inc., Publishers   New York

Library of Congress Cataloging in Publication Data
Main entry under title:

The Scientific evaluation of Freud's theories and
    therapy.

    Includes bibliographies and index.
    1.   Freud, Sigmund, 1856–1939—Addresses, essays,
lectures.   2.   Psychoanalysis—Addresses, essays,
lectures.   I.   Fisher, Seymour.   II.   Greenberg,
Roger P.
BF173.F85S37   150'.19'52   77–90537
ISBN: 0–465–07388–3

To our wives

Rhoda and Vicki

and our children

Eve, Jerid, and Michael

CONTENTS

PART II
ORAL CHARACTER

PART III
ANAL CHARACTER

PART IV

THE OEDIPAL THEORIES

PART V

ORIGINS OF HOMOSEXUALITY

PART VI

PARANOID DELUSION FORMATION

PART VII

PSYCHOANALYTIC PSYCHOTHERAPY

PREFACE

The present collection of papers is intended as a companion volume to our book, *The Scientific Credibility of Freud's Theories and Therapy* (Basic Books, 1977), which presents a detailed analysis of the world scientific literature bearing on Freud's most important ideas.

We have brought together the material in this book to pursue our conviction that the time is ripe for testing the scientific validity of Sigmund Freud's theories and system of psychotherapy as a whole. Although Freud was himself a sensitive observer and was often dedicated to tracing the implications of information collected from his patients, he was resistive to checking the validity of his ideas by means of scientific procedures. To some degree this resistance was aroused by the unfriendly and often unfair criticisms he encountered as he published his views. He seems to have evolved the conviction that the only reasonable way to evaluate psychoanalytic propositions is within the context of psychoanalytic therapy. He felt that only in the course of the special transactions between psychoanalyst and patient could one obtain the complex information about unconscious processes which was pertinent to psychoanalytic propositions.

One of the prime arguments offered by psychoanalysts to oppose scientific evaluation of their theories and operations is that the phenomena involved are too complex to be viewed in an experimental framework. They point out that Freud's theories often implicate numerous causation factors for each specific kind of behavior. They underscore the concept of "overdetermination" which states that a particular symptom, for example, is generated by multiple, interlocking variables. How, they ask, can such complexly patterned events be investigated with a scientific methodology that specializes in studying the effects of changing one variable at a time upon another? There is a certain force to this argument, but it fails insofar as it implies that the phenomena dealt with by Freud are basically more complex than those confronting investigators in many other areas of psychology. Confusing diversity and contradiction threaten to overload every researcher. No one has a monopoly on difficult problems. Take any sector of psychology outside the usual bounds of psychoanalysis and you will find as much complexity as reigns in the most densely packed pages of Freud's monographs. A good example is the concept of intelligence, which has held the attention of psychologists for many decades. As information has accumulated in this area, it has become obvious that what is called intelligence is composed of many factors, affected by both genetic and environmental variables, strongly tied to motivation, perhaps differentially patterned as a function of sex, influenced by psychopathology and central nervous system damage, and likely to fluctuate as a function of how it is measured. One should add that its measurement alone has involved the development of a vast new psychometric technology. After years of work, many problems concerning the nature of intelligence still remain unanswered. But on the other hand we have learned, step-by-step from extensive research, a great deal more concerning this matter than we knew at the beginning. If early investigators in this area had perceived the extraordinarily complicated problems they would eventually encounter, they might have convinced themselves that the whole area was too tough to tackle. Analogously, it has been tempting to accede to the idea that psychoanalytic issues are beyond the reach of systematic exploration.

One must acknowledge that attempts to test theories empirically are often disappointing in their crudity. It is difficult for one or even a cluster of studies to capture the full richness of a complicated theory in experiments that necessarily schematize reality for purposes of laboratory control. The neurophysiologist who develops an elaborate theory about how the nervous system functions cannot but be disappointed at the oversimplified ways in which experimentalists convert his ideas into localized electrode placements on the cortex. Similarly, the sociological theorist who constructs an elaborate model of how multiple institutions interact must feel frustrated when the first empirical tests of its validity are undertaken by examining the relationships of just a few institutions that have been arbitrarily selected. The theorist is rarely satisfied with how the experimentalist treats his creation. So, it is not surprising that psychoanalytic theorists voice disappointment in the way their ideas have been put to the scientific test. But such objections should simply spur investigators to try harder to do justice to the theories in question.

Actually, over the years there has been a growing and probably irresistible movement to subject Freud's theories to dispassionate scientific assessment. Researchers in the areas of psychology, psychiatry, and anthropology have developed a range of rather ingenious methods for probing his speculations. It has turned out to be quite possible to assess Freudian ideas under controlled conditions and still do justice to their complexity. As mentioned earlier, we have documented this fact in our book, *The Scientific Credibility of Freud's Theories and Therapy*, a detailed analysis of the existing empirical findings which test Freud's theories. We have also demonstrated that, despite the antagonistic stance adopted by many psychoanalysts toward "outside" evaluation of what they do, sizable portions of Freud's thinking gain support when judged by the scientific literature. The present book of readings contains extensive samples of this literature and provides the reader with an opportunity to savor it at his convenience, to follow its splendid intricacies, and to judge from personal, detailed knowledge whether it is meaningful. The readings provide an overview of original source materials that have been scattered in diverse journals.

Our selections for this book were guided by several criteria. First of all, we wanted to cover a wide range of pertinent research. We collected clusters of papers dealing with Freud's major theories concerning the following: (1) function of the dream, (2) oral character traits, (3) anal character traits, (4) development and impact of the Oedipus complex, (5) origins of homosexuality, (6) defensive import of the paranoid delusion, and (7) psychotherapeutic treatment. We did not try to cover every significant aspect of Freud's thinking, but did include most aspects for which there was a reasonable amount of experimental data.

A second criterion in selecting papers was that those dealing with a particular theory should convey the gamut of problems that have arisen in the course of researching it and the attempted solutions. They should provide the reader with a clear image of central issues in the empirical evaluation of each theory. No claim is made that the papers are scientifically the "best." Actually, several were included in order to illustrate the kinds of methodological obstacles encountered in testing Freudian hypotheses.

Finally, an attempt was made, where appropriate, to include papers both supportive and nonsupportive of Freud. We wished to avoid a one-sided, biased presentation. As will be seen, the papers range widely, from strong support to negation of Freud's views. We did not intend that the particular weighting of supportive versus nonsupportive studies in this volume should be precisely equivalent to the results available in the full range of the literature. However, it should be acknowledged that there is a definite trend for a majority of the papers presented here to be at least partially supportive of Freud, and this does reflect our judgment concerning what is true. For those who wish to determine the precise situation with regard to the validity of various Freudian theories, see *The Scientific Credibility of Freud's Theories and Therapy*.

There is a general lack of awareness of how much time and energy the scientific community has invested in testing Freud's ideas. Although it is popular to portray the hardheaded empiricist as antagonistic or indifferent to what Freud had to say, numerous papers in this book testify to the contrary. We are convinced that with time it will be possible to delineate confidently which areas of Freud's theorizing are valid and which require revision. This will give welcome relief from the theoretical debates that have raged endlessly between those who are for or against Freud out of simple bias. We particularly hope that the readings in this book will encourage the student who is gaining his first familiarity with Freud's ideas to take a scholarly, nonpolarized attitude.

PART I

THE DREAM THEORY

Freud's dream theory was a rather complex production containing the nuclei of many ideas which he would later expand into novel concepts embracing a number of other areas. He portrayed the dream as a vehicle for the expression of unconscious wishes. He considered that, during sleep, wishes that have been repressed are able to bypass censoring forces that would prevent their expression in the waking state. These wishes are transformed into dream images. However, they are skillfully disguised so that the dreamer will not be disturbed by their content. Freud assumed (quite incorrectly in light of modern research findings) that an important function of the dream is to preserve sleep by permitting potentially disturbing impulses to be vented in a form so disguised that they do not arouse the sleeper. He described the dream, as it is literally told, to be a *manifest* facade. This facade, he said, conceals the inner (*latent*) meaning of the dream, which, with rare exceptions, is supposed to be some form of forbidden wish. In order to uncover the hidden wish one needs to employ a complicated technique which involves first getting the dreamer to free-associate to the various elements of the manifest dream, and then piecing these associations together as one might a jigsaw puzzle, until they provide the necessary interpretative clues. Freud suggested that the manifest images of the dream are often derived from the individual's experiences during the preceding day. Unconscious forces extract elements of these "day residues" and attach latent significances to them. Freud regarded dream interpretation as an important method for uncovering unconscious material in the course of psychoanalytic therapy. His dream theory has received wide acceptance and dream interpretation is usually conducted according to the principles he enunciated.

The accumulated scientific literature concerned with dream phenomena has raised serious questions about two aspects of Freud's dream theory: (1) the idea that the dream is invariably a vehicle for an unconscious wish, and (2) the notion that the manifest content of the dream is mere camouflage and contains little or no meaningful material. There are studies, as described by Fisher and Greenberg in *The Scientific Credibility of Freud's Theories and Therapy*, that indicate the manifest content of dreams can be meaningfully analyzed for significant information about the dreamer. Evidence has been obtained that dreams may serve not only to vent impulses but also to ponder problems, express conscious attitudes, and cope with anxieties. The studies brought together in this subsection will, among other things, convey the nature of some of the research contradicting Freud's dream theory. Brief reviews of these studies follow.

Brender and Kramer (Selection 1) dealt with the issue of whether the manifest content of dreams contains meaningful information and, more specifically, whether this information bears similarities to that obtained from a projective test tapping less conscious levels of response. Thematic Apperception Test stories were obtained from subjects and compared with the contents of their dreams as secured in a dream laboratory setting. Important correlations were found between the themes of the stories and dreams. However, differences were also observed.

Sheppard and Karon (Selection 2) were concerned with a problem quite analogous to that dealt with in the Brender and Kramer paper. They asked whether there are correlations between judgments of dreams based on manifest content and those based on the dreamer's associations. They found significant overlap between the two classes of judgments.

Fancher and Strahan (Selection 3) tested Freud's theory that the portions of a dream which, upon being retold, are most altered from a first version are particularly charged with underlying affect and anxiety. Freud assumed that the alterations in specific sectors of the dream reflected the special unconscious tensions linked to those sectors. Using a galvanic skin response index, Fancher and Strahan determined during a first recital of dreams which passages produced greatest physiological arousal and would therefore be expected to be the ones most often omitted (repressed) or altered when retold. The results did not support Freud's views and, in fact, turned out to be opposite to expectation.

O'Nell (Selection 4) explored in a cross-cultural context the degree to which frustrations involving eating and drinking find expression in the manifest dream content. He found in his comparisons of persons from several different cultures that the greater the oral frustrations resulting from living conditions, the greater the presence of oral themes in dreams. It is important to note that this correlation was established with manifest rather than latent levels of the dreams.

Greenberg et al. (Selection 5) devised an ingenious experiment concerned with testing the proposition that dreams aid in adapting to anxiety-provoking stimuli. They found that persons who were shown a disturbing film of an autopsy on two occasions, with a period of dream deprivation intervening, showed more anxiety on the second occasion than did controls who went through the same procedure, but with no interpolated dream deprivation. These findings, when considered in their full context, add support to the position that dreams may serve other functions besides expressing unconscious wishes.

Carrington (Selection 6) compared the dreams of schizophrenics and nonschizophrenics to find out whether their manifest content could be distinguished. The dreams of the schizophrenics revealed significantly more signs of distortions, threat, and bizarre ideation. Carrington suggested that the appearance of distorted and symbolic thinking in dreams may be a function of the dreamer's maladjustment —rather than being a "*sine qua non* of dreamlife." She speculated that distorted transformations may be minimal in the dreams of normal persons.

Whitman et al. (Selection 7) provided us with an interesting exploratory glimpse of the factors that determine what dreams the patient in psychotherapy relates selectively to his therapist. This paper contains intriguing qualitative observations.

1

William J. Brender & Ernest Kramer

A Comparative Need Analysis of

Immediately Recalled Dreams

and TAT Responses

The purpose of this study is twofold: (1) to demonstrate that content studies of immediately recalled dreams are feasible, and (2) to shed some light on the relationship between TAT (Thematic Apperception Test) responses and dreams by inquiring to what extent these two projective media elicit the expression of similar needs in the same subjects.

The literature contains few studies comparing TAT stories with dreams (10, 4) despite considerable confusion and uncertainty about the general relationship between TAT responses and fantasy. Many workers have been content to assume that the TAT measures "fantasy," following Morgan and Murray's original publication (9). Holt (7), on the other hand, has prepared, on a logical basis, a list of four areas of similarity and fifteen areas of difference between TAT responses and true fantasy. The differences for the most part stem from the consideration that the TAT is a set task with adaptive requirements whereas fantasy arises more spontaneously and effortlessly, generally in an altered state of consciousness. On the basis of his discussion, Holt concludes that the TAT story is not a fantasy. He would confine the meaning of "fantasy" to its usual sense, namely "a product of uncontrolled imagination" (7, p. 36).

One of the most widely utilized sources of an individual's fantasies has been his dreams. The paucity of studies comparing dreams and TAT responses has probably been partly due to the difficulty associated with obtaining good dream data, unbiased by factors such as selective recall and personality characteristics of dream recallers as compared to non-recallers (8, 11, 12, 13). Fairly recently, objective physiological indicants of dreaming have been developed (1, 2). Using these independent in-

Reprinted by permission of the publisher and the authors from *Journal of Projective Techniques and Personality Assessment*, 1967, 31, 74–77.

dicants of dreaming one can determine when during the course of the night a sleeping subject is dreaming. By rousing him during these times it is possible to obtain a fairly complete sample of the subject's nightly dreaming. Furthermore, the dreams are generally reported in vivid detail because the subject is in the midst of the dream experience when he is awakened. This methodological improvement in collecting dream data has made the question of the relationship between TAT stories and fantasy more readily researchable.

METHOD

Subjects

Thirteen subjects, eight male and five female, averaging twenty-one years of age were employed in this study. They were all volunteers, under no inducement beyond their own interest and curiosity. The sample consisted of undergraduate and postgraduate students and graduates.

The experimenter administered six TAT pictures (10, 12M, 12BG, 13G, 16, 19) in the standard manner to each subject and recorded the responses on tape. Approximately one week later, the subject reported at his bedtime to an EEG (electroencephalogram) lab which had been specially equipped for dream collection. The experimenter attached EEG, EOG (electrooculogram), and EMG (electromyograph) leads to the subject's face and scalp in the prescribed manner and allowed him to sleep in the bed provided for him. The physiological measures used as an indication of dreaming were the appearance of emergent Stage One EEG, bursts of rapid eye movements, and absence of muscle potential in the chin. A few minutes were allowed to elapse following these signs, and then the experimenter entered the sleep chamber and abruptly awakened the subject. The subject's report of his previously ongoing dream was recorded on tape. He was then permitted to return to sleep until the physiological criteria again indicated dreaming. The dream data were collected in this way throughout an entire night, of eight hours, for each of the thirteen subjects.

RESULTS

Seventy-eight TAT stories (six for each subject) and thirty-four immediately recalled dreams (averaging approximately two-and-a-half per subject) were collected. Scoring was carried out as follows. The experimenter scored the manifest content of the TAT stories and dreams for presence only, scored +1, of any of a list of twenty of Murray's needs. Hall and Lindzey's (6) text provided the definitions of the twenty needs used. No distinction was made between "need" and "press." A subject's overall score for any given need on the TAT or dreams represents the number of stories or dream reports in which the need was identified.

To test the extent to which the TAT and dreams were evoking similar needs in the same subject, Pearson product-moment correlations were computed between the subjects' scores on the TAT and in the dreams for each need. Five significant correlations were obtained. These are shown in Table 1–1. Two of these, deference and sentience, were dropped from consideration because of their very low frequency of occurrence among subjects. Since need scores based on six TAT stories were being correlated with need scores based on dreams of variable number it was necessary to inquire whether the experimenters had not, in fact, obtained results based on a relationship between TAT need scores and number of dreams rather than dream need scores. No significant correlation between subjects' TAT need scores and number of dreams was found.

The correlations between the appearance of the significantly correlated needs in a subject's TAT and dreams were: affiliation .65, dominance -.63, and play .56. The negative correlation for dominance does not reflect a uniform tendency for all subjects to express more dominance in one medium rather than the other. Subjects in general tended to use both media about equally to express this need, but individual subjects tended to express it in only one of the media. Some support for the stability of the findings presented here on affiliation and play derives from a study by Grotz (5). He compared TAT stories and manifest dream narrations, informally collected, using Combs' scoring system. He reports that both media are used extensively by the individual to express among other things the desire to be with people and the desire to play and do for its own sake.

TABLE 1-1

Significantly Correlated
Needs Appearing in
Individual Subject's
Dreams and TAT Stories

Need	r	p
affiliation	.65	< .02
dominance	−.63	< .05
play	.56	< .05
deference	.64	< .02
sentience	.64	< .02

In the present study an attempt was made to check interscorer reliability. The second scorer was an undergraduate student, with no previous experience with TAT or fantasy material. The resulting estimate of reliability is therefore rather conservative. Interscorer reliabilities in the form of Pearson r's were computed for each need in both the TAT and dreams. That is, the reliability with which each need could be scored in the TAT and in the dreams was obtained. The average reliability across the twenty needs in the TAT and dream data was .52 and .53 respectively. In both projective media, reliability in scoring individual needs varied widely. Ten needs out of the twenty in both the TAT and dreams (five in common) were scored with above chance reliability ($p > .05$). These are shown in Table 1–2. The reliability coefficients ranged from .55 to .93.

TABLE 1-2

Needs Scored With Above Chance (p $<$ *.05) Reliability*

Pearson r	Needs Scored In Dreams	Needs Scored in TAT
.50-.59	Dominance	Dominance, Achievement, Exhibition, Order, Succorance
.60-.69	Nurturance, Play	
	Sentience	Deference
.70-.79	Affiliation, Aggression	Affiliation, Abasement
.80+	Achievement, Defendance	
	Exhibition, Understanding	Play, Sex

CONCLUSIONS

Content studies of immediately recalled dreams, with their fuller content, seem practical. An approximate check of reliability suggests that they can be scored, using Murray's needs, with a reliability comparable to the TAT. By selecting among the needs it seems possible to choose some which would have potentially very satisfactory reliability.

The evidence presented here suggests that the TAT and dreams tend to elicit some similar needs in the same subject but it seems likely that more are dissimilar. Further study of this area seems well warranted. It would be highly desirable to know if these results are replicable. Perhaps some pattern could be discerned among the needs which tend to correlate across individuals' dream reports and TAT stories. Further work would probably benefit by differing selections of TAT cards, perhaps utilizing Eron's normative data on the TAT (3) to select cards which elicit the broadest number of themes.

REFERENCES

1. ASERINSKY, E., & KLEITMAN, N. Regularly occurring periods of eye motility, and concomitant phenomena during sleep. *Science*, 1953, *118*, 273–274.
2. DEMENT, W., & KLEITMAN, N. The relation of eye movements during sleep to dream activity: an objective method for the study of dreaming. *J. exp. Psychol.*, 1957, *53*, 339–346.
3. ERON, L. D. A normative study of the Thematic Apperception Test. *Psychol. Monogr.*, 1950, *64*, 1–47.
4. GORDON, H. L. A comparative study of dreams and responses to the TAT: a need-press analysis. *J. Personal.*, 1953, *22*, 234–253.
5. GROTZ, R. C. *A comparison of Thematic Apperception Test stories and manifest dream narratives.* Unpublished Master's thesis, Western Res. U., 1950.
6. HALL, C. S., & LINDZEY, G. *Theories of personality.* New York: John Wiley & Sons Inc., 1957.
7. HOLT, R. R. The nature of TAT stories as cognitive products: a psychoanalytic approach. In J. Kagan and G. S. Lesser (Eds.), *Contemporary issues in thematic apperceptive methods.* Springfield, Ill.: Chas. Thomas, 1961, 3–43.
8. LACHMAN, F., LAPKIN, B., & HANDELMAN, N. The recall of dreams: its relation to repression and cognitive control. *J. abnorm. soc. Psychol.*, 1962, *64*, 160–162.
9. MORGAN, CHRISTIANA D., & MURRAY, H. A. A method for investigating fantasies: the Thematic Apperception Test. *Arch. neurol. Psychiat.*, 1935, *34*, 289–306.
10. SARASON, S. B. Dreams and Thematic Apperception Test stories. *J. abnorm. soc. Psychol.*, 1944, *39*, 486–492.
11. SCHONBAR, ROSALEA. Some manifest characteristics of recallers and non-recallers of dreams. *J. consult. Psychol.*, 1959, *23*, 414–418.
12. SCHONBAR, ROSALEA. Temporal and emotional factors in the selective recall of dreams. *J. consult. Psychol.*, 1961, *25*, 67–73.
13. TART, C. T. Frequency of dream recall and some personality measures. *J. consult. Psychol.*, 1962, *26*, 467–470.

The authors wish to express their appreciation to Dr. Marco Amadeo, of Montreal's Jewish General Hospital, for providing instruction and equipment for the method of dream collection used here. Our appreciation goes, also, to the Jewish General Hospital for cooperation in providing facilities for this research.

2

Edith Sheppard & Bertram Karon

Systematic Studies of Dreams: Relationship Between the Manifest Dream and Associations to the Dream Elements

Since the publication of Freud's monumental work, *The Interpretation of Dreams* (8a), a vast literature on clinical observations and psychoanalytic interpretations of dreams has supplemented and corroborated Freud's original findings. As the science and technology of psychology have progressed there has been some interest in applications of the new methods to psychoanalytic theories, and, more specifically, to dreams. In this light the dream may be seen as a type of projective datum which can be examined by objective methods in much the same fashion as other forms of projective data.

The present study was undertaken as part of our research project on the investigation of emotional factors in dreams. As previously reported (14) dream rating scales have been constructed and tested for the measurement of hostility and ego strength. Our current report deals with the application of the rating systems to the manifest dream and to the associations to the dream elements for two purposes: to provide some evidence for the validation of the dream rating systems, and to contribute information relevant to the further understanding of the relationship between the manifest dream, dreamer's associations, and dreamer's personality structure. In this manner further supportive evidence may be gained for the corroboration of the construction of the latent dream from dream associations.

Freud (8a) stressed the use of the manifest dream as a starting point in the search for the latent content of the dream, and described a number of facets of the manifest dream which have served as guideposts for the present study. He indicated the relationship between the manifest and latent contents in his statement: ". . . in the case of every dream which I have submitted to an analysis . . . I have invariably found these

Reprinted by permission of Grune and Stratton, Inc., and the authors from *Comprehensive Psychiatry*, 1964, 5, 335–344.

same fundamental principles confirmed: the elements of the dream are constructed out of the whole mass of dream thoughts and each one of these elements is shown to have been determined many times over in relation to the dream thought." Freud described the relevance of the major theme of the dream as: ". . . analysis shows that the most vivid elements of a dream are the starting point of the most numerous trains of thought—that the most vivid elements are also those with the most numerous determinants . . . the greatest intensity is shown by those elements of a dream on whose formation the greatest amount of condensation has been expended."

In particular, Freud drew attention to the significance of affects in the manifest dream: "In the psychic complex which has been subjected to the influence of the resisting censorship, the affects are the unyielding constituent which alone can guide us to the correct completion."

The interest in the manifest dream has received further impetus from more recent authors such as Erikson (6), who wrote: "In addition to a dream's striving for representability, then, we would postulate a style of representation which is by no means a mere shell to the kernel, the latent dream; in fact it is a reflection of the individual ego's peculiar time-space, the frame of reference for all its defenses, compromises and achievements." Erikson further outlined the manifest configurations as: verbal, sensory, spatial, temporal, somatic, interpersonal, and affective.

Previous studies of manifest dreams have correlated aspects of the manifest dream with personality diagnosis. These studies include: our own (14), correlating hostility in manifest dreams with essential hypertension; those of Alexander and Wilson (1) correlating giving and taking tendencies in manifest dreams with gastrointestinal disorders; and those of Miller (11) correlating the occurrence of exhibitionistic and voyeuristic trends in the manifest dreams with skin diseases.

Freud's (8b) interest in experimental investigations of manifest dreams was demonstrated in his citation of Schrötter's studies on the translation of symbols in manifest dreams by hypnotized subjects.

More recent investigations in manifest dreams have indicated a correlation between manifest dreams and Thematic Apperception Test (TAT) stories (10) and correlation between manifest dreams and Rorschach responses presumed to be measures of hostility, anxiety, dependency, positive feelings, and neutral feelings (3).

Reis (13), a student of Hall, instructed subjects in interpreting their own dreams and correlated these interpretations with the manifest content. He found a high correlation between the manifest content and the subjects' interpretations.

METHOD OF PROCEDURE

Two medical students interviewed patients at the New York State Psychiatric Institute and the Eastern Pennsylvania Psychiatric Institute for the purpose of collecting their current dreams and associations to their dreams. The subjects were selected from the various wards randomly with the exception that it was required that they be fairly cooperative and verbally communicative. Subjects were selected who had been hospitalized no longer than one year and no less than one month. Each subject was seen individually once a week for eight weeks by the interviewer at a regularly scheduled time. The interviews were recorded on tape.

DESCRIPTION OF SUBJECTS

A total of thirty-three subjects were interviewed at the two institutions. Among these thirty-three there were nineteen who had given one or more dreams to which there were associations which consisted of material other than a repetition of the dream content. The nineteen subjects whose dreams and associations formed the data of this study are described in the following chart (Table 2–1).

DESCRIPTION OF DATA

From the data which had been collected on each of the subjects chosen as above, one dream and its associations were selected. The bases for the selection of a particular dream were: (1) that there were associations to the particular dream, (2) that the associations to that dream were longer than the associations to any other dream from that subject, and (3) if there were several dreams for a given subject, the associations to which were of equal length, the selection was made by means of a random number table. Thus, one dream and its corresponding associations were selected for each of the subjects. By using only one dream from any one subject the condition that each observation be experimentally independent of each other, which is required for the valid use of chi-square and other common statistical techniques, was met. The dreams were typed on 3x5 cards and then shuffled to arrange them in random order. The associations were also typed on 3x5 cards and

TABLE 2-1

Institute	Age	Sex	Marital Status	Color	Years School	Diagnosis	Weekly PsyRx	No. of Drugs	No. of Dream
EPPI	20	M	Single	White	11	Schizophrenia	2xwk	1	5
EPPI	32	M	Single	White	12	Ac. par. schiz.	0	1	7
EPPI	23	M	Single	White	12	Ac. schiz.	0	0	1
EPPI	20	M	Single	White	14	Ac. schiz.	0	2	8
EPPI	24	M	Single	White	15	Chr. schiz.	0	1	8
EPPI	30	M	Married	White	12	Chr. par. schiz.	0	0	4
EPPI	18	M	Single	White	11	Cat. schiz.	0	3	4
EPPI	41	M	Married	White	7	Par. schiz.	0	1	3
EPPI	36	M	Married	White	20	Paranoid	0	0	5
EPPI	27	M	Married	White	11	Depression	0	1	12
EPPI	32	M	Married	Negro	7	Ac. schiz.	0	0	4
NYSP	37	F	Widowed	White	10	Schiz. pseud.	3xwk	0	7
NYSP	23	F	Single	White	8	Ac. schiz.	1xwk	1	5
NYSP	18	F	Single	White	11	Beh. disorder	1xwk	1	5
NYSP	24	F	Single	White	13	Schiz.	2xwk	1	4
NYSP	23	F	Married	White	16	Schiz.	2xwk	1	5
NYSP	33	F	Single	White	12	B. tumor	2xwk	3	3
NYSP	19	F	Single	White	13	Addiction	0	2	3
NYSP	27	M	Single	White	16	Chr. schiz.	2xwk	2	9

Abbreviations: EPPI: Eastern Pennsylvania Psychiatric Institute.
NYSP: New York State Psychiatric Institute.
F: female; M: male.
PsyRx: Regularly scheduled psychotherapy.
No. of Drugs: Different tranquilizers concomitantly taken.

shuffled. It is critical to note that by the term association we refer to the material given in response to each element of that dream. All words which referred directly to the manifest content of the dream were selected, and no indication was given as to what element a given association had been obtained from. The associations to the sequential elements of the dream were typed in sequential order. The associations were also randomized by shuffling them and retyped as a list, numbered consecutively.

APPLICATION OF SCALES TO DATA

Ratings of the data so ordered were then made by the senior author. The senior author had not taken part in arranging or selecting the dreams so that there was no way for her to know which dream belonged with which association. All ratings were done in this blind fashion on the randomized protocols.

The dreams and associations were checked for presence of the characteristics listed in the scales. A characteristic could only be scored once no matter how many times it appeared in the content. The scoring of one characteristic did not exclude the possibility of scoring of any other characteristic. Arbitrary values were assigned to the categories to signify degrees of intensity and/or impairment. The scales used were: the Hostility, Ego, Orality, Anality, and Genitality Scales. Each scale consisted of a set of subscales measuring different aspects of each of these factors. The following are outlines of those scales which yielded significant results:

Hostility Scale: Hostility may be represented in the story by destructive behavior, inimical interpersonal relationships, disintegration of mind, matter or concepts, or unpleasant feelings.

Degree of Hostility: Scores the intensity of the hostility as a continuous variable:

(4) Maximum: Death or irreparable destruction of important objects.

(2) Medium: Injury or moderate impairment which is reparable.

(1) Minimum: Mild reparable injury or impairment.

Hostile theme: Scores the pervasiveness of hostility.

(4) Repetitive: Repeated hostile themes.

(2) Dominant: Hostile theme dominates story.

(1) Incidental: Hostile theme not important in story.

Roots of Hostility: Scores derivation of hostility.

(4) Id: Themes of bodily pleasure, animals.

(2) Superego: Themes of authority figures or situations.

(1) Ego: Themes about reality, work.

Ego Scale: Ego weakness is scored as reflected in the personae of the story.

Body Image: Scores deviation of body image from healthy.

(8) Bizarre: Personae present bizarre bodily configuration.

(4) Mutilation: Personae present bodily mutilation.

(2) Ill: Personae present ordinary type illness.

(1) Healthy: Personae healthy.

Genitality: Scores degrees of impairment of genital "drive."

(4) Bizarre: Change of sex, animals.

(2) Pursuit of sexual goals: Kissing, petting, games.

(1) Sublimation: Dating, symbolic representations as landscapes, hedges, columns.

EXAMPLE OF SCALING

To demonstrate what types of information the scales provide, the dream and associations of a phobic patient are herewith presented along with their scores.

Dream

"I dreamt of being in a hospital and being in a ward, and of being very sick and totally ignored. No one cared. There were a lot of people on the ward. It made me feel safe to have others suffer. My mother-in-law was the only one who came to see me on her own. She brought my husband as though he were a child. My mother-in-law insisted I should have flowers even if they were plastic. I did not want any."

Associations

"I was trying to get a baby-sitter and called a cousin of the girl next door. Her mother is a nice colorless person. Her husband has recently been fired from his job. He is in his late forties or early fifties. Her reaction is that they won't be able to have so many martinis. That is her way of tightening the purse strings. My other neighbor is upset by her attitude. She said she works at the hospital. I asked her if she enjoys it. She says it would be good for me because it makes her feel better . . . if I were in the hospital I would like a private room and there would be no question about it even if I were lonely. It reminds me of a book review of Marlene Dietrich's book. She said about the Academy Awards that the American public goes for suffering. The one who suffers will get the award. I don't usually like people to insist on giving me something. My daughter does not like to eat at my mother-in-law's. Food is like flowers and cars. They are all lovely things, but if you must have them they are not so nice. It's very odd. I don't know what the great attraction of illness or loneliness is."

TABLE 2-2

Scores	Dream	Associations
Hostility	3	3
Theme	7	7
Roots	2	7
Ego	3	3
Genitality	1	1

By inspection one may see that the above dream closely corresponds in its manifest content to the associations in emotional factors and defensive mechanisms. Table 2–2 reflects this correspondence. In addition to the above scales in which there were significant findings, the above dream and associations appear to correspond also in orality and anality factors.

To understand the significance of these numbers for this subject one would have to compare them with the scores on other dreams from the same subject and then compare the average scores and range of scores of this subject with those obtained from the dreams of other subjects.

The following is a list of scales on which the findings were not significant: Source of Hostility, Object of Hostility, Inhibition of Hostility, Expression of Hostility, Reality of Setting, Interpersonal Relationships, Logical Sequence of Themes, Nature of Dream Problem, Orality Scale, and Anality Scale.

RESULTS

After the protocols were scored, corresponding dreams and associations were reassembled for statistical analysis. The following scales were treated as quantitative scales: Orality, Anality, Genitality, Degree of Hostility, and Pervasiveness of Hostility (Hostile Theme). The other scales were analyzed as categorical data.

The product-moment correlation coefficient for the relationship between the ratings on Degree of Hostility for the manifest content and associations was found to be .65 for the protocols gathered by interviewer A, and .71 for the protocols gathered by interviewer B, and .66 for the total nineteen cases. As Pitman (12) has shown, using the randomization criterion, the product-moment correlation coefficient provides a distribution free test of the significance of correlation. For samples of ten cases or more the distribution of r closely approximates that given by normal curve theory. From this it follows that the relationship between the rated Degree of Hostility of the manifest dream and associations is significant beyond the .002 level.

The product-moment correlation coefficients for the relationship between ratings of Genitality for the manifest content and associations were: .75 for the protocols gathered by interviewer A and .96 for the protocols gathered by interviewer B, and .90 for the combined nineteen cases, which is even more significant ($p < .0006$) than the findings for the Degree of Hostility.

In the Mutilation category of Body Image there was agreement between the manifest content and associations of eleven out of eleven cases for interviewer A, and six out of eight cases for interviewer B, and seventeen out of nineteen cases for the combined series. Tested as a 2x2 table using Fisher's Exact Test (7), the combined series yielded a two-sided significance level of <.04. On the Hostile Theme Scale there is agreement between manifest dream and associations on whether or not hostility is the dominant theme in nine out of eleven cases for interviewer A, five out of eight cases for interviewer B, and fourteen out of nineteen cases in the combined series. Tested as a 2x2 table using Fisher's Exact Test, the combined series yielded a two-sided significance level of <.034. On the Roots of Hostility Scale there was agreement between the latent and manifest content in five out of eleven cases for the protocols of interviewer A, eight out of eight cases for those of interviewer B, and thirteen out of nineteen for the combined series. Inasmuch as this is a matching problem with three categories, the expected number of agreements by chance are 3.82 for interviewer A, 4.25 for interviewer B, and 8.42 for the combined series. The two-sided significance level for the combined series is $< .05$.

There were no other significant findings for the remainder of the scales. The significant findings are summarized in Table 2–3.

TABLE 2-3

Scale	B ($n = 8$)	A ($n = 11$)	Combined ($n = 19$)
Degree hostility	$r = .71$	$r = .65$	$r = .66$ ($p < .002$)
Roots hostility	8/8	5/11	13/19 ($p < .05$)
Hostility dom. theme	5/8	9/11	14/19 ($p < .034$)
Mutilation body image	6/8	11/11	17/19 ($p < .04$)
Genitality	$r = .96$	$r = .75$	$r = .90$ ($p < .0006$)

DISCUSSION

Certain aspects of the relationship between the manifest dream and associations to the dream have been elucidated by the present investigation. It is clear that the degree of hostility, roots of hostility, dominance of hostile theme, genitality, and concern with bodily mutilations as defined by the scales are readily identified from the manifest content by means of the scales and are closely correlated with these factors in the associations to the dream elements.

The lack of correlation of the other scales that we have tested does not necessarily indicate that there is no correlation between the manifest dream and associations in these respects, although this remains a possible explanation. Insofar as the scales in their present form may be inadequate, or the scoring unreliable, a low correlation will be obtained even if the true relationship may be high. An obvious direction for further research, which we are pursuing, is the refining of these other scales to see if appreciable correlations result from a change in the scales. It is noteworthy that the dimensions for which we have adequate scales are those which have been central in the interpretation of dreams from the beginning of psychoanalysis, that is, with those dimensions in which there is the most experience and sophistication in dream interpretation. This suggests that we will find other high correlations between manifest and latent content when our other rating scales are equally sophisticated. In testing for correlations, we are naturally just as interested in negative correlations as in positive correlations.

The lack of correlation in some of the scales may also be due to the particular patient sample which was studied. Evidence for this may be seen in the infrequent scoring of the dreams on the orality and anality scales. A sample of patients with gastrointestinal disorders, as in the Alexander and Wilson study (1), evidently might provide a wider range of variation and hence a firmer basis for correlation of manifest content and associations on these dimensions. Along the same lines, Beck (2) found more masochistic dreams in depressed than in non-depressed subjects. Our failure to obtain a significant correlation in the categories Source and Object of Hostility may thus be related to our sample not consisting of enough depressive subjects. Future studies applying the scales to depressives and nondepressives may clarify this aspect of the scale.

Our positive findings may also be a function of our sample, and it is conceivable that a similar study with neurotic patients would not show the same relationships. This is another obvious line of research we intend to pursue. However, as the scales were constructed on the basis of psychoanalytic experience with neurotic patients, it is doubtful that such a study would yield contradictory results.

One of the problems in this study is that the subjects were seen briefly by interviewers whose announced purpose was research rather than therapeutic interest in the subject. It has been noted by Freud and others that autobiographical dreams, which are commonly seen at the beginning of analysis, occur rarely outside of therapy. Thus, a similar study employing subjects in intensive therapy would be of considerable interest since it may be expected that their dreams would be longer and more revealing than those in our sample. The use of subjects in treatment by several analysts would perhaps control for the possibility of the therapist having a suggestive influence on the dreams.

A further problem in the study consisted in the difference in the interviewers, one of whom customarily obtained rather brief associations to the dream elements, and the other one of whom customarily obtained long associations to the dream elements. It is therefore interesting that our findings still suggest a close relationship between manifest dream and associations to the dream elements.

A further check on our results would be a study of the relationship of the manifest dream to free associations. During the course of analytic therapy some analysts routinely base their analysis of dreams on the dreamer's associations to individual dream elements, whereas other analysts base theirs on free associations given in the hour during which a dream has been reported. Since both methods appear to be applicable, further validation of the scales may be obtained by correlating manifest dreams with the free associations given during the same analytic session.

The work of Dement (5) and others indicating that most people have several dreams a night suggests that future studies should include scaling of dreams of the same night. Such a study might indicate the reliability of the manifest dream particularly in its use as a diagnostic and research tool. The scores for an individual's dreams of a single night may also provide information about the range of variability or fixation within the dreamer's personality.

Inasmuch as the concept of repression embodies to some extent the principle that the repressed is expressed in altered form in the defense mechanism, the present report confirms this view. A notable exception of this occurs when denial, which may be considered a most severe form of repression, is operative. The scales have been designed to reflect this by scores indicating marked weakness of the ego combined with a failure to score in other emotional factors.

A quantitative estimation of the emotional factors in the responses to an association test can be expected to correspond also to the personality disorder of the subject provided that enough data have been presented to the subject. However, this is not felt to invalidate the present study. The subject's own manifest dream offers many advantages as the material to be used as the basis for an association test. Since the manifest dream has been the subject's own product he will more efficiently present material important to his own personality structure. Also, we can expect a reduced possibility of suggested responses from the experiment and experimenter. In this regard, it may be of interest to study the associations that subjects have to dreams other than their own.

To broaden the scales' range of application, we expect to repeat our previous studies of interscorer reliability when the scales are further developed.

This investigation has made a start toward rendering the manifest dream a broader diagnostic, prognostic, and research instrument by indicating some areas of agreement between the manifest dream and associations to the dream elements. The positive correlation found in this study is in accord with clinical observations of these data. Early in analysis subjects view associations and manifest dream content with much the same feeling of estrangement. They are both experienced as events for which the individual does not feel he is responsible.

The analysis of dreams, i.e., the uncovering of the latent content of the dream, is part of the broader process of helping the subject understand and integrate his unconscious motivations into realistic goal-oriented behavior. Thus, the latent content of a thoroughly analyzed dream would present an understanding of the subject's current life problems and his relationship to his analyst against the background of his childhood experience. The scales applied to several dreams of an individual may eventually serve to supplement present knowledge by presenting in quantitative form a measure of the dreamer's emotional factors, ego strength, and ego range. Nonetheless, obtaining patient's associations to dreams and basing interpretations on the associations, therapeutic goals, and the patient's needs, remains, in our opinion, the only way to conduct dream analysis in therapy.

SUMMARY

The relationship between the manifest dream and associations to the dream was investigated by the following method: one dream and its corresponding associations were selected from the data on each of nineteen hospitalized psychiatric patients. The dreams and associations were rated independently and blindly on scales constructed to measure various emotional factors. It was found that the ratings of the manifest content of the dream correlated highly with the ratings of the associations with respect to: Degree of Hostility, Roots of Hostility, Dominance of Hostile Theme, Genitality, and Bodily Mutilation as defined in the scales. The scales by which the manifest dream and associations were correlated are described and some evidence for their validity is presented.

REFERENCES

1. ALEXANDER, F., and WILSON, G. W.:   Quantitative dream studies, a methodological attempt at a quantitative evaluation of psychoanalytic material. *Psychoanalyt. Quart.* IV:371–407, 1935.

2. BECK, A. T.:   A systematic investigation of depression. *Compr. Psychiat.* 2/3: 163–170, 1961.

3. BOLGAR, H.:   Consistency of affect and symbolic expressions: A comparison between dreams and rorschach responses. *Am. J. Orthopsychiat.* 24:538–545, 1954.

4. COCHRAN, W. G.:   The chi-square test of goodness of fit. *Ann. Math. Statist.* 23:315–345, 1952.

5. DEMENT, W., and KLEITMAN, N.:   The relation of eye movements during sleep to dream activity: An objective method for the study of dreaming. *J. Exp. Psychol.* 53:339–346, 1957.

6. ERIKSON, E. H.:   The dream specimen of psychoanalysis. *J. Am. Psychoanalyt. Assn.* 2:5–56, 1954.

7. FISHER, R. A.:   *Statistical Methods for Research Workers,* 12th ed. N. Y. Hafner Publishing Co., Inc., 1954.

8. FREUD, S.:   a: *The Interpretation of Dreams,* trans. by Strachey. N. Y., Basic Books, Inc., 1956. b: *New Introductory Lectures on Psychoanalysis,* trans. by Sprott. N. Y., W. W. Norton & Co., 1933.

9. GILBERT, E. J.:   The matching problem. *Psychometrika* 21:253–266, 1956.

10. GORDON, H. L.:   A comparative study of dreams and responses to the thematic apperception test. *J. Personal.* 22:234–253, 1953.

11. MILLER, M.:   A psychological study of a case of eczema and a case of neurodermatitis. In: *Studies in Psychosomatic Medicine* (Alexander and French). N. Y., Ronald Press Co., 1948.

12. PITMAN, E. J. G.:   Significance tests which may be applied to samples from any population, II. The correlation coefficient test. *Suppl. J. Roy. Statist. Soc.* 4:225–233, 1937.

13. REIS, W. J.:   A comparison of the interpretation of dream series with and without free associations. In: *Dreams and Personality Dynamics* (De Martino). Springfield, Ill., Charles C Thomas, 1959.

14. SAUL, L. J., and SHEPPARD, E.:   An attempt to quantify emotional forces using manifest dreams. *J. Am. Psychoanalyt. Assn.* 4:486–502, 1956.

15. SHEPPARD, E., and SAUL, L. J.:   An approach to a systematic study of ego function. *Psychoanal. Quart.* XXVII: 237–245, 1958.

This study was supported by a grant from the Frank Strick Foundation. The interviews were conducted by John Watt, B.A. and Ira Silverstein, B.A. under USPHS grants in the Medical Student Research Training Program.

The authors gratefully acknowledge the cooperation of the New York State Psychiatric Institute and the Eastern Pennsylvania Psychiatric Institute in the study.

3

Raymond E. Fancher & Robert F. Strahan

Galvanic Skin Response and the Secondary
Revision of Dreams: A Partial Disconfirmation
of Freud's Dream Theory

This research drew its primary inspiration from a passage of Freud's *The Interpretation of Dreams* (1) in which he advises psychoanalysts to pay close attention to a certain kind of "secondary revision" when interpreting particularly difficult dreams.

> If the first account given me by a patient of a dream is too hard to follow, [says Freud], I ask him to repeat it. In doing so he rarely uses the same words. But the parts of the dream which he describes in different terms are by that fact revealed to me as the weak spot in the dream's disguise [p. 553].

The "weak spot," of course, is that part of the first account that least adequately disguises the latent dream thoughts, and Freud suggests that the dream interpretation can most profitably be begun by attacking this weakness. Though his suggestion applies specifically only to the interpretation of *confused* dreams, Freud makes it clear that his general principle—the nonarbitrary and defensive nature of changes in recollection—applies to other dreams as well.

Thus Freud (1) believed that the parts of a first dream account that are changed in a second telling of the same dream, closely associated as they are with the latent and unconscious dream thoughts, are more highly charged with anxiety and emotional arousal than are the unaltered parts. That is, those parts that are changed should reflect more closely and directly the emotional conflicts of the dreamer and be the most upsetting parts of the dream from the dreamer's point of view. It follows from this "dynamic" point of view, then, that those parts of a first account of a dream that are most closely associated with anxiety will be most likely to be altered in a subsequent telling of the dream.

The present research attempted to test this line of reasoning by

Reprinted by permission of the American Psychological Association from *Journal of Abnormal Psychology*, 1971, 77, 308–312. Copyright 1971 by the American Psychological Association.

recording the skin resistances of subjects (Ss) while they tape-recorded accounts of their dreams and then obtaining re-recordings of the same dreams a few mins. later. The passages that were told simultaneously with the occurrence of galvanic skin responses (GSRs) were presumed to be the most emotionally arousing ones in the dreams, and, according to the Freudian hypothesis, they would be the ones most likely to be changed in the second accounts. That hypothesis was tested specifically by comparing the outcomes of first-telling GSR and non-GSR passages in the second accounts.

METHOD

Subjects

The Ss were fifteen female students from an introductory psychology course at the University of Rochester who used their participation toward meeting a research requirement for the course. Two of the Ss ultimately had to be dropped from the sample because they produced undifferentiated GSR records.

Procedure

As each S arrived at the laboratory, she was asked if she could remember a fairly recent dream and if she was willing to tape-record an account of it. In all cases, S responded affirmatively to both questions and was then escorted to a small, sound-deadened room containing a microphone and GSR electrodes. The microphone was connected to one track of a stereo tape recorder and the electrodes to one channel of a Grass Model-7 polygraph. Both recording devices were located in an adjacent room.

An experimenter (E) connected the electrodes as he explained the nature of the GSR recording process. Biocom Ag–AgCl electrodes were placed on the distal phalanges of the index and second fingers of S's right hand. A .05–M mixture of NaCl and Parke-Davis Unibase composed the electrode paste which contacted S's fingers through electrode pads with one-cm.-diameter openings. The regular PGR circuit of a 7P1 preamplifier was used in recording skin resistance.

The S was instructed to wait for approximately one min. after E left the room, then to recite an account of her dream into the microphone. After E left the S chamber, he started the polygraph chart drive in motion. The E then recorded the word "start" on the second (non-S) track of the tape recorder while simultaneously marking the position of the pen on the polygraph record. Since the polygraph record moved at a constant and known rate of speed, as did the stereo tape, it was possible upon playback of the tape recording to synchronize S's dream account with her GSR record.

When S finished recording her dream, she tapped on the door to signal E. The E then said "stop" into the tape recorder while simultaneously marking the position of the polygraph pen. This concurrent noting of a terminal point for both dream and GSR recordings provided a check on the accuracy of their subsequent synchronization. In all cases, that accuracy turned out to be within a sec. or two.

After S was removed from the apparatus, she was asked to fill out a short questionnaire providing information about the date of occurrence of her dream, the number of times it had been told to people, etc. This took about five min., after which S was asked to re-record her dream. The GSR was not monitored during this second telling of the dream, and when S was finished, her participation in the experiment was completed.

Selection of GSR and Control Passages from Dream Accounts

After the data had been collected, a major task was the identification of those specific first-account dream passages that had been accompanied by GSRs. Two Es examined the records of all Ss and located specific GSRs. In most cases, there was agreement between Es in the identification of GSRs. There were five occasions, however, when only one E identified a GSR or where some other doubt existed. These GSRs were identified as "questionable." Two of the records had no identifiable GSRs at all and were removed from further analysis. The remaining thirteen records had between one and seven GSRs each.

Once the GSRs had been identified, an arbitrary decision was made to classify as GSR passages the portions of the dream accounts extending from three sec. before to three sec. after each GSR onset. That is, all verbal content that occurred in the six-sec. periods from three sec. before to three sec. after GSR onset was noted and classified as GSR-related. Though this time interval was arbitrarily imposed, it seemed reasonable in light of the usual GSR latency of 1–2 sec. The six-sec. interval seemed sufficiently wide that it should encompass any GSR-arousing material. A total of forty GSR passages and five questionable passages was identified, ranging in length from five to thirty words.

A *control passage* was obtained for each GSR passage in the following way. A formula using a table of random numbers was employed to select randomly passages from the first dream accounts that were of the same length as the GSR passages but that had not been accompanied by GSRs. Thus, for example, one dream account contained three GSR passages of twenty, twenty-three, and fifteen words, respectively, and, from that same dream, control passages of twenty, twenty-three, and fifteen words were chosen. The table of random numbers was used to locate the first words of the control passages according to a formula by which the first two table entries consulted denoted the lines from the typescript of the dream account, and the third entry denoted the word. If the object was to create a control passage for a twenty-word GSR passage, the table would indicate the word with which to begin the passage. That word and the following nineteen became the control passage, provided that there was no overlap with a GSR passage, a questionable GSR passage, or a previously identified control passage. Thus forty control passages were selected to be used for comparison with the forty GSR passages. Since doubt existed about the status of the questionable GSR passages, they were not included in any analysis.

Analysis of Changes in the Second Dream Accounts

After the GSR and control passages from the first dream accounts had been specified, the task was to determine what became of their content in the second dream accounts. To do this, it was necessary to note each major idea expressed in the GSR and control passages and then to search the corresponding second dream accounts for the *equivalents* of those ideas. For example, one of the control passages from a first account was "they brought me back to campus and I went to Todd Union and was supposed to work." In the second account of the same dream, there occurred the two statements "they brought me back to campus" and "I went to Todd where I was supposed to work" separated by an irrelevant intervening passage. These two passages clearly reflected content comparable to the single passage from the initial control passage, and the two in conjunction were taken to be the equivalent. In many cases, the context suggested that a passage in the second account was clearly an equivalent to a GSR or control passage, even though the specific wording or content was changed. For example, in one of the dreams the passage "I was three people away *from where I was going to be taken*" was cited as the equivalent for "I was three people away *from having my turn*" (italics added to emphasize nonidentical equivalents). In several cases, major ideas from GSR or control passages were omitted entirely from the second accounts, and this was duly noted in the scoring. Thus the fates in the second accounts of the major ideas from all of the eighty GSR and control passages were noted and recorded.

The apparently complicated process described above was in reality quite easily and reliably accomplished. Before the data from the present research were examined, two raters independently identified equivalents for a set of twenty-five first-account passages from dreams collected as part of another study. A coefficient of agreement was computed for each equivalent passage by dividing twice the number of words contained in both raters' versions by the total number of words in both versions. (Thus if Rater A's and B's equivalents contained nineteen and twenty-one words, respectively, and eighteen of the words were common to both versions, the coefficient would be $(2 \times 18)/(19 + 21)$, or .90.) The range of coefficients for the twenty-five passages was .80–1.00, with a median of .96.

Once the equivalent passages were found, it was necessary to determine the extent to which each one represented a change from its original in the first dream account. This was done by examining in detail each major idea or concept in the GSR or control passage, comparing it with its equivalent from the second version, and then exercising one of three scoring alternatives. First, if a major idea was omitted entirely from the second account, an *omission* was scored. Since most passages contained more than one major idea, it was possible for a single passage to be scored for more than one omission. For example, in one case the entire passage "I was over at the other side of the island pulling my sister along" was omitted from the second account. This passage was considered to have two major ideas: "I was over at the other side of the island," and "I was pulling my sister along." The entire passage received a score of two omissions.

The second scoring alternative was to classify part of an equivalent passage as a *substitution* for its counterpart from the first dream version. This category was employed whenever an idea was clearly present but modified in meaning somehow in the equivalent passage. An example of a substitution has already been cited in another context: the equivalent passage "I was three people away from where I was going to be taken" was scored as a substitution for "I was three people away from having my turn." Frequently ideas were expressed in the second accounts in words that were somewhat different from those in the first, but whose meanings were virtually identical. In these cases, substitutions were not scored. Thus, the phrase "a large island" was not scored as a substitution for "a relatively big island."

The third scoring alternative was to regard the two ideas being compared as identical and to score no change at all. It might be pointed out here that a fourth logical scoring category, indicating the *addition* of major ideas to the second versions, was not employed in this study because there was no way of relating such additions to specific GSR or control passages in the first accounts.

The scoring of omissions and substitutions was done by an undergraduate student who had not participated earlier in the study and who had no way of knowing whether individual passages were GSR or control passages. Earlier, this student and another rater had independently scored a series of twenty-five passages taken from another study. The r's between the two raters' sets of scores were .77 for omissions and .73 for substitutions, indicating a fair degree of scoring reliability for the two measures. This degree of reliability on the major scoring categories seemed to suggest that the raters must have substantially agreed as well in selecting the individual major ideas in the passage.

For each S, two sets of two scores were obtained to be used in the data analysis, one set being obtained from the GSR passages, the other from the control passages. The two scores were number of omissions and number of substitutions. The question to be answered, of course, was whether these scores would be higher for the GSR passages, as Freudian theory would seem to predict.

RESULTS

The results, including t tests for the differences between GSR and control passages, are presented in Table 3–1. (The independent difference scores were approximately normally distributed within both omission and substitution categories, justifying use of the test statistic.) The results show that there were almost twice as many omissions from the control passages as from the GSR passages, contrary to the Freudian hypothesis. Substitutions were generally less frequent than omissions and virtually equally likely to appear in GSR or control passages.

TABLE 3-1

Changes in Dream Content

Item	Omissions	Substitutions
Mean no. from GSR passages	1.46	.85
Mean no. from control passages	2.84	.77
Mean difference (GSR minus control)	−1.38	.079
SD of differences	1.86	1.44
t value for differences	−2.57*	.19

Note. — $N = 13$.
*$p < .03$, two-tailed.

DISCUSSION

In interpreting the results of this study, it should be kept in mind that there are three major ways in which dream accounts may be altered from one version to another. First, material from the first version may be dropped altogether from the second account. According to psychoanalytic theory, the part that gets dropped should be especially anxiety-arousing, and the whole process should be referred to as *repression*. Second, material from the first account may be replaced by new material in the later telling. Freud (1) assumed that such a change would serve to replace a particularly "dangerous" idea from the first account with a more "neutral" one in the second. A process like this is usually referred to as *displacement*. Third, entirely new material might be added to the second account. Psychoanalytic theory suggests that such additions might be attempts to "soften" dangerous or anxiety-arousing ideas that are stated baldly in the first version by means of *rationalization* or *intellectualization*.

In the present study, then, omissions should be examples of repressive forces and substitutions should be displacements if the psychoanalytic assumptions are correct. The data, however, indicate that most omissions were *not* examples of repression since most of the omitted ideas originated in the presumably nonarousing and emotionally "indifferent" control passages. In fact, the results suggest the converse of the Freudian hypothesis: that omitted material is especially likely to be minimally emotionally charged and therefore less personally important to the dreamer. The findings with respect to substitutions also fail to support the psychoanalytic position, since GSR and control passages were equally likely to undergo substitutions. Thus there is no evidence to support an interpretation of substitutions as the results of a dynamic process like displacement. Since the design of the study did not permit a test of the hypothesis that additions in the second accounts represented cases of rationalization and intellectualization (since it could not be determined which specific first account passages were being added to), the possibility remains that these changes were of the type suggested by Freud. (1)

Any interpretation of the findings of this study must be made cautiously, of course, because of the restricted nature of the S population as well as the uncertainties inherent in interpreting GSRs. It also should be pointed out that the experimental situation was not a perfect analog of the psychoanalytic setting in which Freud (1) performed his clinical dream interpretations. In the psychoanalytical situation, for example, the patient is encouraged to speak freely about things that would normally be "censored." Before he can do this, however, it is usually necessary that he establish a feeling of particular trust toward the analyst. There was not sufficient time in the present experiment to establish comparable relationships between S and E. Thus the initial accounts of dreams told by psychoanalytic patients may be less heavily censored than those told in the present research. Still another difference may be the fact that in the psychoanalytic setting, the patient clearly understands that his dreams are going to be subjected to the most searching scrutiny, and this may enhance his tendency to make changes of a defensive nature in his second dream accounts. The Ss may not have had such an understanding in the present research. Thus it is possible that defensive forgetting is more likely to occur in the psychoanalytic setting than it was in the present experiment both because the psychoanalytic patients are trained to tell relatively uncensored first accounts (which offer more opportunities for defensive changes) and because greater pressures for defensive changes are experienced by the patients between the first and second accounts.

In spite of these mitigating factors, however, it is difficult to reconcile the findings of the present study with Freud's theory of secondary revision. Some first-account passages were associated with arousal in spite of possible prior censorship, and these passages were less rather than more likely to undergo changes in the second accounts. These results seem more consistent with some of the research that has been done in the area of verbal learning and memory than they do with Freudian theory. Weiner (2), for example, concluded after a literature review that experiments accompanied by intense emotions of any type are more likely to be recalled than are nonemotional experiences. The results with omissions in the present study tend to corroborate that conclusion, even though the experiences in question occurred in dreams rather than real life.

REFERENCES

1. FREUD, S.   *The interpretation of dreams.* New York: Avon Books, 1965.
2. WEINER, B.   Effects of motivation on the availability and retrieval of memory traces. *Psychological Bulletin,* 1966, *65,* 24–37.

The authors' thanks are due to Ronald Kraus, Barbara Meyer, Robert Neems, and John Snavlin, who assisted admirably at various points in the research.

4

C. W. O'Nell

A Cross-Cultural Study of Hunger and
Thirst Motivation Manifested in Dreams

Psychologists and anthropologists have long assumed that manifest dream content might reveal the nature of motivational states in dreamers (10, 3, 5, 9). If the assumption is valid, the manifest dream could be an important behavioral area of study with regard to the development of human motivation.

This study examines how hunger and thirst motivation may be expressed in dream imagery. Since comparatively little empirical work has been done in this area (1, 7, 2), the issue of how hunger and thirst motivation may be expressed in dream imagery stands as a problem of basic research interest.

The present discussion is based on the reported dreams of four groups of respondents. The groups represent four cultures known to differ in patterns of deprivation regarding food and drink. The study attempts to assess the influence of several psychobiological and socio-cultural factors expected to contribute to hunger and thirst motivation and to test the combined weights of these factors against reported manifest hunger and thirst imagery in the dreams of respondents from each of the four groups.

Much of the current research on manifest content in dreams is based upon three somewhat interrelated approaches. The most venerable of these, relative to its contribution to the others, is the psychoanalytic approach initiated by Freud which resulted in the first systematic theory of the origins and dynamics of dream experience. Research in this context has largely been that of the detailed analysis of the reported dream experiences of given individuals in therapeutic settings.

A second approach has been that of the physiologist or experimental psychologist whose interests have centered on the psychological corre-

Reprinted by permission from *Human Development*, 1965, 8, 181–193 (Karger, Basel 1965).

lates of dream experience and the relationship of changes in sleep patterns to changes in nocturnal mentation patterns.

Other behavioral scientists, notably anthropologists and social psychologists, have shown interest in dream reports usually gathered through large sample research.

The study reported here employs the third approach, although it rests heavily upon Freudian theory.

Freud's theory of wish fulfillment in dreams is used as a theoretical base for this research. In Freudian theory the needs for nourishment and drink are seen as primary drives of the organism which find their psychological source in id impulses or wishes. When the satisfaction of such impulses is blocked by reality situations, the impulses are assumed to press for satisfaction in fantasy. Dreams are thought to provide a fantasy experience through which impulses repressed in waking life are asserted. Sleep is seen as the time during which the conscious controls of the ego and superego are greatly relaxed.

One drawback to Freud's theory is that it does not consider the effects of social conditioning upon the development of hunger and thirst motivation. Furthermore, Freud does not discuss the possible consequences of differences in social and cultural settings on the psychological manifestation of hunger and thirst motivation in dreams.

The environmental conditions surrounding the experiences of hunger or thirst complicate the problem of studying these drives. Hunger and thirst in man are subject to social conditioning from earliest infancy. Except for extreme situations man seldom experiences hunger uninfluenced by cultural factors. Food is normally taken in conformity with established customs, at expected intervals, and with only minimal respect to current physiological needs. Hunger and thirst can thus be thought of as subjective experiences, products of organismic adjustment to physiological needs, usually influenced by broad environmental and cultural conditions. Except under highly controlled laboratory conditions, it is not justifiable to conceive of hunger or thirst as purely physiological phenomena. Under the conditions imposed by naturalistic observations one can only conceive of them as products of the complete life situations of the individuals under study.

An important element of this research, therefore, is the assessment of social and cultural conditions which influence hunger and thirst motivation for the four groups included in the study. Certain assumptions are made relating manifest hunger in reported dreams to conditions of food deprivation in the environment. Similarly, manifest thirst in reported dreams is assumed to be related to conditions of drink deprivation in the environment. The study seeks to determine the relationships between measures of hunger and thirst motivation, based upon knowledge of the general life situations of the respondents, and measures of hunger and thirst motivation in the manifest content reported in dreams.

The Sample. The sample consists of 434 male students representing four cultural groups: Ethiopian Orthodox Christians, Fasting Nigerian

Muslims, Nonfasting Nigerians, and Americans.* The mean age of the respondents is 17.3 years.

These four cultures represent wide variation in food and drink patterns. Two of the groups (the fasting Islamic Nigerians and the Ethiopian Orthodox Christians) maintain stringent attitudes and customs with regard to fasting and its public manifestations. The other two groups (the nonfasting Nigerians and the Americans) represent cultures with more relaxed attitudes toward fasting and its public manifestations. These two groups are composed of respondents essentially adhering to western Christian traditions.

The Ethiopians (N=36). For the Ethiopian Orthodox Christian fasting represents the keystone of religious practice and it also pervades the secular cultural ethic. Huffnagel (6) reports that every Wednesday and Friday the Ethiopians fast completely in the forenoon and curtail the kinds and amounts of foods taken in the afternoon and evening. D. Levine (8) maintains that the Ethiopian practice is probably the strictest in the world with respect to the number and harshness of the fasts it prescribes.

Children start to observe fasting practices at seven years of age. Fasting requirements increase with age and station in life. A typical adult layman fasts approximately 165 days per year. The adolescent boys in this sample are expected to follow the customary adult fasting practices (with the exception of being exempted from the forty-eight hours of complete fast expected of their elders prior to Easter).

The fasting Nigerians (N=73). The fasting Nigerians observed the Islamic fasting proscriptions of Ramadan at the time the data were collected. The Koranic injunction is explicit: One may ". . . eat and drink until so much of the dawn appears that a white thread may be distinguished from a black; then keep the fast completely until night" (Koran 2:183). Pregnant women, travelers, and those who are ill are excused from the fast.

R. LeVine's impression is that the fast is strictly observed. Fasting for this group is a public issue. Pressure to obey the fast is exerted by school authorities as well as the community at large. Von Grunebaum (13) states that the Ramadan fast commands widespread and willing obedience among Islamic people and often is adhered to strictly by those who neglect daily prayers and other prescribed duties.

Drink deprivation is an important part of the fast and it is this practice which differentiates the fasting Nigerians from the rest of the sample.

The nonfasting Nigerians (N=270). The nonfasting Nigerians represent various ethnic and religious affiliations. The majority, however, are Christians. This group as a whole has no prevailing fasting customs comparable to those practiced by the Ethiopian Orthodox Christians or the fasting Islamic Nigerians.

---

* R. A. Levine collected the Nigerian data. E. J. Prebis collected the Ethiopian data. The American data were collected by the writer.

There is, however, some evidence of widespread malnutrition among that segment of the Nigerian population from which the sample is drawn. Quinn-Young and Herdman (12) describe the subsistence level of the economy and the great dependence of the population upon root crops such as cassava and yams. They also describe population pressures and overintensive farming methods which deplete the land and lead to lower yields and reduced nutritional values of foodstuffs. According to Niven (11) diseases traceable to poor nutrition are prevalent in the Nigerian population.

The Americans (N=55). The American respondents are drawn from a secondary school in Chicago attended primarily by students from lower middle and upper middle socioeconomic levels. Malnutrition is not a problem. Exact information about the religious affiliation of each respondent is lacking, but the group is known to be predominantly Christian. The fasting issue is judged to be virtually nonexistent for this group.

Study design. Data for this research fall into two categories: (1) two personal dream experiences written in English and by respondents, and (2) descriptive data from library and personal sources concerning the food customs and nutritional status of the populations from which each group was derived.

The reported dream data were coded for measures of manifest hunger and thirst by methods to be described. The data on food customs and nutritional status were useful in establishing estimates of the effects of food and drink frustrations upon the levels of hunger and thirst motivation for each of these groups. Scores based on the estimates were used in the ordering of the groups for testing hypotheses.

Dreams and other personal data were gathered from the Nigerians and Ethiopians in a classroom setting. Because of conflict with examination schedules in their school, the Americans filled out their reports privately, returning them unsigned and in sealed envelopes to the investigator. The Americans were not asked about ethnic background or religious affiliation. These deviations from controlled conditions were considered to impose no significant effects upon the data relative to the problem under study. The respondents were unaware of the nature of the research problem.

One set of hunger and thirst motivation measures is derived from data on food and drink frustrations in the life situations of the groups and another set of hunger and thirst motivation measures is based upon reports of food and drink imagery in dreams. The relations between the two sets of measures are discussed in the section on results. Based on the wish-fulfillment theory of dreams, it was expected that higher levels of hunger and thirst frustration in the environment would result in a greater percentage of respondents revealing manifest hunger and thirst imagery in their dreams.

Research into such matters as formalized fasting customs, food preferences and taboos, the socialization of food denial, and the relative undernutrition and malnutrition for each group suggests six issues of food frustration upon which judgments are made for each group. Each of these issues is treated as a separate component (see Table 4-1) for purposes of judging. There is, however, considerable overlap among them. The first three components directly concern participation in formalized fasting and serve to emphasize the fasting issue in this study.

A distinction is made in this study between undernutrition (Component 5) and malnutrition (Component 6). The standard adopted by the Food and Agricultural Organization of the United Nations defines malnutrition as the condition which prevails when roots, grains, and sugars supply two-thirds or more of the total caloric intake per capita. This definition of malnutrition is accepted for the study. Undernutrition is defined as insufficient intake of calories.

Judgments are made on the relative presence or absence of each given frustration component in the life situation of each group. The measures for each component issue, therefore, are dichotomous and admittedly gross oversimplifications of reality. The information on each group and the source materials on each component are too general to allow for the application of scaling methods in judging their relative strengths.

The dichotomous measures for each component are cumulatively handled, with each positive judgment receiving a weight of one and each negative judgment receiving a weight of zero. The totals thus derived (Table 4-1, Column 7) are called cultural deprivation scores. These scores are used to rank-order the four groups on food deprivation and the rank order is used to predict the percentage of individuals in each group likely to express manifest hunger in their dream reports.

Thirst is treated as a single component issue separating the fasting

TABLE 4-1

Food Deprivation Components for the Four Groups

Groups	Food Frustration Components*						Cultural Deprivation Score
	(1)	(2)	(3)	(4)	(5)	(6)	(7)
Ethiopian Christians	+	+	+	+	−	+	5+
Fasting Nigerians	+	−	+	+	−	−	3+
Nonfasting Nigerians	−	−	−	−	−	+	1+
Americans	−	−	−	−	−	−	0

*The food frustration components indicated by column numbers: (1) Participation in a formalized fast. (2) The intensity, prolongation or frequency of the fasting experience. (3) The stringency of enforced sanctions accompanying the fast. (4) Other negative food behaviors including well-defined food taboos. (5) Evidence of chronic undernutrition. (6) Evidence of chronic malnutrition.

Each (+) sign represents a judgment in a positive direction and is scored 1. Each (−) sign represents a judgment in a negative direction and is scored 0. The total score accumulated by each group is in column 7 and is the *cultural deprivation score*.

Nigerians from the rest of the sample. The *drink deprivation score* for the fasting Nigerians is one; for the rest of the sample zero.

Measures of manifest hunger and thirst in dreams. The instrument which was developed for coding manifest hunger and thirst imagery in dreams is reproduced here.

INSTRUCTIONS FOR CODING HUNGER AND THIRST IMAGERY

I. General Instructions

Read each dream report completely at least once before attempting to code it. It is important to note that a distinction is always made between waking activity and dream activity as reported by the dreamer.* Only *dream activity* is coded; waking activity is *not* coded. If no distinction can be drawn, it is to be assumed that the reported activity is dream experience and it is coded accordingly.

These elements are being discriminately coded in the reports: accounts of eating and/or drinking on the part of *any* dream character inclusive of the dreamer; the mention of food and/or drink and the specific occasions of which food and/or drink are of central importance.

In cases of ambiguous meaning be as objective as it is possible for you to be. Use the general context of the dream report as your guide.

II. Particular Instructions

(1) Eating. If the dreamer or any dream character is described as eating, wanting to eat, preparing to eat or is specifically given food by another, put a check in the *manifest hunger column* of your coding sheet just opposite the number of the dream you are coding.

If the dreamer or any dream character is described as not eating, not wanting to eat, refusing food or being deprived of food, put a check in the manifest hunger column of your coding sheet as directed above.

(2) Drinking. If the dreamer or any dream character is described as drinking, wanting to drink, preparing to drink or is specifically given drink by another, put a check in the *manifest thirst column* of your coding sheet opposite the number of the dream you are coding.

If the dreamer or any dream character is described as not drinking, not wanting to drink, refusing or being deprived of drink, put a check in the *manifest thirst column* of your coding sheet as directed above.

(3) Food and its contexts. The mention of food in general terms, i.e., "dinner," "nourishment," "something to eat," as well as specific names for food, i.e., "mangoes," "meat," "yams," etc. are coded by placing a check in the *manifest hunger column* of your coding sheet. *Food contexts* (See Section III) are similarly coded even though eating may not be specifically indicated by the dreamer.

(4) Drink and its contexts. The mention of general and specific terms descriptive of drink and its contexts (See Section III) are coded by placing a check in the *manifest thirst column* of the coding sheet.

(5) Combined themes. Eating and drinking may be reported as separate or combined activities. One must be careful to code for both themes when they occur jointly, e.g., "I ate the meat and then I drank the wine," is coded in both columns.

---

* Many dream respondents included in their reports certain events or activities preceding or following their sleep and dream experiences.

III. Special Instructions

The context of the dream is of importance in determining the definitions of food, food contexts, drink, and drink contexts in most cases.

(1) For an animal, spirit or ogre to attack and eat a victim is described as a hunger theme although the attack is obviously aggressive. Since it is equally possible for such a being to attack and dismember a victim *without* eating it the hunger dynamic is made manifest. The implications of *condensation* in dream theory are important here.

(2) Fruits, vegetables and the trees, bushes, etc. upon which they grow are considered food elements for coding purposes.

The activity of fishing is coded as food context if it is clear that the fish are to be eaten or if no particular explanation is given. Fishing is *not* coded if the dreamer explicitly describes it as a sportive activity only.

Hunting is *not* coded as food context unless it is clear that the animal or victim is to be used for food.

The above distinctions made for hunting and fishing are based upon their apparent differences in meaning in the dreams. Fish are often described as food in a fishing context. However, many animals which are hunted are rarely suitable as food objects, i.e., lions, tigers, etc.

Picnics, feasts, banquets are coded as food contexts; ceremonies, festivals, etc., are *not* coded as food contexts unless the dreamer describes food as an explicit part of them

The mere mention of animals, even potential food animals is *not* coded as food. Their use as food has to be clear and unambiguous.

(3) Beverages to be coded as drinks are what one would normally expect them to be, i.e., water, milk, wine, beer, etc.

Water is coded if one drinks it, seeks it, fetches it from a pool, etc. Water is *not* coded as a drink context if it is mentioned only as a part of the landscape, something for bathing, something on which one travels, etc.

The drinking of unusual and bizarre liquids constitutes a drink theme, e.g., an ogre drinking the vital fluids of his victim, a person drinking the juice of a magical herb to ward off witches. The theory of *condensation* is important in these instances.

The reports were coded by the writer and one other individual who was uninformed of the hypotheses under study and the character of the groups in the sample.

Intercoder reliability of the instrument was tested by a comparison of the judgments of the two coders working independently on a set of forty-five dream reports randomly drawn from the total sample. Agreement between the two coders of 93% on the manifest hunger measure and 91% agreement on the manifest thirst measure was statistically significant ($p < 0.001$).

A sample recording sheet for the dream reports is reproduced here.

Name of Coder _____	Date _____	
Dream Number	Manifest Hunger	Manifest Thirst
485		
170		
032		

Although multiple codings for each category can be determined, each dreamer is scored on the simple presence or absence of thematic material in his two dream reports. The proportion of respondents who reveal manifest hunger in their dreams for any given group is the measure of *manifest hunger motivation* for that group. *Manifest thirst motivation* is measured in similar fashion.

Selected excerpts from some of the dreams with manifest hunger and thirst imagery follow. A fasting Nigerian youth reports a dream in which, after riding his horse through green grass, he encounters a beautiful girl from whom he requests water for his horse. The dream narrative follows:

. . . She at last said, "Well, I am sorry for you there is no water near here. If you need water seriously, you have to travel at least fifty-five miles."
I said, "I don't agree with you. If it is so, how do you get water on which you live?"
She said, "I am sorry we are not using water in my village. We are using milk instead."
"Do you mean you are quenching the thirsts of your cattle, donkeys, horses, dogs, goats and yourselves by drinking milk?"
She said, "If you doubt it you can follow me. If we go there you will be surprised when you see your horse drinking milk."

An Ethiopian respondent reports:

. . . I found people setting around a fire. They bade me sit down near the fire by the mere movements of their hands. I sat down and was entertained in friendly fashion with very delicious foods of all kinds. . . .

Another Ethiopian respondent includes the following description within a long and complicated dream:

. . . After I went for some miles (following a heavenly light) I reached a place where different types of foods were stored. As I was hungry I went on to eat the sweetest foods and to drink. I enjoyed doing this very much. . . .

Typically, the American respondents' references to eating are more casually inserted in the dream reports. For example, one boy includes the following reference to eating:

. . . and while I was at dinner one evening one of my teachers came over and told my father I was going to be flunked. . . .

In a dream about being in a rush to get to school one American writes:

. . . I hurried downstairs after I got my clothes on. Then I rushed through my breakfast also. . . .

Another American, reporting a dream of his first date, includes the following:

. . . The dance was over and I took her to dinner. There was nothing about the dinner. We drove out to the lake. . . .

Less casual is the report of a nonfasting Nigerian boy who reports dreaming of one of the food staples of his country:

. . . About two nights ago I dreamed that the people of my family were on a harvest day . . . when they bring the yams from the farm to the home. Every member of the family was very happy. Our yams had grown very big and work for the year had been successful. My brothers and myself were harvesting the yams. My mother and the other women and children were carrying the yams home.

That day was a great day for our family and everyone of us was proud. Everything that is usually done on a harvest was done that day. Some women took pieces of yam to their kitchens which is usually done when the yams have grown big. I never had such a dream before. . . .

RESULTS AND DISCUSSION

The data were treated as follows: The groups were rank-ordered on the basis of their cultural deprivation scores. These scores predicted the rank order of these groups relative to manifest hunger, Table 4–2. (Manifest hunger is defined as the percentage of dreamers in each group who show manifest hunger motivation in their dreams.)

The rank-order prediction is significant on the basis of permutation tests, $p=0.04$ (i.e., the single predicted alignment of four units taken four at a time).

Two groups, the nonfasting Nigerians and Americans, are differentiated on only one component, malnutrition. (The potential malnutrition of the nonfasting Nigerians has been discussed in a previous section.) As expected, manifest hunger is revealed in the dream reports of proportionately more nonfasting but malnourished Nigerians than Americans ($x^2=7.9$; 1 df; $p<0.005$).

Drink deprivation differentiated the fasting Nigerians from the rest of the sample. The expectation that the fasting Nigerians would have proportionately more dreamers reporting thirst imagery in their dreams is confirmed ($x^2=4.6$; 1 df; $p<0.05$) (See Table 4–3).

The results tend to support Freud's wish-fulfillment theory regarding the manifestations of hunger and thirst motivation in dreams. The

TABLE 4-2

The Rank Order of the Groups with Respect to Cultural Deprivation Scores and Manifest Hunger Motivation in Dreams

Groups*	Total Respondents	% of Respondents Showing Manifest Hunger
Ethiopians	36	63.8
Fasting Nigerians	73	43.8
Nonfasting Nigerians	270	33.7
Americans	55	14.5

*Ordered to cultural deprivation scores, Table 4-1.

TABLE 4-3

*The Relationship between Drink Deprivation
and Thirst Imagery in Dreams*

Groups	Total Respondents	% of Respondents Showing Manifest Thirst
Fasting Nigerians (Drink deprived)	73	19.1
All others (nondrink deprived)	361	10.2

findings should lend encouragement to efforts to study the development of human motivational states through the use of reported dreams.

The results also point to the usefulness of looking at broadly defined sociocultural situations in studying manifest dream content.

The finding that malnutrition seemingly contributes to hunger motivation in dreams is of interest. The effect may be either *direct*, i.e., stimulated by tissue needs, or *indirect*, i.e., the secondary result of some sociocultural adaptation to the physical environment. A discrimination between these effects is not possible within the context of the present study.

Whiting (14) has reported evidence that prolonged nursing of infants and small children is most commonly the pattern in tropical societies where there is inadequate protein in the diet. Prolonged nursing may represent an adaptation to a basic nutritional condition imposed by the physical environment. It may also have profound effects on personality development—effects which may have influenced the dream reports of the malnourished Nigerians.

SUMMARY

The question of how motivational states might be revealed in manifest dream content is viewed as a potentially important research area. The present study has focused upon the manifestations of hunger and thirst motivation in dreams. Freud's wish-fulfillment theory is reinterpreted within a broad biocultural perspective to supply the underlying hypothesis for the study.

Four groups differing significantly from one another in their food and drink customs and in their nutritional states were selected for study ($N=434$). Two sets of motivational measures were developed to test the assumption that hunger and thirst motivations are contingent upon conditions of food and drink deprivation, and to test the hypothesis that hunger and thirst motivations are revealed in dreams.

The findings indicate that rankings of food and drink deprivation, derived from cross-cultural data, are positively associated with the levels at which hunger and thirst motivations are made manifest in groups of dreamers.

REFERENCES

1. BENEDICT, F. G.; MILES, W. R.; ROTH, P. and SMITH, H. M.:   *Human vitality and efficiency under prolonged restriction diet* (Carnegie Institute, Washington 1919).

2. DEMENT, W. and WOLPERT, E. A.:   The relation of eye movements, body motility, and external stimuli to dream content. *J. exp. Psychol.* 55: 543–553 (1958).

3. EGGAN, D.:   The manifest content of dreams: a challenge to social science. *Amer. Anthropol.* 54: 469–485 (1952).

4. FREUD, S.:   *The interpretation of dreams* (Science Editions, Inc., New York 1961). Originally published 1900.

5. HALL, C.:   *The meaning of dreams* (Harper Brothers, New York 1953).

6. HUFFNAGEL, H. P.:   *Agriculture in Ethiopia* (Food and Agricultural Organization of the United Nations, Rome 1961).

7. KEYS, A.; BROZEK, J.; HENSCHEL, A.; MICKELSON, O. and TAYLOR, H. L.: *The biology of human starvation, vol. II* (Univ. of Minnesota Press, Minneapolis 1950).

8. LEVINE, DONALD N.:   Identity, Authority and Realism. In W. PYE LUCIAN and VERBA SNYDER (Ed.), *Political culture and political development* (Princeton Univ. Press, Princeton, N.J. 1965).

9. LeVINE, ROBERT A.:   *Achievement motivation in Nigeria: a study of personality and social structure* (Committee on Human Development, Univ. of Chicago, Chicago, Ill. 1964).

10. MURPHY, G.:   *Personality: a biosocial approach to origins and structure* (Harper Brothers, New York 1947).

11. NIVEN, C. R.:   *Nigeria, outline of a colony* (Thomas Nelson & Sons Ltd., London 1945).

12. QUINN-YOUNG, C. F. and HERDMAN, T.:   *Geography of Nigeria, 2nd ed.* (Longmans, Green & Co., London 1949).

13. VON GRUNEBAUM, G. E.:   *Muhammadan festivals* (Henry Schuman Inc., New York 1951).

14. WHITING, JOHN W. M.:   Effects of climate on certain cultural practices. In WARD L. GOODENOUGH (Ed.), *Explorations in cultural anthropology: essays in honor of George Peter Murdock* (McGraw-Hill, Inc., New York 1964).

5

Ramon Greenberg, M.D., Richard Pillard, M.D.,
& Chester Pearlman, M.D.

The Effect of Dream (Stage REM)
Deprivation on Adaptation to Stress

The concept that dreaming serves to fulfill wishes, presented by Freud in the *Interpretation of Dreams,* eclipsed all previous theories about dreaming, but subsequent writers have frequently commented on the limitations of this hypothesis as a total theory of dream function. Maeder (1), Garma (2), and Piaget (3) have proposed that dreaming is involved in adaptation to traumatic (anxiety-arousing) experiences. French and Fromm (4) elaborated this concept into a theory that dreaming is concerned with the formulation of solutions to current "focal conflicts" of the dreamer.

Studies based on current psychophysiologic concepts of sleep have also led to the idea that dreaming during Stage Rapid Eye Movement (REM)-sleep* is involved in processing new experiences. Breger (5) formulated dreaming as a working over and integration of recently perceived input into already existing structures. Gaarder's (6) hypothesis also included the idea of adding recent experiences to existing structures for adaptive purposes. Dewan (7) characterized REM as a programming process for the brain. We recently presented a similar hypothesis (8). We stated that daily experiences may arouse repressed conflicts, memories, or feelings. In the dream, these new experiences interact with the previously repressed material with a resultant reinstitution of characterologic defense patterns that previously have been used to deal with this kind of experience.

The aim of the present study was to investigate the role of dreaming (Stage REM sleep) in adaptation by normal persons to an anxiety-provoking experience. Previous work (9) had shown that viewing a film

Reprinted by permission of American Psychosomatic Society from *Psychosomatic Medicine,* 1972, *34,* 257–262.

* Mental content has frequently been recorded following awakening from non-REM sleep but, for most persons, it is easily distinguishable from the dream experiences associated with REM sleep.

of a medical autopsy usually aroused anxiety in a normal medically unsophisticated subject. Most normal subjects subsequently adapted to the experience so that a second exposure produced much less anxiety.

In this study, we compared the influence of REM-deprived sleep, normal sleep, and interrupted (but not REM-deprived) sleep on the subjects' capacity to adapt to the second viewing of the film. From our hypothesis about the function of dreaming, we predicted that subjects deprived of REM sleep between the first and second viewing would be more anxious and show less adaptation to the second viewing than those who had normal sleep or interrupted sleep without REM deprivation.

METHOD

Twenty college students (male and female) were involved in this study. Those who had interrupted sleep were paid $30, and those who had undisturbed sleep received $25. Subjects began the study with a session at the Psychopharmacology Laboratory at Boston University's School of Medicine. There they became familiar with the psychophysiologic measurements which involved attachment of electrodes to measure heart rate, respiration rate, skin potential, and finger sweat (FSP). They also were given the Psychiatric Outpatient Mood Scale (POMS) test (10). After these measurements, they were shown a short, interesting film about computer generated tones.* Physiologic measurements were made for three-min. periods before and during the film. Following the film the POMS was again administered. That night, they reported to the Sleep Laboratory at the Boston VA Hospital where electroencephalogram (EEG), electrooculogram (EOG), and electromyogram (EMG) recording was performed throughout a night of undisturbed sleep. This was a practice session to acquaint subjects with the procedure and to allay nonspecific apprehension.

A week later, each subject returned to the Psychopharmacology Laboratory where the same procedure was repeated, except that on this occasion the movie was an eight-min. excerpt from a medical film, "Basic Autopsy Procedures." It showed a pathologist examining a cadaver, making an abdominal incision, a scalp incision, sawing and chiseling away the calvarium and making an incision along the spine. Sound was turned off to increase opportunity for fantasy. That night, they again reported to the Sleep Laboratory where five were allowed undisturbed sleep, nine were REM deprived by being awakened at the first signs of REM sleep, and six were awakened from non-REM sleep

* "A Pair of Paradoxes" by R. N. Shepard and E. E. Zajac. Furnished through the courtesy of Bell Telephone Laboratories.

the same number of times as a paired member of the REM-deprived group had been awakened. The next morning they returned to the Psychopharmacology Laboratory where the same film and measurements were repeated. The psychophysiologist did not know the subjects' sleep group. Following this session, each subject was interviewed to elicit his feelings and impressions of the experience.

RESULTS

We first assessed the stressfulness of the autopsy film. Increases were registered in heart and respiration rates, skin potential, finger sweat, and those factors on the POMS which describe "tension anxiety" and "disgust shock." Of these, the increases in FSP and POMS were significant ($P = <.01$) (Figure 5–1).* By contrast, most subjects did not develop any change in these variables when they saw the computer tone film. Thus, the stressful nature of the autopsy film in comparison to the computer tone film was clearly demonstrated in the increases in FSP and POMS scores; thus we assumed the tests were measuring an increase in anxiety.

Most subjects also reported that the first viewing of the autopsy film bothered them. During the period of time between viewing the film and reporting to the Sleep Laboratory, they felt (1) "Shocked and surprised," (2) "I couldn't be alone after watching it," (3) "It was a shock treatment. . . ," (4) "I was tempted to ask you to stop it," "Repulsive. . . horrible." One subject requested that the film be stopped halfway through.

The POMS and FSP results showed the stress reaction for most but not all of the subjects. Those who failed to show greater anxiety with the first autopsy film than with the computer film were dropped from further analysis. For the POMS this included two control sleep, one control awakening, and one REM-deprived subject. For the FSP this included one control awakening and four dream-deprived subjects. Without a definable measure of stress from the first viewing of the autopsy film, we assumed that the effects of dreaming on the stress could not be assessed. The excluded subjects were not necessarily the same for the POMS and the FSP. This seems understandable because people manifest anxiety in different ways.

The next question involved the difference in sleep patterns between REM-deprived and control groups. The REM-deprived group had seven to nineteen mins. of REM sleep. The control awakening and control subjects had from fifty-three to ninety-seven mins. of REM. Sleep pa-

---

* POMS "tension/anxiety" scored as described by McNair et al. (10) with some items added to reflect feelings of disgust and shock. FSP scored from a photographic density scale described in reference 9.

FIGURE 5-1

*Comparison of Responses of All Subjects to Computer
Tone and Autopsy Films on the POMS and FSP Scores*

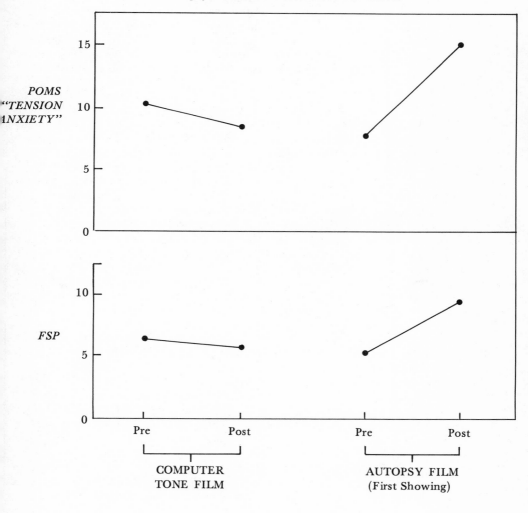

rameters of the control awakening and unawakened subjects did not differ significantly and these groups were combined for comparison with the REM-deprived group. The combined control group had an average of 360 mins. of sleep and the REM-deprived group averaged 265 mins. Of this ninety-five min. difference, about seventy are accounted for by the difference in REM.

We now turn to a comparison of the effects of viewing the autopsy film a second time on the combined-control and REM-deprived groups (Figure 5–2). (There was no difference between the control awakening and undisturbed sleep groups.) Using the tension-anxiety scores of the POMS, both groups had a significant increase in anxiety in response to first viewing the autopsy ($t = 3.92$; $df = 15$; $P < .002$) and a lesser increase to the second viewing ($t = 1.90$; $P < .10$). Thus, both groups showed some adaptation to the second viewing. The REM-deprived sub-

FIGURE 5-2

Comparison of POMS Anxiety Scores for REM-deprived and Control Groups on the First and Second Viewings of the Autopsy Film

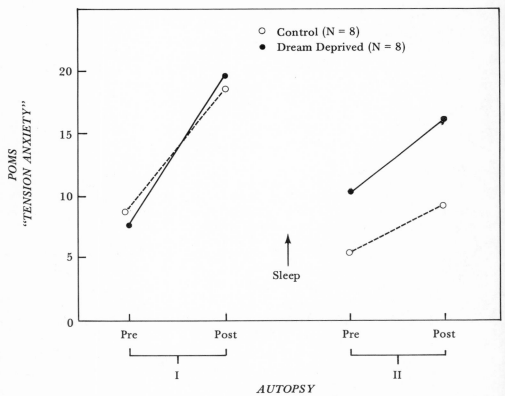

jects were more anxious, however, especially on the postfilm measure ($t = 2.14$; $P < .05$).

Another way to test this effect is by a 2×2 analysis of covariance using the scores after the first autopsy viewing as the covariate. This permits an estimate of whether the *change* in anxiety for the two groups was different. Analysis of the data in this fashion shows that while both groups have an increase in anxiety on the second viewing ($F = 3.42$; $P < .10$), the REM-deprived group is made more anxious than the control by the second viewing ($F = 5.41$; $P < .05$), almost approaching the levels they showed after the first viewing. The interaction term was not significant, showing that the anxiety increase for the two groups was not of different magnitude.

A final way of viewing the data is to compare the difference between responses to the first and second viewing for each subject. Six of the eight control subjects were affected less by the second viewing than by the first, one showed no change, and one was made more anxious. In contrast, five of the eight REM-deprived subjects were made more anxious by the second viewing than by the first, two were less affected, and one showed no change. The Mann-Whitney U test showed this difference to be significant ($P < .05$).

The FSP scores were analyzed in the same fashion. Our criterion for excluding subjects who failed to show greater increase in FSP to the autopsy than to the tone film left only four subjects in the REM-deprived group. The results parallel those on the POMS test, but because of the small number of subjects the difference between control and REM-deprived groups is nonsignificant.

DISCUSSION

This study was designed to explore the relationships of dreaming to adaptation to an anxiety-provoking situation. The results showed that, with a stress that clearly induced anxiety, a second experience of the stress revealed significantly less adaptation by the REM-deprived group than by the control group. That is, the REM-deprived group was significantly more anxious following the second viewing than the control group. Our hypothesis suggests the following explanation of this finding. When an individual meets a situation which is stressful for him, the stressfulness is due to the arousal of memories of prior difficulties with similar situations. The person's initial defensive reaction is usually of an emergency or generalized type (such as global denial or repression). Then, during the dream experience, these feelings from the past and the current stressful stimulus are integrated, and the individual's characteristic defenses for that particular set of emotions and memories are used to deal with the current threat. If the stress is reexperienced, he now has available his characteristic (for him most efficient) means of dealing with the threat. Thus, reexposure to the stress should not produce the initial degree of anxiety.

Another possible explanation for the poorer adaptation is that the subjects were in a sensitized state due to increased drives as a result of the REM deprivation procedure. While this interpretation is consistent with classic psychoanalytic concepts of dream function, there is no evidence confirming the development of increased drives with one day of REM deprivation. A study in our laboratory revealed that rats REM-deprived for one day showed neither an increase in exploratory behavior nor increased bar pressing for food. The Rorschach protocols in our study of REM deprivation in humans also failed to show a consistent increase in drive state (8).

Although the results show a significant impairment of adaptation by the REM-deprived subjects, some adaptation did occur. A possible explanation for this is that they all did some dreaming during the night. In a similar study, Breger et al. (11) found that REM-deprived subjects reported dream fragments incorporating elements from the stressful film. This implies an immediate attempt to deal with the anxiety-provoking stimulus in the dream. It would be extremely difficult to evaluate just how much dreaming is necessary to deal with the stressful situation. It is also possible that some REM-deprived subjects continued to use emergency defenses (e.g., intellectual understanding of the situation) which permitted some reduction in anxiety.

Two other observations in this study are worth noting. There was a tendency for anxiety and fatigue in the REM-deprived subjects to be increased prior to viewing the second autopsy film. Most studies of REM deprivation have not shown a generalized increase in anxiety (12, 13). Why, then, did we observe some increased anxiety? The unique aspect of this REM-deprivation study is that the subjects were presented with an anxiety-provoking stimulus prior to the REM deprivation. The increase in anxiety may well represent defective handling of the anxiety aroused by the stimulus. In other words the individual is presented with a specifically labeled task and, without REM, the anxiety continues. The fatigue might represent unusual efforts to deal with the anxiety due to prevention of the usual mechanism—i.e., dreaming. While this explanation is speculative, it fits our hypothesis and also offers a new way of studying REM deprivation—i.e., by presenting subjects with the task before the deprivation procedure. For example, wearing inverting prisms has been shown to lead to an increase in REM. Would REM deprivation during the period of wearing the prisms lead to impaired adaptation?

In discussing the psychoanalytic psychology of adaptation, Joffe and Sandler (14) emphasized the continual development by the ego of new organizations of the "ideal state of the self" to preserve the feeling of safety and to avoid being traumatically overwhelmed. A stressful experience is a demand for such an alteration, and a traumatic experience involves a demand for greater change than the individual is capable of at the time. It is a truism that successful adaptation requires time.

The reasons for this are not so clear. Experiments with the learning of cognitive material suggest that such a learning is completed soon after the learning experience. Some defensive operations occur in a similar close relation to emotionally stressful experiences. Thus, why adaptation or emotional learning requires so much more time is puzzling. Thinking about the stressful experience or discussing it with other people may facilitate adaptation, but anxious brooding, usually accompanied by sleep disturbance, indicates the limitations of conscious thinking as a mechanism of adaptation. It is also commonly observed that adaptation occurs relatively independently of the conscious action of the subject. It "just happens." In attempting to determine when it happens, one might propose that during waking life unconscious processes of psychic adaptation occur which are analogous to other processes of growth and homeostasis. In our opinion, such a simple model does not do justice to clinical experience. The vivid example of the posttraumatic dream suggests another model. Posttraumatic dreams reveal, over a period of time, an evolution from repetition of the traumatic event to a change in the content which reveals some of the elements from the past which have been aroused by the traumatic event. The past and present become woven together and the traumatic event is gradually mastered. When this fails to happen, as in the repetitive war dream, the patient continues to have a symptomatic neurotic illness.

SUMMARY

In this study we have examined the hypothesis that a critical intervening process in adaptation to a stressful situation is dreaming or the REM stage of sleep. We studied a group of volunteer subjects who, after adaptation to the laboratory conditions, were shown a stressful movie on two consecutive days. During the night between these two viewings, some subjects were REM-deprived, some awakened an equivalent number of times during non-REM sleep, and some allowed to sleep undisturbed. Psychologic and physiologic measures of anxiety were obtained in relation to the two viewings. The results showed that the subjects who were REM-deprived showed significantly less habituation to the second viewing than the control subjects. These findings were discussed in relation to the hypothesis that REM sleep serves to integrate memories of similar experiences with the current stress, allowing the use of the individual's characteristic defenses. When the film is viewed for a second time, those subjects who have been allowed to dream were made less anxious than the REM-deprived group because they could now use their characteristic, and probably more efficient, defenses to deal with the anxiety-provoking aspects of the film. REM-deprived subjects, on the other hand, showed a decreased ability to adapt to the specific stress.

REFERENCES

1. MAEDER, A. E.:   The dream problem. *Nerv. Ment. Dis.*, Monograph No. 22, 1916.

2. GARMA, A.:   The traumatic situation in the genesis of dreams. *Int. J. Psychoanal.* 27:134–139, 1946.

3. PIAGET, J.:   *Play, Dreams and Imitation in Childhood.* New York, W. W. Norton & Company, Inc., 1951.

4. FRENCH, T. M., and FROMM, E.:   *Dream Interpretation: A New Approach.* New York: Basic Books, Inc., Publishers, 1964.

5. BREGER, L.:   The function of dreams. *J. Abnorm. Psychol.*, Monograph No. 641, 1967.

6. GAARDER, K.:   A conceptual model of sleep. *Arch. Gen. Psychiatry* 14:263–270, 1966.

7. DEWAN, E.:   *Programming (P) hypothesis for REM sleep, Sleep and Dreaming, International Psychiatric Clinics.* Edited by E. Hartman. Boston, Little, Brown and Company, 1970. pp. 295–307.

8. GREENBERG, R., PEARLMAN, C., KAWLICHE, S., et al.: The effects of dream deprivation. *Br. J. Med. Psychol.* 43:1–11, 1970.

9. PILLARD, R., ATKINSON, K., and FISHER, S.:   The effect of different preparations on film induced anxiety. *Psychol. Record* 17:35–41, 1967.

10. McNAIR, D. M., LORR, M., and DROPPLEMAN, L. F.:   *Manual Profile of Mood States.* San Diego: Educational Industrial Testing Service (In press).

11. BREGER, L., HUNTER, I., and LANE, R. W.:   The effects of stress on dreams. *Psychol. Issues* 27, 1971.

12. KALES, A., HODEMAKER, F. S., JACOBSON, A., et al.: Dream deprivation: an experimental reappraisal. *Nature* 204:1337–38, 1964.

13. SAMPSON, H.:   Psychological effects of deprivation of dreaming sleep. *J. Nerv. Ment. Dis.* 143:305–317, 1966.

14. JOFFE, W. G., and SANDLER, J.:   Comments on the psychoanalytic psychology of adaptation. *Int. J. Psychoanal.* 49:445–454, 1968.

From the Boston Veterans Administration Hospital and the Boston University School of Medicine.

Supported by Research Scientist Development Award Grant No. MH-32896.

6

Patricia Carrington, Ph.D.

Dreams and Schizophrenia

So striking are the elements of the bizarre and the unreal in certain dreams, that dreams in general are apt to be looked upon as a form of noctural madness that regularly overtakes the normal person. Despite its popularity, we might question this view. Can we identify differences between nonschizophrenic and schizophrenic dreams which are as striking as their similarities? If so, then not all dreams are equally "mad"—some may even be quite rational.

While some experimental attempts have been made to answer this question, investigators have generally sought to identify a dream pathognomonic of schizophrenia, and researchers (1–3) seeking to demonstrate unequivocally specific characteristics either in dream content or structure have had to conclude that a diagnostically unique entity, the "schizophrenic dream," does not exist.

Unfortunately, failure to discover a uniquely "schizophrenic" dream can easily lead to the assumption that *no* differences exist between the dreams of schizophrenics and others. Clinical observation suggests, however, that this conclusion may be as unwarranted as the idea that a schizophrenic *always* dreams "differently" from a nonschizophrenic. A systematic investigation of the differences between dreams with respect to variables related on theoretical and clinical grounds to the schizophrenic process is needed.

METHODOLOGY OF PREVIOUS STUDIES

Several studies of schizophrenic dreams were published between 1936 and 1959 using *clinical inspection* as a research technique (4–8). Although these studies could not give a conclusive answer as to content

Reprinted by permission of the American Medical Association from *Archives of General Psychiatry,* 1972, *26*, 343–350. Copyright 1972 by the American Medical Association.

TABLE 6-1

*Characteristics of Schizophrenic
and Nonschizophrenic Subjects*

	Schizophrenic Subjects $N = 30$	Nonschizophrenic Subjects $N = 30$
Religion		
Catholic	5	4
Jewish	17	9
Protestant	8	15
Other	0	2
Race		
Negro	2	1
White	28	29
Age in Years		
Mean age	20.4	21.6
Median age	19	21
Modal age	19	21
Age range	15-39	18-44
Parents' Occupation		
Professional	10	15
Business	13	14
White collar	2	0
Skilled labor	3	0
Unskilled labor	1	1
Unemployed	1	0
Education Completed		
1 yr High School	1	0
2 yr High School	5	0
3 yr High School	7	0
4 yr High School	12	1
1 yr College	3	4
2 yr College	1	9
3 yr College	1	10
4 yr College	0	2
1 yr Graduate School	0	4
Marital Status		
Single	28	29
Married	2	1

differences, they were the first attempts at confirming a frequent clinical observation, namely that schizophrenic dreams have a "flavor" or quality discernible to the trained person.

While affording valuable leads, none of these studies used "blind" evaluations or objective scoring to control for experimenter bias. A number (4, 7, 8) failed to include comparison groups.

More recently, schizophrenic dreams were studied under more standardized conditions (1–3, 9). However, the only studies to date aimed specifically at investigating schizophrenic dream *content* with objective scoring methods (1, 3, 9) either do not report reliabilities or report some as low as 50% (3). The Hall-Van de Castle scoring system has high reliability but, as it was developed on a college population, it is not geared specifically to measurement of psychopathology, and so far has not differentiated clinical groups (9). A fully acceptable, widely applicable scoring system to investigate schizophrenic dream content has not as yet been devised.

This study was designed as the first in a series on the dreamlife of the schizophrenic. It uses a scoring system devised to reflect certain commonly recognized symptoms of schizophrenia (10).

RESEARCH DESIGN

The clinical criteria selected for study had to be generally recognized by qualified authorities, reflective of commonly encountered schizophrenic traits, and identifiable in dream *content*. Probably only about one-third of the commonly recognized schizophrenic traits can be readily studied in dreams. Comparison of Beck's rather exhaustive list of schizophrenic traits (11) with the categories used here (10) suggests that, of those common schizophrenic traits potentially identifiable in dream *content* (rather than dream *structure*), about 80% are covered by the items used in the present study.

HYPOTHESES

This study investigated three broad areas of dysfunction commonly associated with schizophrenia: (1) disturbed interpersonal relationships, (2) disintegrative trends, and (3) impaired reality sense.

A fourth area included an additional maladaptive trait (anhedonia), and two categories to be compared with previous studies but for which results were not predicted.

Several areas of interpersonal functioning were considered: (1) the schizophrenic's need for interpersonal contact (even though in fantasy), (2) his avoidance of mutually shared experience, (3) his tendency to view others as hostile toward himself, and (4) to experience a hostile attitude *toward* others.

Certain disintegrative trends, such as thought disorders, are not readily studied in dreams; it was extremely difficult to separate a present waking thought disturbance from one which might have occurred *during* the dream. Disintegrative trends which could be studied in dream content were: (1) the schizophrenic's anxieties about world destruction (catastrophic environmental threats), (2) his anxieties of bodily disintegration, and (3) impaired control over his impulse life (dyscontrol).

Only certain types of impaired reality testing could be investigated in dreams (since the dream world represents an inner, distorted "reality" to begin with). Two categories of reality disturbance were studied: (1) the patient's tendency to overlook the limitations of objective reality and operate outside of culturally accepted frames of reference (bizarre imagery), and (2) a tendency for paranoid coloring in his thinking.

One more hypothesis seemed worthy of investigation. On theoretical grounds we were led to predict a more pleasurable tone in the dreams of *nonschizophrenic* subjects.

In addition to the hypotheses, two other main categories, "friendly" and "presence of dreamer's relatives" were investigated for purposes of comparison with former studies. (The "friendly" category is based on the Hall-Van de Castle (12) scoring for "friendly interactions" and involves a deliberate, purposeful attempt on the part of a character to express friendliness toward the dreamer.)

It was predicted that schizophrenic subjects would obtain higher scores on the following variables: *others act with dreamer, aggression against dreamer, aggression against others or objects, environmental threat, human physical deficit state, dyscontrol, bizarre imagery*, and *paranoid ideation*. It was predicted that schizophrenic subjects would obtain *lower* scores for *gratifying content*, and that the two groups would show no differences (prediction of the null hypothesis) for the category *other persons appear in the dream*. The present study may be viewed as a test, in a very broad sense, of the hypothesis that dream content is consistent with waking psychopathology, or waking normality.

PROCEDURES

Since certain aspects of dream recall are sex linked (12, 13) and women may be better dream recallers than men (14), the subjects were women volunteers (thirty schizophrenics and thirty nonschizophrenics).

The patients (S group: mean age 20.4, median 19, range 15 to 39) were chosen from a hospital population diagnosed as schizophrenic by the staff (15). Most were in an acute state, 70% being first admissions. None had organic disease, electroconvulsive therapy within three months of study, or thought disorders of a severity which would impair ability to communicate dreams. They were of average or superior intelligence. Twenty-one of the thirty were taking medication (nineteen were taking tranquilizers). None were taking imipramine hydrochloride, which has been shown to increase hostility in dreams (16).

The control group was composed of twenty-five female university

TABLE 6-2

Schizophrenic (S) vs. Nonschizophrenic (NS) Group
(N = 30, Each Group)*

Variable	S Group Mean	SD	NS Group Mean	SD	Z Value	Significance Level
I. Interpersonal Disturbance						
Hypothesis 1. Other persons appear in dream	4.63	0.76	4.67	0.55	−0.19	NS
Hypothesis 2. Others act *with* dreamer	42.17†	23.66†	62.94†	25.75†	−3.25	< .0007
Hypothesis 3. Aggression against dreamer	23.17†	22.72†	10.33†	12.93†	2.69	< .004
Hypothesis 4. Aggression against others or objects	1.20	1.09	0.77	0.86	1.70	< .04
II. Disintegrative Trends						
Hypothesis 5. Environmental threat	1.40	1.10	0.77	0.77	2.58	< .005
Hypothesis 6. Human physical deficit state	1.63	1.30	0.73	0.78	3.25	< .0007
Hypothesis 7. Dyscontrol	1.33	1.12	0.37	0.61	4.13	< .00003
III. Impaired Reality Sense						
Hypothesis 8. Bizarre imagery	2.47	1.57	1.30	1.23	3.20	< .0007
Hypothesis 9. Paranoid ideation	0.80	0.80	0.20	0.41	3.64	< .002
IV. Other						
Hypothesis 10. Gratifying content	0.53	0.73	0.30	0.59	1.35	NS
Comparative Category Friendly toward dreamer‡	13.33†	14.22†	7.94†	12.09†	1.58	NS
Comparative Category Presence of relatives‡	37.28†	29.14†	31.17†	26.58†	0.85	NS

*Comparison of means (one-tailed test) using normal curve.
†Expressed as a percentage of the number of positive scores for Hypothesis 1 (presence of others).
‡Two-tailed test.

students (NS group: mean age 21.6, median 21, range 18 to 44). Sociological comparisons of the groups are given in Table 6–1. Each NS group subject completed a Minnesota Multiphasic Personality Inventory (MMPI) (self-administering form).

Schizophrenic subjects slept in their own rooms in open sections of a private hospital, and control subjects slept in their dormitory rooms. Five dream reports (from five different nights of sleep) were obtained on tape from each subject by asking the subject to report dreams in the morning in accordance with a standardized interviewing procedure. The subjects and the interviewers were unaware of the purpose of the study.

The dream reports were transcribed verbatim, disguised by eliminating obvious identifying elements, such as "hospital," and were randomly ordered. Five judges, who had five preliminary training sessions with the scoring manual, independently scored the reports.

The first dream reports were obtained from the nonschizophrenic subjects. It was then learned that the schizophrenic subjects were too disorganized and negativistic in the early morning to report dreams immediately after waking. They did cooperate and report in midmorning. Since the different time of dream reporting may have influenced dream content, a comparison of dream categories was made between my controls and dreams obtained later in the day by Hall from another group of college women (mean age 21.6, median 21, range 19 to 40) (17).

Scoring System. The present study rests on the use of a scoring system designed to identify the selected clinical criteria (10). In addition to the ten hypotheses and the two comparative categories, the scoring manual in its final form also contained nineteen qualitative scores (subvariables) which qualified the main categories. These nineteen scores had been pretested and refined on sample dreams during the formal training of the judges and are described in detail elsewhere (10).

Hypotheses 3 and 4 (aggression against dreamer and aggression against others or objects) were each separately characterized as consisting of either (1) rejection, (2) chase, (3) violence, (4) heterosexual aggression, or (5) homosexual aggression. Hypothesis 5 (environmental threat) was characterized as consisting of either a "passive" or an "active" threat. Hypothesis 6 (human physical deficit state) was characterized as consisting of a deficit involving either mutilation or death, and Hypothesis 7 (dyscontrol) was characterized as consisting of either an actual or potential loss of balance. One category (morbid) qualified Hypothesis 8 (bizarre imagery) as consisting of a form of bizarreness which included deathlike, decadent, ugly, sickening, or "unwholesome" qualities. Hypothesis 9 (paranoid ideation) was characterized as consisting of paranoid imagery which was either "grandiose" or "projective."

Scoring Procedures. The dream was the unit of scoring with dreams scored for *presence* or *absence* of each of the twelve main variables and nineteen subvariables. Qualitative categories were scored only when the main variable in question had already been given a positive score. These qualitative categories represented areas in which the experimenter was particularly interested. They did not by any means represent *all* the qualifying comments that could have been made about any one category, and when they did not apply they were not scored.

Interjudge Agreement. The mean interscorer agreement for all pairs of judges was 90% or above on all main categories, and 88% or above on all qualitative categories. Range of interjudge agreements, mean interjudge agreements for the combined categories, and percentage agreement computed for each category separately are reported elsewhere (10).

Obtaining Subject Scores. In cases of disagreement between the three judges, the final classification for each dream on any one variable followed the majority opinion (two out of the three opinions). Following determination of these consensus scores for each separate dream, the dreams were decoded and recombined according to subject, and a *sub-*

TABLE 6-3

Schizophrenic (S) vs. Nonschizophrenic (NS) Qualitative Categories*
Which Showed Significant Differences Between Groups

Variable	S Group			NS Group			t- = Value	Significance Level
	N	Mean	SD	N	Mean	SD		
I. Interpersonal Disturbance Hypothesis 3. Aggression against dreamer: violence	19	38.60	39.30	13	7.69	27.74	2.44	.05
Hypothesis 4. Aggression against others or objects: violence	20	59.17	42.05	16	18.75	40.31	3.92	.01
II. Disintegrative Trends Hypothesis 5. Environmental threat: active	23	64.49	39.02	17	23.02	39.10	3.25	.001
Hypothesis 6. Human deficit: mutilation	23	22.83	35.02	16	3.13	12.50	2.15	.05
I. Impaired Reality Sense Hypothesis 9. Bizarre: morbid	26	24.49	30.52	20	0.00	0.00	3.58	.001

*Means of qualitative categories are expressed as a percentage of the number (N) of positive scores received or the main category which they qualify.

ject score for each of the twelve main variables was determined by counting the number of dreams (out of each subject's dream series) in which this variable occurred. Possible scores for each subject on each variable thus ranged from zero to five.

When each subject's subject score had been determined for all the variables, means and standard deviations of these subject scores were computed on each variable. Subject scores were also computed for the qualitative categories. These scores were expressed as percentages of the main subject score for the category qualified. For example, if a subject had received a subject score of three on the main category bizarre, and if two out of her three bizarre dreams subsequently received the qualitative score of morbid, she would receive a qualitative subject score of 66% for the category morbid.

Statistical Operations. Means and standard deviations were computed for the main scores in each group and tests of significance were carried out. Because of the large number of degrees of freedom (fifty-eight), the curves were taken from the normal table, and results are reported accordingly.

Since each qualitative category was dependent on the presence of the main category which it qualified, each qualitative score was expressed as a percentage of its respective main category. Numbers were therefore smaller for the qualitative categories, and differences between means were evaluated for their significance by referring to student's distribution.

RESULTS

As detailed in Tables 6–2 and 6–3, all but one of the nine testable hypotheses were confirmed at better than the 0.05 level of significance, with three of these categories showing differences where P was < 0.0007. Five qualitative categories also showed differences between the groups. For the two comparative categories, friendly toward dreamer and presence of relatives, no differences were found.

Factors Affecting Results. No significant differences between experimental and control groups were found in length of dreams. The effects of differences in education and religion, of medication, and of the time of day when dreams were collected were negligible. Further, the scoring categories were found to correlate no more frequently than could be expected on the basis of chance (10).

Subgroup Comparison. On the basis of their MMPI protocols, non-schizophrenic subjects were classified by digital computer, using a program developed by Kleinmuntz (18), into the subgroups: "well-adjusted" (nineteen subjects) and "maladjusted" (ten subjects). One subject was unclassifiable by this method, and her data were omitted. Mean dream scores for the well-adjusted and maladjusted subgroups and for the schizophrenic group were then compared.

On most of the dream parameters considered, sharp differences were found between the schizophrenic group and either the well-adjusted or maladjusted subgroups (while scores of these subgroups generally resembled each other). Some blurring of the distinctions found in the first study occurred, however, when schizophrenic and maladjusted groups were compared on such variables as depiction of the dream environment as threatening, and of human beings as being in a state of physical deficit. Both of these categories showed higher scores for the maladjusted than for the well-adjusted group, with means for the maladjusted group falling roughly midway between those of the well-adjusted and schizophrenic groups. This suggests that traits which these dream variables reflect may be distributed along a continuum of increasing maladjustment, rather than reflecting schizophrenia per se. Dreams which depict violence against the dreamer may also be distributed in this fashion. The *manner* in which environmental threats, human physical deficit states, or violent assaults are perceived and reacted to by the schizophrenic may be unique to the latter group, however (10).

COMMENT

The hypothesis of consistency between waking and dreamlife is supported by the present study. Schizophrenic subjects displayed symptomatology commonly associated with schizophrenia in their dreams significantly more often than did nonschizophrenic subjects.

In general, the findings suggest that the dreams of the schizophrenic subjects represent a state of emergency or stress. Schizophrenic subjects tended to view their dream environment and the persons depicted in it as overwhelmingly threatening. Their dreams were replete with mutilation imagery and morbid themes. They were more aggressive, more bizarre, and more often reflective of ego dyscontrol than were the dreams of control subjects. The impression was that the sleeping schizophrenic subject was struggling, often futilely, with massive disruptive forces in her personality. By contrast, the dreams of the controls seemed to have an "everyday," practical quality, and to be only mildly stressful.

Theoretically, one might expect some overlap between the dreams of other psychiatric groups and those of our patients, although this possibility remains to be tested. The "emergency" quality here observed in the schizophrenic subjects' dreams might also be seen transitorially in the dreams of persons under intensive stress due to severely disrupting emotional or physical states, for example, or in persons with central nervous system damage. It may, in fact, be found that what we have observed in the schizophrenic subjects is, in part, the degree of stress under which the organism operates, and the manner in which such stress affects personality disorganization. Such a stress-adaptation measure might be expected to overlap a number of clinical entities, relating them theoretically one to the other. Only systematic research can clarify this issue.

A more detailed study of the dream protocols collected seemed to be in order to fully understand the significance of the statistical results, and analyses of the previously collected data were therefore undertaken with attention directed to the qualitative aspects of the dream protocols (10). Some of the more important qualitative findings are discussed below.

Aggression Against Dreamer and Against Others or Objects. Inspection of dream protocols indicates that *physical* aggression directed against the dreamer is relatively rare in the NS (nonschizophrenic) dreams as compared to the S (schizophrenic) group dreams. Supporting an interpretation of the dreams of the schizophrenic subjects as representing an emergency stance is the fact that roughly one-half of these S group dreams of physical aggressions against the dreamer explicitly indicated the dreamer's *life* to be in danger. In some instances, the dreamer was actually killed in her dream. The remaining half of the S group dreams of physical assault on the dreamer involved sexual assaults, rapes, and other nonlethal attacks such as someone throwing a jar of spiders over the dreamer. In such dreams, while the dreamer's life was not explicitly described as being at stake, they often seemed to *imply* danger to life. In contrast, danger to life was depicted in only one of the two NS dreams of physical assault against the dreamer.

In those dreams where aggression was turned against others or objects instead of against the dreamer, the total percentages of physical aggression increased for *both* groups, but the schizophrenic subjects still showed the preponderance of physical responses. Nonschizophrenic subjects most frequently attacked others *verbally* in their dreams and in four instances (28% of the NS group's dreamer-as-aggressor dreams) the NS subjects described themselves in the dream as merely *feeling* angry but not *acting* on the feeling, a form of impulse control which did not occur in any of the schizophrenic dreams. These observations may attest to the relative ego intactness, even during sleep, of the dreaming NS subjects. The schizophrenic dreamer's frenzied dream attacks upon others were not delayed or considered actions, and were seldom modulated.

Environmental Threat. The dreams of the schizophrenic group depicted environmental threat significantly more often than did NS group dreams, and in addition, the judges scored S group threat dreams as more active and overwhelming in nature than those of the NS group. Qualitative study of the protocols reveals a further difference—the *outcomes* of the threatening situations appear to differ for the two groups.

The S group appeared generally less able to cope with the environmental threats with which they confronted themselves in their dreams. Helpless surrender to an overwhelming disaster, or entrapment in a dangerous situation with no escape in sight, comprised 72% of S group threat dreams, while such a bleak outcome occurred in only 21% of NS group threat dreams. Conversely, mild environmental nonsupport, where the dreamer depicts such mildly threatening or inconvenient occurrences as standing near the shoreline in an ocean which is "somewhat rough," stepping into a puddle, a boy with a hole in his coat (which the dreamer sews up), or a dilapidated home with "rickety stairs," were entirely absent from the dreams of the schizophrenic subjects. The S group did not dream of mild discomforts at all, perhaps because S group subjects were overwhelmed by the urgent problems of survival they faced in their dreams and had no time for comparatively trivial discomforts. In the midst of a tornado, for example, one does not usually worry about whether one's coat is torn or whether one's shoelaces are tied.

Disasters occasionally occurred in the dreams of NS subjects as well, but these were most often mitigated, as, for example, in an NS dream where a tunnel collapses and the dreamer describes *most people* as escaping, although *one* girl gets killed. In another NS disaster dream, there was a scene of men who have lost their families in a storm but who are *now trying to fight the storm.*

In the schizophrenic group, the disasters tended to be overwhelming and ruthlessly demolishing in nature. A volleyball hits a girl and pulverizes her into a million pieces; an alligator eats the dreamer alive; a dreamer's head is pressed into quicksand; nuclear wars and world-destructive cataclysms are common.

While only a single nonschizophrenic dream depicted continuing danger from which no escape has been found by the end of the dream, this hopeless state prevailed in a large number of the S group dreams, in which characters were trapped and lost on a tiny island or in a grotesque amusement park by a vicious dog. They choke on stringy food, are "impaled under a pole," closed in by slowly crushing walls, or unable to escape from man-eating fish. There is a general sense of helplessness and terror that typifies these "no escape" dreams. For example, a dream of a sea of spiders with no escape in sight; the dream ends with the dreamer helplessly "just screaming and screaming."

Human Physical Deficit State. Human physical deficit states were depicted significantly more often in the dreams of the S group and only one NS subject showed a particular *type* of deficit which was quite common among the S group subjects, namely, mutilation imagery. This suggested the possibility that closer investigation of the human deficit state dreams might reveal further qualitative differences between the two groups.

The single nonschizophrenic mutilation dream depicted a little girl without legs who had to walk with crutches. The subject who reported the dream had been classified as "well-adjusted" on the basis of her MMPI. Other "deficit" (but *nonmutilation*) dreams of NS subjects depicted a blind character, a severe stutterer, an ill friend, and a "stupid" friend who could not drive a car well. These NS human deficit states did not involve bizarre or jarring dismemberment of persons or the rendering asunder of living creatures. Even the little girl without legs was described as a normal cripple with crutches. We do not see the legs ripped off in the dream nor find ourselves immersed in grisly details.

By contrast, a large proportion of the schizophrenic group deficit

TABLE 6-4

Degree of Bizarreness in Nonschizophrenic Dreams*

Group	Bizarre Dreams Rated as "Mild"		Bizarre Dreams Rated as "Extreme"	
	No.	Proportion	No.	Proportion
NS Group	16	76% of bizarre dreams	5	24% of bizarre dreams
NS Subgroup: *Normal*	14	88% of "mildly" bizarre dreams	1	20% of "extremely" bizarre dreams
NS Subgroup: *Maladjusted*	2	12% of "mildly" bizarre dreams	4	80% of "extremely" bizarre dreams

*Number bizarre dreams in NS group = 21.

dreams contained outright mutilation imagery, often savage and brutal. Such dreams were not reported by NS group subjects. For example, in S group dreams a penis is torn off leaving a big hole "with blood oozing out and pus"; a dreamer burns her arm which then falls off exposing raw veins and bloody flesh; a woman kills her husband and stuffs parts of his body into camels' heads; a girl kills and throws dissected body parts down the toilet; cut-up pieces of people are hung on racks with blood oozing and mingling with the sawdust on the floor, etc.

The following schizophrenic group dream is typical: "I was decapitated. My ribs were picked clean, no skin, no muscle. My body was cut in half. I was just a pile of bones. They didn't know who it was, but I still knew who I was. I wanted to pull myself together but I couldn't."

Schizophrenic mutilation dreams usually did not make attempts at restoration of the object and seemed to carry destructive impulses to excess, as though the situation was brought to an ultimate point of symbolic humiliation and degradation of the mutilated object. Such destructive excesses suggest a strong lack of inhibitory controls in the dreaming schizophrenic subject.

Dyscontrol. The schizophrenic group subjects frequently reported a type of dyscontrol dream ("insanity") which was reported by only one NS subject, in one isolated instance. Fourteen schizophrenic dreams (roughly 35% of the S group's dyscontrol dreams) depicted loss of sanity, variously described as "craziness," "catatonic stupor," "going beserk," and the like. Awareness of loss of control over their own mental processes evidenced by the schizophrenic subjects may largely account for the large difference between groups ($P = < 0.00003$) on the dyscontrol category.

Bizarre Imagery. The fact that bizarre dreams occur at all in normal persons is sometimes cited as an argument against any difference between normal and schizophrenic dreams (5). Accordingly, the nature of nonschizophrenic-group bizarre dreams (representing about one quarter of all the NS group dreams) was explored. Are these dreams very jarring and "far out," or are they only "mildly bizarre"? And does the degree of bizarreness perhaps vary with adjustment (as measured on the MMPI)?

I blindly rated each nonschizophrenic bizarre dream as being either "mildly" or "extremely" bizarre. Schizophrenic dreams could not be similarly rated because I was able to identify their source due to my familiarity with those protocols. Later informal scanning of the S group dreams, however, gave the distinct impression that the overwhelming majority of this group's dreams would have been rated "extremely bizarre" using the same criteria that were applied to the NS dreams.

These blind ratings of the nonschizophrenic protocols revealed a disparity between the well-adjusted and maladjusted subgroups with respect to the extremity of the bizarreness in their dreams (Table 6–4): Of the twenty-one NS subjects reporting bizarre dreams, sixteen (76%) had reported dreams which I rated as "mildly bizarre." Such "mildly bizarre" dreams included references to a strange car that could float on water and also burrow down into sand, the dreamer spying on a dachshund, someone walking over an overpass on stilts, a trunk filled only with plastic boxes, the dreamer bouncing about a room slowly on a big balloon, a table that was not a square or rectangle but had odd projections, and cola bottles with POW (prisoner of war) printed on them. Of the sixteen subjects reporting such "mildly bizarre" dreams, only two (12%) had been classified as maladjusted according to the MMPI, while fourteen of these subjects (88%) had been classified as well-adjusted.

The remaining five nonschizophrenic subjects had reported dreams which I rated as "extremely bizarre." Such dreams included situations where a dreamer ate pieces of rocks "like birds do," where a steel marker shaped like a beaver's tail projected two feet out of a dreamer's crotch, where a dreamer's father appeared in triplicate, where hundreds of people were fighting and eating potato chips at the same time, where two green pellets enclosed in plastic were actually secret explosives, where the dreamer died then came alive again, and where the dreamer was observing herself from "outside" (in the third person). Of the five subjects who reported these "extremely bizarre" dreams, four (80%) had been rated as maladjusted on the basis of the MMPI; only one had been rated as well-adjusted. Since extremity of bizarre imagery thus correlated highly with ratings of maladjustment in this tentative investigation of the nonschizophrenic dreams, it is possible that the *extremity* of bizarre imagery in dreams may, on further investigation, be found to be at least as important an index of the degree of maladjustment in the dreamer as the *presence* of bizarre imagery per se. Three other studies (all conducted in the sleep laboratory) have indicated a positive correlation between "dreamlike" (i.e., more hallucinatory or distorted-dramatic, or a combination of both) mentation reported on awakenings from sleep and personality pathology as measured on the MMPI (19–21).

Nonschizophrenic dreamers failed to report any bizarre imagery scored as "morbid" by the judges. Morbid dreams appeared as a peculiarly schizophrenic manifestation in this study. These "morbid" dreams of the schizophrenic group subjects were often repugnant. They included a man sweeping up a girl's bones and throwing them into a sanitation truck, dead flesh decaying in layers, the dreamer lying down in a coffin from which her dead parents had just risen, people turning into skeletons, the dreamer raking up a huge ten-foot piece of decaying feces which was wrapped in a white sheet, and the dreamer taking a blanket off a corpse and finding it to be a sewed up banana.

Gratifying Content. There was no significant difference between the groups in the frequency of gratifying dreams, contrary to the expectation that S group subjects would depict pleasurable content in their dreams less often than NS group subjects. Breakdown of scores into percentages further revealed that the baseline for gratifying content was exceedingly low, with only 6% of the NS group and 12% of the S group dreams depicting content rated by the judges as gratifying.

When inspection of dream protocols rated as gratifying was undertaken, there were certain qualitative differences between the groups. The "gratifying" dreams of the schizophrenic group frequently contained seemingly implausible changes of mood, with an idyllic scene followed abruptly by a traumatic one, or even more often, with some nightmarish situation suddenly transformed into an exaggeratedly "beautiful" experience. Other schizophrenic dreams depicted pleasurable and anxiety-provoking content occurring simultaneously. Quite frequently the gratification in the schizophrenic dreams appeared highly unrealistic, precipitate, and magical (10).

On the other hand, the gratifying dreams of the nonschizophrenic subjects tended to be consistent in mood, with pleasure logically accounted for and described in relatively moderate language. When the NS subject described pleasure in a dream, she often documented it convincingly with realistic details. The gratifying content of NS dreams tended to be confined to specific objects and not to present a generalized mood of ecstatic gratification. The awake NS subject might also retrospectively view her own dream gratifications and be somewhat skeptical of them. Such waking reassessment of dream gratification did not occur in any of the schizophrenic dream reports.

Since the gratifying dreams of the schizophrenic group tended to have an unreal quality, with gratifications frequently juxtaposed with anxiety-laden dream content, it may be that the pleasurable reactions in schizophrenic dreams serve as denials. The S group gratifying dream content may therefore be spurious and very defensive in nature.

The very low baseline for gratifying dreams in both groups, and the fact that more schizophrenic (43%) than nonschizophrenic subjects (23%) reported at least one gratifying dream in their series of five dreams, suggests the interesting possibility that gratifying dreams may be suspect whenever and in whomever they occur. Can it be that even normal persons tend to have frankly pleasurable dreams only when under stress? A study designed to relate the current mood of the subjects to the mood of their dreams, with particular reference to gratifying content in dreams, might be useful in clarifying this question.

Other Categories. Further qualitative findings indicated that NS group subjects dreamed about their fathers and male relatives almost twice as often as did S group subjects, and that friendly-toward-dreamer dreams were largely confined to the "maladjusted" nonschizophrenic and to the schizophrenic subjects, rarely occurring among "well-adjusted" subjects. In contrast to nonschizophrenic subjects who saw others as performing simple friendly acts toward themselves, schizophrenic dreamers most frequently depicted the "friendly" others in their dreams as rescuing them from danger or offering them reassurance against extreme anxiety or guilt. These findings are discussed elsewhere (10).

CHARACTERISTICS OF NONSCHIZOPHRENIC DREAMS

Certain characteristics of nonschizophrenic dream life were highlighted by the contrast between the groups. On the whole, nonschizophrenic dreams tended to be practical, realistic, and detailed, and often gave the impression that the dreamer might be relating experiences from her waking life, were it not for a few changes of scenes, occasional confusions, or somewhat bizarre elements that identified these commonplace stories as dreams. Nonschizophrenic subjects described shopping, cooking, attending classes, dressing, sewing, participating in family gatherings, going to parties or on dates, and indulging in any number of other everyday occurrences, with a sensitivity and involvement typical of young women of similar socioeconomic level when they describe such events occurring in waking life. The exact layout of a store and the list of items purchased, the careful itemizing of food on a table, the artful delineation of clothing worn by others or by the dreamer herself, nuances of interpersonal relationships—all were abundantly described in NS dreams.

By contrast, the schizophrenic dreams seemed stark and tragic. In these dreams, detail was minimal and subordinated to tense drama. It seemed that S group subjects could not afford the emotional luxury of an awareness of detail such as the NS subjects showed.

The nonschizophrenic dreams evidenced a rich repertoire of coping techniques, with NS dream characters typically arguing their way out of situations, making excuses, insisting on their own way, and being wont to try any number of various solutions to the same problem. While these maneuvers of the dream characters were not invariably successful, NS dreamers were almost always highly resourceful in their attempts to solve dream problems. Such a repertoire of ego resources was strikingly absent from the S group dreams, with S group dreamers tending either to resort to violent outbreaks in order to deal with dream problems, or else being overwhelmed by them.

The NS dreams were, therefore, highly realistic, with reality concerns and problems carefully attended to and dealt with, within the confines of dream life. The practical and efficient quality of NS dreams seems to attest to an active participation of the dreamer's ego during the dreaming state, while evidence of such ego participation was minimal in S group dreams.

THEORETICAL IMPLICATIONS OF THE STUDY

The present findings are seen as consistent with theories of dreaming which emphasize the role of the ego in the dream process (22–26). It appears that a strong ego in waking life may lead to an effective, highly integrated, and resourceful dream, and vice versa.

The present results suggest, then, the interesting possibility that the primary process thinking of dream life may be in large part a function of the degree of maladjustment of the dreamer, and not necessarily a *sine qua non* of dream life. A number of nonschizophrenic (and a few schizophrenic) dreams in the present study showed no discernible symbolic transformation of a distorted nature in their manifest content. Often these dreams seemed like an account of something the dreamer had done the other day. While all subjects studied showed *some* dreamlike transformations or bizarre elements in *some* of their dreams, these elements were both more numerous and more extreme in the schizophrenic dreams. As indicated, among NS subjects there was a difference in the extremity of primary process, or bizarre, material according to the personality adjustment of the dreamer, with extremity of bizarreness positively correlated with maladjustment as measured on the MMPI.

The well-adjusted dreamer, then, may not have terribly "dreamlike" dreams on the whole. This possibility raises a question with regard to dream theories developed on the basis of clinical samples alone, as, for example, during psychoanalytic treatment with neurotic or psychotic persons. While the psychic *mechanisms* involved in dreaming appear common to all persons (viz. the failure of experimenters to find an exclusively "schizophrenic" dream mechanism), the degree to which the dream process makes use of distorted transformations may, in the past, have been overestimated on the basis of sampling bias. Maladjusted persons undergoing treatment for emotional problems may draw heavily on archaic and regressive problem-solving techniques in their dreams (and hence produce many striking and bizarre combinations of dream elements) because the more effective ego solutions or "coping devices" are not readily available to them, because they may temporarily regress in the service of the ego during psychoanalysis, or for both reasons. Conceivably, relatively well-adjusted persons not undergoing psychoanalytic treatment may only turn to such regressive dream devices when under particular stress.

In conclusion, one might say that the present findings are consistent with the notion that, other things being equal, the greater the resources of the awake ego, the more successfully will the dream deal with emotional conflicts, and achieve ego reintegration during sleep.

REFERENCES

1. CAPPON, D.: Morphology and other parameters of phantasy in the schizophrenias. *Arch. Gen. Psychiat.* 1:17–34, 1959.

2. RICHARDSON, G. A., and MOORE, R. A.: On the manifest dream in schizophrenia. *J. Amer. Psychoanal. Assoc.* 11:281–302, 1963.

3. LANGS, R. J.: Manifest dreams from three clinical groups. *Arch. Gen. Psychiat.* 14:634–643, 1966.

4. SUSSMAN, L.: Beitrag Zum Problem Der Traume Der Schizophrenen. *Der Nervenarzt* 9:453–466, 1939.

5. BOSS, M.: The psychotherapy of dreams in schizophrenia and organic psychosis (1938), Peter Rabe (trans.), in DeMartino, M. F. (ed.): *Dreams and Personality Dynamics.* Springfield, Ill., Charles C Thomas, Publisher, 1959, pp. 156–175.

6. TRAPP, C. E., and LYONS, R. H.: Dream studies in hallucinated patients. *Psychoanal. Quart.* 11:253–266, 1937.

7. KANT, O.: Dreams of schizophrenic patients. *J. Nerv. Ment. Dis.* 95:335–347, 1942.

8. NOBLE, D.: A study of dreams in schizophrenia and allied states. *Amer. J. Psychiat.* 107:612–616, 1950.

9. HALL, C. S.: A comparison of four groups of hospitalized mental patients with each other and with a normal population. *J. Nerv. Ment. Dis.* 143:135–139, 1966.

10. CARRINGTON, P.: *Dream Reports of Schizophrenic and Nonschizophrenic Women,* thesis. Teachers College Columbia University, Ann Arbor, Mich., University Microfilms, 1969, No. 70–6947.

11. BECK, S. J.: *The Six Schizophrenias: Reaction Patterns in children and adults.* New York, Research Monograph of the American Orthopsychiatric Association, pp. 76–79.

12. HALL, C. S., and VAN DE CASTLE, R. L.: *The Content Analysis of Dreams.* New York, Appleton-Century-Crofts, 1966.

13. COLBY, K.: *The Skeptical Psychoanalyst.* New York, Ronald Press Co., 1959.

14. SCHONBAR, R. A.: Differential dream recall as a component of "life style." *J. Consult. Psychol.* 29:468–474, 1965.

15. American Psychiatric Association, Committee on Nomenclature and Statistics: *Diagnostic and Statistical Manual: Mental Disorders,* Washington, D.C., American Psychiatric Association, 1952.

16. WHITMAN, R. M., PIERCE, C. M., and MASS, J. W., et al.: Drugs and dreams: II. Imipramine and prochlorperazine. *Compr. Psychiat.* 2:219–226, 1961.

17. HALL, C. S.: Dreams of American college students, in Barker R., Kaplan, B. (eds.): *Primary Records in Psychology, No. 2.* Lawrence, Kan., University of Kansas Social Science Studies, 1963.

18. KLEINMUNTZ, B.: MMPI decision rules for the identification of college maladjustment: A digital computer approach. *Psychol. Monogr.* 77/44: whole No. 577, 1963.

19. FOULKES, D., and RECHTSCHAFFEN, A.: Presleep determinants of dream content. *Percept. Motor Skills* 19:983–1005, 1964.

20. PIVIK, T., and FOULKES, D.: Dream deprivation: Effects of dream content. *Science* 153:1282–1284, 1966.

21. FOULKES, D.: Nonrapid Eye Movement Mentation. *Exp. Neurol* 4(suppl.): 28–38, 1967.

22. FEDERN, P.: The awakening of the ego in dreams. *Int. J. Psychoanal.* 15: 296–301, 1934.

23. JEKELS, L.: A bioanalytical contribution to the problem of sleep and wakefulness. *Psychiat. Quart.* 14:169–189, 1945.

24. FRENCH, T. M., and FROMM, E.: *Dream Interpretation: A New Approach.* New York, Basic Books, Inc., Publishers, 1964.

25. JONES, R. M.: *Ego Synthesis in Dreams.* Cambridge, Mass., Schinkman Publishing Co., 1962.

26. EPHRON, H. S., and CARRINGTON, P.: Ego functioning in rapid eye movement sleep: Implications for dream theory, in Masserman, J. (ed.): *Science and Psychoanalysis.* New York, Grune & Stratton, Inc., 1967, Vol. 9, pp. 75–102.

From the Postgraduate Center for Mental Health, New York. This study is based upon a dissertation submitted to Teachers College, Columbia University, in partial fulfillment of the requirements for the degree of Doctor of Philosophy.

Grateful acknowledgment is extended to the dissertation committee, Rosalea A. Schonbar (Chairman), Paul E. Eiserer, and David R. Ricks. Rosedith Sitgreaves assisted with statistical procedures; Calvin S. Hall supplied the dream protocols used in the second comparison group; and Hillside Hospital, Glen Oaks, N.Y., the Psychiatric Treatment Center, New York City, Roosevelt Hospital, New York City, and Barnard and Teachers Colleges, Columbia University participated in the data collection.

7

Roy M. Whitman, M.D., Milton Kramer, M.D.,
& Bill Baldridge, A.B.

Which Dream Does the Patient Tell?

INTRODUCTION

A number of investigators utilizing the dream collecting technique of Aserinsky and Kleitman (1, 2) and Dement and Kleitman (3, 4) have demonstrated that individuals have episodes of dreaming three to five times a night. Goodenough et al. (5) showed that even "nondreamers," when monitored by electroencephalogram (EEG) and eye movement tracings and awakened throughout the night, report dreams several times a night.

These observations are in marked contrast to clinical experience in which psychotherapists are accustomed to having one or two dreams, but rarely more, presented to them in psychotherapeutic sessions. The purpose of this study is to determine what factors of selection are operative in determining which dreams are told and which are not in a psychotherapeutic setting.

METHOD

Two subjects, one male hospital patient and one female volunteer graduate student of a nearby university each slept overnight in a "dream laboratory" two times a week for eight weeks. During the night, their EEG and eye movements were recorded via scalp electrodes and leads coming from the outer canthi of each eye. When there was an indication that the subject was dreaming, he was allowed to continue for five mins. and then awakened to report the dream to the experimenter (B. B.).

Reprinted by permission of American Medical Association from *Archives of General Psychiatry*, 1963, 8, 277–282. Copyright 1963 by American Medical Association.

He was then asked to give associations to parts of the dream. After the dream night the subject was interviewed by a psychiatrist (M. K.) and asked to relate his night's dreams. In order to assess the effect of time lapse on the quality and quantity of the dreams as recounted to the psychiatrist, the psychiatrist alternated his interviews so that the subject was seen either one hour or one full day after the night of dreaming.

The first subject, the male inpatient at a nearby hospital, reported few dreams without the explicit request by the psychiatrist for the dreams. He seemed to view the dream collection as an experiment for which he had volunteered and separate from his psychotherapy. On the other hand, there were indications that the other subject, the female graduate student, who had volunteered as an experimental subject, adopted a relationship to the psychiatrist which was in many respects similar to what one would expect in therapy. Barad et al. (6) have confirmed our clinical experience that the telling of dreams to a psychiatrist leads to the development of a relationship quite similar to a therapeutic one. What might appear then to be different conditions were, in fact, viewed by the two subjects as quite similar; i.e., they were simultaneously experimental and therapeutic subjects.

The male patient entered the hospital with the chief complaint of nightmares. He manifested a personality disorder characterized by temper outbursts, alcoholism, and anxiety attacks. The female subject was a very verbal, compliant graduate student who manifested no symptoms other than character traits of shyness, introversion, and social inhibition.

RESULTS

The dream data consisted of the dreams collected from sixteen nights of sleep for the male hospital patient and from thirteen nights for the female volunteer. The male subject reported one or more dreams to the experimenter during the night on thirty-four of forty-six awakenings. In the first ten therapy sessions, during which the therapist did not ask for dreams, the patient alluded to the content of only two of nineteen dream awakenings. In the last six sessions, in which the therapist specifically asked for dreams, the patient referred to five of fifteen dream awakenings. The female subject reported dreaming on fifty-four of sixty awakenings, and retold forty-one of these to the psychiatrist who, in this instance, had asked for dreams from the initial session on.

Major changes or deletions occurred three times more frequently than did the complete forgetting of an awakening. Unexpectedly, a number of dreams from the experimental night were reported to the psychiatrist which had not been told during the dream night.

The dream material was examined for the complete omission of an awakening and for major deletions or changes during the retelling of

TABLE 7-1

Dream Data

	Male Subject	Female Subject
Total night awakenings	46	60
Awakenings from which dreams were told to the experimenter ("dream awakenings")	34	54
Awakenings from which dreams were told to the psychiatrist	7	41
Dreams told to the psychiatrist and not to the experimenter	3*	7

*This patient reported these additional dreams to the psychiatrist, but he clearly stated that these were from other nights or from naps he took during the day.

the dreams to the psychiatrist. Complete omissions were judged to occur when no part of an awakening could be identified in the retold dreams. Major changes or deletions included the omission of one or more dream scenes from a multiple dream, changes of situations or characters within a dream, or the omission of prominent details. The manifest content and associations of the omitted or altered dreams were then analyzed for their psychodynamic implications.

In formulating these dreams, we utilized both the manifest content and the associations given to both the experimenter and the psychiatrist. Since we felt that even this amount of material was not sufficient for a precise formulation of the exact latent content of the dream, we settled on the concept of "theme" as expressing a translation of the dream in the direction of the dynamic latent content.

(1) *Male Subject.* The dreams *retold* by the male patient to the psychiatrist often tended to highlight his capabilities as a man. The dreams *omitted* by the male patient dealt primarily with homosexual impulses. For example, from Night 11, he *retold* the following dreams to the psychiatrist:

Night 11:

11–3*

"This girl had her dog trained so well she was afraid to let anyone near it. It was gone and I was helping her look for it."

(Theme: Takes the role of an adequate masculine figure helping a woman.)

11–4a†

"I dreamed I was in prison. When I was gone my wife and family was left unattended. When I got out I went to search for them."

* The second number refers to the number of the awakening during the night.
† The letter refers to the dream scene if several occur in an awakening.

(Theme: Continues role of responsible head of family but can't perform this because "they put him in prison.")

These dreams of the same night, although told to the experimenter, were *not told* to the psychiatrist:

11–2

"I was with a buddy of mine. We went on a tour of a big factory . . . new automobiles being built. When I came out of the factory, it wasn't a buddy of mine anymore—it was Jack Benny."

(Theme: Closeness to another man.)

11–4b

"We were out walking along with a man. He was an officer in the Service."

(Theme: Similar to Dream 11–2, closeness to a man.)

Quotations from subsequent nights of dreaming told to the experimenter but *not told* to the psychiatrist were:

Night 14:

14–2

"A guy, I don't know who he was, he came up to school and wanted to look at my drawings."

(Theme: Intimate contact with a man—"Come up and see my etchings.")

14–4

"A guy, who had been an F.B.I. man, shows a picture of a man, after they had been shot, where the bullet went in."

(Theme: A man examines another man who had been penetrated.)

Night 16:

16–3

"Some fellow giving me a tattoo."

(Theme: A man being penetrated rhythmically by another man.)

The only dream *told* to the psychiatrist from sessions 14 through 16 was:

Night 16:

". . . about being out with another woman . . ."

(Theme: Takes out a woman other than his wife.)

We see from these examples that dreams that seem to be heterosexual or demonstrate masculinity are told by the male patient to a male psychiatrist and homosexually oriented dreams are not. The hypothesis suggests itself that left-out dreams seem to contain material which would be most ego alien to this male subject in his current relationship to the male psychiatrist.

(2) *Female Subject.* The material from the dreams of the female graduate student also illustrated a pattern of telling and not telling, and, in addition, clearly showed a change in her relationship to the psychiatrist during the course of the experiment.

(a) From the early sessions she *told* the following dreams to the male experimenter who awakened her but *not* to the male psychiatrist the next day:

Night 1:
1—2
"I was washing my fingers—hands several times."
(Theme: Concern about dirty hands—mastubatory guilt.)
1—4
"Thinking about morals, some have good, some bad."
(Theme: Problem with morals—sexual guilt.)
Night 2:
2—5
"In someone's bedroom, I and another girl were in bed."
(Theme: Intimate setting with a woman: potential homosexual situation.)

In later sessions, however, she *told* a dream of a clearly homosexual nature to the psychiatrist but *not* to the experimenter:
Night 7:
7—3
". . . I was sitting there and another girl was sitting over there and I leaned over and kissed her and I said to myself 'you've never had a homosexual impulse before' . . ."
(Theme: Greater acceptance of her homosexual impulses.)

(b) Throughout the series there were numerous examples of dreams *told only to the experimenter* which made thinly disguised critical or sexual references to the psychiatrist:
Night 5:
5—3
"Asking for an appointment. He was only in two days a week. It was a doctor. I was wearing a bathing suit and was real embarrassed."
(Theme: Resentment about the infrequency of appointments and also sexual exhibitionistic wishes.)
Night 6:
6—5
"The doctor was not able to treat the patient because he was not properly licensed."
(Theme: Depreciation of the psychiatrist's qualifications.)

(c) Hostile and sexual dream scenes about the experimenter were not told to the experimenter but were *told only to the psychiatrist* as additions to larger dream episodes:
Night 3:
3—3
"A boy was lost; he didn't know anything. I said the little dog knows more than he does."
(Theme: Associations clearly suggested her competitive depreciation of the experimenter.)
Night 4:
4—2
"I was embarrassed because I didn't want to sleep close together (with a male)."

(Theme: Sexual feelings of wanting to sleep close to the experimenter.)

(d) Most striking were fifteen instances of dream scenes *told to the experimenter* in which this subject expressed her fears of psychiatry and denied her need for treatment but which she did *not tell the psychiatrist*:

Night 6:

6–4

". . . a patient did not need a doctor after all. She started out thinking she needed a doctor but she didn't need a doctor or nurse."

(Theme: Denies her need for treatment.)

Night 7:

7–1

"There was a patient and a doctor. They were talking about the effects of being embarrassed in psychoanalysis."

(Theme: Points out potential "pain" of treatment.)

7–2

". . . I remember thinking his method wasn't good. It might cause depression in the patient."

(Theme: Suggests possible harm from treatment.)

12–2

"They couldn't get to sleep or were hurt . . . They (patients) had to convince people they were sick."

(Theme: Other people need treatment, not she.)

While there were a considerable number of dreams which dropped out and a still larger number of changes which occurred, the fidelity with which the subjects retold most of their dreams seemed to indicate that ordinary forgetting played only a minor role. An analysis of the data revealed little difference in the number of dreams not recalled immediately after the night of dreaming, as compared to the number omitted a full day later. That is, the number of dreams not recalled to the psychiatrist one hour after the dream night was eleven, while twenty-four hours after the dream night twelve dreams were recalled.

There was a slight tendency for dreams omitted in recall to the psychiatrist to come from the early portion of the night's dreams rather than from the later portion. Thus there were thirteen dreams omitted which came from the first half of a night's awakenings and ten which came from the last half of the night's awakenings.

The psychiatrist was more likely to get an "extra" dream after twenty-four hours than he was the morning following the dream night. According to the subjects, these additional dreams were dreamt by the female subject during the experimental night but by the male subject during naps or intervening nights.

COMMENT

We now have three categories to consider: (1) dreams told to the experimenter but not to the psychiatrist, (2) major changes or deletions in the retelling of the dreams, (3) additional dreams told to the psychiatrist but not to the experimenter.

(1) Our findings indicate that the forgetting of dreams had much less to do with the time of night of dreaming than with the content of the dreams; recall is affected by the current interpersonal relationship with the person to whom the dream is told or not told. We inferred that there is, in many instances, a preconscious or unconscious recognition of the meaning of the dream and of the ability of the listener to decipher it. Thus the initial hand-washing dream could be told to the experimenter but not to the psychiatrist who, the subject felt, might be able to see through the sexual content of the dream. It may also be that the unconscious transference attitude toward the experimenter and the psychiatrist may determine remembering and forgetting. Thus the experimenter might be seen as a brother figure and the psychiatrist as a father figure who, in this example, would not tolerate masturbation.

(2) Major changes and partial omissions could be formulated in the same dynamic framework. For example, as part of a much longer dream, a scene about a hypodermic needle turning into an ice-cream bar which was fed to her was not told to the psychiatrist. This could be understood in the context of repressing a dependent-hostile-sexual orientation to the psychiatrist. These needs, seen by her as so shameful, interfered with her acceptance of the relationship with the psychiatrist as a more explicitly therapeutic one. Similarly, a reference to being given gingerbread cookies was not told to the psychiatrist, although the rest of the dream containing this allusion was reported in exact replication of the night's dreaming. It should be pointed out that at the conclusion of the experiment, she refused his recommendation for psychotherapy, deciding she did not need it.

(3) The third category, of additional dreams told to the psychiatrist but not to the experimenter, could be divided into two parts: those suppressed (because of conscious or preconscious recognition) and those repressed (because of unconscious resistance). For example, later in the course of the experiment the woman subject had manifest sexual dreams about the experimenter which she told only to the psychiatrist, admitting that they were too embarrassing to tell the experimenter. As an example of the preconscious recognition, she told a dream of "hot whipped cream coming from a cut over her eye" only to the psychiatrist. We felt that this was perceived by her as a strong statement about her own sexual excitation which she did not wish to reveal to the experimenter. As an example of her repression of a dream, she recalled a previously forgotten dream to the psychiatrist of "kidding the experimenter about being an undergraduate rather than a graduate student."

We can now see that the order of the dream in the night's dreaming, or the time of its being dreamt, had less to do with its being retold to the psychiatrist or forgotten than had the dynamic thematic content of the dream. Early night dreams could be retained almost as easily as any others once the subject was wakened to tell it, provided it did not deal with material considered by the dreamer as unacceptable to the psychiatrist.

Another observation made during the experiment was the amount of secondary elaboration occurring in the dreams told to the psychiatrist versus those told during the night. During the night, dreams were often very fragmentary, sometimes inarticulate, and had very little of a coherent thread running through them. The dreams were much better organized the next day. An organized theme ran through them in the form of a story, and minor places and unidentified people dropped out. This seemed to reach a rapid level of organization during the night of the dream, with only minor improvements one day after the night's dreaming.

THEORETICAL IMPLICATIONS

One of the problems implicit in this research concerns the hypothesis that the dreamer at some level knows the meaning of his dream. It would seem, from the repetitive pattern of omitted dreams that we observed, that the dreamer does have some understanding of the meaning of the dream. Our study seems to support Freud's statement (7),

> It is not only quite possible, but highly probable, that the dreamer really does know the meaning of his dream; only he does not know that he knows, and therefore thinks that he does not.

For purposes of understanding repression of these once-remembered dreams, the crucial variable seems to be the communicative function of the dream as it is affected specifically by the current and/or transference relationship between the dreamer and the listener and the fantasy of how the listener will receive certain content. One of Freud's analogies (8) seems more appropriate than even he realized.

> We have gathered an impression that the formulation of obscure dreams occurs *as though* one person who was dependent upon a second person had to make a remark which was bound to be disagreeable in the ears of the second one; and it is on the basis of this simile that we have arrived at the concepts of dream distortion and censorship. . . .

Considering the dream as an interpersonal communication in which the person being told the dream is likely to "read" the communication, the internal censor involved in the dream work is once more projected to this listener and his response anticipated.

We hypothesize from this research study that the recollection of dreams in a therapeutic relationship would be dependent on four factors in addition to dream content: (1) the process of awakening and recording the dream, (2) the specifically stated interest of the therapist in the patient's dreams, (3) the relationship between the patient and the therapist at the time of the interview, and (4) least importantly, the time of night of the dream.

Since all dynamic psychotherapies utilize the dream as a diagnostic, investigative, and therapeutic tool, it is important to recognize that there may be an automatic selection process determining which dreams are presented by the patient to the therapist. As we have suggested, the changing climate of the therapeutic session should permit dreams dealing with different problems to emerge. It is usually taken for granted that the dream reported in the therapeutic session contains one of the major conflicts that the patient is struggling with at that time. Our findings suggest, however, that therapists should maintain a high degree of suspicion that one or more of the major interpersonal conflicts of the patient may well be contained in the dream that is not told.

Diagnostic formulations of the psychodynamics of patients might include the collection of dreams via the Kleitman technique which the patient could not otherwise recall, thus enlarging and sharpening the scope of future exploratory psychotherapy. Another research project would be one which made immediately available to the therapist "forgotten" dreams which he could utilize to increase his understanding of the resistance in sessions with the patient, thereby perhaps expanding or speeding up the process of therapy.

SUMMARY

A psychodynamic investigation was made of dreams experimentally obtained during the night's dreaming which were not told to a psychiatrist in a subsequent interview. Dreams containing an orientation or attitude which the dreamer anticipates will bring forth a negative response from the psychiatrist are not recalled. For a male patient these were strong homosexual feelings. For a female subject this was initially guilty sexuality, and later on an intense denial of dependency. Four factors, in addition to the expected one of the content of the dream, influence the process of dream report to the psychiatrist: (1) the process of having been awakened and immediately telling the dream, (2) the stated interest of the psychiatrist in the dreams of the night, (3) the relationship between the patient and psychiatrist at the time of the interview, and (4) of least significance, the time of night of the dream, later dreams of the night being slightly better remembered than earlier dreams.

REFERENCES

1. ASERINSKY, E., and KLEITMAN, N.: *Eye Movements During Sleep,* Fed. Proc. 12:6–7, 1953.

2. ASERINSKY, E., and KLEITMAN, N.: Regularly Occurring Periods of Eye Motility and Concomitant Phenomena During Sleep, *Science* 118:273, 1953.

3. DEMENT, W., and KLEITMAN, N.: Cyclic Variations in EEG During Sleep and Their Relation to Eye Movement, Body Motility and Dreaming, Electroenceph. *Clin. Neurophysiol.* 9:673–690, 1957.

4. DEMENT, W., and KLEITMAN, N.: The Relation of Eye Movements During Sleep to Dream Activity: An Objective Method for the Study of Dreaming, *J. Exp. Psychol.* 53:339–346, 1957.

5. GOODENOUGH, D. R.; SHAPIRO, A.; HOLDEN, M., and STEINSCHRIBER, L.: A Comparison of "Dreamers" and "Nondreamers," *J. Abnorm. Soc. Psychol.* 59:295, 1959.

6. BARAD, M.; ALTSHULER, K. Z., and GOLDFARB, A. P. I.: A Survey of Dreams in Aged Persons, *Arch. Gen. Psychiat.* 4:419, 1961.

7. FREUD, S.: *General Introduction to Psychoanalysis,* translated by Joan Riviere, New York, Garden City Publishing Company, 1943.

8. Freud, S.: *On Dreams,* Standard Edition, translated by James Strachey, London, The Hogarth Press, 1953, Vol. 5, p. 677.

Read at the 118th Annual Meeting of the American Psychiatric Association, Toronto, Canada, May 7-11, 1962. This study was supported by an NIMH Grant entitled, The Psychophysiology of Dreaming (MY-3033).

The participation of Theodore Striker as a member of our research team is gratefully acknowledged.

PART II

ORAL CHARACTER

The papers contained in this section deal with oral sensations, needs, and fantasies. They seek in different ways to evaluate the validity of theories originated by Freud (and also Abraham)[1] concerned with how early oral experiences involving sucking, eating, and the use of the mouth, shape personality. These theories proposed that if a child is unusually deprived or overgratified orally during the first year of life, this will have consequences for his long-term personality formation. First of all, the child's ability to progress along the scale of psychosexual maturity will presumably be impaired. If he or she cannot learn to master and integrate oral wishes, the child may become fixated at the oral level or be rendered susceptible to regression to that level. He or she may be left without the energy to cope successfully with the problems that are linked with later developmental phases (for example, anal and phallic). Secondly, extreme oral gratification or deprivation may result in the long-term shaping of personality in certain directions. Indeed, it was proposed that an "oral character" pattern evolves which reflects both special oral needs and defenses against these needs. The oral character is said to be unconsciously preoccupied with ways of gratifying the urges to incorporate. He or she is depicted as intent on being close to people to be assured of obtaining supplies from them and to guarantee gratification of dependent fantasies. Taking, getting, and receiving are highlighted as dominant motifs in the oral character's life. This orientation can diversely take the form of an optimistic expectation of always being fulfilled, a suspicion that scarcity will prevail, or a compensatory generosity which conceals an underlying "avarice." It is presumed that unsatisfied oral needs can motivate the individual to develop compensatory oral outlets like smoking and excessive eating. Such oral wishes are described as permeating the whole fabric of his or her life. They affect social relationships, degree of optimism-pessimism, amount of ambivalent feeling toward others, openness to new experience, creativity, and vulnerability to specific kinds of psychological dysfunction. Numerous attempts have been made to evaluate the validity of different facets of the oral character concept. The success of these attempts has been evaluated systematically elsewhere[2] and was found to be encouraging overall.

Examples of empirical attempts to test the influence of oral variables on behavior are provided by the papers presented here. The study of Goldman (Selection 8) represented a direct effort to trace oral traits in the adult to his infant breastfeeding experience. Early weaning was found to be positively correlated with a pessimistic orientation as an adult and late weaning positively linked with optimism.

Blum and Miller (Selection 9) described an elaborate research design in which they examined the correlations between mouth activity in the child and such variables as amount of interest in food, need for liking and approval, need to be ingratiating, dependency and suggestibility. Their findings were mixed and difficult to summarize succinctly.

Masling et al. (Selection 10) probed the relationships between oral fantasies, as they appear in inkblot responses, and dependent behavior. They defined dependency in terms of responses to a situation in which the individual is pressured to abandon his own judgmental standards for apparently contradictory judgments made by a group. The results were supportive of the theory that orality and dependency are positively correlated.

Lazare et al. (Selection 11) determined whether the traits and attributes presumed to be manifestations of an oral type of personality do actually cluster together in a fashion consistent with the "oral character" theory. Their results conformed only moderately to expectation.

Rosenblatt (Selection 12) went to cross-cultural data to find out if those who are orally deprived at an early stage look to special satisfaction of their dependent needs through romantic love involvements. Oral socialization practices in numerous cultures were compared to the importance of romantic love as a basis for marriage in those cultures. The emphasis placed on romantic love proved to be positively tied to the amount of early oral frustration experienced. The varied impact of oral variables upon personality as reported in these papers is a true reflection of what one finds in the total range of scientific literature bearing on this issue.

NOTES

[1] Freud formulated the basic concepts relating to the possibility that oral wishes influence behavior and affect personality formation. But Karl Abraham gave body and detail to these concepts, in a fashion meeting Freud's approval.

[2] Fisher, S., and Greenberg, R. P. *The Scientific Credibility of Freud's Theories and Therapy.* New York: Basic Books, 1977; Kline, P. *Fact and Fantasy in Freudian Theory.* London: Methuen and Co., 1972.

8

F. Goldman

Breastfeeding and Character Formation: The Etiology of the Oral Character in Psychoanalytic Theory

As to the etiological assumptions which underlie the psychoanalytic classification of oral character traits, they are in no way unequivocal and universally agreed on among psychoanalysts. On the question of the type of experience most likely to induce an oral fixation Abraham considers early frustration or overindulgence of equal effect.

In either case the child would take leave of the sucking stage with difficulty "and aim at compensation at the next stage" since its need for pleasure has either not been sufficiently gratified or has become too insistent (1). Glover, while taking into account the question of oral disposition and of the *relative* length of an individual optimum period of oral-primacy," considers that "the shortening of this period is more likely to prove traumatic" (5) than the lengthening.

Edmund Bergler (2) takes Abraham's point of view of the equivalence of frustration and overindulgence as traumatic factors and quotes Freud in support of the thesis that "the greed of the child after his first feed is altogether insatiable, that he never resigns himself to his loss," also referring to the latter's caustic remark that he would not be surprised if the analysis of a primitive who was given the nipple even when he could walk and talk, would reveal a grudge of having been deprived of the breast.

However, in his later writings Freud stresses the importance of the external situation as a traumatic factor, viz., "frightening *instinctual* situations can in the last resort be traced back to *external* situations of danger"; and he adds that it is not the objective injury that is feared but a state of traumatic excitation (previously experienced) "which cannot be dealt with in accordance with the norms of the pleasure principle" (4).

Sandor Rado (9), referring to Freud, points out that "the deepest fixation point in the melancholic (depressive) disposition is to be found in the 'situation of threatened loss of love,' more precisely, the hunger situation of the suckling baby." Thus according to this point of view it would, in the last resort, not be the endopsychic instinctual situations such as the greed and insatiability of the child but the external deprivation (hunger and loss of love), which, via an unpleasurable emotional excitation, would be the traumatic basis of depression.

Against this view Klein maintains that the actual experience of the "loss of the loved object" already meets with an intrapsychic situation of a successful or unsuccessful introjection of the "good" object which decides whether the loss of the breast before and during weaning will result later on in a depressive state. "No doubt, the more the child can at this stage develop a happy relationship to its real mother, the more will it be able to overcome the depressive position. But *all* [italics mine] depends on how it is able to find its way out of the conflict between love and uncontrollable hatred and sadism" (8). This depressive position characterized by cannibalistic desires directed at the mother and the guilt feelings arising therefrom Klein places between the third and fifth month. (6).

THE PROBLEM

The implications of the etiological hypotheses of these writers seem to be fundamentally twofold:

(1) That the weaning trauma with its psychological manifestations of melancholia and oral pessimism is induced by an external situation which may be that of frustration manifested in early weaning rather than late, according to Glover, or that of frustration as well as of over-indulgence (taking an overlong period of breastfeeding as a measure of the latter), according to Abraham and Bergler, and

(2) That the intrapsychic *instinctual* situation, the child's greed and his capacity to overcome his inner conflict between love and hatred of the object will in the last resort determine whether he will remain fixed to the oral level, or, as Klein terms it, in his depressive position.

The above survey throws the speculative character of psycho-analytic views concerning the etiology of oral depression clearly into focus. References are made by Abraham (1), Glover (5), Stärke (11), Bernfeld (3)—in full consciousness of the tentativeness of their views—to supporting material gained from the analyses of patients. It cannot, however, be assumed that these analyses have unearthed memories directly connected with the experiences of early frustration, particularly weaning, the first year of life being hardly accessible to psychoanalytic anamnesis. These authors rather seem to refer to later fantasies containing the motif of weaning, the relation of which to the original trauma (of weaning) must be considered too uncertain to warrant its value as evidence. The analyses of children from which Klein derived her hypothesis again are based only on fantasy material and its interpretation, no steps having been taken to ascertain the objective data concerning the child's early feeding.

This is, of course, not surprising as it is not part of the orthodox psychoanalytic technique to ascertain data outside the therapeutic process by which the patient produces material. However, discussing Rank's theory of the "trauma of birth," Freud emphasized that with an etiological theory which "postulates a factor whose existence can be verified by observation, it is impossible to assess its value as long as no attempt at verification has been made" (4, p. 35).

Weaning, a frustration imposed on the child from the outer world and assumed to be a traumatic impact is an objectively verifiable factor. The above quoted etiological hypotheses concerning oral depression can thus be put to an objective test.

In this part of our study* we tested two of the psychoanalytic hypotheses concerning the etiology of oral character:

(1) Glover's assumption that the shortening of the period of breastfeeding, i.e., early weaning, is more likely to prove traumatic than the lengthening, i.e., late weaning, and (2) Abraham's that an overlong as well as too short a period was traumatic.

The problem now arose how to define early and late weaning.

Referring to the literature we find that Ribble (10) with due consideration of the factors of individual differences in the rate of development and the effects of frustrating situations on this development has "found definitely that the sucking impulse spontaneously wanes as new oral activities become differentiated and are brought into momentum around the fourth month of life." Ribble feels that if sucking has been satisfactory up to that period weaning does not present problems, and in fact becomes spontaneous. On the basis of her observations she thought it justified to assume that, under normal conditions, weaning after a sucking period of four months would meet with a more favorable instinctual situation than weaning before that period. The same critical period in the instinctual development is also indicated by Klein, who places the depressive position between the third and fifth month.

In setting up our hypothesis that oral pessimism (depression) is a function of early weaning, it was therefore the fourth month which was chosen to separate the two groups to be tested. Early weaning we define as weaning at the ages of up to four months, and late weaning as weaning at five months of age and more. Caution may, however, be advised as to this definition with respect to the intermediate months in the age-scale of weaning, i.e., 5–8 months, since the possibility that *individual differences in rate of development* may blur the picture of the effect of weaning in these months on character formation is to be

* The first part (7) dealt with the descriptive aspect in the psychoanalytic exposition of the oral character.

considered. A clearer picture of this effect might be expected from comparing the early weaning group as defined above with the group of those subjects who were taken off the breast at not earlier than nine months of age, i.e., who were given what in the general medical opinion is the optimum period of sucking.

DATA

The data for this investigation were:

(1) scores for oral pessimism obtained on the basis of the verbal rating scales for nineteen character traits administered to 100 adult subjects and the type pattern derived therefrom, as described in the first part of this paper (7), and (2) information obtained from the mothers of these subjects as to whether the child had been breastfed or bottlefed from the start; and, if breastfed, at what age it was taken off the breast.

An analysis of variance testing the scores of the two groups of early and late weaners (referring to both of the definitions of late weaning given above) for the significance of their differences was then computed.

TYPE SCORES

In order to measure each person's standing with respect to the type factor or pattern of oral pessimism or optimism, the individual measurement for each of the nineteen character traits were correlated with the measurements of the standard pattern. The coefficients thus obtained express to what degree the person approximates to the oral pessimist type. The figures ranged from $+ .97$ to $- .88$ and may actually be taken as the person's coefficients of saturation with the oral type factor. It should be noted that they do not depend on the *level* of response but that they are a measure of the approximation of the pattern of traits within each person to the standard pattern regardless of the size of the individual scores.

The question addressed to the mothers of the 100 subjects as to whether the child had been breastfed or bottlefed from the start; and, if breastfed, at what age it was taken off the breast, yielded the distribution of periods, shown in Table 8–1, of weaning in the sample investigated:

This distribution shows the largest frequencies in the first two weaning groups (B and C) and the last two weaning groups (I and J). This

TABLE 8-1

	Age	No. of Subjects	Group
Bottlefed from the start		10	A
Breastfed	Two months and less	18	B
	Three months and less	9	C
	Four months and less	3	D
	Five months and less	4	E
	Six months and less	10	F
	Seven months and less	7	G
	Eight months and less	3	H
	Nine months and less	23	I
	Over nine months and less	13	J
		100	

may perhaps give some weight to the deliberations that certain general factors come into play determining the time of weaning, which in the intermediate months are complicated by other individual factors. What these factors determining the time of weaning might be is at present a matter of mere speculation. To the writer it seems that the attitude of the mother, either rejecting or accepting, might be one. It may be likely that a rejecting mother would have thrown off the burden of breastfeeding by the third or fourth month rather than drag on further. Mothers who carry on would probably be of the type who, discounting interference of other factors, would go through with breastfeeding to the conventionally approved and medically advised age of nine months. This question calls for investigation, in order to throw more light on any relation between weaning and character which might be found. Other factors precipitating weaning might arise from the child's constitution and the intensity of the demands he makes on the mother, necessitating his being taken off the breast.

TREATMENT OF DATA AND RESULTS

An analysis of variance was then computed to test any possible difference in the scores on oral pessimism in the early and late weaning groups whereby both definitions of late weaning described above (five months and more, and nine months and more) were referred to successively. In Table 8–2 are set out the corresponding tables, F-ratios and correlated coefficients.

We see that the difference in oral pessimist scores between early and late weaning whereby late weaning is defined in the two above

TABLE 8-2

Analysis of Variance Testing the Difference between Early Weaners·
(Weaned at Not Later than Four Months of Age)
and Late Weaners (Weaned at Five Months and More)

Source	Degrees of Fr.	Sum of Squares	Mean Square
Within weaning group	88	22.267	.253
Between early and late weaning group	1	2.033	2.033
	89	24.300	.2730

$F = 8.04$ (F for 1 & 80 df at 1% level = 6.96)
$= E^2 .073$ $E = .271$[1]

[1] Epsilon is a measure of correlation based on the analysis of variance (see Peters and Van Voorhis, *Statistical procedures and their mathematical bases.* New York: McGraw-Hill, 1940, pp. 325, 353).

described ways is significant, as tested through the F-ratio in both cases, beyond the 1% level. The correlation between early weaning and oral pessimism, using the whole distribution of weaning groups and separating early and late weaning at the fourth month, is .271; if in the late weaning group only those taken off the breast at nine months and after are included, the correlation is slightly higher, viz., .305.

Testing Abraham's and Bergler's assumption that frustration as well as overindulgence determines oral pessimism, by comparing the early weaners with those subjects whose breastfeeding was continued after their ninth month of age we find the following results: the mean score for the former group in oral pessimism is + .138, for the latter group − .346. In other words, those who experience early frustration in breastfeeding tend in their adult character makeup to lean toward the oral pessimist end of our type pattern, while those who have enjoyed an

TABLE 8-3

Analysis of Variance Testing the Difference between Early Weaners
(as Above) and Late Weaners (Weaned at Nine Months and More)

Source	Degree of F.	Sum of Squares	Mean Squares
Within weaning group	64	16.271	.254
Between early and late weaning groups	1	1.904	1.904
	65	18.175	.280

$F = 7.50$ (F for 65 df at 1% level = 7.04)
$= \Sigma^2 .093$ $\Sigma = .305$

overlong period of breastfeeding show a marked tendency to develop oral optimist character traits. The correlation between early weaning and oral pessimism on the one hand and overlong breastfeeding and oral optimism on the other is .368, significant beyond 1%.

This result supports Glover's contention that the shortening of the weaning period must be regarded as traumatic factor rather than the lengthening, if by traumatic we mean inducing oral pessimism or depression. At the same time the above result also coincides with the observations of those anthropologists that a long period of breastfeeding and optimism, generosity, etc., were related.

DISCUSSION

Attempting to answer our question concerning the influence of breast-feeding on character formation from our data, we can therefore say: that a significant (beyond the 1% level) correlation has been found between early weaning and oral pessimism. Or, in other words, early weaning tends to be associated with oral optimism to the extent of $r = .27$, respectively, .31.

These results seem therefore to indicate that the length of breast-feeding is a significant factor in the etiology of oral pessimism and probably depression; but the size of the correlation also shows that there are other factors involved in oral pessimism which account for it to a greater extent, and which still await investigation.

As to the effect of the weaning trauma itself, neither do we suggest that the duration of breastfeeding as such need be regarded as a last cause in the etiological chain; for it may equally be only a symptomatic manifestation of more fundamental factors, such as the attitude of the mother, the constitution of the child, and the interaction of both. Here too we need further investigation.

REFERENCES

1. ABRAHAM, K. The influence of oral erotism on character formation. In *Selected Papers,* Hogarth Press, London, 1942.

2. BERGLER, E. Zur Problematik des "oralen" Pessimisten. *Imago,* 1934, *20,* 330–376.

3. BERNFELD, S. *The psychology of the infant.* London: Kegan Paul, Trench, Trubner & Co., Ltd., 1929.

4. FREUD, S. *Inhibition, symptom and anxiety.* London: Hogarth Press, 1936.

5. GLOVER, E. Notes on oral character formation. *Int. J. Psycho-Anal.,* 1925, *6,* 131–154.

6. GLOVER, E. Examination of the Klein system of child psychology, *The psychoanalytic study of the child. Imago,* London, 1945, *1,* 75–118.

7. GOLDMAN, F. Breastfeeding and character formation. Part I. *J. Personal.,* 1948, *17,* 83–103.

8. KLEIN, MELANIE. The psychogenesis of manic-depressive states. *Int. J. Psycho-Anal.,* 1935, *16,* 145–174.

9. RADO, SANDOR. The problem of melancholia. *Int. J. Psycho-Anal.,* 1928, *9,* 9–32.

10. RIBBLE, MARGARET A. Infantile experience in relation to personality development. In J. McV. Hunt (ed.), *Personality and the behavior disorders.* New York: Ronald Press, 1944. Vol. II, pp. 621–651.

11. STÄRKE, A. The castration complex. *Int. J. Psycho-Anal.,* 1921, *2,* 179–201

Acknowledgments should be made to Mr. Alubin, from whose interest in this work the writer has derived invaluable stimulation and instruction.

9

Gerald S. Blum & Daniel R. Miller

Exploring the Psychoanalytic Theory
of the "Oral Character"

In these days of sophisticated discussion on how to study psychoanalytic theory we feel somewhat defensive concerning the methods we
are about to describe. Not only did we confine ourselves to conventional techniques in psychology's stockpile but we used as many as we
could. This approach was designed to test whether the theory *can* be
phrased in operational terms amenable to traditional types of
experimentation.

The topic we chose to investigate was the theory of "oral character."
On one hand, there is sufficient agreement in the psychoanalytic literature to provide a starting point from which to formulate hypotheses. On
the other, this aspect of the theory is admittedly incomplete. The
combination made the area seem especially promising for experimental
exploration.

Various clinical manifestations of oral passivity are summarized
by Fromm in the following selected excerpts describing what he calls
the "receptive orientation":

> In the receptive orientation a person feels "the source of all good" to be outside,
> and he believes that the only way to get what he wants—be it something material,
> be it affection, love, knowledge, pleasure—is to receive it from that outside source.
> In this orientation the problem of love is almost exclusively that of "being loved" and
> not that of loving. . . . They are exceedingly sensitive to any withdrawal or rebuff
> they experience on the part of the loved person. . . . It is characteristic of these people
> that their first thought is to find somebody else to give them needed information rather
> than to make even the smallest effort of their own . . . they are always in search of
> a "magic helper." They show a particular kind of loyalty, at the bottom of which is
> the gratitude for the hand that feeds them and the fear of ever losing it. Since
> they need many hands to feel secure, they have to be loyal to numerous people. It is
> difficult for them to say "no," and they are easily caught between conflicting loyalties
> and promises. Since they cannot say "no," they love to say "yes" to everything and
> everybody, and the resulting paralysis of their critical abilities makes them increas-
> ingly dependent on others.
>
> They are dependent not only on authorities for knowledge and help but on people

Reprinted by permission of the publisher and the author from *Journal of Personality*,
1952, *20*, 287–304. Copyright 1952, Duke University Press, Durham, North Carolina.

in general for any kind of support. They feel lost when alone because they feel that they cannot do anything without help. . . .

This receptive type has great fondness for food and drink. These persons tend to overcome anxiety and depression by eating or drinking. The mouth is an especially prominent feature, often the most expressive one; the lips tend to be open, as if in a state of continuous expectation of being fed. In their dreams, being fed is a frequent symbol of being loved; being starved, an expression of frustration or disappointment. . . . (4, pp. 62–63)

COLLECTION OF DATA

Having delimited our field of investigation, we were then faced with decisions concerning subjects and specific techniques. In regard to subjects, we chose to work with humans rather than animals. Generalizations from animal behavior are largely by way of analogy. Furthermore, the complexities of interpersonal relationships cannot be fully duplicated in animal work. A second decision concerned normal versus abnormal subjects. We chose the former because of the frequently heard objection that a theory derived largely from abnormal subjects must be shown to be applicable to normals. A third decision involved the desired age level of the subjects. The selection finally centered on eight-year-olds, since children in the latency period have the double advantage of being relatively free of the rampant psychosexual conflicts of earlier childhood on one hand, and of crystallized adult defenses on the other. The experimental group consisted of the eighteen boys and girls in the third grade at the University of Michigan during 1948–49.

To test the hypotheses formulated from the literature, we first had to select a criterion measure of orality. This operational definition consisted of nonpurposive mouth movements recorded at various times over the three-week period of research. Trained observers followed the children individually during eight two-minute intervals as part of a time-sampling procedure. They tallied such oral activities as thumbsucking, licking the lips, tongue-rolling, and bubbling. In addition to these routine classroom observations, the same activities were noted in an experiment on boredom tolerance (see Section X). All children were ranked on both measures and a final average ranking computed.*

Data on the dependent variables were collected by the following methods: teacher ratings, time-sampling, sociometrics, and experimental situations. Wherever feasible, we employed several approaches to test each hypothesis. Since the theory postulates that all individuals fall along a continuum of orality, rank-order correlations (corrected for ties) were calculated to measure the association between variable and criterion.

* These two measures of mouth movements correlated .61 with each other.

TESTING THE HYPOTHESES

Each of the following sections presents the statement of a hypothesis, the design worked out to test it, and the subsequent results.

I. Extreme Interest in Food

(A) Hypothesis
Since the oral character is emotionally involved with eating beyond the dictates of simple hunger, he will consume extreme amounts of oral supplies and evince great interest in related activities. Accordingly, positive correlations are predicted between the orality criterion (mouth movements) and variables measuring interest in food.

(B) Methods
(1) Ice cream consumption. Our measure of consumption of oral supplies was the amount of ice cream eaten after hunger satiation. The children all ate lunch together. The meal, provided by the school, was dietically planned and ample for all the children. Upon conclusion of a short rest period which followed lunch, they were offered an unlimited supply of vanilla ice cream contained in one-ounce paper cups packaged especially for the study. The carton of ice cream was placed on a table in the center of the room by a female graduate student who supervised the distribution of the cups. Each child was allowed to take one whenever he wished. However, only one cup at a time was permitted and that in return for an empty one. No limit was placed on how much a child ate. The carton was kept in the room for the entire forty minutes devoted to arts and crafts, during which period observers recorded the exact number of cups consumed by each child. This procedure was repeated daily over three weeks. From these data averages were computed. The range in any one day's session was quite startling, varying all the way from no cups to thirty-nine for a single child. The absence of any parental complaints concerning illness or lack of appetite was a pleasant surprise in view of the inability of the observers, even at the end of the most frustrating days of the experiment, to eat more than five or six cups without discomfort.

(2) Eagerness at lunch time. The regular teacher and five practice teachers were given a scale describing various kinds of behavior typical of oral children. They were asked to write the names of the children who occurred to them spontaneously as they read each of fourteen items.*

---

* Following is the complete list of questions: (1) Which children do you think get discouraged or give up most easily when something is difficult for them? (2) Which children do you think are most able to take care of themselves without the help of adults or other children? (3) Which children get the blues most often? (4) Which children would you most like to take with you on a two-week vacation? (5) Which children tend to ask the teacher for help most often, even when they know how to

At the completion of the form they were asked to reconsider each item and to increase all shorter lists of names to five. Among the questions was: "Which children appear most impatient to eat at lunch time, as if eating were particularly important to them?"

(C) *Results*

Mouth Movements

1. Ice cream	.52	$P < .05$
2. Eagerness at lunch time	.51	$P < .05$

These figures strongly support the predicted association between orality (mouth movements) and interest in food.

II. *Need for Liking and Approval*

(A) *Hypothesis*

In terms of the theory, a significant relationship should be found between degree of orality and the need for liking and approval.

(B) *Methods*

(1) "Which children are most eager to have other children like them?" (Teacher item 6)

(2) "Which children make a special effort to get the teachers to like them?" (Teacher item 12)

(3) Approaches to teachers for approval. (Time-sampling item)

(4) Approaches to children for approval. (Time-sampling item)

(5) Attention to observers. (Time-sampling item)

Mouth Movements

1. Eagerness for others' liking	.68	$P < .01$
2. Efforts for teachers' liking	.10	$N S$†
3. Approaches to teachers for approval	.44	$P < .10$
4. Approaches to children for approval	.24	$N S$
5. Attention to observers	.36	$P < .20$

---

do the task? (6) Which children are most eager to have other children like them? (7) Which children display their affections most openly to the teachers? (8) Which children's feelings seem to be most easily hurt? (9) Which children seem to be always eager to help even when they are inconvenienced? (10) Which children seem to accept the suggestions of others almost without thinking twice? (11) Which children appear most impatient to eat at lunch time, as if eating were particularly important to them? (12) Which children make a special effort to get the teachers to like them? (13) Which children would you least like to take with you on a two-week vacation? (14) Which children seem most concerned with giving and receiving things?

† Not significant.

Viewing these correlations as a whole, the hypothesis seems to be fairly well supported. Although only two are significant beyond the 10% level, all are in the positive direction.

III. Dependency

(A) Hypothesis
Closely allied to the preceding hypothesis is the prediction of a positive correlation between orality and dependency.

(B) Methods
(1) "Which children do you think are most able to take care of themselves without the help of adults or other children?" (Teacher item 2)
(2) "Which children tend to ask the teacher for help most often, even when they know how to do the task?" (Teacher item 5)

(C) Results

	Mouth Movements	
1. Doesn't take care of self	.50	$P < .05$
2. Asks teachers' help	.10	$N S$

These results tend to be equivocal, with one correlation being significant and the other not.

IV. Concern Over Giving and Receiving

(A) Hypothesis
Since gifts represent a form of "supplies" to the oral character, it is predicted that concern over giving and receiving varies with degree of orality.

(B) Methods
(1) "Which children seem most concerned with giving and receiving things?" (Teacher item 14)
(2) Generosity without promise of supplies in return. A related prediction held that oral children would be reluctant to give unless attractive supplies were forthcoming. After the distribution of ice cream on the second gift day (see Section 3 immediately following) the class was allowed to use the colored pencils in a drawing period. Shortly before the end of this session, a strange adult wearing a large, yellow badge marked "Pencil Drive" entered the room and made a very stirring appeal to give as many pencils as possible to the poor children of the neighborhood. Each child then went behind a screen and secretly deposited his pencils in the slot of a colorful box marked "Pencil Drive." All the new pencils had been marked with pin points, so that the contributions of each subject were readily identifiable. Unfortunately, this coding system was of little aid since only three in the entire class gave new pencils.

The rest of the collection consisted of a varigated assortment of battered, chewed-up stumps with broken points—all without identification marks. In order to locate the pencil contributors, a new procedure was developed which provided the basis for the added experiment described in Section 4 following.

(3) Gifts as the equivalent of food. The term "oral supplies" connotes, in addition to food, tokens of personal recognition. It was hypothesized that, if gifts and food are equivalent supplies, receipt of gifts should result in a diminution of ice cream consumption for the group as a whole. On one occasion the children were each given a box of crayons; another time they received seven colored pencils which they had chosen as their most desired gift in a rating session the preceding day.

(4) Guilt over not giving. The theory leads to the prediction that guilt, typically experienced as a deprivation of supplies, should bring about an increase in the consumption of ice cream. The day after the pencil drive, the teacher agreed to deliver a stern lecture telling how ashamed she was of their stinginess. She was so effective that, before she finished, one boy blurted out that he had meant to give more new pencils and ran to the box to deposit a few. Next the teacher asked the group to retrieve their donations and observers tallied the number of pencils each pupil took back, which provided the data missing in Section 2 immediately above. Shortly afterward the ice cream was distributed and the number of cups counted as usual.

To relieve the guilt, the pencil solicitor returned later to proclaim happily that the school drive had been 100% successful. He then apologized for not having announced previously that old pencils were not wanted.

(C) Results

Mouth Movements

1. Concern over giving and receiving	.46	$P < .10$
2. Lack of generosity	.22	$N S$

(3) Gifts as the equivalent of food. On the crayon day, fourteen of the sixteen subjects decreased in the number of cups consumed ($X^2 = 9.00$, $P < .01$); and on the pencil day, twelve out of fifteen dropped ($X^2 = 5.40$, $P < .02$).

(4) Guilt over not giving. While there were no significant increases in the actual amount of ice cream consumed after the "guilt" lecture, certain qualitative observations were noted. The five most oral children in the group sat on the table next to the ice cream carton throughout the whole period, in contrast to their usual wandering around the room. Since they had apparently been eating up to maximum physical capacity, it was virtually impossible for them to eat significantly more cups than before. Another exceptional feature was the fact that none of the ice cream was left over this time.

Considering the above experiments as a whole, there seems to be fair support for the hypothesis that orality is related to concern over giving and receiving.

V. Need To Be Ingratiating

(A) Hypothesis
The oral character, by virtue of his never-ending search for love and approval, tends to behave toward others in a very ingratiating manner.

(B) Methods
(1) "Which children display their affections most openly to the teachers?" (Teacher item 7)
(2) "Which children seem to be always eager to help even when they are inconvenienced?" (Teacher item 9)
(3) Going out of way to do favors. (Time-sampling item)

(C) Results

Mouth Movements

1. Displays affection openly	−.28	N S
2. Always eager to help	−.24	N S
3. Goes out of way to do favors	.16	N S

These results clearly negate the predicted association between orality and the need to be ingratiating.

VI. Social Isolation

(A) Hypothesis
According to the theory, the oral character should be infrequently chosen by his peers in view of his passivity, his excessive demands for attention, and his hostility when these demands are not gratified.

(B) Methods
In a private interview each child was asked to answer a number of sociometric questions to determine his favorites among his classmates: (1) "Which children in your classroom do you like best?" (2) "Which of the children in your classroom would you most like to invite to a party?" (3) "Which teachers do you like the most?"* (4) "Which children in your class are you good friends with?" Class members were then ranked according to the number of times their names had been mentioned.

(C) Results
Mouth Movements

1. Social isolation	.68	P < .01

* Included only for use in Section VII.

This correlation strongly supports the theoretical deduction that orality and social isolation go hand in hand.

VII. Inability to Divide Loyalties

(A) Hypothesis

The theory leads to the hypothesis that the more oral child has greater difficulty choosing between two friends, inasmuch as both represent potential sources of supply.

(B) Methods

Several days after the socioeconomic ratings a measure of divided loyalty was obtained. Each child was interviewed individually and asked to make a number of choices between his two best friends as noted on the sociometric ratings and also between his two best-liked teachers. The interviewer recorded decision time plus comments, actions, and expressive movements. The protocols were then rated blindly by three judges for degree of indecision.

(C) Results

Mouth Movements		
1. Inability to divide loyalties	−.28	N S

The correlation of this variable with the criterion contradicts the hypothesized association between orality and the inability to divide loyalties.

VIII. Suggestibility

(A) Hypothesis

From the theory it was anticipated that the oral child, in view of his excessive need for love and approval, would be suggestible in the presence of a potentially supply-giving adult.

(B) Methods

(1) Upon his arrival in the testing room, the child was told: "We have some things which we want you to help us try out in order to see if they are right for school children of your age." The experiment consisted of three parts: tasting a hypothetical cherry flavor in candy, smelling perfume from a bottle of water, and feeling nonexistent vibrations in a metal rod attached to some apparatus.

(2) "Which children seem to accept the suggestions of others almost without thinking twice?" (Teacher item 10)

(C) Results

Mouth Movements

1. Taste	.50	$P < .05$
Touch	.00	N S
Smell	.03	N S
2. Accepts suggestions	.11	N S

Except for taste, suggestibility does not appear to be related to degree of orality. The discrepancy between results with taste and with the other items is most easily accounted for by the specifically oral quality of the taste measure.

IX. Depressive Tendencies

(A) Hypothesis
Self-esteem in the oral child is presumed to depend upon external sources of love or supplies. Therefore, the unavoidable frustration of oral demands is said to be experienced as a feeling of emptiness or depression.

(B) Methods
(1) "Which children do you think get discouraged or give up most easily when something is difficult for them?" (Teacher item 1)
(2) "Which children get the blues most often?" (Teacher item 3)
(3) "Which children's feelings seem to be most easily hurt?" (Teacher item 8)

(C) Results

Mouth Movements

1. Get discouraged	.32	$P < .20$
2. Get the blues	.05	N S
3. Feelings easily hurt	.13	N S

The low correlations between mouth movements and personality characteristics relevant to depression do not support the theoretical prediction.

X. Boredom Tolerance

(A) Hypothesis
Boredom is assumed to be especially disturbing to the oral child because it signifies a lack of available supplies. Therefore he would be expected to show very little tolerance for a boring, unrewarded activity.

(B) Methods

In this experiment the child was taken into a room where he was shown a large sheaf of papers containing lines of Xs and Os. The examiner then said: "Your class is being compared with another class in another town to see which class can cross out the most circles." After giving the instructions, the examiner added: "There are several pages [the examiner leafed through all the sheets]. Don't write your name on the paper. We don't care how much you yourself can do, but how much the class can do. All right, you may begin."

The examiner then left the room. As soon as the child began, an observer casually entered the room, sat at a distance, and recorded all the actions of the subject, such as number of mouth movements and work interruptions. The child was stopped after twenty minutes. Ranks were based on number of lines completed. As mentioned previously, this experiment also contributed to the criterion measure of nonbiting mouth movements, which were tallied throughout.

(C) Results

Mouth Movements

1. Boredom Tolerance	.45	$P < .10$

While not very high, this figure does provide some support for the prediction that orality and boredom tolerance are positively associated.

XI. Summary of Results

Ten hypotheses concerning oral character structure have been tested. The results can be summarized in tabular form as in Table 9–1.

TABLE 9-1

Strong Support	Fair Support	Unsupported	Equivocal
1. Extreme interest in food 2. Social isolation	1. Need for liking and approval 2. Concern over giving and receiving 3. Boredom tolerance	1. Dependency 2. Suggestibility	1. Need to be ingratiating 2. Inability to divide loyalties 3. Depressive tendencies

The goal of this phase of the research is to check the existing status of the theory, and to make revisions wherever dictated by the evidence. The above data represent the initial tests of hypotheses deduced from the psychoanalytical literature on orality. In general, a fair number of predictions have been supported, some remain questionable, and still others are clearly not supported. Before evaluating specific hypotheses, however, we prefer to await the returns from successive attempts to measure the same variables. It is very possible that any one of the significant correlations may still reflect the influence of chance factors. Too, any one of the insignificant findings may be a function of faulty experimentation rather than incorrect theory. Both of these possibilities suggest the necessity for repeated research along similar lines. Apart from the fate of specific hypotheses, the overall results hold promise for the investigation of psychoanalytic theory by conventional psychological methods.

RELATED EMPIRICAL OBSERVATIONS

Intercorrelations of Major Variables

In addition to providing data concerning specific hypotheses, the study lends itself to an overall analysis of correlations among the major variables. This supplementary approach seems worthwhile in view of the postulated communiality of the variables. If each variable really measures oral passivity, the table of intercorrelations should demonstrate positive relationships beyond chance expectancy. These data, grouped according to pure oral measures, experimental situations, and behavioral measures, are shown in Table 9–2.

From Table 9–3 we see that the total numbers of significant positive correlations at the 10%, 5%, and 1% levels clearly exceed the chance expectancies. These results suggest the possible existence of a general "factor" of orality.

Comparative Evaluation of Methodological Approaches

Table 9–4 presents a breakdown of the personality variables into two general types—experimental situations and behavioral measures. The number of significant correlations for each type with the major variables suggests a probable difference in their relative efficacy. It is true that the same operational variables are not measured in both types. Nevertheless, the large number of significant behavioral correlations warrants speculation concerning possible causes. Three alternative explanations come to mind. One, the experimental designs were adequate and the negative results are a contradiction of the hypotheses. This possibility does not seem very plausible in light of the positive theoretical findings with other techniques. Two, the hypotheses are valid and the designs inadequate. No evidence exists for rejecting this alternative, but the marked discrepancy between results with the two approaches, both of which were carefully designed and pretested, leads us to question the explanation. Three, the difficulty lies, not in experimental design or theory, but in unreliability inherent in the settings in which the experi-

TABLE 9-2

Intercorrelations of Major Variables

| | Pure Oral Measures | | | | Personality | | | | | | |
| | | | | | Experimental Situations | | | | Behavioral Measures | | |
	1. Ice Cream	2. Eagerness at Lunch (T.R.)	3. Mouth Activity (T.S.)	4. Mouth Activity (B.T.)	5. Suggestibility	6. Boredom Tolerance	7. Divided Loyalty	8. Generosity	9. Sociometrics	10. Combined Teacher Ratings[1]	11. Combined Time Samples[2]
1.	—	19	67‡	32	30	31	−07	−29	40*	−09	43*
2.	—	—	41*	50†	11	34	−18	15	44*	20	01
3.	—	—	—	61‡	04	39	−21	19	61‡	15	55†
4.	—	—	—	—	25	44*	−18	32	71‡	20	17
5.	—	—	—	—	—	12	44*	−33	36	07	−11
6.	—	—	—	—	—	—	04	25	35	10	−04
7.	—	—	—	—	—	—	—	−33	03	04	−31
8.	—	—	—	—	—	—	—	—	18	45*	09
9.	—	—	—	—	—	—	—	—	—	23	12
10.	—	—	—	—	—	—	—	—	—	—	−01

$* = P < .10$
$† = P < .05$
$‡ = P < .01$

[1] Does not include 2 [Eagerness at Lunch (T.R.)]
[2] Does not include 3 [Mouth Activity (T.S.)]

ments were conducted. The number of observations involved in the experiments were necessarily limited to one session, whereas the behavioral measures were usually accumulated over several time periods. Unavoidable and unpredictable obstacles are bound to arise in the course of experimentation in a natural setting, such as a schoolroom, where the success of each design hinges upon the precision and cooperation of a large number of individuals.

Cases in point are the Love Withdrawal and Can't Say No experiments, both of which had to be abandoned. The hypothesis in the former stated that the oral child should be highly sensitive to withdrawal of love. The "ice-cream lady" first asked the children in the class to make drawings using themes of their own choice. When the drawings were finished she circulated around the room, praising them all freely. Then she instructed the group to draw a house, each child individually to bring his drawing to her upon its completion. She lauded half of the drawings, and held them up before the class while commenting on their merits and naming the artists. The other half were received with casual in-

TABLE 9-3

*Number of Significant Positive Correlations
among Major Variables*

Probability Level	Number Expected by Chance	Number Obtained
.10	2.75	13
.05	1.38	6
.01	0.28	4

difference but no criticism. This was the love withdrawal procedure. Finally, she asked the class to draw a picture of a child. The aim of the experiment was to determine the effects of the withdrawal of love upon both drawings and behavior as recorded by observers.

The experiment was to have been repeated several days later, with a reversal of the treatment of the previously praised and ignored halves. In the actual administration it turned out to be impossible to maintain any kind of order in the class. The children were all excited about an Indian play which they had performed that day before the entire school, and their drum pounding and war whooping precluded any systematic, experimental procedure.

The Can't Say No hypothesis dealt with the inability of the oral character to refuse requests from adults for fear of losing their approval. Nine observers entered the library while the class was listening to a fascinating record. Each observer approached a child, tapped him on the shoulder, and said in a neutral tone: "Come with me." The reactions to this request were later reported in detail. Like the preceding experiment this one was disrupted by an unforeseen complication. At the last

TABLE 9-4

*Personality Measures Broken Down by the
Type of Approach vs. Major Variables*

Personality Measures	Probability Level	Number Positive Correlations Expected by Chance	Number Obtained
Experimental	.10	1.70	3
Situations	.05	0.85	0
	.01	0.17	0
Behavioral	.10	1.35	7
Measures	.05	0.68	3
	.01	0.14	2

minute the librarian was unable to schedule a record session when the other nine children in the group were to be asked to leave.

In contrast to the above illustrative experiments, the cumulative behavioral measures, on the other hand, were not as susceptible to unforeseen disruptions, since accidental influences on any one day tended to average out in the course of time. For example, differences occured when ice cream was delivered late, yet this did not seriously alter the final ranking of subjects on the number of cups consumed.

From these speculations, it seems preferable that research designs, when dealing with something as complex as character structure, involve a series of measurements over a period of time.

Exploration of Projective Instruments

The following four projective techniques were included to explore their suitability as measures of orality: the Rorschach Test (8), Thematic Apperception Test (TAT) (7), Blacky Pictures (1, 2) and a specially constructed Story Completion Test which had been found to be significantly related to sociometric status in a previous study (6). Since there had been no previous applications of the techniques to this topic and age range, attempts at explicit predictions were not made.

Table 9–5 presents the correlations of the various projective methods with the major variables. Analysis of the projectives can be grouped

TABLE 9-5

Correlations of Projective Methods with Major Variables

| | Pure Oral Measures | | | | Personality | | | | | | |
| | | | | | Experimental Situations | | | | Behavioral Measures | | |
	1. Ice Cream	2. Eagerness at Lunch (T.R.)	3. Mouth Activity (T.S.)	4. Mouth Activity (B.T.)	5. Suggestibility	6. Boredom Tolerance	7. Divided Loyalty	8. Generosity	9. Sociometrics	10. Combined Teacher Ratings	11. Combined Time Samples
Rorschach (Objective)	28	19	20	−05	11	41	−03	−11	−13	−10	45
TAT (Objective)	−40	−58	−34	−59	01	−37	33	−21	05	−02	−05
Story Completion (Objective)	−11	−45	−29	−36	08	−20	60	−06	−11	−12	−05
Story Completion (Interpretive)	47	06	33	48	40	37	23	−34	19	−12	06
Blacky (Interpretive)	21	−23	16	25	41	−06	16	−20	28	15	21

under two broad headings, objective and interpretive. The Rorschach, TAT, and Story Completion (Objective) were all scored by counting the number of oral references, e.g., "food," "hunger," "eating," etc. The Blacky and Story Completion (Interpretive) protocols were ranked according to global impressions of oral passivity. While none of the correlations is very high, it should be noted that the "objective" approach yielded twenty-two negative and eleven positive correlations, whereas the "interpretive" produced only five negative and seventeen positive $(X^2 = 10.19$ $P < .01)$. Whether this difference can legitimately be attributed to type of scoring approach can be answered only by further investigation.

SUMMARY

This project was designed to explore the feasibility of testing psychoanalytic theory by conventional psychological methods. Hypotheses concerning the "oral character," deduced from statements in the literature, were examined by means of teacher ratings, time-sampling, sociometrics, and experimental situations conducted in a third-grade class. The operational definition of orality consisted of nonpurposive mouth movements recorded by observers. The eighteen subjects were ranked on the criterion and on a series of variables related to specific hypotheses.

The resulting correlations lent strong support to hypotheses dealing with (1) extreme interest in food and (2) social isolation. Fair support was given (1) need for liking and approval, (2) concern over giving and receiving, and (3) boredom tolerance. Unsupported hypotheses were (1) need to be ingratiating, (2) inability to divide loyalties, and (3) depressive tendencies; while remaining equivocal were (1) dependency and (2) suggestibility. Apart from the currently tentative nature of these specific findings, the overall results were interpreted as holding promise for the investigation of psychoanalytic theory by traditional techniques.

REFERENCES

1. BLUM, G. S. A study of the psychoanalytic theory of psychosexual development. *Genet. Psychol. Monogr.*, 1949, 39, 3–99.

2. BLUM, G. S. *The Blacky Pictures: a technique for the exploration of personality dynamics.* New York: The Psychological Corporation, 1950.

3. FENICHEL, O. *The psychoanalytic theory of neurosis.* New York: W. W. Norton and Co., 1945.

4. FROMM, E. *Man for himself*. New York: Rinehart, 1947.

5. MILLER, D. R., and HUTT, M. L. Value interiorization and personality development. *J. Soc. Issues*, 1949, 5, No. 4, 2–30.

6. MILLER, D. R., and STINE, M. E. The Prediction of Social Acceptance by Means of Psychoanalytic Concepts. *J. Pers.*, 1951, 20, 162–174.

7. MURRAY, H. A. *Thematic Apperception Test manual*. Cambridge: Harvard University Press, 1943.

8. RORSCHACH, H. *Psychodiagnostics* (translation) Bern: Hans Huber, 1942.

9. THOMPSON, C. *Psychoanalysis: evaluation and development*. New York: Hermitage House, 1950.

10. THORNTON, G. R. The significance of rank-difference coefficients of correlation. *Psychometrika*, 1943, 8, No. 4, 211–222.

This project was supported by a grant from the Rackham School of Graduate Studies at the University of Michigan. The following individuals participated in the planning and execution of the study: Edith B. Bennett, Marvin A. Brandwein, James Chabot, Elizabeth Douvan, Stanley C. Duffendack, Glenn D. Garman, Maizie Gurin, J. Edwin Keller, Louise Morrison, Otto Riedl, E. Robert Sinnett, Ezra H. Stotland, William D. Winter, and Marion P. Winterbottom.

"This article is based on a paper presented at the 1950 American Psychological Association symposium on "Experimental Approaches to Psychoanalytic Theory."

10

Joseph Masling, Lillie Weiss, & Bertram Rothschild

Relationships of Oral Imagery to
Yielding Behavior and Birth Order

The psychoanalytic notion of the oral dependent character stresses the need the individual has for support and approval from others. The oral character "is extremely dependent on others for the maintenance of his self-esteem. External supplies are all-important to him, and he yearns for them passively." (4, p. 160) In his discussion of the "receptive orientation" as a means of coping with the demands of the world, Fromm (7) stated:

it is characteristic of these people that their first thought is to find somebody else to give them needed information rather than to make even the smallest effort of their own. . . . They are always in search of a "magic helper" [p. 62].

In addition to their passivity, those with a receptive orientation are also compliant:

Since they need many hands to feel secure, they have to be loyal to numerous people. It is difficult for them to say "no," and they are easily caught between conflicting loyalties and promises. Since they cannot say "no," they love to say "yes" to everything and everybody, and the resulting paralysis of their critical abilities makes them increasingly dependent on others [pp. 62–63].

A situation which frequently results in "paralysis of critical abilities" and forces some subjects to rely increasingly on others is the Asch (1) conformity experiment, in which subjects are required to choose between the information furnished by their own sensory apparatus and the information available from other people. The psychoanalytic theory of character formation clearly indicates that the oral-dependent person will look to others for information rather than trust his own judgment.

Following this reasoning it was hypothesized that oral dependent subjects yield more frequently in a conformity situation than nonoral dependent subjects. A method of scoring Rorschach responses for oral imagery was used to define the independent variable; this scoring method had previously demonstrated validity in discriminating between obese and nonobese populations (8) and between alcoholic and non-alcoholic populations (3).

A second goal of this study was to investigate the relationship between oral dependence and birth order. Schachter (11) reported that emotionally disturbed nursery school pupils who were firstborn or only children were seen by their teachers to be more dependent than later-born children, and Sears (13), in discussing birth order and dependency, concluded that firstborn and only children were more dependent on both their mothers and nursery school teachers than those born later. However, this relationship is by no means clearly established. While several experiments (2, 6) have demonstrated that firstborn and only subjects are more conforming (e.g., are more dependent on the judgment of others), partially or completely nonsignificant findings have been reported in at least three other studies (9, 10, 14).

Because of the contradictory nature of many of the results of studies on birth order and dependency, no specific hypothesis was formulated, the goal being only to examine this relationship without specifying the direction of differences.

METHOD

Sample. The subjects (Ss) were sixty-six male undergraduates at Syracuse University who were required to participate in experiments as part of the introductory psychology course. Nineteen of the Ss could not be used in the conformity experiment: eleven guessed they had been part of a conformity study, seven could not count the stimuli rapidly enough, and one was not used because of equipment failure. For the comparison of birth order and Rorschach responses a firstborn twin was eliminated together with three Ss who failed to give at least ten responses.

Apparatus and procedure. The method is described fully in Roths-child (9). The Ss were first given individual administrations of the Rorschach, including inquiry. The conformity experiment was introduced as an Army study on communication and began after S took the Ror-schach test. Each S listened to a tape recording of a series of clicking sounds. He was led to believe that four other Ss were also listening to the sounds and would report their estimates of the number of clicks before his turn to announce his estimate. The voices of the other four Ss were prerecorded, and the estimates the voices gave differed on five trials from the actual number of clicks. The yielding score for each S was the number of times he agreed with the other voices on the five critical trials.

Examiners. The third author and another experienced clinical psychologist administered the Rorschach tests; the first two authors scored them with the identification of Ss removed. At the time the conformity data were being collected, the Rorschach test was used to test hypotheses concerning movement, vista, color, and surface responses (9). The idea of relating oral Rorschach content to conformity behavior did not occur until three years after the tests were given, so there was no possibility of operant conditioning of desired responses.

Scoring for oral imagery. A complete description of the scoring method is reported in Masling et al. (8). Briefly, all responses were scored for presence or absence of either oral dependent or oral sadistic images following the suggestion of Schafer (12). Simple scoring manuals were prepared by defining each category and listing various examples. The following categories were used:

Oral dependence—food; food sources; food objects; food provider; passive food receiver; food organs; beggars and supplicants; nurturers; gifts and gift givers; good luck symbols; needing help or being passive; pregnancy and female reproductive anatomy; oral activity.

Oral sadism—percepts involving destruction, aggression, sadism, maiming; overwhelming figures; depriving figures; deprivation or the loss of some vital part or function; faulty oral capacity; oral assault; burdens.

Any response which met one of these criteria was given a score of one.

RESULTS

Reliability. The Rorschach records were scored blind. There were 819 responses on the forty-four Rorschach protocols; of this number, there were eighty-seven disagreements on presence of an oral percept, producing 89% agreement on this dimension. Correlation coefficients were obtained for the agreement of the two raters' scores on the categories of oral dependence and oral sadism. For oral dependence the correlation was .89, and for oral sadism the correlation was .87. Disagreements between the raters were settled without reference to group membership of the subject.

Oral imagery and yielding. The subjects were placed in rank order on the basis of frequency of yielding, and a median split was obtained. It was found that yielding subjects ($n = 23$) produced a mean of 15.3 Rorschach responses, while the nonyielders ($n = 21$) produced 22.2 responses, a difference significant at the .10 level. In order to eliminate the effect of the number of responses each subject made to the Rorschach, the scores were transformed into percentages. Using percentages as the comparison, it was found that yielding subjects gave more oral dependent responses ($M = 19.17\%$) than the nonyielders ($M = 13.33\%$). These data produced a chi-square of 4.46 ($p = .025$, one-tailed test). The hypothesis that oral dependence and yielding were positively related was, therefore, confirmed. A comparison was made of the distribution of responses among the various subcategories, but no differences between groups were found for any of the subcategories considered singly; the significant difference between groups was due to the generally more frequent use of all the subcategories by yielding subjects. There were no significant differences between groups on oral sadism, nor were differences predicted.

Oral imagery and birth order. A chi-square comparing birth order and oral dependence demonstrated that the later-born subjects gave more oral dependent responses than subjects who were firstborn or only children ($x^2 = 5.17$, $p = .05$, two-tailed test). There was no relationship between birth order and oral sadistic responses.

Yielding behavior and birth order. The relationship between yielding and birth order was the subject of the original study (9). A chi-square relating these two variables failed to reach statistical significance ($p = .20$).

DISCUSSION

As predicted from psychoanalytic speculation regarding the oral-dependent character, a positive relationship was found between conforming behavior and the perception of oral-dependent images on the Rorschach test. The finding that later-born subjects saw more oral-dependent images than firstborn and only subjects is contradictory to studies discussed by Sears (13) and Schachter (11). The present results may have occurred because the overt behavioral dependency seen by nursery school teachers and mothers is different from the dependency inferred from Rorschach responses, or the findings may provide a bridge between Blum and Miller's (5) observation that dependent third-grade children are socially isolated and Schachter's (11) conclusion that second– and later-born subjects do not seek affiliation with others to resolve anxiety as frequently as those born first. If later-born subjects tend to withdraw from social contact and if withdrawal from social contact is an oral trait, then those born later should produce more oral dependent responses, as was found in the present study.

REFERENCES

1. Asch, S. E. Studies of independence and conformity: I. A. minority of one against a unanimous majority. *Psychological Monograph,* 1956, 70(9, Whole No. 416).
2. Becker, S. W., & Carroll, J. Ordinal position and conformity. *Journal of Abnormal and Social Psychology,* 1962, 65, 129–131.

3. BERTRAND, S., & MASLING, J.   Oral imagery and alcoholism. *Journal of Abnormal Psychology*, 1969, *74*, 50–53.

4. BLUM, G.   *Psychoanalytic theories of personality*. New York: McGraw-Hill, 1953.

5. BLUM, G., & MILLER, D. R.   Exploring the psychoanalytic theory of the "oral character." *Journal of Personality*, 1952, *20*, 287–304.

6. CARRIGAN, W. C., & JULIAN, J. W.   Sex and birth-order differences in conformity as a function of need affiliation arousal. *Journal of Personality and Social Psychology*, 1963, *3*, 479–484.

7. FROMM, E.   *Man for himself*. New York: Rinehart, 1947.

8. MASLING, J., RABIE, L., & BLONDHEIM, S. H.   Obesity, level of aspiration, and Rorschach and TAT measures of oral dependence. *Journal of Consulting Psychology*, 1967, *31*, 233–239.

9. ROTHSCHILD, B.   Response style: A basis for Rorschach construct validity. *Journal of Projective Techniques and Personality Assessment*, 1964, *28*, 474–483.

10. SAMPSON, E.   Birth order, need achievement, and conformity. *Journal of Abnormal and Social Psychology*, 1962, *64*, 155–159.

11. SCHACHTER, S.   *The psychology of affiliation*. Stanford: Stanford University Press, 1959.

12. SCHAFER, R.   *Psychoanalytic interpretation in Rorschach testing*. New York: Grune & Stratton, 1954.

13. SEARS, R. R.   Ordinal position in the family as a psychological variable. *American Sociological Review*, 1950, *15*, 397–401.

14. STAPLES, F., & WALTER, R.   Anxiety, birth order, and susceptibility to social influence. *Journal of Abnormal and Social Psychology*, 1961, *62*, 716–719.

The authors are indebted to Marilyn Rothschild, who helped in all phases of the conformity experiment, particularly in the administration of the Rorschach test.

11

Aaron Lazare, M.D., Gerald L. Klerman, M.D.,
& David J. Armor, Ph.D.

Oral, Obsessive, and Hysterical

Personality Patterns

An Investigation of Psychoanalytic Concepts by
Means of Factor Analysis

This study is an attempt to explore the empirical basis of three personality types frequently discussed in the psychiatric literature—oral, obsessive, and hysterical. More specifically, the trait patterns which historically have been said to characterize each of the three personality types will be reexamined by means of factor analysis, and a self-rating form will be offered as a measure of these personality types.*

In order to understand the significance, the limitations, and the theoretical framework of this research, we shall first describe the content out of which it emerged, including a preliminary experiment which partially failed. Our interest in personality arose from our observations of the relationship between personality and symptom formation in depressed women (19). We noted, for instance, that depressed women with hysterical personalities differed from depressed women with obsessional personalities in their prehospital adjustment, in their patterns of depressive symptomatology, in the frequency of their hysterical symptoms, and in their therapeutic responses to electroconvulsive therapy. In these studies, personality was assessed by the clinical judgments of psy-

Reprinted by permission of the American Medical Association from *Archives of General Psychiatry*, 1966, *14*, 624–630. Copyright 1966 by the American Medical Association.

* In this study, "personality type" refers to a constellation, cluster, or pattern of descriptive personality traits which can be distinguished from other such constellations. It should be noted that "personality type" may elsewhere refer to a stage of libidinal development or a pattern of ego defenses. An obsessive personality, for example, would be fixated at the anal stage of libidinal development, while using the predominant ego defenses of isolation and reaction formation. In this study, obsessive personality refers only to the trait constellation of severe superego, orderliness, perseverance, etc.

chiatrists who had interviewed the patient several times. Because of the practical limitations of personality assessment by interview, the preliminary experiment began as an attempt to assess personality by patients' self-reports validated against clinicians' judgments. Our current approach to the trait patterns which characterize each of the three personality types emerged from the partial failure of this preliminary work.

PRELIMINARY EXPERIMENT

The plan of the preliminary experiment was to validate a self-rating form against the clinical judgments of psychiatric residents. The trait definitions of the three personality types were derived from extensive review of the literature. The residents were then asked to select patients typical of one of the personality types and then to assign a quantitative rating for each patient on all three types. Meanwhile, each patient was given a 200-item self-rating form designed to measure twenty personality traits which in turn defined the oral, obsessive, and hysterical personality types. Using the technique of multiple regression, the correlations between the clinical judgments and the self-ratings did not exceed 0.30. This was regarded as a research failure.

To understand these low correlations, we questioned the three assumptions on which this experiment had been based. These assumptions were:

(1) That the clinical judgments made by relatively inexperienced psychiatric residents are valid.

(2) That the trait descriptions of the personality types presented to the resident psychiatrists are valid; in other words, that the traits, which define each type, cluster statistically as they are presumed to.

(3) That the self-rating method of personality assessment is valid.

As Regards Assumption One. Discussions with the psychiatric residents and a reexamination of the patients they rated convinced us that the residents' judgments were not valid. These judgments were often based on one or two traits which lent a "halo" effect in the global rating of the personality type. For instance, a young, attractive, sexually provocative female was usually considered to be hysterical in personality regardless of the presence or absence of other hysterical traits. We also found that a high rating in one personality type would automatically lead to low ratings by the resident in the two other types.

As Regards Assumption Two. There is recent evidence to suggest that the classical trait descriptions of the personality types are not valid. Goldman-Eisler (14), for example, has demonstrated by factor analysis that the oral traits of aggression and passivity are found in two distinct factors. In addition, the current thinking of the hysterical personality is undergoing revision with an emphasis on the admixture of oral and hysterical traits (20).

As Regards Assumption Three. Self-ratings are always subject to the criticism that the subject will answer in a way that will place her in a favorable light, or that she will see herself not as others see her. Nevertheless, there is no a priori evidence that this particular self-rating form is not valid. Earlier studies by Murray (25) and Goldman-Eisler (14), both of whom conceived many of the items used in this self-rating form, achieved partial validation.

Based on these considerations, we undertook an analysis of personality trait constellations which was not dependent upon assumptions one or two but which instead utilized multivariate statistical methods to define patterns of personality traits independent of clinical judgment or prior definition.

METHODOLOGY

Research Questions and Overall Plans. The main body of this paper reports a reexamination of assumptions two and three, on which the preliminary study was based. These two assumptions became the following research questions.

(1) Can personality traits and personality types be measured by means of patients' self-reports?

(2) If so, will the personality traits thus measured form distinct statistical clusters, and will the clusters correspond in any degree to those described in the classical literature?

To answer these questions, the data from self-reports collected in the preliminary experiment were reanalyzed. Twenty personality traits were measured by a 200-item, self-rating form. The scoring of each trait was examined for internal consistency by measuring item-to-trait correlations. Finally, the twenty trait scores were subjected to factor analysis, and the factors derived were compared to the predicted clustering of traits. Having found internal consistency and having found that the trait clusters derived from the factor analysis had theoretical meaning, we regard self-ratings as a valid measure of personality.

Definitions of Personality Types. Oral personality: For the purpose of this study the seven personality traits which define the oral (ungratified) personality are: *pessimism, passivity, oral aggression, rejection of others, aggression, dependence,* and *parsimony.* This trait definition of the oral personality is based on the writings of Glover (13), Abraham (2), Fenichel (9), and Goldman-Eisler (14).

Obsessive Personality: For this study the nine personality traits which define the obsessive personality are: *orderliness, obstinacy, parsimony, rejection of others, emotional constriction, self-doubt, severe superego, rigidity,* and *perseverance.* This definition is derived from Freud (11), Abraham (1), Jones (18), Fenichel (9), Reich (28), Henderson and Gillespie (16), Ewalt et al. (8), Mayer-Gross et al. (22), Rado (27), Munroe (24), Noyes and Kolb (26), Masserman (21), Sandler (29), and the APA *Diagnostic Manual* (5). From these sources all the adjectives used to describe the obsessive personality are grouped into nine categories (see Table 11–1), each of which may be said to represent a personality trait. Several of these adjectives and several of these traits may be viewed as overlapping, but this is to be expected with adjectives or traits which are theoretically related.

Hysterical Personality: For the purpose of this study the seven traits which define the hysterical personality are: *egocentricity, exhibitionism, emotionality, suggestibility, dependence, sexual provocativeness,* and *fear of sexuality.* This definition is derived from Bleuler (7), Reich (28), Fenichel (9), Marmor (20), Ziegler and Paul (34), Henderson and Gillespie (16), Alexander and Ross (4), Abse (3), Ziegler et al. (35), Millar (23), Mayer-Gross et al. (22), Noyes and Kolb (26), Janet (17), Sullivan (32), Wechsler (33), Fitzgerald (10), Siegman (30), Berblinger (6), Stephens and Kamp (31). From these sources all the adjectives used to describe the hysterical personality are grouped into seven categories (see Table 11–2), each of which may be said to represent a personality trait.

Selection of Patients. Ninety female inpatients and outpatients at the Massachusetts Mental Health Center participated in this study. All inpatients were tested within ten days of discharge in order to minimize the psychological effects of acute illness and hospitalization. The patients were referred to the project by their resident physicians, who were asked to select female patients between the ages of eighteen and sixty-five. The patients could be classified by any APA diagnosis, excluding organic brain conditions, but could not be out of contact with reality at the time of testing. They were to be nearly typical of at least one of the three psychoanalytic personality types as described in the preliminary study.

The mean age of the ninety patients studied was thirty-four years (SD of 13). Thirty-six percent (thirty-three) were single, 46% (forty-one) were currently married, 17% (fifteen) were separated or divorced, and 1% (one) was widowed. With regard to religion, 41% (thirty-seven) were Catholic, 33% (thirty) were Protestant, 20% (eighteen) were Jewish, and 6% (five) claimed no religion. At the time of the study 8% (seven) were inpatients, 66% (fifty-nine) were former inpatients, and 27% (twenty-four) were outpatients with no previous psychiatric hospitalization. The most recent admission represented the only psychiatric hospitalization for 37% (thirty-three) of the patients. Thirty-nine percent (thirty-five) had more than one hospitalization and 24% (twenty-two) had never been admitted as a psychiatric inpatient. The

TABLE 11-1

Adjectives Defining Obsessive Personality Traits

Orderliness.—Love of order which develops to pedantry, pleasure in details of work, compulsive listing, pleasure in indexing and cataloguing, thorough, accurate, meticulous, fastidious, perfectionistic, organized, precise, excessive and inappropriate orderliness, punctilious.

Obstinacy.—Obstinacy which may become defiance, stubborn, stands on rights, self-righteous, highly opinionated, one way of doing things.

Parsimony.—Avarice, parsimony which develops to miserliness, thriftiness, frugality, tendency to collect things, fondness for collecting or hoarding, all object relations are like possessions, take pleasure in possessing things nobody else has, impulse to collect and look at possessions.

Rejection of Others.—Convinced they can do everything better than other people, sadistic love for power, oversevere to others, self-centered, scornful of others, grudge in trivial matters, proud of superior intelligence, spiteful, destructively critical.

Emotional Constriction.—Narrow range of affective reactions, warm outgoing contacts difficult, cold, abstract, emotionless, morose expression, lacks charm and grace, interest in fine arts is slight or pretended, keen sense of reality, avowed rationality.

Self-doubt.—Self-doubting, cannot make decisions, in doubt what to do, regrets choice already made, tendency to hairsplitting, indecision, doubt, distrust, overcautious, circumstantial thinking.

Severe Superego.—Severe superego, exaggerated sense of duty, scrupulous, conscientious, oversevere superego, love of discipline, dependable, reliable, punctual, ascetic, overconscientious, compliant and correct behavior, tendency to literal obedience, superego functions are severe, addicted to rules of conduct, over-idealistic, unswerving integrity.

Rigidity.—Rigid, lack of adaptability, not imaginative or creative, conservative, propriety, formal, unable to carry on under pressure, reserved, guarded, inflexible.

Perseverance.—Persistence and endurance, lacks normal capacity for relaxation, great perseverance with tendency to put things off till last minute, nonproductive perseverance, tremendous capacity for work.

TABLE 11-2

Adjectives Defining Hysterical Personality Traits

Egocentricity.—Egocentric, childish egocentricity, self-engrossed, self-absorbed, contempt for others, self-centered, egoism, vanity, craves attention, compulsive need to be loved and admired, self-indulgent.

Exhibitionism.—Stagy dramatic quality, everything valued in superlatives, incapacity to distinguish between genuine and assumed, self-deception, bid for sympathy and attention, great liars to no purpose, histrionic, pseudologic, pathological lying, inclination to make oneself noticeable, exaggerating, dramatization, self-dramatization, theatrical, desire to impress and gain sympathy, play-acting, role does not quite fit, self-display.

Emotionality.—Easy excitability, inconsistency of reactions, unbridled affectivity, labile affectivity, irrational emotional outbreaks, chaotic behavior, intensity of expression of feelings, lack of persistence of emotions, shallowness of feeling, goes through the motions of feeling, emotional incontinence, no depth to emotions, love lacks warmth and tenderness, quick but evanescent enthusiasm, infatuations, extravagance of emotional color, fleeting moods, deficient in emotional control, excessively irritable, lack of emotional inhibition, profusion of affects, volatility and lability of affects, compulsive quality to emotions.

Suggestibility.—Strong suggestibility with strong tendency to disappointments, capacity for autosuggestion.

Dependence.—Dependent, greater than normal need for personal relationships, dependence on the approval of others for self-esteem, excessive demand for security, dependency and immaturity, possessive, another must make every sacrifice, feels neglect keenly.

Fear of Sexuality.—Often frigid or negativistic toward sex but very sensitive psychosexually, sexual striving may be repressed, no increases in sexual experience with increased activity, disgust for sex, sexually immature, sexual relations marred by immaturity.

Sexual Provocativeness.—Obvious sexual behavior, body agility with sexual nuance, coquetry, lasciviousness, pseudohypersexuality, sexualization of all nonsexual relationships, intense erotic interest, hostile seductiveness, may have sexual excess, passionate feelings, and autoeroticism.

resident physician had diagnosed 60% (fifty-four) as having an affective disorder, 26% (twenty-three) as having a personality disorder, and 14% (thirteen) as having a schizophrenic disorder. In summary, the modal patient was a thirty-four-year-old married Roman Catholic woman who had recently been discharged from her second psychiatric hospitalization for the treatment of an affective disorder.

Measurement of Personality Traits. The twenty personality traits were measured by a self-rating form in which the subjects responded "yes" or "no" to items which reflected their behavior. Initially 200 items were used to measure the twenty personality traits. The random arrangement of the items made it difficult for the patient to understand the purpose of the rating form.

The patients were contacted by phone or mail and asked to participate in a research program which would take up to one hour. They were told they were selected randomly from all hospital patients. Although their participation was voluntary, only three patients who were contacted refused to participate. Each patient was given the self-rating form in a private office with the following instructions both read to her by the administrator and printed on the coversheet.

> Please read each of the following statements carefully. If you agree with the statement or if it is generally true for you, write *TRUE* on the line after it. If you do not agree with it or if it is generally not true for you, then write *FALSE* on the line after it. Please make a response for each statement.

The form was completed in thirty to sixty mins. by all but two patients.

Seventy percent of the items were adapted from two sources: Murray (25) and Goldman-Eisler (14). These authors were also measuring personality traits as part of a different experiment. Some of the names of the traits were changed, so that for instance, Murray's "succorance" was changed to "dependence," and "narcism" was changed to "egocentricity." The remaining 30% of the items were original.*

The contribution of each item measuring the trait was calculated by correlations of the item to the total score for the respective trait. For each trait of the original ten items, the seven with the highest correlations were used in the final self-rating form. Three items had higher correlations to trait scores other than the ones they were said to measure. In these instances, the items were used in the measurement of the new trait. Only 20% of the final 140 items had correlations to

---

* The items composing the self-rating form and the statistical material regarding correlations between individual items and traits can be obtained from Gerald L. Klerman, M.D.

their traits of less than 0.50. In these calculations, the trait score included the item with which it was being correlated.

Factor Analysis of Trait Scores. Ninety patients were each scored for twenty traits which were then factor-analyzed using principle axis solution with Varimax Rotation. Although five unrotated factors were extracted, the first three accounted for 90% of the common variance.

RESULTS

Three distinct factors were extracted. In addition, the clustering of traits was such that each factor could easily be compared to one of the personality types.

Table 11–3 compares factor I with the predicted hysterical traits. Of the seven traits which yielded loadings greater than 0.39, five were

TABLE 11-3

Comparison of Traits Derived From
Factor I and Predicted Hysterical Traits

Predicted Traits	Traits Derived From Factor	Factor Loading
	Aggression	0.70
Emotionality	Emotionality	0.64
	Oral Aggression	0.61
Exhibitionism	Exhibitionism	0.59
Egocentricity	Egocentricity	0.58
Sexual provocativeness	Sexual provocativeness	0.57
Dependence	Dependence	0.40
	Obstinacy	0.36
	Rejection of others	0.17
Fear of sexuality	Fear of sexuality	0.10
	Pessimism	0.07
	Passivity	0.08
	Parsimony	0.01
	Perseverance	−0.01
	Rigidity	−0.05
Suggestibility	Suggestibility	−0.08
	Orderliness	−0.17
	Severe superego	−0.23
	Self-doubt	−0.23
	Emotional constriction	−0.61

predicted from the psychoanalytic descriptions of the hysterical personality type. Two predicted hysterical traits ("suggestibility" and "fear of sexuality") had loadings of less than 0.11, while two traits which were not predicted ("aggression" and "oral aggression") did load. Although (negative) "emotional constriction" was not listed as a hysterical character trait, it may be regarded as an equivalent of the hysterical trait "emotionality."

Table 11–4 compares factor II with the predicted oral traits. Of the nine traits with the highest loadings, five ("dependence," "pessimism," "passivity," "rejection of others," and "oral aggression") were predicted from the psychoanalytic descriptions of the oral ungratified personality. Two predicted traits ("aggression" and "parsimony") did not load, while four traits which were not predicted ("self-doubt," "fear of sexuality," "suggestibility," and "egocentricity") did load.

Table 11–5 compares factor III with the predicted obsessive traits. All eight traits that yielded loadings greater than 0.36 were predicted from the psychoanalytic description of the obsessive personality type. One predicted obsessive trait ("self-doubt") had a loading of only 0.12.

TABLE 11-4

Comparison of Traits Derived From
Factor II and Predicted Oral Traits

Predicted Traits	Traits Derived From Factor	Factor Loading
Dependence	Dependence	0.66
Pessimism	Pessimism	0.65
Passivity	Passivity	0.61
	Self-doubt	0.54
	Fear of sexuality	0.53
	Suggestibility	0.53
	Egocentricity	0.39
Rejection of others	Rejection of others	0.32
Oral Aggression	Oral aggression	0.29
	Rigidity	0.26
	Sexual provocativeness	0.06
Parsimony	Parsimony	0.06
	Emotionality	0.03
	Severe superego	0.03
	Exhibitionism	−0.01
	Emotional constriction	−0.04
	Orderliness	−0.11
Aggression	Aggression	−0.19
	Obstinacy	−0.23
	Perseverance	−0.26

TABLE 11-5

Comparison of Traits Derived From
Factor III and Predicted Obsessive Traits

Predicted Traits	Traits Derived From Factor	Factor Loading
Orderliness	Orderliness	0.74
Severe superego	Severe superego	0.62
Perseverance	Perseverance	0.54
Obstinacy	Obstinacy	0.54
Rigidity	Rigidity	0.50
Rejection of others	Rejection of others	0.38
Parsimony	Parsimony	0.37
Emotional constriction	Emotional constriction	0.35
	Egocentricity	0.21
	Fear of sexuality	0.12
Self-doubt	Self-doubt	0.12
	Aggression	0.07
	Emotionality	0.02
	Pessimism	0.00
	Oral aggression	−0.04
	Exhibitionism	−0.05
	Passivity	−0.05
	Sexual provocativeness	−0.07
	Suggestibility	−0.10
	Dependence	−0.12

COMMENT

Methodological Issues. The two major methodological problems in this study are the use of self-rating forms and the use of factor analysis.

Regarding the problem of using the self-rating forms, one might ask whether a patient will honestly and accurately record traits of his personality, some of which might not be favorable. This is a valid consideration. However, in this study, the traits were not measured directly. The patient was not asked if she had a severe superego; instead, the trait of "severe superego" was assessed by a series of questions such as, "I carry a strict conscience with me wherever I go." Furthermore, when she was asked to comment on six other statements of superego function which were scattered throughout the rating form, these statements had high item-to-trait correlations and only rarely correlated better with other traits. Despite this test of internal consistency, it could still be argued that the items do not measure what they are said to measure. If this were true, it would be extremely difficult to explain how the three factors which emerged resemble so closely the personality descriptions made by clinicians over fifty years ago, and how the discrepancies are so compatible with more recent personality theory, as will be described below.

Factor analysis is a recently developed statistical tool, having been employed by psychologists for little more than twenty years. The major factor studies of character have been conducted by psychologists such as Eysenck and Cattell, neither of whom focused on psychoanalytic theory. The criticisms of these and other factor studies are reviewed by Hall and Lindzey (15), who summarize with a quotation from Allport: ". . . that seldom do the factors derived in this way resemble the dispositions and traits identified by clinical methods when the individual is studied intensively." In this paper, the specific *traits selected* were *derived from the intensive clinical study of the individual.* Then, using these building blocks, the traits of psychoanalytic theory, we have asked whether the edifice constructed by the factor analysis resembles the edifice constructed by the mind of the clinician as he observes the patients. In other words, rather than factoring random traits, signs, and symptoms, we factor only those items relevant to the research hypothesis.

The Hysterical Personality and Factor I. The agreement between factor I and the hysterical personality is relatively good. This is consistent with the clarity and agreement in the literature on the description of the hysterical personality.

Most interesting in factor I is the addition of two oral traits ("aggression" and "oral aggression") with the loss of two predicted traits ("suggestibility" and "fear of sexuality") to factor II. This leaves factors I and II with mixtures of oral and hysterical personality traits. At first glance, this does not make sense. Theoretically, the oral personality with its presumed fixation at the earliest stage of development seems far removed from the hysterical personality with its fixation at the Oedipal phase. On the other hand, the close relationship between the oral and the hysterical personality has been noted clinically. Currently there is much rethinking of the classical concepts of libidinal development and fixation. In an important paper, Marmor (20) has attempted to show the theoretical relationships between these two personality types. He concludes that, "Oral fixations are of basic importance in the hysterical personality," and furthermore that, "These oral fixations give the subsequent Oedipus complex of the hysteric a strong pregenital cast." Our findings indirectly support Marmor's observations.

The presence of "aggression" and "oral aggression" in factor I is also consistent with most of the other traits which reflect an active, assertive attitude, rather than a passive, receptive, withdrawing one. This seems to be a basic difference between factors I and II.

The Oral Personality and Factor II. Factor II (oral) had the least correspondence with the predicted traits. This is consistent with the marked variations in the writings about oral personality. Of the three personality types, it has been the most difficult to delimit, the last to be described, and the least written about. The limitations were understood by Abraham (2) and Glover (12), who pointed out that oral eroticism does not need to be sublimated or changed to personality traits to the same extent as anal eroticism does, since oral elements may more easily persist as erotic activities. Furthermore, adult regression, except in the major psychoses, usually comes to a stop at the anal stage, and if it proceeds further, a mixture of oral and anal traits will remain. And finally, oral traits are contradictory and may be subdivided many ways, such as sucking vs. biting, active vs. passive, gratified vs. ungratified, fixation due to shortening vs. fixation due to prolongation of sucking.

The higher loadings of "aggression" and "oral aggression" on another factor confirm the work of Goldman-Eisler (14), who by factor analysis first demonstrated that these two traits separate from the other oral traits. This is also consistent with Abraham's (2) division of the oral stage into the sucking and the biting with fixations at either substage. "Aggression" and "oral aggression" could be viewed as oral biting, while the traits of factor I could be viewed as oral sucking. A review of the traits of factor II, *including those not predicted*, reveals attitudes of pessimism, passive receptiveness, and withdrawal, which are said to belong to ungratified fixations of the oral sucking stage. *Pessimism* is reflected in "pessimism" and "self-doubt;" *passive receptiveness* is reflected in "passivity," "dependence," and "suggestibility;" *withdrawal* is reflected in "rejection of others," "fear of sexuality," and perhaps "egocentricity."

The Obsessive Personality and Factor III. The near identity between the predicted clustering of obsessive traits and the traits of factor III represents strong evidence of the validity of the obsessive personality type; that eight personality traits which are said to occur together do in fact cluster. This agreement between the factor and the type mirrors the consistency of the textbook descriptions of the obsessive personality type. The clarity and clear delineation of this type might well account for its being the first to be described by psychoanalysts (11).

Other Conceptual Issues. The comparison of factor with types raises an important conceptual issue. In this study, a factor refers to a cluster of intercorrelates or covarying traits which are independent of other trait clusters. When patients are given three factor scores, however, the score in one factor in no way predicts the scores in the other two factors. In terms of factors, then, the patient is described by means of a *profile* of three factor scores. At first glance, this would seem to be inconsistent with the concept of the personality type, which, both in its descriptive and dynamic meanings, has often been used to designate one type to the *exclusion* of another. The question is then raised whether a profile concept of the factor can be compared with a "pure" concept of the type. Only a small proportion of persons represent pure type, that is are high on one pattern but low on the others. These persons of course represent ideal teaching cases but poor statistical sampling instances.

Current Status of the Self-Rating Form. This study has demonstrated the use of psychological and mathematical techniques in the testing of a psychoanalytic concept. These tools have been employed in the partial validation of three trait patterns frequently discussed in the psychiatric literature. The self-rating form which emerged from this study has the items separated out according to traits. The applicability of this form is dependent on research now in progress involving cross-validation with consecutive psychiatric hospital admissions and several nonpatient groups.

SUMMARY

The purposes of the current study were: (1) to test whether the traits which are said to define the oral, obsessive, and hysterical personality types do in fact statistically cluster into three distinct and predictable factors; and (2) to construct a self-rating form to measure these three personality types. The three personality types were defined by a total of twenty personality traits which were obtained by a review of the literature. Ninety female patients were measured for the twenty personality traits by means of a self-rating form. The trait scores of the ninety patients were subjected to factor analysis. There were three factors which accounted for 90% of the common variance. Each of the factors resembled one of the personality types. The obsessive personality was nearly identical to its factor while the oral and hysterical personalities corresponded to lesser degrees to their factors. Of interest was the mixture of traits in the oral and hysterical factors so that each had traits of both personality types. This was discussed in terms of recent psychoanalytical theory. The rationale for the use of the self-rating form was discussed.

This study represented a partial validation of the descriptive aspects of the psychoanalytic concepts of personality types and demonstrated the potential utility of psychological and mathematical techniques in the testing of a psychoanalytic concept.

REFERENCES

1. ABRAHAM, K.: "Contributions to the Theory of the Anal Character," in *Selected Papers on Psychoanalysis*, New York: Basic Books, Inc., 1948, pp. 393–406.

2. ABRAHAM, K.: "The Influence of Oral Eroticism on Anal Character Formation," in *Selected Papers on Psychoanalysis*, New York: Basic Books, Inc., 1948, pp. 370–392.

3. ABSE, D. W.: *American Handbook of Psychiatry*, New York: Basic Books, Inc., 1959, vol. 1, pp. 272–292.

4. ALEXANDER, F., and ROSS, M.: *Dynamic Psychiatry*, Chicago: University of Chicago Press, 1952.

5. American Psychiatric Association: *Diagnostic and Statistical Manual—Mental Disorders*, Washington, D.C.: American Psychiatric Association, 1952.

6. BERBLINGER, K. W.: Hysterical Crisis and the Question of the Hysterical Character, *Psychosomatics* 1:270–279, 1960.

7. BLEULER, E.: *Textbook of Psychiatry*, New York: Macmillan Co., 1924.

8. EWALT, J. R., et al.: *Practical Clinical Psychiatry*, New York: McGraw-Hill Book Co., Inc., 1957.

9. FENICHEL, O.: *The Psychoanalytic Theory of Neuroses*, New York: W. W. Norton & Co., Inc., 1945.

10. FITZGERALD, O. W. S.: Love Deprivation and the Hysterical Personality, *J. Ment. Sci.* 94:701–717, 1948.

11. FREUD, S.: *Collected Papers*, London: Hogarth Press, 1950, vol. 2, pp. 45–50.

12. GLOVER, E.: Notes on Character Formation, *Int. J. Psychoanal.* 6:131–154, 1925.

13. GLOVER, E.: *On the Development of Mind*, New York: International University Press, 1956.

14. GOLDMAN-EISLER, F.: *Personality in Nature, Society, and Culture*, New York: Alfred A. Knopf, 1955, pp. 146–184.

15. HALL, C. S., and LINDZEY, G.: *Theories of Personality*, New York: John Wiley & Sons, Inc., 1957.

16. HENDERSON, D. K., and GILLESPIE, R. D.: *A Test Book of Psychiatry for Students and Practitioners*, London: Oxford University Press, 1950.

17. JANET, P.: *The Major Symptoms of Hysteria*, New York: Macmillan Co., 1907, pp. 277–316.

18. JONES, E.: *Papers on Psychoanalysis*, London: Baillière, Tindall & Cox, 1948, pp. 413–437.

19. LAZARE, A., and KLERMAN, G. L.: *Hysteria and Depression*, Harry C. Solomon Award Manuscript, unpublished, Massachusetts Mental Health Center, 1964.

20. MARMOR, J.: Orality in the Hysterical Person, *J. Amer. Psychoanal. Assoc.* 1:656–671, 1953.

21. MASSERMAN, J. H.: *Practice of Dynamic Psychiatry*, Philadelphia: W. B. Saunders Co., 1955.

22. MAYER-GROSS, W., et al.: *Clinical Psychiatry*, Baltimore: Williams & Wilkins Co., 1955.

23. MILLAR, W. M.: Hysteria—A Reevaluation, *J. Ment. Sci.* 104:813–821, 1958.

24. MUNROE, R.: *Schools of Analytic Thought*, New York: Dryden Press, 1955.

25. MURRAY, H. A.: *Exploration in Personality*, London: Oxford University Press, 1938.

26. NOYES, A. P., and KOLB, L. C.: *Modern Clinical Psychiatry*, Philadelphia: W. B. Saunders Co., 1948.

27. RADO, S.: *American Handbook of Psychiatry*, New York: Basic Books, Inc., 1959, vol. 1, pp. 324–344.

28. REICH, W.: *Character-Analysis,* New York: Orgone Institute Press, 1949.

29. SANDLER, J., and HAZARI, A.: The "Obsessional": On the Psychological Classification of Obsessional Character Traits and Symptoms, *Brit. J. Med. Psychol.* 33:113–122, 1960.

30. SIEGMAN, A. J.: Emotionality—A Hysterical Character Defense, *Psychoanal. Quart.* 23:339–354, 1954.

31. STEPHENS, J. H., and KAMP, M.: On Some Aspects of Hysteria: A Clinical Study, *J. Nerv. Ment. Dis.* 134:305–315, 1962.

32. SULLIVAN, H. S.: *Clinical Studies in Psychiatry,* New York: W. W. Norton & Co., Inc., 1956.

33. WECHSLER, I. S.: *A Textbook of Clinical Neurology,* Philadelphia: W. B. Saunders Co., 1947.

34. ZIEGLER, F. J., and PAUL, N.: On the Natural History of Hysteria in Women, *Dis. Nerv. System* 15:301–306, 1954.

35. ZIEGLER, F. J., et al.: Contemporary Conversion Reactions: A Clinical Study, *Amer. J. Psychiat.* 116:901–910, 1960.

This article is a revision of a paper read before the American Psychiatric Association, New York, May 3–7, 1965.

This study was supported in part by grant No. MH-04586 from the US Public Health Service, Bethesda, Md.

Mrs. Louise Lazare, RN, assisted in the construction of the self-rating forms.

12

Paul C. Rosenblatt

A Cross-Cultural Study of Child-Rearing
and Romantic Love

In the classic cross-cultural study of Whiting and Child (3) considerable evidence was presented in support of the Freudian hypothesis of negative fixation: frustration of a need in childhood is correlated with expressions of the need in adult behavior. Evidence for positive fixation, overindulgence in a behavior system producing a surplus of adult concern and interest in the area of behavior, was much weaker. The differential evidence for the two kinds of fixation could be due to differences in opportunities for their development—frustrating environments perhaps being more common and more consistent than indulgent environments —or in opportunities for their prevention through subsequent learning— frustration-based motives being more difficult to unlearn than indulgence-based motives (2). One expectation that can be derived from the differential evidence for positive and negative fixation in the Whiting and Child data is that negative fixation is more likely to occur than positive fixation in cross-cultural comparisons where either could occur.

Perhaps because of their interest in measures that could be used with a variety of behavior systems, Whiting and Child did not test directly one of the most important specific predictions that can be made from Freudian fixation theory. It is a prediction that can be made on the assumption that negative fixation is far more common than positive and one that has important implications for human social behavior: early frustration of oral and dependency needs, needs which are most closely related to affection, is reflected in adult concern for affection. It is the purpose of the present paper to report a cross-cultural test of the hypothesis, using ratings by Whiting and Child of initial satisfaction of oral and dependency needs and subsequent severity of oral and dependence socialization as measures of infancy and childhood experiences. The measure of adult concern for affection used is importance of romantic love as a basis for choice of marital partner. Before the specific methods are reported, a problem of difference between the Whiting and Child data on oral socialization and their data on dependence socialization must be mentioned.

Whereas Whiting and Child's ratings of initial indulgence and later severity of socialization in the area of oral behavior correlate strongly, the two kinds of ratings do not correlate significantly in the area of dependence behavior. They report the former correlation to be $-.60$, which with thirty-seven cases is significantly different from .oo beyond the .oo1 level, and the latter to be $-.18$, which with twenty-seven cases is not significantly different from .oo (3, p. 108). Thus, across cultures, oral socialization from infancy into childhood is rather consistent, while dependence socialization is not. The difference in consistency seems reasonable in that postinfancy dependence-independent socialization has been shown to respond strongly to demands of technology (1), while postinfancy oral socialization appears to be much more free to respond to the same factors as infant socialization. An obvious implication of the difference in developmental consistency between oral socialization and dependence socialization is that if prolonged frustrative experiences are necessary for negative fixation to occur, stronger support for a negative-fixation hypothesis would come from cross-cultural data on oral socialization than from data on dependence socialization.

METHOD

The initial sample consisted of twenty-one societies which had been rated by Whiting and Child on at least one of the four oral or dependence socialization variables, this information being available from the Human Relations Area File microcards at the University of Missouri library. Of these twenty-one societies, two, Malekula and Marquesan, were dropped because the information available on importance of romantic love as a basis for marriage was inadequate. The number of cases involved in each of the correlations performed was reduced further because Whiting and Child were unable to rate confidently each aspect of socialization of interest in the present study for one or more of the nineteen remaining societies in our sample.

For the rating of importance of romantic love as a basis for marriage, extracts were made of ethnographic materials in categories 581 (Basis of Marriage) and 831 (Sexuality) of the Human Relations Area File microcards. Two raters independently rated the extracts on an eleven-point scale, the end points being "zero—active avoidance of marital unions based on romantic love; virtually no unions based on romantic love" and "ten—virtually all unions based on romantic love; romantic love extremely important in the culture." The major criteria for judging the presence of romantic love were ethnographers' specific statements about romantic love, presence of nonarranged marriage or frequent elopement where marriages are traditionally arranged, idealization of those characteristics of members of the opposite sex which are not directly relevant to subsistence activities such as cooking or planting, and belief in predestination for marriage partners.

The ratings of the two judges, which correlated .72 ($p < .001$) for the nineteen societies which could be rated on importance of romantic love, were added together, giving scores on importance of romantic love as a basis for marriage* that could range from zero to twenty.

RESULTS AND DISCUSSION

Importance of romantic love as a basis for marriage was rather strongly related to the two measures of oral frustration. In the case of initial oral indulgence, the rank correlation was −.54, which with eighteen societies is significantly different from .00 beyond the .05 level. In the case of later severity of socialization the rank correlation was .37, which with sixteen societies is different from .00 at the .08 level (one-tailed test), not significant but nearly so. Both of these correlations fit the negative-fixation hypothesis. However, for the two measures of dependence frustration, the correlations with importance of romantic love as a basis for marriage are virtually zero. In the case of initial dependence indulgence, the correlation is .07 ($N = 18$); in the case of later severity of socialization, the correlation is .10 ($N = 16$).

Although the correlations for oral frustration fit the negative-fixation hypothesis, the ones for dependence frustration do not. Since, as was mentioned above, oral socialization practices in infancy and early childhood are consistent, while dependence socialization practices are not, the fact that the correlations with romantic love were strong for oral frustration but not for dependence frustration may be interpreted as reflecting the importance of prolonged frustration in producing negative fixation.

* The combined ratings of importance of romantic love as a basis of marriage were as follows: Abipón, 2; Alorese, 11; Andamanese, 11; Azande, 6; Chagga, 17; Ifugao, 4; Jivaro, 13; Kurtatchi, 2; Lepcha, 4; Manuans, 1; Marshallese, 10; Murngin, 4; Papago, 7; Pukapukans, 15; Rwala, 17; Samoans, 13; Tikopia, 14; Trobrianders, 18; Wogeo, 15.

REFERENCES

1. BARRY, H., III, CHILD, I. L., & BACON, M. K.   Relation of child training to subsistence economy. *American Anthropologist,* 1959, *61,* 51–63.

2. LAWRENCE, D. H., & FESTINGER, L.   *Deterrents and reinforcement.* Stanford: Stanford University Press, 1962.

3. WHITING, J. W. M., & CHILD, I. L.   *Child training and personality.* New Haven: Yale University Press, 1953.

This study was supported by a grant from the Graduate School Research Council of the University of Missouri. Robert E. Cowan and John Stuart Garrity made the extracts and ratings of importance of romantic love.

PART III

ANAL CHARACTER

Freud assigned great importance to anal variables in his developmental explanatory scheme. He hypothesized that what happens to the child during the toilet-training period has a reverberating impact in later years. He called attention to the conflicts that develop between parents and child as the parents impose controls on the anal sphincter. The intensity of these conflicts presumably affects the child's ability to achieve stability and maturity. Freud speculated that anal drives and fantasies play a role in the etiology of homosexuality. He also formulated the notion that intense conflicts about gratifying anal impulses result in the defensive development of a personality type which he designated as the "anal character." He defined the anal character as one who, under the impact of stringent parental demands for anal control, reacts with extreme denial of his or her own anal wishes. This denial takes the form of proving that one has no interest in anything dirty (fecal). Therefore traits are cultivated which demonstrate that one is clean, orderly, and not messy.

Freud stated that the trait of parsimony also typifies the anal character. He accounted for this in terms of an assumed equation between money and feces. Presumably, those who have been anally frustrated are interested in holding onto money (being parsimonious) as a means for maintaining contact with a substance having secret fecal significance.

Freud associated still a third major trait with the anal character, namely, obstinacy. He reasoned that such obstinacy derives from the child's antagonism to the demands of toilet training. The pressure for obedience presumably makes him or her resentful and therefore generally set to be resistive. Anal attitudes were often portrayed as playing a significant role in various forms of psychopathology, for example, obsessive-compulsive symptomatology and paranoid delusions.

Freud's formulations concerning anality were among his most original. If anything, they were even more novel than his theories about genital sexuality. They simultaneously called attention to the erogenous capabilities of the anal zone, the conflicts incited by the toilet-training period, and the importance of attitudes individuals develop toward their body openings. Of course, these theories also provided a framework for understanding the ambivalent attitudes so pervasive in our culture toward that which is dirty or has anal connotations.

The papers presented in this section span a wide gamut. Rosenwald (Selection 13) experimentally tested a number of hypotheses derived from the anal character model. He measured reactions to coping with a fecallike substance, evaluated anxiety about anal themes, and related these measures to such variables as aggression, attitude toward money, persistence, and orderliness. Mixed results emerged, but the major trend was in the direction of supporting Freud's anal concepts.

Timmons and Noblin (Selection 14) employed an ingenious conditioning design to investigate logically derived differences between the oral and anal character orientations. They exposed persons who had been classified as oral or anal, on the basis of their responses to a projective test, to a conditioning procedure whose effectiveness depends on the individual's need to win approval from an authority figure. Since orals are presumed to be dependent and suggestible and anals rather obstinate, it was assumed the former would condition better. The results fitted this expectation.

Noblin et al. (Selection 15) elaborated the design just described by exposing orals and anals in a conditioning paradigm to positive and negative reinforcements. They assumed the positive reinforcement would be more effective with orals and the negative with anals. In general, the findings followed the expected pattern.

Adelson and Redmond (Selection 16) classified persons as anal retentive or anal expulsive on the basis of their responses to a projective test and then evaluated their ability to recall verbal material. They predicted that the anal retentives would, because of their defensive system, which is based on systematization and investment in words, display a superiority to the anal expulsives in recalling verbal material they have been asked to learn. The findings proved to be supportive of the hypothesis.

Centers (Selection 17) explored the question of whether anal traits influence certain social attitudes. The relationship of anality (as measured by a questionnaire) to social attitudes toward teenagers and welfare recipients was appraised. It was anticipated that the underlying hostility linked with the obstinacy of the anal character would find expression in negative, disapproving social opinions. Modest support for the hypothesis was obtained. The generally positive results obtained in the studies just cited fit with the somewhat confirmatory tenor of the total scientific literature dealing with anal character concepts.

13

George C. Rosenwald

Effectiveness of Defenses Against
Anal Impulse Arousal

In an earlier article (12), the concept of defense effectiveness was introduced to account for the complex relationship between psychic conflict and overt anxiety. The theoretical model was first applied to aggression. In a subsequent investigation, findings related to anal impulses were collected (13). It was found that subjects (Ss) with ineffective defenses against anal impulse arousal are more indecisive and have a lower threshold for anally toned associations. Defense effectiveness was assessed alternatively with an anal anxiety questionnaire and with a performance criterion based on the mastery of anal impulse arousal. Although the two assessment measures were significantly correlated with each other, the relationship was not strong, and there is some suggestion that they yielded partially nonoverlapping findings. The experiment reported is an extension of this work, seeking to confirm a broader range of hypotheses drawn from the clinical literature on the anal personality (1, 5, 6, 7, 11, 14).

DEFENSE EFFECTIVENESS: CONCEPTS AND MEASURES

With respect to a given measure of conflict about a drive, for instance, anal impulses, one can set an intensity value such that Ss falling below it are designated as uninvolved in conflict and Ss falling above it are designated as having a conflict. The latter group can be divided into two subgroups: effective defenders, those who are not overtly troubled or constrained by the conflict, and ineffective defenders, those who are afflicted with symptoms, anxiety, or inhibitions.

Reprinted by permission of the publisher and the author from *Journal of Consulting and Clinical Psychology*, 1972, 39, 292–298. Copyright 1972 by the American Psychological Association.

The present study employs two alternative measures to identify ineffective defenders, but makes no attempt to distinguish uninvolved individuals from effective defenders. Findings pertaining to this distinction will be presented on another occasion. One of the two measures is based on an inhibition criterion, the other on an anxiety criterion.

Inhibition Measure

The measure of defense effectiveness based on the inhibition criterion was drawn from the oil test described by Rosenwald et al. (13). In this test, it was S's task to match tactile impressions with a visual standard. Three flat, irregularly shaped pieces of aluminum were placed at the bottom of a pail. At S's eye level hung a display of the pencil outlines of six such aluminum pieces. The pail was filled with water, and S sat with his arm immersed to the elbow, attempting to determine, by feeling only, which outlines on the display matched the pieces in the pail. After two trials in the water medium, he was administered two trials in a viscous, malodorous mixture of crankcase oil and flour. Accuracy and speed of performance were recorded. The oil test was employed to yield an estimate of S's defense effectiveness on the assumption that the oil medium mobilizes anal impulses and that performance inhibition under these conditions indicates ineffective defenses against anal arousal.

Two quantitative expressions were derived from the oil test: (1) oil efficiency, based on a regression model, and (2) oil matchings, based on an after-only model. As for oil efficiency, each S's performance in water was expressed as total time required divided by number of correct aluminum identifications. Using the water–oil regression coefficient, each S's oil score was projected on the basis of his prior water score. The S's who tended to be more efficient in oil than was projected were designated as high oil efficient, whereas Ss falling below their projected oil efficiency score were designated as low oil efficient. As for oil matchings, Ss falling above the median of correct aluminum identifications in oil were designated high oil-matching Ss; those below the median are referred to as low oil-matching Ss.

Anxiety Measure

The measure of defense effectiveness based on the anxiety criterion was drawn from a questionnaire designed for this purpose. This represents a revision of the instrument used by Rosenwald et al., containing 224 true–false items altogether. Of these, 14 refer directly to anal anxiety (e.g., "When I have been in a dirty place, I feel contaminated") and 10 to derived anal anxiety (e.g., "I frequently get upset because my routines are interfered with"). Also included in the questionnaire were the Taylor Manifest Anxiety Scale (15), the Buss-Durkee Aggression Inventory (3), and a number of other items which are not discussed in the present report.

Through an item-selection procedure described by Gulliksen (9), one item was dropped from the *direct* anal anxiety scale, leaving thirteen items, and two from the derived anal anxiety scale, leaving eight items. In testing hypotheses, the extremes of the four distributions were as follows: oil efficiency—fourteen high versus fourteen low Ss; oil matchings—fourteen high versus fourteen low Ss; direct anal anxiety—fourteen high versus fourteen low Ss; derived anal anxiety—fourteen high versus fourteen low Ss.

HYPOTHESES, DEPENDENT VARIABLES, AND MEASURES

To facilitate exposition and reference, the seven hypotheses tested in the study are presented together with the pertinent measures.

Subjects

The Ss were forty male undergraduate students enrolled in the introductory psychology course at the University of Michigan. They served in this experiment as part of a course requirement. The experiment was conducted in single individual sessions lasting about one-and-a-half hours. Twelve tasks were administered, each pertaining to a dependent variable involved in a hypothesis or to the independent variable, defense effectiveness.

Hypothesis 1

Hypothesis 1 postulates that ineffective defenders (in relation to anal conflicts) manifest unbalanced patterns of constructiveness when the task necessitates surrendering products in keeping with an imposed schedule. This prediction drawn from Abraham (1) does not specify the nature of the imbalance. The dilemma of retention versus expulsion of feces, deemed to underlie this trait, causes hypermeticulousness and retentiveness in some instances and careless overproduction in others.

Method

Clay. The S was presented with a cylindrical piece of dark brown modeling clay about six inches long and three-quarters of an inch in diameter and eight balls of clay of comparable mass. The task was introduced as a measure of manual dexterity. He was asked to mold the lumps into sticks resembling the model and to work quickly as well as accurately. After three minutes he was interrupted. The time required for the molding of each clay object was recorded.

Hypothesis 2

Hypothesis 2 postulates that ineffective defenders manifest a retentive attitude toward goods (especially money) which have come into their possession. Clinicians (7) have frequently commented on the hoarding and characteristic stinginess of anal personalities not only with respect to physical goods, but also feelings and ideas.

Method

Betting. At the time when S was given his testing appointment, he was instructed to bring with him $.50. He was given the choice of betting $.10, $.20, or $.30 and was told he would be able to keep whatever he won. He then drew a lot from a jar after being told that he would win by a factor of two if his lot bore an X. All lots were marked, assuring a win. The S was paid and, depending on his first bet, was told he could bet any amount from only his winnings to all he now held. The odds were to be the same. The S's bet was recorded, but he was not permitted to draw again. The data were recorded as the amount bet on the two trials of this task.

Hypothesis 3

Hypothesis 3 postulates that ineffective defenders (1) cultivate fantasies of physical damage, but (2) are inhibited upon instigation to direct physical aggression. Reich (11), in particular, has commented on the anal character's "frozen" sadistic attitudes.

Method

Two tests were used for 1—*story of violence* and *cartoons*—and one for 2—*doll*. The Buss-Durkee Aggression Inventory also bears on the hypothesis.

Story of Violence. The S was asked to write a "descriptive passage of violence such as might be found in a book about adventure, crime, or espionage." He was given the first two sentences of the story and told he would have five minutes to write an ending:

The passage begins: "Finally Ivan Lenkov, the Russian agent, caught up with his victim in a dark alley. He drew a knife from his pocket and planned his attack." Continue from there, and make it as horrible and bloodcurdling as you can.

The obtained stories were rated on three-point scales as to their degree of violence as well as quality of composition.

Cartoons. The experimenter (E) presented S with twenty-four cartoons clipped from various paperback collections and asked him to sort them into three equal piles: liked, indifferent, and disliked. The cartoons had been selected for aggressive and neutral contents in equal numbers and were presented in the same random order to all Ss. The data were expressed as the number of aggressive cartoons placed in each of the three piles.

Doll. The E seated S at a table remote from himself, facing a window, and said:

In this test you will be given a doll and a knife. I want you to imitate a small boy in destructive, temper-tantrum behavior and to demolish the doll. Put yourself in the little boy's place. Demolish the doll completely and let me know when you are through.

A soft plastic doll and paring knife were provided. The E remained out of sight, but timed and observed S's behavior. During the test, E made ratings concerning the amount of S's bodily movement and aggressive vigor and counted the number of destructive methods employed (tearing, stabbing, cutting, wrenching). Further ratings were made after the experimental sessions of the amount of damage inflicted on the doll, which body parts had been attacked, the distribution of cuts on the doll's body, and the number of pieces of debris. Performance was timed.

Hypothesis 4

Hypothesis 4 postulates that in pursuing a course of action, especially one which involves the person's self-esteem or ambition, the ineffective defender exhibits an exaggerated sense of autonomy and persistence. Erikson (4) discussed how the sense of autonomy reaches a critical developmental stage during the modal age of toilet training. Rigid insistence on self-determination as an adult is thought to derive from the refusal to obey others at that critical stage of child development.

Method

Puzzle. Fifteen pieces of an insoluble jigsaw puzzle were placed before S. The E presented the task as a test of motor skill and of insight:

It's quite a difficult test, and we've found that very few people can solve it without help. The way we give the test is to offer you help at various times. You will have five minutes to complete the whole test.

The E offered help at one-minute intervals. Shortly after help had been offered for the fifth time, S was stopped with reassurance. Whenever S accepted help, E juxtaposed two puzzle pieces. The data from this task consisted of the number of hints accepted by S.

Hypothesis 5

This hypothesis postulates that ineffective defenders are exaggeratedly critical. This attitude is probably originally directed by the compulsive character at himself and later spreads to others often under the guise of being helpful to them (1).

Method

Brightness. This task was introduced as follows:

I am going to flash two lights of the same brightness. However, when we ran this study last year we had a lot of trouble getting the lights to *appear* of the same brightness to the subject. People kept thinking one or the other flash was brighter. We have improved the apparatus this year. I want you to look closely and tell me how it looks to you. Please report even small differences in apparent brightness. We are trying to get the lights to look exactly the same. If they don't, please say so. There will be ten pairs of flashes.

By means of an electronic timing device, two flashes of the same brightness and duration were produced with an ordinary lamp. The number of pairs reported as unequal were recorded as a measure of criticalness.

Hypothesis 6

This hypothesis postulates that ineffective defenders proceed from distorted notions regarding orderliness. The self-imposition of, and consequent rebellion against, a principle of order have been frequently attributed to the anal character (e.g., Angyal, 2). This trait is first mentioned by Freud (5) in a discussion of reaction formation against disorderly and destructive impulses associated with anal interests.

Method

Magazines. At the start of the testing session, S was ushered into the experimental room by E, who pretended to be distracted and hurried. The E asked S casually to straighten out a pile of magazines scattered on one table and move them to another. The time for completing this task was measured with a concealed stopwatch.

Hypothesis 7

This hypothesis postulates that ineffective defenders tend to be obstinate. The trait was first noted by Freud in 1908 and described as a "direct continuation" of the anal impulses.

Method

Medical practices. For this task, adapted from a study by McGuire (10), E handed S a sheet with eight opinion statements concerning the usefulness or harmfulness of brushing one's teeth after each meal and undergoing periodic medical examinations. Each statement was followed by a scale broken down into fifteen intervals, ranging from "definitely disagree" to "definitely agree." The items were counterbalanced as to meaning and direction. The E then asked S to mark all the scales in accordance with his opinion on these issues. After a few other tasks were administered, E handed S several pages containing "specialized, scientific information not usually available to the general public." The communications contained bogus messages attributed to fictitious dental or medical authorities. One message detailed the hazards of excessive tooth brushing; the other argued against periodic medical checkups in the absence of specific health problems. The S was then handed the opinion questionnaire containing his previously stated opinions and was asked to fill it in again on the basis of this new information:

We are interested in the formation of beliefs. Beliefs are a combination of attitudes and objective knowledge. We want to see how much this new knowledge you just got will affect your beliefs.

The S's performance was evaluated in terms of attitude change in the direction advocated by the message.

RESULTS

As to the relationship between the S classification based on the anxiety and inhibition criteria, the present findings approximate those reported in the earlier study (13). While oil efficiency did not correlate significantly with direct anal anxiety or derived anal anxiety, the other measure derived from the oil test, oil matchings, was significantly related to both anxiety scales. Low oil-matching Ss obtained significantly higher direct anal anxiety scores than high oil-matching Ss ($F = 4.95$, $df = 1/26$, $p < .05$). That is, Ss who identified the aluminum pieces inaccurately in the oil medium score significantly higher on the anal anxiety scale.

Hypothesis 1 (Constructiveness)

Performance of the clay task was expressed as the ratio of the total time spent by S in processing clay objects to the number of processed objects. Low oil-efficient Ss spent significantly less time per object than high oil-efficient Ss ($t = 2.18$, $p < .05$). In order to determine whether this finding rested primarily on a time or an output factor, since both of these are involved in Hypothesis 1, the two groups were compared with regard to total times spent at the clay task (regardless of productivity) and number of objects processed (regardless of time spent). Both comparisons yielded significant differences: Low oil-efficient Ss processed more clay objects ($t = 2.55$, $p < .02$) and spent less time at the task ($t = 2.95$, $p < .01$) than did high oil-efficient Ss. Since the oil and clay tasks appear superficially similar to each other, both involving contact with a substance reminiscent of feces, it is noteworthy that low oil-efficient Ss, who are defined by their generally slow performance in the oil medium, performed quickly in the processing of brown clay. Since no quality ratings were made of the S's submitted clay objects, it cannot be determined whether the low oil-efficient Ss performed quickly at the expense of accuracy. This finding is discussed further.

Hypothesis 2 (Retentiveness)

Contrasting fourteen high and fourteen low derived anal anxiety Ss, it was found that the former wagered a smaller average amount in the betting task ($t = 2.24$, $p < .05$). Ineffective defenses, as measured by anal anxiety, are associated with a parsimonious attitude in this situation.

Hypothesis 3 (Aggression)

The Ss scoring high on the direct anal anxiety scale disliked aggressive cartoons significantly more than did those Ss scoring low as measured by a Mann-Whitney test ($U = 37.5$, $p < .05$).

Performance on the doll task was correlated with the oil test measures as well as with the questionnaire scales. The fourteen high oil-efficient Ss used a significantly larger number of methods of destruction ($t = 2.37$, $p < .05$). *Physical* rigidity seems also to be associated with ineffective defenses in that the fourteen high derived anal anxiety Ss were rated as showing greater bodily constriction than the low derived anal anxiety Ss ($t = 1.99$, $p < .03$, one-tailed). Furthermore, they required more time to complete the task of destruction ($t = 2.33$, $p < .05$). This finding regarding speed is replicated by comparing the fourteen high Ss with the fourteen low direct anal anxiety Ss ($p < .01$).

Another finding bearing on the aggression hypothesis concerns the association between Ss' self-reported aggressiveness and performance in the oil task. Low oil-matching Ss described themselves as significantly less assaultive than high oil-matching Ss ($t = 2.44$, $p < .026$). Table 13–1 displays the intercorrelations between the two anal anxiety scales and the subscales of the Buss-Durkee Aggression Inventory and the Taylor Manifest Anxiety Scale. There is a significant positive correlation between each of the anal anxiety scales and the Buss-Durkee Resentment and Irritability subscales. In addition, the derived anal anxiety scale is significantly correlated with the Negativism subscale. Interestingly enough, there are no significant correlations between the anal anxiety scales and the two subscales which measure *direct* aggression: assault and verbal aggression. The ratings of the story of violence task yielded no differences between effective and ineffective defenders.

Hypothesis 4 (Autonomy) and 5 (Criticality)

Neither performance in the oil test nor anal anxiety scores on the questionnaire were associated with the number of "hints" accepted in

TABLE 13-1

Correlations of Two Anal Anxiety Scales with Buss-Durkee Inventory
Subscales and the Taylor Manifest Anxiety Scale

Scale	Assault	Verbal	Indirect	Resent-ment	Nega-tivism	Irrita-bility	TMAS
Direct anal anxiety	−.00	−.12	−.01	.30*	.08	.48**	.49**
Derived anal anxiety	−.12	.16	.17	.44**	.33*	.59**	.68**

Note.—TMAS = Taylor Manifest Anxiety Scale.
  *p < .05.
  **p < .01.

the puzzle task or with the number of flashes seen as unequal. There is no positive support for either hypothesis.

Hypothesis 6 (Orderliness)

The fourteen Ss scoring high on the derived anal anxiety scale required more time to straighten the magazines out to their satisfaction than did the fourteen low-scoring Ss ($t = 2.05$, $p < .05$).

Hypothesis 7 (Obstinacy)

A shift in ratings from the first to the second trial of the medical practices task indicates Ss' susceptibility to persuasion as against obstinacy. After establishing that high oil-efficient Ss and low oil-efficient Ss did not differ in their initial opinions regarding the advisability of periodic health exams or of brushing one's teeth frequently, the two groups were compared in regard to opinion *change* as against *persistence* in the original opinion. Low oil-efficient Ss changed an average of 2.3 out of 8 possible opinions, while high oil-efficient Ss changed 3.8. The difference, tested by a Mann-Whitney U test, was significant at the .045 level. Comparing high oil-matching and low oil-matching Ss yielded identical results ($t = 2.07$, $p < .05$). The results appeared equally reliable for the two topics, brushing teeth and medical checkups.

In sum, the inhibition criterion of defense effectiveness produced positive results for Hypotheses 1, 3–2, and 7. The anxiety criterion yielded support for Hypotheses 2, 3–1, 3–2, and 6. Two hypotheses, the ones concerning autonomy and criticality, were not supported.

As a control for generalized anxiety effects, high and low scores on the Taylor Manifest Anxiety Scale were compared with respect to the dependent variables. Only two significant differences were noted, both involving a time variable. High scorers on the Manifest Anxiety Scale required more time to destroy the doll and to straighten out the magazines than low scorers.

DISCUSSION

The correlates of ineffective defense, as defined by the inhibition and anxiety criteria, are (1) a distinctive pattern of productivity (clay), (2) reduced susceptibility to persuasion (medical practices), (3) constricted approach to physical aggression (doll, cartoons), (4) covert hostility (Buss-Durkee), (5) conservative attitude toward money (betting), and (6) accentuation of orderliness (magazines). Together with earlier findings by Rosenwald et al. (13) regarding indecisiveness and a lowered threshold for anality-related ideas, the results conform to the traditional sketch of the anal or compulsive personality.

Freud (8) discussed inhibition as an arrangement whereby the experience of anxiety can be avoided. One might, thus, expect a relationship of mutual exclusion to obtain between the two criteria. Those who successfully avoid encountering drive-relevant situations may not ordinarily become anxious about the drive in question. Those who do become anxious about it have, by definition, failed to avoid the situation in which it is aroused. The Ss who neither avoid the drive stimulus nor are made anxious by it may fall in the class of "uninvolved Ss" described earlier. It may be an artifact of laboratory procedure that individuals who would normally choose to avoid a drive-relevant situation are forced to confront it, at least by degrees. These contingencies suggest a two-fold criterion of classification for the prediction of overall adjustment with respect to drive demands. The best results in predicting daily adjustment would be obtained if *both* anxiety and avoidance potential were taken into account.

In concrete terms, one wonders what psychological processes mediated the low oil-efficient Ss' inefficient response in the oil? Did they feel acutely anxious in the oil medium or did they "freeze" or "block" so as to minimize the sensory encounter with the substance? Since no systematic observations were made of this, a definitive answer is impossible. However, an ad hoc dirt-avoidance scale was drawn from among the questionnaire items (other than the direct anal anxiety and derived anal anxiety scales). Included were seventeen questions which seemed to tap feelings of discomfort in unclean or unhygienic situations. It was found that low oil-efficient Ss scored significantly *lower* on dirt avoidance that did high oil-efficient Ss ($p < .05$). A possible explanation of this finding is that performance decrement in this setting is not brought about by the familiar sequence of defensive breakdown resulting in anxiety, but that a counterphobic attitude is mobilized when avoidance is impossible, and that this interferes with performance through psychomotor rigidity and the like. Another possible explanation is that low oil-efficient Ss subjectively enjoyed the messiness of the oil and paid more attention to this than to the assigned task.

A surprising result was that concerning the low oil-efficient Ss' performance on clay. It might have been expected that they would process fewer objects and do so more slowly, especially since they were, by definition, slowpokes in a fecallike medium. The opposite was the case. Perhaps the task was too obviously childish in comparison with oil; perhaps its fecal implications were sensorily too blatant and caused the low oil-efficient Ss to escape the situation as quickly as possible. A line of research, suggested by this problem, concerns the role of insight in triggering or altering defensive patterns. Action tests are well suited to such investigations since they permit a finer manipulation of stimulus quality than do paper-and-pencil tests. Another explanation of the finding is that the clay test involved an active transformation of the fecallike substance, whereas the latter played the role of an irrelevant (to S) medium in the oil test, the aluminum pieces being of greatest interest.

The distinction between aggressive fantasy and action has not been borne out in the obtained relationships. Ineffective defenders were constricted in dealing with the doll; they also disliked aggressive cartoons. However, they admitted to more indirect aggressiveness in the Buss-Durkee questionnaire than did effective defenders. The implication may be that direct as against indirect aggression is a more fruitful distinction in this context than fantasy as against action. This seems all the more plausible when one considers that putting a cartoon in a pile of liked cartoons may appear to some Ss as an overt commitment.

Although it has been shown above that general anxiety does not account for the reported correlations between anal anxiety and various dependent variables, further observations are needed to determine the contributions of conflict to these same correlations. It is possible to compare three groups with each other: (1) high anxious, (2) low anxious with *high* underlying conflict, and (3) low anxious with *low* underlying conflict. Thus, the dimensions of conflict about anality and of defense effectiveness in relation to such conflict can be distinguished more clearly. Findings will be reported elsewhere which indicate the justification of this distinction. For the time being, it is worthy of consideration that ineffective defenses can be identified, and not only by the well-known index of anxiety.

REFERENCES

1. ABRAHAM, K.   Contributions to the theory of the anal character. In *Selected papers on psychoanalysis*. London: Hogarth, 1949. (Originally published: Berlin: Berlin Psychoanalytical Society, 1921.)

2. ANGYAL, A.   *Neurosis and treatment*. New York: Wiley, 1965.

3. BUSS, A. H.   *The psychology of aggression*. New York: Wiley, 1961.

4. ERIKSON, E. H.   Growth and crises of the "health personality." In M. J. E.

Senn (Ed.), *Symposium on the healthy personality*. New York: Josiah Macy, Jr., Foundation, 1950.

5. FREUD, S.   On transformations of instinct as exemplified in anal erotism. In J. Strachey (Ed.), *Standard edition of the complete psychological works of Sigmund Freud*. Vol. 17. London: Hogarth, 1955. (Originally published: *Internationale Zeitschrift für Psychoanalyse*, 1917, 4, 125–130.)

6. FREUD, S.   The disposition to obsessional neurosis. In J. Strachey (Ed.), *Standard edition of the complete psychological works of Sigmund Freud*. Vol. 12. London: Hogarth, 1958. (Originally published: *Internationale Zeitschrift für Psychoanalyse*, 1913, 1, 525–532.)

7. FREUD, S.   Character and anal erotism. In J. Strachey (Ed.), *Standard edition of the complete psychological works of Sigmund Freud*. Vol. 9. London: Hogarth, 1959. (a) (Originally published: *Psychiatrisch-Neurologische Wochenschrift*, 1908, 9, 465–467.)

8. FREUD, S.   Inhibitions, symptoms and anxiety. In J. Strachey (Ed.), *Standard edition of the complete psychological works of Sigmund Freud*. Vol. 20. London: Hogarth, 1959. (b) (Originally published: Vienna: Internationaler Psychoanalytischer Verlag, 1926.)

9. GULLIKSEN, H.   *Theory of mental tests*. New York: Wiley, 1950.

10. McGUIRE, W. J.   Resistance to persuasion conferred by active and passive prior refutation of the same and alternative counterarguments. *Journal of Abnormal and Social Psychology*. 1961, 63, 326–332.

11. REICH, W.   *Character-analysis*. New York: Noonday Press, 1949. (Originally published: Vienna: Author, 1933.)

12. ROSENWALD, G. C.   The assessment of anxiety in psychological experimentation: A theoretical reformulation and test. *Journal of Abnormal and Social Psychology*, 1961, 62, 666–673.

13. ROSENWALD, G. C., MENDELSOHN, G. A., FONTANA, A., & PORTZ, A. T.   An action test of hypotheses concerning the anal personality. *Journal of Abnormal Psychology*, 1966, 71, 304–309.

14. SHAPIRO, D.   *Neurotic styles*. New York: Basic Books, 1965.

15. TAYLOR, J. A.   A personality scale of manifest anxiety. *Journal of Abnormal and Social Psychology*, 1953, 48, 285–290.

Financial support of this investigation by the Foundations' Fund for Research in Psychiatry is gratefully acknowledged. Diane Rogow, Maris Monitz, and Joel Hencken contributed major efforts to the analysis of the data collected in this investigation.

14

Edwin O. Timmons & Charles D. Noblin

The Differential Performance of Orals and Anals in a Verbal Conditioning Paradigm

Through the years the overwhelming majority of concepts used to explain human behavior and to guide the course of psychotherapy have originated from the writings of Freud. Sears (12), after reviewing the attempts to quantify the tenets and principles of psychoanalytic theory, concluded that experimental psychology had yet to make a major contribution toward stripping away the subjectivism of psychoanalytic concepts. Many consider Sears' judgment too harsh and point to the heuristic value in the experimental analogues of defense mechanisms as evidence (6, 7, 9, 10, etc.). Further, more or less complete systems of personality and psychotherapy have been offered by Shoben (13), Dollard and Miller (3), Mowrer (8), and Pascal (11), in which they substituted learning terms for dynamic terms to offer broader understanding and to suggest research approaches to the psychoanalytic system.

The method of verbal operant conditioning, however, has been largely neglected as a tool for directly studying the theoretical concepts which are basic to much of the applied work being done in clinical settings. Obvious advantages of the operant conditioning approach are its empirical, near atheoretical nature and the marked flexibility it allows the experimenter in choosing both independent and dependent variables.

The present study attempted to utilize operant conditioning techniques to test the predictive efficiency of two of Freud's most venerable personality concepts—the characterological types of *oral* and *anal*. The writings of Freud's followers contain numerous references to the etiology of these character types and to the personality and behaviors expected of them. For instance, Fenichel (4) and others have suggested that oral character types—being dependent—are highly susceptible to

Reprinted by permission of the publisher and the author from *Journal of Consulting Psychology*, 1963, 27, 383–386. Copyright 1963 by the American Psychological Association.

suggestion from authority figures on whose assurance they depend for self-esteem, while anal characters tend to maintain their self-esteem through obstinacy and resistance to authority figures. Consequently, it was hypothesized for this experiment that oral subjects would condition markedly better than anal subjects when mild, affirmatory words from an authority figure were used as reinforcing stimuli. A second hypothesis was that more anals than orals would be able to verbalize the reinforcement contingency due to the obsessive-compulsive or even paranoid method of approaching problems ascribed to anal types by Freudian theory.

METHOD

The Blacky Test was administered to two undergraduate psychology classes ($N = 90$) from which fifteen oral and fifteen anal subjects were selected for a Taffel-type verbal conditioning experiment. All the protocols were administered and scored by E_2; E_1 conducted all the conditioning portion of the experiment. E_1, who was the instructor of both classes, did not know which subjects were orals or anals until after the conditioning data were completely collected. The scoring was done according to the method developed by Blum (1). In assigning subjects to oral or anal experimental groups, it was necessary to ignore indicators of other areas of conflict (e.g., masturbation guilt, sexual identification problems, castration anxiety) which are also afforded by the Blacky Test. Blum's method of scoring entails weighing (1) the subject's spontaneous story, (2) answers on a multiple-choice questionnaire, and (3) cartoon preference. Only indicators of orality and anality from these sources were used as criterion measures for this study.

The experimental procedure was standard and simple. The subjects were seen individually, with orals and anals randomly intermixed. Each subject was seated in a chair with the experimenter behind and slightly to the left to obviate extraneous reinforcing cues by the experimenter. A series of 120 5×7 cards were presented to each subject one at a time. On each at the top were two pronouns—one first (I or we), and the other third person (he, she, they). At the bottom of each card was a sentence fragment which, when preceded by either of the pronouns, made a complete sentence. This deck of cards has been refined, and each type of pronoun is equally represented and randomized as to position within each of the twelve blocks of ten cards.

The first thirty cards were used to establish an operant level for each subject's choosing the selected class of pronoun. (For this experiment, first person pronouns were designated as the "correct" response.) During the next sixty trials mild, affirmatory utterances such as "Um-hmm," "That's fine," "Good," etc., were administered following correct responses

FIGURE 14-1

*Performance Curves in Taffel-type Conditioning Situation for 15 Subjects
Rated as "Anals" and 15 Subjects Rated as "Orals" on Blacky Test
(Data plotted in four blocks of 30 trials each)*

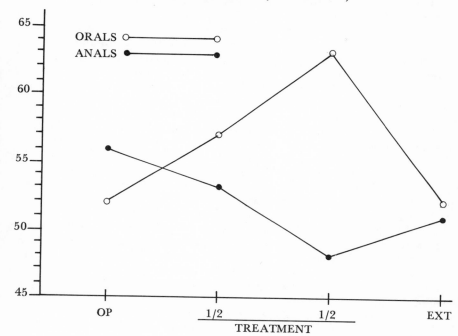

on a 75% variable ratio schedule. The schedule was employed to help minimize the number of subjects who might verbalize the reinforcement contingency. The last thirty cards constituted the extinction phrase in which no reinforcements were given for either choice.

After each subject's responses had been collected and recorded, he was asked the following three questions in an attempt to assess awareness: (1) Now, what do you think this experiment was all about; what was the general idea? (2) Did you notice MY saying or doing anything? (answer) Why was I doing that? (3) Did you notice any change in YOUR responses from the first of the cards to the last? (answer) How did you change? (answer) Why did you change?

Any subject who verbalized the experimental principle was omitted from the analysis of the conditioning data.

RESULTS

Figure 14–1 shows the conditioning data for each experimental group plotted in blocks of thirty trials. The curve generated by the oral subjects shows the typical verbal conditioning curve: a level of response near chance during the operant phase, a continuing increase in the dependent variable throughout the treatment phase, and a drop back to near-operant level during extinction. Friedman's nonparametric analysis of variance for correlated data showed the overall effect of treatment to be significant beyond the .01 level. Wilcoxon's matched-pair T tests applied to the points along the curve reveal that the source of the significance is due to the difference between the operant level and the second half of treatment level ($p < .01$), and to the drop from the second half of treatment to the extinction level ($p < .05$). The other three comparisons failed to reveal significant differences.

A marked contrast is noted when the performance of the anal subjects is plotted. The anal subjects started at a high level (56%) in choosing the personal pronouns during operant, then dropped nearer chance (53%) during the first thirty treatment trials, and then dropped to a below chance frequency (48.6%) during the second thirty treatment trials. When the experimenter discontinued reinforcement during extinction, the frequency of the dependent variable rose to near chance again (51.5%). The curve approached, but did not reach, the accepted significance level.

Direct comparison *between* the two groups at the four points along the curves was afforded by the Mann-Whitney nonparametric T test for independent data. The oral and anal groups' operant levels, the extinction levels, and the first half of treatment for each all failed to yield significance; but the difference between the orals' 63% and the anals' 48% during the second half of the treatment phase was significant beyond the .05 level. All p levels reported are two-tailed.

DISCUSSION

Hypothesis 1 was supported by the data, for two groups of students treated exactly alike and differentiated only by oral and anal scores on the Blacky Test showed strikingly different performance on a standard verbal conditioning problem.

Hypothesis 2 was not supported. It had been predicted that the suspicious, precise approach to problems said to be associated with the anal character would lead to more anals than orals verbalizing the idea of the experiment. Actually, six subjects verbalized the experiment concept—three orals, three anals.

A post hoc reanalysis of the data was made to see how consistently one could have predicted subjects' oral or anal rating on the Blacky Test from the conditioning data alone. Following the method used by Matarazzo et al. (5), each subject was tallied in a 2×2 table as having "gone up" from his mean number of personal pronouns given during operant to his mean number given during the treatment phase, or having "gone down" from operant to treatment phase. Oral and anal subjects were tallied separately. The resulting table showed that of the fifteen oral subjects, twelve showed an increase and three stayed the same; none went down. Of the fifteen anal subjects, four increased from operant to treatment phases and the remaining eleven showed a decrease over the same comparison. A chi-square comparison of these data yielded a p value considerably less than .01, reflecting the consistency of the data.

Since the execution of this experiment, closely related findings have been reported by Cairns and Lewis (2). These investigators used the Edwards Personal Preference Schedule to divide subjects into high and low dependency groups, then placed the entire group in a verbal conditioning situation very similar to ours. The two sets of findings were almost identical, for their low dependency subjects in showing a sharp decrement in emission of the reinforced verbal class; their high dependency subjects showed a conditioning effect, though not as pronounced as our orals. Further, an extension of the oral-anal predictor type experiment has just been completed by one of our students which replicated the findings of both this and the Cairns and Lewis study. It would appear that verbal operant conditioning can be a useful tool in investigating clinical concepts.

REFERENCES

1. BLUM, G. S. *The Blacky pictures: A technique for the exploration of personality dynamics* (manual). New York: The Psychological Corporation, 1950.

2. CAIRNS, R. B., & LEWIS, M.   Dependency and the reinforcement value of a verbal stimulus. *J. consult. Psychol.*, 1962, *26*, 1–7.

3. DOLLARD, J., & MILLER, N. E.   *Personality and psychotherapy.* New York: McGraw-Hill, 1950.

4. FENICHEL, O.   *The psychoanalytic theory of neurosis.* New York: Norton, 1943.

5. MATARAZZO, J. D., SASLOW, G., & PAREIS, E. N.   Verbal conditioning of two response classes: Some methodological consideration. *J. abnorm. soc. Psychol.*, 1960, *61*, 190–206.

6. MILLER, N. E.   Theory and experiment relating psychoanalytic displacement to stimulus-response generalization. *J. abnorm. soc. Psychol.*, 1948, *43*, 155–178.

7. MOWRER, O. H.   An experimental analogue of regression with incidental observations on reaction formation. *J. abnorm. soc. Psychol.*, 1940, *35*, 56–87.

8. MOWRER, O. H.   *Learning theory and personality dynamics*. New York: Ronald Press, 1950.

9. MURRAY, E. J., & BERKUN, W. M. Displacement as a function of conflict. *J. abnorm. soc. Psychol.*, 1955, *51*, 47–56.

10. O'KELLEY, L. I.   An experimental study of regression, I. and II. *J. comp. Psychol.*, 1940, *30*, 41–53 and 55–95.

11. PASCAL, G. R.   *Behavioral change in the clinic—A systematic approach*. New York: Grune & Stratton, 1959.

12. SEARS, R. R.   Experimental analysis of psychoanalytic phenomena. In J. McV. Hunt (Ed.). *Personality and the behavior disorders*. New York: Ronald Press, 1944.

13. SHOBEN, E. J.   Psychotherapy as a problem in learning theory. *Psychol. Bull.*, 1949, *46*, 366–393.

14. ZELLER, A. F.   An experimental analogue of regression. I. Historical summary. *Psychol. Bull.*, 1950, *46*, 39–51.

15

Charles D. Noblin, Edwin O. Timmons, & Howard C. Kael

Differential Effects of Positive and Negative Verbal Reinforcement on Psychoanalytic Character Types

Although psychoanalytic theory has exerted a large influence on contemporary psychology, it is generally agreed among psychologists that the strength of psychoanalytic contributions has been lessened by its subjective methods of investigation. In a recent publication, an eminent psychoanalyst (5) echoed this long-held sentiment when he pointed out that Freudian methods do not lend themselves to objective recording, reproduction, quantification, or control of observations, making it difficult to assess the validity of psychoanalytic theorizing.

The need to define psychoanalytic concepts in more testable form has, through the years, given impetus to various experimental tacks and methods of investigation. In an important early work, Mowrer (8) attempted to operationally define Freud's concept of anxiety as a form of conditioned response. Experimental analogues of defense mechanisms have been suggested by numerous investigators (6, 7, 9, 10, 12).

Skinner (15) suggested that the refinement of operant-conditioning techniques makes it possible to construct interactions between systems of behavior as are seen in Freudian dynamisms. Brady and Lind's (4) operant analysis of hysterical blindness clearly demonstrated that operant techniques and dynamic theory can be utilized together in psychological investigations. The usefulness of operant techniques for studying psychoanalytic concepts is further attested to by investigations of the behavioral effects of psychoanalytic-type interpretations (1, 2, 11).

Timmons and Noblin (17) utilized operant-conditioning techniques to test the predictive efficiency of two Freudian personality concepts—oral and anal character types. They demonstrated that positive verbal reinforcement led to a significant increase in a reinforced-response category for orals, but to a significant decrease in the same reinforced-response category for anals. The rationale for their study was provided

Reprinted by permission of the publisher and the authors from *Journal of Personality and Social Psychology*, 1966, *4*, 224–228. Copyright 1966 by the American Psychological Association.

by the writings of psychoanalysts who stated that oral character types are dependent, compliant, and submissive to suggestions from authority figures, while anal characters are negative, hostile, and resistant to suggestions from authority figures. Consequently, they predicted that oral subjects would condition markedly better than anal subjects when mild affirmatory words from an authority figure were used as reinforcing stimuli.

The present study was designed to test the general hypothesis that oral and anal character types respond differentially to negative as well as positive verbal reinforcement in an operant-conditioning paradigm. It is in part a replication and in part an extension of the work of Timmons and Noblin (17). In view of the psychoanalysts' statements regarding oral and anal characters and the previous research concerning the effect of *positive* verbal reinforcement on these two character types, it seemed reasonable to predict that *negative* verbal reinforcement would lead to an increase in the reinforced response for anal subjects but to a decrease in the reinforced response for orals. Using positive reinforcement, results comparable to those of Timmons and Noblin were expected.

METHOD

The Blacky test was administered to four introductory psychology classes from which twenty-four oral and twenty-four anal subjects were selected for this study. The administration and scoring of the Blacky test followed the method of Blum (3). In assigning subjects to oral and anal experimental groups it was necessary to ignore indicators of other areas of conflict (e.g., masturbation guilt, sexual identification problems, castration anxiety, etc.) which are also afforded by the test. Accordingly, after each test protocol was scored on the spontaneous stories, inquiry, and cartoon preference, only the indicators of orality and anality were used as criterion measures for assigning subjects to treatment groups.

In the experimental procedure the subjects were divided into four groups in such a manner that half the subjects of each character type would receive positive verbal reinforcement and half would receive negative verbal reinforcement. By enlisting the aid of an assistant it was possible to keep the experimenter from knowing which subjects were orals and which were anals until after the conditioning data were completely collected.

A modified Taffell (16) procedure was used in presenting the stimulus materials. These were 120 5×7-inch cards. Two pronouns were printed at the top of each card—one first person (I or we), and one third person (he, she, or they). Below the pronouns a group of words was printed which, when preceded by either pronoun, made a complete sentence. The cards were presented in the same order to all subjects.

Each type of pronoun was equally represented and randomized as to position within each block of ten cards.

The forty-eight subjects were seen individually, and all were given the following instructions:

These cards [experimenter shows subject cards] are all alike in that they have two pronouns at the top followed by a sentence fragment. I want you to choose one of the two pronouns at the top of each card and complete the sentence fragment below, reading aloud, much in this manner [experimenter demonstrates]. Choose either pronoun. If you have any questions please ask them now, because once you begin, I do not want you to ask questions or make comments regarding any of the cards until you have finished. Any questions? OK; let's begin.

The first thirty cards were used to establish an operant level for choosing the selected class of pronouns. The pronoun class to be reinforced was first person (I or we) for half the subjects within each experimental treatment condition, and third person (he, she, or they) for the other half.

The next sixty cards constituted the conditioning or acquisition phase. During this phase, the subject was reinforced on a 75% variable-ratio schedule for making the "correct" response. Such a schedule was employed to help minimize the chances that the subjects would verbalize the contingencies of reinforcement. The type of reinforcement given was appropriate to the experimental treatment condition to which the subject was assigned. Positive reinforcement consisted of mild affirmatory words or phrases as are typically employed in verbal conditioning experiments (such as "um-hm," "That's fine," "OK," "Good," etc.), and negative reinforcement consisted of mildly critical words and phrases (such as, "You can do better," "um—no," "um, not quite," etc.).

The final thirty cards constituted the extinction phase; during this time no verbal reinforcement was given for either response.

Following the experiment, each subject was asked the following questions in an attempt to assess awareness:

(1) "Now, what do you think this experiment was all about?" [If "Don't know":] "Take a guess."

(2) "Did you notice my doing anything in particular?" [If "Yes":] "Why was I doing that?"

(3) "Did you notice any change in what you were saying from the first of the session to the last?" [If "Yes":] "Why did you change?"

As is conventional in verbal conditioning studies, protocols of subjects who could verbalize the contingencies of reinforcement were not included in the formal analysis of the conditioning data.

RESULTS

Figure 15–1 represents the percentage of correct responses during operant, acquisition, and extinction phases for oral subjects reinforced positively and for oral subjects reinforced negatively. The acquisition

FIGURE 15-1

Differential Effects of Positive and Negative
Verbal Reinforcement on Oral Character Types

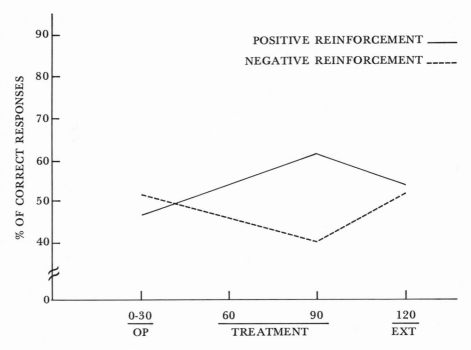

period of sixty trials has been divided into two blocks of thirty trials to better illustrate the effects of the experimental treatments.

The positively reinforced oral group displayed an increase in frequency of the dependent variable with the advent of reinforcement, then a decrease when reinforcement was terminated. A Friedman two-way analysis of variance by ranks (14) showed that the overall effect of treatment was significant beyond the .01 level. In order to analyze the origin of the effect a series of Wilcoxon matched-pairs signed-ranks tests (14) was used. The major source of significance, yielding a probability beyond the .01 level, was between the operant level and the second half of acquisition. Though the typical decline is evident during extinction, it was not found to be significant in this case.

The presentation of negative reinforcement to the oral subjects resulted in a decrease in production of the reinforced response, while discontinuing reinforcement resulted in an increase in correct responses. A significant response decrement was found between the operant period and the second half of the treatment phase. When Wilcoxon matched-

FIGURE 15-2

*Differential Effects of Positive and Negative
Verbal Reinforcement on Anal Character Types*

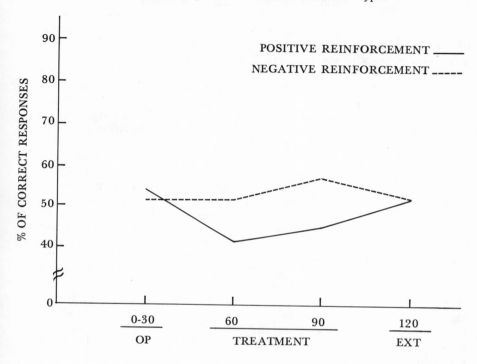

pairs signed-ranks tests were applied, this difference was shown to fall beyond the .05 level. A comparison of the second half of acquisition and extinction yielded a difference beyond the .01 level, reflecting the rise in the dependent variable following cessation of the negative responses by the experimenter.

A comparison between the curves shown in Figure 15–1 indicates that the two classes of reinforcement have differential effects on the verbal behavior of oral character types. Mann-Whitney U tests (14) yielded no significant differences between the groups for operant or for extinction phases; neither was significance generated during the first half of acquisition. However, difference beyond the .02 level was found between the two groups during the second half of acquisition.

Figure 15–2 represents the percentage of correct responses for anal subjects positively reinforced and for anal subjects negatively reinforced. Here again, acquisition trials are presented in two equal blocks.

The positively reinforced anal group was affected by the treatment in a manner converse to that which is typically found in verbal conditioning studies using positive reinforcement. There was a decrease in percentage of correct responses from the operant to the treatment or "acquisition" phase, and an increase during extinction. A Friedman analysis showed that the overall effect of the treatment was significant beyond the .01 level. Wilcoxon analyses indicated that the percentage of correct responses during both phases of acquisition was significantly less than during the operant period, with probabilities beyond .02 and .01, respectively. Operant and extinction levels were not significantly different, nor was a difference found between acquisition and extinction.

The anal group under negative reinforcement presented a response profile typical of that seen in verbal operant-conditioning studies using positive reinforcement. While not significant by Friedman analysis for overall effects, these data did show a significant increase in responding from the operant period to the second half of acquisition ($p < .05$). Extinction responses were less than treatment responses at a probability level beyond .05. Mann-Whitney U tests indicated significant differences between acquisition phases for the two anal treatment groups with a probability beyond .05 for the first phase and beyond .02 for the second phase. These data demonstrate that anal character types respond differentially with respect to positive and negative reinforcement, but not in the direction implied by the nature of the reinforcement.

Further comparisons with regard to the relationship between character types and type of reinforcement were afforded by recombining the four groups on the basis of type of reinforcement received. Statistical analysis indicated that the negatively reinforced anal group and the negatively reinforced oral group did not differ significantly with regard to either operant or extinction phases. A difference was found during the second half of acquisition ($p < .02$) indicating that the negatively reinforced anal group was significantly higher in response frequency when disapproving phases followed the selected-response category. When oral positive and anal positive groups were compared, it was found that they differed with respect to operant level. In order to make the groups comparable, difference scores were computed between the operant level and the first half of acquisition for each group, and these differences were compared utilizing the Mann-Whitney test. It was found that the oral positive group emitted the selected response at a significantly higher rate than the anal positive group during the treatment phase.

These comparisons clearly illustrate that what served as a positively reinforcing agent for one character type served as negative reinforcement for the other. These results were shown consistently for the two classes of reinforcers presented to the two different character types.

A final comparison of the four curves showed that the positively reinforced oral group and the negatively reinforced anal group were not significantly different. Nor were differences found when comparisons were made between the positively reinforced anals and the negatively reinforced orals, indicating that, under the conditions of this study, the effects of positive and negative reinforcement, per se, on verbal behavior do not differ.

Seven subjects, five anal and two oral, verbalized the contingencies of reinforcement and were replaced by standby subjects of the same character type. The data presented are for forty-eight subjects who did not indicate awareness of the experimental principle.

DISCUSSION

Oral subjects demonstrated a marked rise in responding when mildly affirmatory words were used as reinforcers and a marked decrease in responding when mildly critical words were used. Conversely, anal subjects decreased in frequency of responding when reinforced with affirmatory words and increased when reinforced with critical phrases. The verbal behavior of the oral group appeared to be contingent on the approval of the experimenter, while anals demonstrated an apparent resistance to the suggestions of the experimenter.

When the presentation of mild affirmatory words to anal subjects was discontinued, the frequency of previously reinforced responses showed an increase, an effect previously found with the cessation of punishing verbal stimuli (13, 18), while cessation of critical words as reinforcers resulted in a decrease in responding typically found with the cessation of positive reinforcement. It was also shown that the effects of critical words on anals was not significantly different from the effects of affirmatory words on orals. These findings suggest that the reinforcing effects of affirmatory words are not determined by the nature of the stimulus alone, but also depend upon personality variables of the individual subject.

In a recent review of research in the conditioning of verbal behavior (19), the analogy between traditional psychotherapy and the verbal conditioning paradigm is discussed. In studies using verbal operant conditioning to investigate psychotherapy, the therapist is thought of as a source of reinforcement contingent upon classes of patient verbal behavior. The findings of the present study indicate that subject personality variables play a part in verbal conditioning. If the results of verbal conditioning studies of psychotherapy are to be adequately assessed, personality factors must be controlled.

In summary, the results of this study demonstrated the differential effects of positive and negative reinforcement on oral and anal character types. The findings of Timmons and Noblin (17) were confirmed and extended. These results strengthen the psychoanalytic assertions that orals are dependent, compliant, and submissive to suggestions from authority figures, while anals are negative, hostile, and resistant to authority figures.

REFERENCES

1. ADAMS, H. E., BUTLER, J. R., & NOBLIN, C. D.   Effects of psychoanalytically derived interpretations: A verbal conditioning paradigm? *Psychological Reports*, 1962, 7, 691–694.

2. ADAMS, H. E., NOBLIN, C. D., BUTLER, J. R., & TIMMONS, E. O.   The differential effect of psychoanalytically derived interpretations and verbal conditioning in schizophrenics. *Psychological Reports*, 1962, *11*, 195–198.

3. BLUM, G. S.   *The Blacky Pictures: A technique for the exploration of personality dynamics (manual).* New York: Psychological Corporation, 1950.

4. BRADY, J. P., & LIND, D. L. Experimental analysis of hysterical blindness. *Archives of General Psychiatry*, 1961, *4*, 331–339.

5. COLBY, K. M.   *An introduction to psychoanalytic research.* New York: Basic Books, 1960.

6. DOLLARD, J., & MILLER, N. E.   *Personality and psychotherapy.* New York: McGraw-Hill, 1950.

7. MILLER, N. E., & BUGELSKI, R.   Minor studies in aggression: II. The influence of frustrations imposed by the ingroup on attitudes expressed toward outgroups. *Journal of Psychology*, 1948, *25*, 437–442.

8. MOWRER, O. H.   A stimulus-response analysis of anxiety and its role as a reinforcing agent. *Psychological Review*, 1939, *46*, 553–565.

9. MOWRER, O. H.   An experimental analogue of regression with incidental observations on reaction formation. *Journal of Abnormal and Social Psychology*, 1940, *35*, 56–87.

10. MURRAY, E. J., & BERKRUN, H. M.   Displacement as a function of conflict. *Journal of Abnormal and Social Psychology*, 1955, *51*, 47–56.

11. NOBLIN, C. D., TIMMONS, E. O., & REYNARD, M. C.   Psychoanalytic interpretations as verbal reinforcers: Importance of interpretation content. *Journal of Clinical Psychology*, 1963, *19*, 479–481.

12. O'KELLY, L. I.   An experimental study of regression: I. Behavioral characteristics of the regressive response. *Journal of Comparative Psychology*, 1940, *30*, 55–95.

13. SANDLER, J.   *The effect of negative verbal cues upon verbal behavior.* Unpublished doctoral dissertation, Florida State University, 1959.

14. SIEGEL, S.   *Nonparametric statistics for the behavioral sciences.* New York: McGraw-Hill, 1956.

15. SKINNER, B. F.   *Cumulative record.* New York: Appleton-Century-Crofts, 1959.

16. TAFFELL, C.   Anxiety and the conditioning of verbal behavior. *Journal of Abnormal and Social Psychology*, 1955, *51*, 496–501.

17. TIMMONS, E. O., & NOBLIN, C. D.   The differential performance of orals and anals in a verbal conditioning paradigm. *Journal of Counseling Psychology*, 1963, *27*, 383–386.

18. WALDER, L.   *The effect of three postacquisition procedures on a verbal avoidance response.* Unpublished doctoral dissertation, Columbia University, 1959.

19. WILLIAMS, J.   Conditioning of verbalization: A review. *Psychological Bulletin*, 1964, *62*, 383–393.

16

Joseph Adelson & Joan Redmond

Personality Differences in the
Capacity for Verbal Recall

When we think of the topic "psychoanalysis and memory" we are likely to bring to mind Freud's theory of repression; and we are also apt to think of that curious scatter of experiments—some of them knowing and clever, some of them innocent of understanding—which have striven to confirm or confute Freud's observations. Many of these studies concentrate on the stimulus: they ask whether a certain type of stimulus —"disturbing," "unpleasant"—can, by evoking anxiety, bring into play the ego's defenses so as to inhibit or distort recall. Other studies center on the experimental subject: by inducing a momentary state of distress, they seek to bring about some disturbance in recall.

Our research approaches psychoanalysis and memory from a somewhat different perspective. It focuses on the problem of individual differences in the *capacity* for recall. The topic is much neglected in an otherwise extensive tradition of research; there have been few studies of differences in recall capacity; and there appear to have been none that look to personality as a source of such differences. At a first glance, psychoanalytic theory seems to offer no explicit statement on the problem, but a closer examination yields this hypothesis: individuals fixated at the late anal phase (the so-called anal retentives) have a greater ability to recall verbal material than those fixated at the early anal phase (anal expulsives).

Surely a farfetched idea; but it may gain plausibility if we take the retentive-expulsive dimension to specify, not psychosexual fixation points per se, but differing forms of ego organization.* To begin with the anal retentive: (1) He has developed fairly stable techniques for coping with aggressive impulses. The dominant defenses are reaction-formation, undoing, and the various forms of isolation (including intellectualization).

Reprinted by permission of the publisher and the authors from *Journal of Abnormal and Social Psychology*, 1958, 57, 244–248. Copyright 1958 by the American Psychological Association.

* The discussion will follow a line of approach suggested by Fenichel (1, pp. 295–300) and Rapaport (3, pp. 622–625).

The isolation defenses are especially relevant here: their use gives a systematic and orderly cast to the thought process; verbal stimuli can be effectively organized and codified; when countercathexes are directed against affects, ideation proper remains undisturbed. (2) His defensive style is characterized by a peculiar absorption in words and concepts. As Fenichel puts it: "He flees from the macrocosm of things to the microcosm of words" (1, p. 295). Cathexes are directed toward language, ideas, the thinking process itself.

These processes occur among (indeed, partly define) the obsessional neuroses. In the severely obsessional personality, however, we generally find that cognitive functioning is seriously burdened by the strenuous demands of defense; among "normal" retentives, cognitive style is in the obsessional direction—systematic and orderly—yet is spared the brittleness and rigidity, the vulnerability to breakthrough that we see among the clinically obsessional.

Far less is known about "anal expulsive" normals, and so we must offer here a more hesitant formulation. We take it that in this group, too, character structure has developed out of the struggle between parent and child on the issue of aggression. The anal retentive tames his hostile drives by turning against them, or by isolation; the expulsive person shows a less thorough, less efficient regulation of these impulses. Aggression continues to be discharged, but in a muted, modified way, the dominant defenses being aim-inhibition and displacement. The original aims—aggression and disorder—are, so to speak, blunted, and find a modulated continuation in messiness, rebelliousness, impulsiveness.

The intrapsychic system, then, shows a *relative* failure to neutralize aggressive drives or to bind them adequately through countercathexes. A persistent imbalance between impulses and defense produces sporadic inefficiencies in certain types of cognitive performances. Leakages of aggression elicit anxiety and so bring about momentary disruptions of attention and concentration.

We are now in a position to turn to the problem of recall. Among retentives, the use of isolation permits a heightening of attention to external stimuli; unwelcome impulses and affects, which would disturb attention, are warded off. Equally important, we find a tendency to hypercathect words, an increased alertness to them. In concert, these processes produce a peculiar efficiency in the apprehension of verbal stimuli. Expulsives, on the other hand, are characterized by defensive processes that lead to a decreased capacity for verbal recall; the manner of handling impulses and affects brings about momentary disturbances of attention and concentration.

METHOD

Subjects. The sample consisted of sixty-one college women, all of them first-year students at Bennington College.

The Criterion for Anality. The Blacky Test was used to determine the type of anal fixation. Several weeks prior to the experiment itself, the test had been administered on a group basis to all entering students at the college. A subject (S) was designated "Expulsive" if she received a score of $++$ (very strong) or $+$ (fairly strong) on Anal Expulsion, and a score of zero on Anal Retention; the reverse was true for the scoring of retentiveness. Ss receiving scores on both dimensions were not included. An S was rated "Neutral" if she received zero scores on both dimensions. The experimental group was composed of thirty-two expulsives, eighteen retentives, and eleven neutrals.

The Stimuli. Two prose passages were used, one with innocuous, the other with disturbing content. We wanted to determine whether the hypothesized differences in recall would be present only when the material was of a nature to evoke defenses, or whether they would also be found with relatively neutral material.

(1) "Disturbing" passage. Here we wanted a passage which would be threatening enough to elicit defenses, yet sufficiently decorous to permit its presentation to young ladies in a classroom setting. So we devised a passage which stated, rather crudely, Freud's theory of psychosexuality. It follows:

Psychoanalysis is the creation of Sigmund Freud, who was born in 1856 and died in 1939. Beginning with the attempt to cure neurotic patients, Freud developed one of the most significant systems for understanding human behavior. His psychology has had widespread influence to the extent that it has completely revised the previous understanding of human nature. At the center of his system is the idea that early childhood experiences influence later personality. This is called the Theory of Psychosexual Development, the major features of which follow:

During the first oral stage, the child receives intense pleasure sucking the mother's breast. There is a desire to eat everything and resistance to being deprived of this pleasure when weaned.

During the second oral stage, intense pleasure is received through using the teeth to bite and devour, desiring to chew and gnaw at the mother, with fear of punishment in return.

During the anal stage, pleasure is obtained through retaining bowel movements and through eliminating them. The child resists being trained to be neat and clean, and would rather smear his feces.

During the Oedipal stage, the female child feels sexually attracted to her father, is jealous of her mother for possessing him, and wishes for the death or disappearance of her mother.

Between the third and fifth year, children experience intense pleasure through masturbation, by playing with their sexual organs. Along with this there is a strong fear of being caught and punished.

During this same period, female children become aware that they lack a penis. They feel inferior, believing that its absence is a punishment, and are jealous of the male's sexual organ.

Children sometimes feel intense hostility and jealousy toward a sibling. They feel that they are being neglected in favor of the other child, and wish for the sibling's death or disappearance.

(2) *"Innocuous" passage.* Here we wanted didactic, colorless prose, and so chose the following passage:

> Undoubtedly the most famous brick house in seventeenth century New England was that built for Peter Sergeant in Boston. Sergeant, who had come to Boston in 1667, became a wealthy merchant and later served as a judge and a member of the Governors Council. The land he bought on October 21, 1676, a large tract extending halfway from Washington to Tremont Street, included a fine garden and orchard, stable, and coach house. The big house which he built with brick walls about two-feet thick, was completed by 1697. The Sergeant House was early accustomed to society. Governor and Lady Bellomont visited it for several months in 1697, and Sergeant's third wife, whom he married in 1707, was Lady Phips, widow of the former Governor Sir William Phips. After Sergeant's death in 1714 the mansion was purchased by the province (in 1716) to serve as a residence for the royal governors. It was thenceforth known as the Province House.

(3) *Scoring.* Because of differences in the sentence structures of the two passages, we used a separate scoring system for each. The "disturbing" passage had been written so as to permit its being scored by phrases, or thought units; S was given one point for each phrase precisely or substantially correct. In the scoring of the "innocuous" passage, one point was given for each word (except for conjunctions and prepositions) correctly reproduced; dates and numbers accurately recalled were given two points. Since the scoring of the "innocuous" passage was more or less mechanical, requiring only the counting of words, no study of interjudge agreement seemed necessary. For the scoring of the "disturbing" passage, scoring criteria were first established for each phrase; then a sample of the protocols was scored separately by two judges. Agreement between them was nearly complete and formal testing of interjudge agreement was therefore omitted.

Administration. The recall tasks were administered to five classes in freshman literature which met at the same hour. The experimenter introduced the task in these words: "Read these papers carefully twice. You will be asked questions on them later." Ss were then given the passages to read. The passages were printed on separate sheets of paper. The classes were allowed about ten minutes to read the material. The passages were then collected, writing paper distributed, and Ss told: "Now write down all you can remember about what you have just read." This was a test of immediate recall. We were also interested in learning what differences, if any, would be present in delayed recall. One week later, the experimenters therefore returned to the classes and asked the Ss to reproduce all they could now remember about the passages.

There were seventy-eight Ss in the five classes; all are included in the analysis, except those with Blacky scores on both anality dimensions, and those who were absent from either or both of the class meetings when the recall testings were done.

RESULTS AND DISCUSSION

Anal Retention vs. Expulsion and Recall

In Table 16–1, we find the results for both passages and for immediate and delayed recall. Retentives show a significant superiority in reproduction of both types of material; their advantage persists over time.

We may gain a more graphic impression of the differences if we look at the data from the point of view of quartile extremes. For example, when we consider the distribution of scores for "disturbing passage—immediate recall," we find that retentives, who make up 36% of the total sample, contribute 69% of the scores in the top quartile and only 9% in the bottom quartile. Roughly equivalent distributions are found for the other passage and other testings.

We made no specific hypothesis about the eleven neutral Ss; however, we wanted to determine the recall performance of this group. If we take these Ss to represent average functioning in recall, we would have some basis for judging whether the expulsive-retentive differences are due to the superior recall capacity of retentives, the inferior capacity of expulsives, or both. We found that for all four comparisons the neutral group is located midway between the other two. This finding suggests that both the retentive and expulsive Ss occupy extreme positions in recall performance.

Other Possible Sources of the Differences

(1) Other psychosexual dimensions. We next considered whether differences in recall are associated exclusively with anality; could it

TABLE 16-1

Differences Between Expulsives and Retentives in Verbal Recall
(Expulsives N = 32; Retentives N = 18)

Tests	Group	M	SD	t	P
Innocuous passage— Immediate recall	Expulsive Retentive	19.9 28.3	12.84 12.08	2.25	.05
Innocuous passage— Delayed recall	Expulsive Retentive	9.9 15.1	6.00 8.66	2.60	.02
Disturbing passage— Immediate recall[a]	Expulsive Retentive	21.6 28.7	9.59 12.29	2.68	.02
Disturbing passage— Delayed recall[a]	Expulsive Retentive	11.1 19.3	5.92 8.94	3.66	.001

[a]The mean scores for the disturbing passages refer to thought units.

be that anality is one of several psychosexual dimensions where we would find similar differences? To test this possibility, we looked for recall differences (both passages, both testings) on all of the other Blacky dimensions; that is, we compared the recall scores of high and low groups on Oral Sadism, Oral Eroticism, Oedipal Intensity, and so on; we also compared high and low groups on Total Pregenitality. Of forty differences tested, only two were significant at the .05 level: the high group on Oedipal Intensity has better recall scores for the "innocuous passage—delayed recall"; the low group on Ego-Ideal has higher recall scores on "disturbing passage—immediate recall." These results (two of forty at the .05 level) are what we would expect by chance alone.*

It is interesting to note that no Blacky group receives recall scores (on each of the four passage-testing comparisons) as high as those received by the retentives; and only one Blacky group has a mean recall score as low as those received by the expulsives.

(2) *Intellectual capacity.* Another possible explanation of the results is that expulsives and retentives are intellectually unequal, and that the differences in recall performance are due to intellectual differences associated with the type of anal fixation. To check this, we compared the SAT scores (V and M) of both groups; these were available for most of our Ss. For both V and M there are no significant differences between the groups; indeed, their means are almost identical.

A Partial Replication

An unpublished study by Nahin (2) supports some of these findings. Nahin's research was on a somewhat different topic, but a portion of her study duplicates some elements of the present one. The criterion for anality was the Blacky Test; Ss were Bennington College freshmen. However, she used only a "disturbing" prose passage (basically equivalent to the one reported here) and tested only for immediate recall. She found significant differences between expulsive and retentive Ss.

Nonverbal Recall

What about the recall of nonverbal stimuli? Should we expect to find expulsive-retentive differences here as well? The question is relevant to some parts of the theory underlying this research. The retentive S is presumed to be sensitive to words, at least in some respects: he tends to reduce the anxiety inherent in "things" by capturing them verbally, by transposing them into the safer, more tractable realm of language: taming by naming, let us say. There develops, then, a peculiar efficiency in certain (though surely not all) verbal performances, as this study has suggested. Now one might wonder whether this capacity is operative

---

* The tables which report these and other results described here may be found in Redmond (4).

only when the stimuli are verbal (or can be made so by being "named" or "labelled"), or whether we are dealing with a more general disposition.

We cannot, unfortunately, provide a satisfactory answer to the question. Although we carried out a study of the recall of nonverbal stimuli, circumstances did not allow a precise enough duplication of the conditions of the verbal recall research. It is reported here briefly.*

A set of twenty abstract line drawings were developed. The pictures were simple enough in design to permit ready reproduction by the experimental Ss, and were so drawn that they did not resemble common forms or objects; consequently, they could not be "labelled." In the experiment, the drawings were projected on a screen, one at a time, for fifteen seconds. Ss were students in a large lecture class at the University of Michigan, all of whom had earlier been tested for expulsion-retention. Except for slight and necessary changes in wording, the instructions were the same as in the verbal recall study. After the drawings had been exposed, the group was asked to reproduce them. The reproductions were scored by a six-category scheme (e.g., perfect reproduction, one slight error, etc.). Male and female Ss were treated separately, since they distribute differently on expulsion-retention; there were thirty-three female retentives and twenty-two expulsives, twenty-one male expulsives and ten retentives. Expulsion-retention differences, within sex, were tested for each of the six scoring categories and for various combinations of categories. No significant differences were found; in fact, recall scores throughout are highly similar.

But the variations in experimental procedure are too marked to allow us to treat the two recall studies as comparable. In all likelihood, recall performance can be significantly influenced by differences in motivational conditions, experimental set, testing atmosphere, and so on. It seems the most judicious course to take the findings on nonverbal recall as, at best, suggestive.

Discussion

The study has demonstrated that under certain conditions we can obtain personality differences in verbal recall. Yet all of our experience in the area of personality and cognition warns us to caution in generalizing the findings. The results may very well be tied to a particular set of experimental conditions: change the stimuli, in length or content; change the experimental instructions; change the method of testing recall, from reproduction to recognition, as an example; use a different sampling of Ss; make any of these changes and, for all we know, the differences may fail to appear. Our understanding of the expulsion-retention variable and of the influence of personality on recall is still too uncertain to allow us to extrapolate the findings with any sense of confidence.

* The authors are grateful to John Hirtzel for carrying out the analysis of the data.

There are, then, a great many occasions for speculation offered by the research. The stimuli, the details of administration, the experimental atmosphere (especially the role of anxiety in producing the results) — each of these gives us an opportunity to reconsider the meaning of the experiment. But perhaps the most critical question to be raised concerns the expulsion-retention variable itself.

In formulating the central hypothesis of the research, we took the position that recall differences are based on capacity differences; equivalent motivation was assumed for both groups of Ss. The assumption, however, is open to challenge: can we explain the findings equally well as arising from motivational differences between expulsives and retentives?

A considerable body of unpublished data makes this a highly credible alternative. Anal retentives, it appears, show a marked disposition toward compliance and conformity, especially so in the presence of authority; anal expulsives are distinguished by an edgy, often sullen independence. Thus we can well imagine the retentives, solemn, *bürgerlich*, eager to do well, bending to the experimental task with dedication and gravity; and it is quite as easy to see the expulsives, skeptical or diffident or rebellious, giving the task only cursory attention.

There is, at this moment, no way of choosing between the motivational and cognitive interpretations of the findings; they are equally plausible. If the nonverbal recall experiment had been comparable to the earlier study, then we would have some reason for believing that motivational differences are not the source of the recall differences. (Even so, it could be argued that nonverbal stimuli do not engage motivation or interest to the same degree that words do.) As it is, the question must remain open, awaiting further research.

The position we take on this issue—motivation vs. capacity—will determine whether we view the recall differences as a function of differences in acquisition, or retention, or performance. If a motivational factor is involved we can regard it as influential at any or all points between stimulus presentation and reproduction. The contrast between eager and indifferent attitudes toward the task might operate in the amount of attention given the stimuli, or in the intention to retain what was learned, or in the degree of interest in reproducing the stimuli.

Our own approach is derived from the cognitive concepts of psychoanalytic theory, and so we interpret the findings as an outcome of variations in cognitive style. From this viewpoint, one is led to stress differences in the capacity for attention and concentration, which would operate with particular force during the process of acquisition. We would then see the experiment as a study of incidental learning, rather than retention or performance.

SUMMARY

It was hypothesized that "anal retentive" individuals have a greater ability to recall verbal material than "anal expulsive" subjects. The hypothesis was derived from an analysis of differences in ego organization between the two groups.

The subjects were sixty-one first-year college women. The criterion of anality" was the Blacky Test; there were thirty-two expulsives, eighteen retentives, and eleven neutrals. Subjects were asked to read two prose passages, each of several hundred words. One passage discussed sexual and aggressive themes and was considered "disturbing" in content; the other was an "innocuous" description of colonial architecture. Subjects were asked to reproduce the passages immediately after presentation and again one week later.

Retentives showed a significant superiority over expulsives in the reproduction of both passages, immediately and one week later. Neutrals scored midway between the two extreme groups on all four testings. There were no differences in intellectual capacity between retentives and expulsives, as measured by the SAT, V, and M. None of the other Blacky dimensions is associated with recall differences. The findings have been partially corroborated in another study. A study of the recall of nonverbal stimuli showed no differences between expulsives and retentives; since the research methods of this study differed in some possibly critical respects from the investigation of verbal recall, the findings are offered as suggestive rather than definitive.

REFERENCES

1. FENICHEL, O. *The psychoanalytic theory of neurosis.* New York: Norton, 1945.

2. NAHIN, BARBARA. *Psychosexuality and memory.* Unpublished thesis, Bennington College, 1953.

3. RAPAPORT, D. *Organization and pathology of thought.* New York: Columbia Univer. Press, 1951.

4. REDMOND, JOAN. *Anality and memory.* Unpublished thesis, Bennington College, 1954.

17

Richard Centers

The Anal Character and Social

Severity in Attitudes

It is surprising, in view of renewed interest in the relationship between personality and politics as exemplified in two recent issues of *The Journal of Social Issues* (5, 4) that a significant lead contributed to this area by Farber (1) over a decade ago is apparently completely overlooked. This is especially puzzling in view of the fact that Farber's work demonstrated a substantial correlation between anal character traits and what he terms political aggression, the latter being defined by him as "the tendency to advocate violent solutions to political problems, to think in terms of the use of power rather than law or compromise" [p. 487].

Freud (3), in describing what has since come to be called the anal character type, pointed out that "such personalities are remarkable for a regular combination of the three following peculiarities: they are exceptionally *orderly*, *parsimonious*, and *obstinate*. Each of these words really covers a small group or series of traits which are related to one another. 'Orderly' comprises both bodily cleanliness and reliability and conscientiousness in the performance of petty duties; the opposite of it would be 'untidy' and 'negligent.' 'Parsimony' may be exaggerated to the point of avarice; and obstinacy may amount to defiance, with which irascibility and vindictiveness may easily be associated. The two latter qualities—parsimony and obstinacy—hang together more closely than the third, orderliness; they are, too, the more constant element in the whole complex. It seems to me, however, incontestable that all three in some way belong together" [pp. 27–28].

Such a character structure Freud found to be marked by early difficulties in toilet training; persons possessing it being prone to refuse to empty the bowel when placed on the chamber, because they derived an incidental pleasure from the act of defecation. Such early anal eroticism was, Freud noted, absent in the adult marked by this trait triad, and the

Reprinted by permission of the publisher and the author from *Journal of Projective Techniques and Personality Assessment*, 1969, 33, 501–506.

traits themselves were seen as developments associated via sublimation and reaction formation with the disappearance of anal eroticism. Farber (1) drawing on both Freud and Fenichel (2) indicates that orderliness develops from the acceptance of the parental attempts to regulate bowel evacuation; parsimony (or frugality) from the continuance of the early tendency toward retention of feces due to erogenous pleasure and fear of losing, and obstinacy from resistance to the parental demands.

PROBLEM

The study to be reported, like Farber's, which it partially replicates, deals not with the origin of these so-called anal traits themselves, but rather with attempting to determine whether or not the possession of certain social attitudes and beliefs implied by the anal character structure may be predicted from a measure of the traits embodied in it.

Farber was able to demonstrate a positive and substantial relationship between anality and antipathy toward communism, which he considers an aspect of "political aggressiveness." The aggressiveness which he postulated apparently is deduced as an elaboration and extension of the irascibility, defiance, and vindictiveness associated with obstinacy. He hypothesized, further, that "aggressive conventionality" (or being reactionary) would be found to be the dominant political characteristic of the anal personality type.

The hypothesized rigid conventionality and reactionariness seem psychologically plausible; yet one can hardly consider them to have been adequately demonstrated through a found antipathy to communism, for the latter trait is quite compatible with even ultraliberalism in attitude. Certainly the hypothesis would be greatly strengthened if it could be shown to have some confirmation under a wider set of conditions than that within which previously tested.

Another context in which the anal's rigid conventionality, conformity to tradition and reactionariness might be expected to express itself is in attitudes toward contemporary problems involving teenagers, delinquency, and social welfare dependency. More specifically, from his ungiving, order-loving and vindictive nature, the anal character, it was hypothesized, would take a "hard line" rather than a permissive and lenient position, and manifest what for want of a better term will be called *social severity of attitude*.

METHOD

Another limitation of the Farber study which the present one sought to overcome was in the nature of his sample, composed as it was of 130 college students. His data were collected by means of anonymous questionnaires given in classrooms. The present study was designed for data collection from a cross-sectional sample of nonstudent adults in person-to-person interviews. There were a total of 562 interviews conducted in 1968 by a corps of interviewers trained by the writer and using a standard interview schedule prepared for the purpose.

Although it was desired to use the same scale as developed by Farber to measure anality, for it had the several advantages of brevity, good internal consistency, and face validity, two of the five items were unsuitable for use with nonstudent subjects and hence required either modification or replacement. The items, presented in their order of appearance in the interview schedule follow: (The symbols OB, OR, and P are intended to indicate which of the three traits, obstinacy, orderliness, or parsimony the item is supposed to embody.)

(1) In general I like to spend my money very carefully, P, OR.

(2) I get irritated by people who can't seem to make up their minds or come to definite conclusions about things, OR.

(3) It bothers me a great deal when I lose or break something of mine, P, OR.

(4) I usually feel annoyed when things around me are not neat and orderly, OR.

(5) I pride myself on always trying to be on time, OR.

(6) I like to take very good care of things that belong to me, OR, P.

(7) Generally, I like to give relatively few gifts, P.

(8) Once I have made up my mind on something I almost never change it, OB.

Items 4 and 8 are essentially duplicates of Farber's items. Item 2 substitutes *people* for *professors*. Items 1 and 7 represent a division of a single item in the original wherein spending and giving are lumped together. Items 3, 5, and 6 are new. In Table 17–1 are shown the intercorrelations of the several statements. The correlations are not high, but all are positive, with few exceptions statistically significant (.01 level), and suggestive that Freud was correct in his observation that the traits of obstinacy, orderliness, and parsimony "belong together."

The following items were those employed as the measure of severity in attitude:

(1) Do you think teenagers today are less well behaved, about the same, or better behaved than in the past?

(2) In general, do you think the morality of teenagers is higher or lower than in the past?

(3) Some people say that if our courts weren't so lenient we would

TABLE 17-1

Intercorrelations* of Items on Anality Scale

Item No.**	1	2	3	4	5	6	7	8
1								
2	.04							
3	.11	.17						
4	.22	.11	.24					
5	.26	.10	.04	.18				
6	.28	.08	.11	.34	.18			
7	.17	.08	.09	.05	.08	.05		
8	.12	.18	.11	.16	.13	.14	.13	

*Correlations larger than .08 are significant at the .05 level.
Those of .11 and above are significant at the .01 level or higher.
**Item numbers correspond to the order of listing in the text.

have less juvenile delinquency. Do you agree or disagree with this view?

(4) Some people say many of our problems with teenage youth are due to the fact that parents have spoiled them by being too easy and permissive. Do you agree or disagree with that?

(5) How do you feel about teenage boys and youths wearing beards? Does this please or annoy you?

(6) What about teenage boys and youths wearing long hair? Do you feel pleased or annoyed at this?

(7) In general do you approve or disapprove of the way Reagan is handling his job as Governor?

(8) Do you agree or disagree that nowadays people expect the government to do too much for them?

(9) Do you think anyone who really wants to work can find a job these days?

(10) With which of these two points of view do you tend to agree more?

(a) Most people on welfare relief are truly victims of circumstances and can't be blamed for their condition.

(b) Most people on welfare relief are really just too lazy and irresponsible to take care of themselves even though they really could do so if they were willing to make the effort.

The intercorrelations of these items are presented in Table 17–2. They are all positive, and all but five of the forty-five correlations are significant (most of them at better than the .01 confidence level). Actually there were fifteen items which were originally on an intuitive basis expected to belong together, but five were eliminated because on analysis they were found to have either negligible or negative correlations with the retained ones. These items all related to the respondent's opinions about the honesty and integrity of government officials, and while

TABLE 17-2

Intercorrelations* of Items on Social Severity Scale

Item No.**	1	2	3	4	5	6	7	8	9	10
1										
2	.26									
3	.22	.36								
4	.16	.12	.23							
5	.27	.13	.20	.18						
6	.18	.16	.24	.21	.63					
7	.05	.11	.13	.16	.16	.10				
8	.06	.05	.19	.22	.16	.18	.22			
9	.07	.01	.09	.13	.12	.14	.15	.14		
10	.11	.09	.15	.14	.18	.16	.22	.16	.27	

*Correlations larger than .08 are significant at the .05 level or higher. Those of .11 and above are significant at the .01 level or higher.
**Item numbers correspond to the order of listing in the text.

positively correlated with each other, had virtually no commonality with the ten items in the above severity list.

The interviewer also obtained information from each respondent with regard to age, birth order, and education.

RESULTS AND DISCUSSION

In Figure 17–1 is presented in graphic form the relationship obtaining between anality scores and scores on the social severity scale. The generally positive progression in the relationship is quite clear. The graph, however, perhaps overstates the case because of the plotting of average scores on social severity for each level of anality. Since both sets of scores, anality and severity, were approximately normally distributed in the sample, a product-moment coefficient of correlation was also computed. The resulting .30, while not quite so impressive, does indicate at least modest support for the hypothesized relationship. With an N of 562 this correlation figure is significant at the .001 confidence level. It is evident from these data, too, that anality in the general adult population manifests less linkage or determinance in relation to social severity than in the case of Farber's college students with regard to anticommunism, where the correlation was .37. Social severity, of course, is a quite different variable from anticommunism in respect to the objects of reference involved, namely behavior of adolescents and welfare recipients. Also, as indicated from their correlations with the other items in the scale, the items constituting it elicit a greater variation in responses than that activated by Farber's items, which were focused so highly on communism as the attitude object.

Actually, the discrepancy in findings is not nearly so large when only the responses of the subsample of college educated people in the present sample are compared with Farber's. There were eighty-eight respondents in the present total sample who had at least some college education and were under thirty years of age. For this subsample the correlation of anality scores and social severity scores was .33.

As mentioned earlier, information from respondents was obtained which permitted them to be classified according to age, sex, order of birth, and education. Groupings of subjects in terms of these "background" variables were systematically examined to ascertain whether or not any of them differed significantly on the anality variable. The results of a one-way analysis of variance revealed that there were no significant differences between sexes, nor among age, educational or birth order groupings. Differences among the various categories mentioned above were always quite small as well, hence lead to confidence that none of

FIGURE 17-1

Mean Scores on Social Severity at Various Levels of Anality

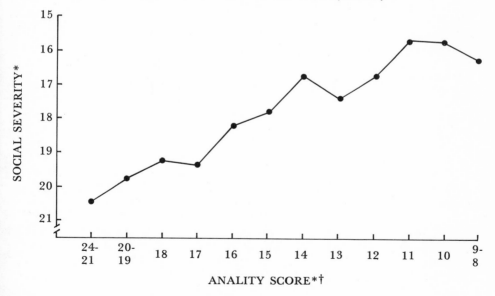

*High scores represent a low degree of the trait.
†Scores represented by fewer than 10 respondents were cumulated until at least that number was obtained.

them taken singly could have played any large role in the relation of anality to the social severity variable.

It must be acknowledged of course, that correlations of the modest magnitudes revealed here between anal character traits and social severity of attitudes, even if plausibly inferred to have causal signifi- cance, account for but a small portion of the variance in social severity. This is quite typical of psychological relationships. It would be naive to expect that one could, by measuring any given trait of personality, pre- dict response to any social object with great precision except where the target area was highly identified with the trait itself. Social severity cer- tainly does not have this character.

Social severity of attitude toward teenagers and welfare recipients might be viewed also as quite a different sort of response from anti- communism or political aggression, and, as was pointed out above, the object clearly is. Yet, at a deeper level, what is involved in both anti- communism and social severity is being tough, taking a hard line, an attitude of stubborn resistance, toward people whose policies or behavior threaten to disturb the established order and traditional ways.

The present results measurably extend the significance of Farber's findings with regard to anal traits and political and social attitudes, but of course leave many other aspects of the total relationship of anal traits and social behavior to be explored. It is hoped that others will be as intrigued by the possibilities as the writer. One of the reasons that anality is such an interesting variable, incidentally, is that it is highly visible, even without psychometric techniques. Even scant acquaintance and observation often are enough to reveal the orderliness of a person, his stubbornness, his frugality. To the extent that such traits are prominent, moreover, many of such a person's everyday behaviors and expressions of opinion become highly predictable.

REFERENCES

1. FARBER, M. L.   The anal character and political aggression. *Journal of Ab- normal and Social Psychology*, 1955, *51*, 486–489.

2. FENICHEL, O.   *The psychoanalytic theory of neurosis*. New York: Norton, 1945.

3. FREUD, S.   Character and anal eroticism (1908). In Rieff, A. (Ed.). *Character and culture*. New York: Collier Books, 1963.

4. GREENSTEIN, F. I. (Ed.) Personality and politics: Theoretical and methodo- logical issues. *The Journal of Social Issues*, 1968, *24* (Whole No. 3).

5. SAMPSON, E. E. (Ed.) Stirrings out of apathy: Student activism and the decade of protest. *The Journal of Social Issues*, 1967, *24* (Whole No. 3).

PART IV

THE OEDIPAL THEORIES

A key aspect in Freud's account of how the personality structure evolves is anchored in the Oedipal concept. He theorized that during a period embracing the third through fifth years of life the child becomes confronted with an acute dilemma growing out of attraction to the parent of the opposite sex and antagonism toward the parent of the same sex, who is perceived as a competitor. He specified that the child wants to take the opposite-sex parent as a sex object and sees the same-sex parent as standing in his way. This is the Oedipal confrontation. Freud indicated further that the child gradually finds that such a situation creates untenable conditions and tensions. In the case of the male child he postulated that his antagonistic stance vis-a-vis his father leads to the fantasy that his father will retaliate by castrating him. This castration anxiety, said Freud, becomes a prime motivating agent which leads the male child to give up his sexual intent toward his mother and to identify with his father. He decides to become like his father rather than fighting him. At this point when he identifies with his father he also presumably takes over (introjects) his father's superego values. The resolution of the Oedipal conflict involves, for the boy, retreating from his mother and adopting the orientation of his father. Eventually he finds another woman to replace his mother as a love object.

Freud's account of the girl's Oedipal problems and her mode of resolving them is less clear than his formulation of the boy's. In fact, he not only considered that the girl's Oedipal confrontation is less definite and intense than the boy's, but also that she resolves it less conclusively. He hypothesized that she originally turns away from her mother and takes her father as a love object out of disappointment with her mother, whom she blames when she discovers she lacks a penis. She is said to develop fantasies that a sexual union with her father will result in conceiving a child who can provide compensation for her lost penis. But she finds her antagonistic relationship with her mother increasingly uncomfortable because she fears a total loss of her mother's love and support. So she presumably retreats from her intense involvement with her father and eventually accepts another male as a substitute. There are various ambiguities in this account that cannot be discussed here, but they do render empirical testing of the Oedipal concepts, as they apply to the female, difficult.

Freud portrayed the resolution of Oedipal conflicts as one of the most arduous of developmental tasks. He assumed that few emerged from the Oedipal period without psychological scars, and he focused on persistent Oedipal conflicts as being central to many forms of psychopathology that appear in the adult. He particularly called attention to Oedipal conflicts as interfering with heterosexual relationships and sexual functioning. The so-called Oedipal theory is actually a congeries of theories. Freud's account of what happens during the Oedipal phase touches on a number of major areas. It includes a string of hypotheses diversely dealing with the problems of intimacy and conflict in the family, how sex role identification evolves, the sources of conscience or superego, and the transition to mature sexuality. The studies presented for consideration in this section reflect this diversity.

The paper by Ammons and Ammons (Selection 18) examined the parental preferences of Oedipal-age children. Preferences were determined both by doll-play techniques, supposedly tapping an unconscious level, and by means of direct questioning. No consistent trends were found that would indicate that the child felt relatively more positive toward the opposite-sex than toward the same-sex parent. This was considered to contradict Freud's Oedipal theory.

Leichty (Selection 19) tested several hypotheses concerned with the basic proposition that a boy whose father is absent during the Oedipal phase will have unusual difficulty in resolving his Oedipal conflicts. A projective test was used to compare a group of males whose fathers had been absent with a control group whose fathers had not been absent. Disturbance about Oedipal themes was found, as predicted, to be greater in the father-absent group.

Mussen and Distler (Selection 20) interviewed mothers to investigate the child-rearing antecedents of masculine identification and conscience in kindergarten boys. Degree of masculine identification was measured by means of a semiprojective test. The more masculine boys were found to have had a warm, rather nurturant relationship with their fathers. This pattern does not fit Freud's concept that male identification is basically energized by a threatening stance on the father's part.

Sarnoff and Corwin (Selection 21) cleverly validated Freud's theory that sexual stimuli have the power to incite castration anxiety in males. They were able to show that exposure to erotic pictures significantly increases fear of death, which is depicted as an indirect index of castration anxiety.

Levin (Selection 22) studied the amount of castration anxiety in women invested in masculine roles as compared to those who are more conventionally feminine. A quantitative scoring system based on Rorschach inkblot responses demonstrated, as predicted, the presence of relatively greater castration concern in the masculine-oriented sample.

Cameron (Selection 23) obtained preferences for male versus female symbols from large numbers of children of both sexes over a wide range. He concluded that the preference patterns conformed surprisingly well to theoretical expectations derived from Freud's Oedipal scheme.

These papers provide only brief glimpses of the multiple approaches that have been taken to checking Oedipal propositions. The literature is replete with pertinent objective studies concerned with the determinants of identification, superego formation, response to sexual stimuli and symbols, cross-cultural correlates of specific parent-child interaction patterns, and so forth.

18

R. B. Ammons & H. S. Ammons

Parent Preferences in Young Children's Doll-Play Interviews

Whether or not there is a universal factor of sexual attachment of a child to the cross-sex parent has been the basis for much speculation and often emotional debate among people interested in the study of human behavior. Although a considerable amount of evidence on this point has been gathered and many of the studies have shown provocative trends, conclusive results are nowhere to be found.

Present Information on Parent Preferences. Opinion as to the origin of parent preference has ranged from the inherited pattern inherent in Freud's concept of the "Oedipus complex" to Watson's purely learning theory based on chance factors in the environment. Freud (6, 7, 8) constructs parts of his personality theory on the supposed fact of the sexualizing of the Oedipus complex where "the small son develops a tenderness for the mother, the small daughter loves the father." Beliefs similar to those of Freud have been held by such writers as White (26), Moll (15), Homburger (10), and Seligman (23).

Adler (1) disagrees with the concept of the Oedipus feeling as an inherited trait in all children. He believes that where it is shown to exist it has come about solely through the experiences of the child. Putting this point of view in a different way, Mursell (16) believes that both boys and girls prefer the mother because she is a "complex of food signs."

A more extreme environmental point of view is stated by Katz and Katz (12) and Watson (25). Katz and Katz believe that the child's preferences depend on his experiences, often shifting from one to the other parent. Watson points to learning as the only factor which will cause the child to love anyone.

Very few studies giving systematic observational evidence on the incidence and nature of parent preferences have been reported. Hamilton (9) asked 100 men and 100 women about their childhood relationships with their parents. He reported the results shown in Table 18–1.

Reprinted by permission of the publisher and the authors from *Journal of Abnormal and Social Psychology*, 1949, *44*, 490–505. Copyright 1949 by the American Psychological Association.

TABLE 18-1

Men	Women	
19	28	fonder of father
39	19	fonder of mother
52	52	always on friendly terms with father
54	28	always on friendly terms with mother
33	29	irritability toward father
32	44	irritability toward mother
36	36	never irritable toward father
39	14	never irritable toward mother

These data show a certain degree of cross-sex parental preference.

Newell (17), in a questionnaire study of family attitudes of juvenile delinquents, found that 80% of the boys preferred their mothers and that 10% preferred their fathers. Of the girls, 53% preferred the father and 33% preferred the mother. In a similar study, Yarnelle (27) analyzed the records of forty problem children between the ages of eight and ten and also found that the boys generally preferred their mothers. Only when the mother definitely rejected them was their preference less marked. The girls, on the other hand, preferred the parent who overprotected them and who dominated in the family. In attacking the same kind of problem, Busemann (3) obtained compositions from children between ten and eighteen years of age on the subject, "an episode in which I was punished; another in which I was praised by my parents." Boys mentioned father as punisher in 52% of the compositions, mother in 33%. In only 27% of the girls' stories the father punishes them, the mother in 55%.

A more direct approach to the problem was made by Simpson (24). Besides asking direct questions, e.g., "Whom do you like best at home?", responses to a set of nine pictures, two stories, and reports of the child's dreams were used. It was found that children have very definite preferences for one parent or the other. Children as a group preferred the mother (127—father; 327—mother; 46—no preference). This tendency was more marked on the part of the boys than on the part of the girls: more boys than girls preferred the mother; more girls than boys preferred the father. By ten years, both sexes showed an overwhelming mother preference. In the possibly more "projective" preference scores, the boys showed the same preferences as they did in answer to direct questions. However, the girls showed a much more pronounced mother preference by this method than in answer to direct questions. Throughout the entire study the boys were much more stable in their preferences than were the girls. On the basis of reasons given by children for their preferences Simpson concluded that they like: (1) the parent best who best caters to their material wants; after that, the parent (2) who is nice to them, (3) plays with them, (4) spanks them least, and (5) whom they are taught to like best. These results seem to justify the conclusion that at least on the "conscious" level parent preferences are fairly closely related to the child's experiences.

Doll-play Approaches to the Study of Personality Structure. Although projective techniques have been used extensively for some time in the study of personality, only recently have adequate methods for studying younger children been developed. These methods depend upon the observation and analysis of behavior during play, particularly doll play.

The potentialities of the doll-play situation are indicated by the work of Sargent (22), Levy (13), and Despert (5). In studying the spontaneous doll play of a normal nine-year-old boy in a natural setting Sargent observed that the child appeared to be projecting his personal problems. Levy, after intensive work using the play technique to study hostility patterns in sibling rivalry experiments, concluded that

the feelings of children can be revealed through activity in play situations, so organized as to satisfy the requirement of experimental procedure and yet sufficiently flexible to allow abundant variety of behavior.

Despert reported that children dramatized their home life in factual and fantasied situations and that the associated emotional expressions were not always the same as those observed in their overt social behavior.

Doll play often brings out feelings on the part of the child which are not available from case histories, parents' reports, or even from the child's own responses to questions about them. Conn (4) explains how the child reveals himself:

It is not the child himself, but the doll, who is afraid of the dark. It is not he who is jealous or hates, but the doll character. . . . He can describe the emotions and imaginations that may explain the doll's behavior and consequently his own.

In this connection, Jeffre's results (11) demonstrate empirically that the child's doll-play dramatizations tend to reflect actual parent-child relationships, and in a much less inhibited way than the child himself responds in a comparable non-doll-play situation.

In the doll-play situation the doll child was often aggressive, at times to the extent of spanking the mother doll or cooking her on the stove.

Studies reported by Sears' students (2, 11, 18, 19, 20, 21, 28) have dealt mainly with problems of methodology in an attempt to discover the important variables in doll-play experimentation. Well-organized observational and analytic procedures have led in their studies to high observer agreements. Certain of their general findings have potential importance for any further work with doll play. Bach (2) found that "normal" children produced intensively aggressive fantasies during doll play. Pintler, Phillips, and Sears (20), in studying sex differences in the doll play of preschool children, found that

girls had reliably greater amounts of stereotyped thematic play than boys. Boys significantly exceeded girls in amount of nonhuman thematic play, number of theme changes, and amount of nontangential aggression. No reliable sex differences were found in amount of exploratory and organizational activity, self-thematic play, non-stereotyped thematic play, tangential play behavior, or tangential aggression.

They interpret the data in terms of "a sex-typing process dependent on social learning during early childhood."

Doll play can thus be considered as a reliable avenue to the understanding of children's underlying and often repressed motivations and feelings.

PROBLEM

This study attempts to determine the relationships between parent preferences indicated by preschool-age children and the following variables: (1) degree to which the child is aware of being asked for "his own" preference, (2) age, (3) sex, (4) situation with respect to which a preference is to be expressed, and (5) related home experiences.

OBSERVATIONAL DESIGN

Subjects. Fifty-eight children attending four public day care centers and a kindergarten were used as subjects. This includes all children in these groups meeting the following criteria:

1. Between the ages of 3–0 and 6–0.
2. Living with both natural parents. If S (subject) was adopted or if the parents were separated for any reason, S was eliminated.
3. At least third-generation "Americans." Homogeneity of cultural background was also obtained by eliminating all Negro and Spanish-American children.

Ten children were eliminated for various reasons: three with whom rapport could not be maintained because of a generalized fear of new situations, two because even with considerable encouragement and assurance they did not seem to understand what was expected of them, and five because they were not available for the second session within the maximum time limit of fourteen days after the first session.

The final group of forty-eight Ss (subjects) consisted of six sub-groups of eight children each arranged as shown in Table 18–2.

A tabulation of fathers' occupations showed that approximately one-third were from the professional group, one-third were engaged in sales or clerical work, and one-third could be considered to be skilled workmen. It can be seen that the group is urban, of above average socio-economic status, and excludes farmers and unskilled workmen. On the

TABLE 18-2

Composition of Subgroups

Subgroup	Number	Sex	Average Age (Years)
3B	8	Boys	3.3
3G	8	Girls	3.7
4B	8	Boys	4.5
4G	8	Girls	4.6
5B	8	Boys	5.5
5G	8	Girls	5.4

other hand, a rather wide range of occupational levels is included, and all occupational groups are quite evenly represented in the three age groups.

The day care center children were available from approximately 8 AM to 5 PM, while those in the kindergarten attended only in the afternoon. The amount of time the children spent with each parent was found to be approximately the same when parents were subsequently questioned.

All of the children were familiar with E (experimenter), who spent some time in each group becoming acquainted with them, learning their names, and establishing suitable rapport. All of the Ss were naive to this form of doll play.

Procedure. Two distinct methods were used in attempting to discover the children's preferences for either parent. The first consisted of direct questioning in a free-play situation, and the other was the projective method of having the child give the preferences of the child doll (with whom he had presumably identified) in a doll-play situation. In this manner an attempt was made to discover relatively "conscious" and "unconscious" preferences.

In the free-play situation S was approached by E while he or she was playing alone, and was asked several questions, including "Whom do you like best at home?" If S named someone other than one of the parents, the question was repeated, "Whom do you like best, Mother or Father?"* With the younger children it was necessary to use a slightly different form of the question. E asked S if he lived with his mother and daddy at home and then asked, "Which one do you like best?" If he answered that he liked both, the question was repeated, "Which one do you like *best*?" ("Best" used rather than "better," for the sake of emphasis.)

Each S participated in two doll-play interview sessions. For the first,

* The form of this question was taken directly from Simpson (24), who found that with older children (CA's 5 to 9) it called forth very definite statements of preferences.

S was approached at a time when he was not too preoccupied with or involved in some activity and it was felt he would welcome a change. He was asked if he would like to see "some things I brought over for boys and girls to play with." Most of the Ss were eager to leave with E; those who showed any reluctance were told, "Well, some other time you can come. I'll see if . . . . wants to go now." E then picked someone who, it was felt, would be happy to go.

On the way to the observation room (a distance of a short block in one center and in the other locations the distance of a large play room) E talked with S, attempting to gain his confidence and to appear in the role of a sympathetic, noncensoring individual. As often as possible hostile and aggressive feelings were recognized and accepted in an attempt to make S feel free to bring out as much suppressed feeling as he desired without fear of punishment.

When S and E entered the doll-play room, S was presented with furniture arranged in a model house, and three dolls. He was told, "Here is a little boy just about as old as you are and here are his daddy and mommy. Which one does the little boy like best?" After S answered, E said, "Now let's see what they do." E then had the child doll go through actions following in general the daily routine of S: he got up, went to the toilet, dressed, was punished by and reconciled with each parent, ate his breakfast, helped in the home, played, went walking and riding, bought a present, was read to by both parents, had a bath and went to bed and to sleep. Aside from the standard situations, the mother and father were not mentioned, nor was there any E action involving them. No mention was made by E of the relationship between the parents. During the dramatization the following questions were asked if they seemed to fit into the action and not interfere with the child's on-going play:

(1) *Toilet:* "Which one does the little boy want to take him to the toilet?"
(2) *Dressing:* "Which one does the little boy want to help him get dressed?"
(3) *Punishment:* "The mommy spanks the little boy. Which one does he like best now?"
(4) *Reconciliation:* "Now the mommy is through spanking the little boy. The little boy feels all right now. Which one does he like best now?"
(5) *Eating 1:* "Which one would he like to fix his breakfast?"
(6) *Eating 2:* "Which one does the little boy want to sit next to at the table?"
(7) *Helping:* "The mommy is washing the dishes and the daddy is fixing the stove. Which one does the little boy want to help?"
(8) *Play:* "Which one does the little boy want to play with?"
(9) *Punishment* (father): (same as for mother)
(10) *Reconciliation* (father): (same as for mother)
(11) *Walking:* "Now they're all going for a walk. Whose hand does the little boy want to hold?"
(12) *Riding:* "When they go riding on the streetcar, which one does the little boy want to sit next to?"
(13) *Present:* "The little boy has enough money to buy one present. Which one does he buy it for?"
(14) *Story* (mother): "The mommy reads a story to the little boy. Which one does he like best now?"
(15) *Story* (father): (same as for mother)

(16) *Bath:* "Which one does he want to give him a bath?"
(17) *To bed:* "Now the little boy is going to bed. Which one does he want to put him to bed?"
(18) *Sleeping:* "If the little boy could sleep in the big bed over here, which one would he like to get in bed with and sleep with?"

In the case of girls, the word "girl" was substituted for "boy." Care was taken to see that in these situations the mother and father were rewarding or punishing an equal number of times. Care was also taken to see that each situation was separate to avoid any carryover from the preceding situation. A reconciliation situation was brought in in an attempt to neutralize the feeling of the "little boy," so that the punishment situation would not carry over into the next situation; i.e., the child might want to hold his mother's hand because his daddy had just spanked him—making the father suffer twice for the same punishment.

After all the situations had been given in as natural a manner as possible S was allowed to play freely with the dolls for a maximum of ten mins., E saying, "You may play with them any way you like. You may let the little boy do anything he wants to." S was allowed to terminate the session at any time. During this period and also during the dramatization any spontaneous positive or negative doll action toward either parent was recorded. Due to the small number of these responses, these data are not included in this paper. At the end of the free play, S was again asked, "Which one does the little boy like best?" After S answered, E said, "Would the little boy like to marry his . . . .?" (naming the last preference given.) As a check on whatever answer was given S was then asked if the boy would like to marry the other parent.*

The second doll-interview session was in all practical respects the same as the first, coming 6 to 14 days later, with a total group mean of 8.1 days. It was felt that this repetition would provide a check on the reliability of Ss' responses over a period of time. Also, since it had previously been found that aggressive responses increase from first to second sessions (28), it was hoped that S might reveal more of his "true" feelings in the second session.

Each of the sessions lasted about twenty mins. The same Es (the authors) conducted all the sessions, testing equal numbers of boys and girls at each age level.

Since it was hoped to check the relationship between the child's preferences as expressed in the doll-play interviews and his home experiences, pertinent information was collected from the parents by the experimenters (fourteen children) and by head teachers (thirty-four children). Parents were asked which more frequently carried out the following twelve activities with the child: taking to toilet (Q_1), dressing

---

* The responses to the marriage questions are not included in the "preference score" but are treated separately, because they are "leading" questions of a highly structured nature. In addition to the 18 standard items, general preferences were asked for at the beginning and end of each session, making a total of 20 scorable items in the doll interview.

(Q2), cooking for (Q5), sitting next to at table during eating (Q6), having child help with household task (Q7), playing with (Q8), holding hand while taking a walk with (Q11), sitting next to on a streetcar (Q12), child buying present for parent (Q13), giving bath (Q16), putting to bed (Q17), sleeping with (Q18). Numbers following items refer to questions used in the doll-play interview with respect to which information was collected from parents. Thus Q1 in each case dealt with which parent was associated with going to the toilet. In the doll play, the child was asked his preference; in the subsequent questioning, the parents indicated which parent most often actually took the child to the toilet.

It was hoped that this method would allow the measurement of the child's parent preferences by a projective technique, and the comparison of those preferences with the child's actual experiences.

Materials. No special materials were needed in the free-play situation which was conducted informally on the playgrounds of the school and centers. For the doll play three pipestem-cleaner dolls were used, a mother, a father, and a child doll the same sex as S. They were seven, six and one-half, and three and one-half inches tall, respectively, and were flexible and easy to manipulate. Each was made clearly identifiable by means of clothing and facial features.

The furniture used was appropriate in size and consisted of: stove, refrigerator, sink, kitchen table, three kitchen chairs, dining table, three dining chairs, double bed, vanity, child's bed, dresser, bathtub, toilet, lavatory, couch, two easy chairs, living room table, radio, and sixteen sections of walls. The dolls and furniture were arranged in a standard plan of six rooms at the beginning of each session in order to decrease the amount of organizational behavior and to facilitate the dramatization necessary.

RESULTS

Results and their analyses are presented as follows: (1) scoring and observer reliability, (2) consistency of doll-play responses within a session and from one session to the next, (3) comparison of "conscious" and "unconscious" preferences, (4) deviations of groups from equal preferences for both parents, (5) age and sex differences in preferences, (6) comparison of responses to specific items in the preference scale, (7) relation of preferences to actual home experiences.

Scoring and Observer Reliability. In order to give a "preference score," the following method was used to evaluate the responses obtained in the doll-play sessions: each mother-preference response was given $+1$ and each father-preference response was given -1. Neutral responses ("both" or "neither" preferred) were scored zero. The scores were then added arithmetically for each S and a constant of thirty was added to make all scores positive.

An experimenter and an assistant observed ten of the experimental sessions and independently recorded all responses to questions and all positive or negative doll action. These were scored by the above method and reliability determined by a rank-order correlation between the scores of the ten sessions. The correlation coefficient was found to be .99.

All forty-eight records were scored independently by the two observers, and the two scorings were found to agree perfectly. Thus both observational and scoring reliabilities were found to be nearly perfect in this rather simple interview situation.

Consistency of Doll-Play Responses from One Session to the Next. Two preference scores were obtained for each of the groups from the doll-play sessions: a first session score and a second session score. The correlations between first and second session scores are given in Table 18–3. It can be seen that the three-year-old boys were the least consistent of all the groups from first to second session, showing a correlation which is very nearly zero. Of the other groups, the five-year-old boys show the highest correlation, with the three-year-old girls second highest. There seems to be an increase with age in consistency of preference for the boys and a slight decrease with age for girls.

Odd-Even Reliabilities of the Doll-Play Interview by Groups. As there was good reason to believe the total group was not homogeneous, in view of its being stratified by age, correlations were computed individually for the six groups. Table 18–4 gives the reliabilities based on the correlation of mother-preference score on the odd items ($N = 10$) of the scale with this score on the even items ($N = 10$). Both rank-order and product-moment correlation coefficients are given because of the small number of subjects ($N = 8$) in each group. The correlations are

TABLE 18-3

Correlations between First and
Second Session Preference Scores

Groups	Correlations*	
	Rank Order	Product Moment
3B	−.05	.01
3G	.62	.78
4B	.51	.43
4G	.49	.54
5B	.79	.86
5G	.49	.68

*Both types included because of small size of samples.

TABLE 18-4

Odd-Even Reliabilities of Doll-Play Interview by Groups

Group	Session I			Session II		
	Rank-order Correlation	Product-moment Correlation	Corrected* Product-moment Correlation	Rank-order Correlation	Product-moment Correlation	Corrected* Product-moment Correlation
3B	.64	.65	.79	.69	.76	.87
3G	.70	.69	.81	.58	.60	.75
4B	.20	.62	.76	−.52	−.77	−.87
4G	.32	.55	.71	.68	.62	.76
5B	.51	.55	.71	.64	.73	.84
5G	.88	.78	.88	.58	.24	.39
Medians	.58	.64	.77	.61	.68	.75

*Since the correlations were between two sets of ten items, the reliability for all twenty items can be estimated from the Spearman-Brown prophecy formula.

almost all positive and fairly large. The median product-moment correlation corrected to twenty-item length was .77 for Session 1 and .75 for Session 2. It can be seen that the reliability of the method is quite high enough for group investigations such as the present one, is apparently not affected appreciably by age or sex, and is equally high in both sessions.

Comparison of "Conscious" and "Unconscious" Preferences. In order to determine the relationship between "conscious" and "unconscious" preferences, the mother responses to the direct question, "Which one do you like best?", and for the second doll-play session to the last preference question, "Which one does the little boy like best?", were tabulated for each group. These data are given in Table 18–5. They seem to show that there is no consistent tendency for boys to show more preference for the mother in their unconscious responses or the girls for the father. The percentage of self-agreement between conscious and unconscious responses was computed for each age-sex group by dividing twice the number of agreements between the two answers for each S by the total number of responses for that S. The percentages obtained were:

Group:	3B	3G	4B	4G	5B	5G
Percentage:	.25	.25	.50	.625	.50	.625

Agreement was defined as where the same response was given to the two questions by the same S: Mother-Mother; Father-Father; or Both-Both. The percentages of agreement show a trend toward greater conscious-unconscious agreement with increasing age which may be due to an increasing reliability of responses (see Table 18–4), or an actual change in the relationships of conscious and unconscious preferences toward greater agreement. It is to be noted, however, that even at the points of greatest agreement only slightly more than 50% agreement is found.

Differences of Groups from No Preference. Table 18–6 shows the mean scores and standard deviations for the two sessions for the various groups. Since a constant of thirty was added to all scores, scores below thirty show a father preference and those above thirty show a mother preference. We see first from Table 18–6 that three- and four-year-old boys show a father preference; four- and five-year-old girls show a mother preference; and that three-year-old girls and five-year-old boys seem to be relatively neutral. Table 18–7 shows the statistical significance of the deviations from equal preference by testing the hypothesis that the true mean preference score is thirty (equal preference).

If our "true" mean were thirty we would expect the second-session scores to "regress" toward the mean. It can be seen from Table 18–6 that except in Group 5B there is a slight increase of the preference in the same direction from first to second sessions for all groups. This shows a possible trend in the direction of less "inhibition" in the second session and perhaps reveals "truer" feelings on the part of the Ss, a possibility mentioned previously.

Age and Sex Differences. In order to test for differences between age and sex groups, *t*'s [see (14)] were figured for all different combinations

TABLE 18-5

Responses to Direct and Indirect
Questions Concerning Preference

| | Mother-Preference Scores* | |
| | Conscious | Unconscious |
Group	Direct Question	(Second Session Doll Interview)
3B	2.5	3.0
3G	5.5	3.0
4B	3.5	3.5
4G	5.0	6.0
5B	5.0	3.5
5G	6.5	5.0

*This figure represents number of Ss expressing a preference for the mother. Since there were eight Ss in each group, the maximum possible "mother preference" would be eight while the maximum "father preference" would be zero. A score of four would indicate an equal number of children in the group preferring each parent.

TABLE 18-6

Means and Standard Deviations for First and Second Doll-Interview Session Preference Scores*

Group		Session I	Session II
3B	M	25.0	24.1
	SD	4.6	7.6
3G	M	29.9	26.6
	SD	8.9	10.2
4B	M	28.4	27.4
	SD	5.1	2.7
4G	M	37.1	39.5
	SD	5.7	7.0
5B	M	31.4	30.0
	SD	7.6	7.5
5G	M	35.9	36.5
	SD	7.2	6.3

*Score represents the sum of the pluses and minuses and zeros, where a mother preference adds +1 to the child's score, a father preference adds a −1, and no preference, a zero. Since thirty was added to each score, "equal preference" would be represented by a score of thirty; extreme father preference, ten; extreme mother preference, fifty.

TABLE 18-7

Significances* of Preferences Shown by Various Groups ($df^\dagger = 7$)

Group	Session	M	σ_M	$t^\dagger$	Percentage Level of Confidence†
3B	1st	25.0	1.7	2.9	5
	2nd	24.1	2.9	2.0	20
3G	1st	29.9	3.4	.0	—
	2nd	26.4	3.8	.9	—
4B	1st	28.4	1.9	.8	—
	2nd	27.4	1.0	2.6	5
4G	1st	37.1	2.1	3.3	2
	2nd	39.5	2.6	3.6	1
5B	1st	31.4	2.9	.5	—
	2nd	30.0	2.8	.0	—
5G	1st	35.9	2.7	2.1	20
	2nd	36.5	2.4	2.7	5

*This is tested by assuming that if there were an equal preference, the true mean score would be 30. Scores below this would favor the father, above this would favor the mother.
†See Lindquist (14).

TABLE 18-8

*Significance of Differences between Groups
in Second-Session Preference Scores*

Groups*	t	Degrees of Freedom	Percentage Level of Confidence
3B vs. 3G	.5	14	—
3B vs. 4B	.8	14	—
3B vs. 5B	1.5	14	20
3G vs. 4G	3.0	14	2
3G vs. 5G	2.3	14	5
4B vs. 4G	4.3	14	0.1
4B vs. 5B	.9	14	—
5G vs. 4G	.8	14	—
5B vs. 5G	1.8	14	20
3 yrs. vs. 4 yrs.	2.9	30	1
3 yrs. vs. 5 yrs.	2.8	30	1
5 yrs. vs. 4 yrs.	.1	30	—
All B vs. All G	2.6	46	2

*The groups listed in the left-hand column showed a greater father preference than those in the right.

of groups plus total age and sex groups.* Table 18–8 shows the t's obtained, using the second-session preference scores.

We see that there were statistically significant differences between three- and four-year-old girls; three- and five-year-old girls; and four-year-old boys and girls. There are also possibly significant differences between three- and five-year-old boys, and five-year-old boys and girls. Three-year-olds together differed significantly from both four- and five-year-olds. Taken together, boys differed significantly from girls. In all cases the group mentioned first in the above showed a greater father preference.

Comparison of Responses to Specific Items in the Preference Scale. In Table 18–9 are summarized the responses of different groups to the specific items which made up the scale. Here the minimim score (extreme father preference) for the total group would be zero (i.e., no one in any of the groups showing preference for the mother). The maximum score (extreme mother preference) would be forty-eight (i.e., all Ss in all the groups showing preference for the mother and none for the father). If the preference were equally divided, the total score would be twenty-four (i.e., twenty-four Ss showing mother preference and twenty-four showing father preference). The obtained mean for the total score distribution was 24.4 and the standard deviation was 6.5. Scores in the other columns represent scores obtained in an analogous

* The authors are well aware of the fact that computing many t's, assuming that each group is a random sample from the same population, increases the probability of obtaining a "significant" t.

TABLE 18-9

Item Responses* by Groups in the Second Doll-Interview Session

Item	Total (Equal pref = 24)	Sex (Equal pref = 12)		Age (Equal pref = 8)		
		Boys	Girls	3	4	5
Preference	21.0	9.0	12.0	6.0	6.0	9.0
1. Toilet	29.0	14.0	15.0	7.0	12.0	10.0
2. Dressing	24.0	8.0	16.0	4.0	9.0	11.0
3. Punishment (M)	7.5	3.0	4.5	5.0	1.5	1.0
4. Reconciliation (M)	26.5	13.0	13.5	3.5	12.5	10.5
5. Cooking	31.5	17.0	14.5	7.0	13.0	11.5
6. Sitting beside	22.0	8.0	14.0	7.0	7.0	8.0
7. Helping	23.0	6.0	18.0	5.0	8.0	10.0
8. Playing	15.5	4.0	11.5	3.0	9.5	3.0
9. Punishment (F)	39.5	18.5	21.0	9.5	14.0	16.0
10. Reconciliation (F)	22.0	7.0	15.0	9.0	5.5	7.5
11. Holding hand	31.0	15.0	16.0	9.5	10.0	11.5
12. Sitting beside	23.0	8.0	15.0	5.5	10.5	7.0
13. Present	26.5	10.0	16.5	7.5	8.0	11.0
14. Story (M)	30.0	14.5	15.5	7.5	12.0	10.5
15. Story (F)	16.5	9.0	7.5	4.5	5.5	6.5
16. Bathing	30.0	15.0	15.0	7.0	10.0	13.0
17. To bed	24.5	11.0	13.5	5.5	11.0	8.0
18. Sleeping	23.0	7.0	16.0	5.5	8.0	9.5
Preference	24.0	10.0	14.0	6.0	9.5	8.5
Marriage (M)	40.0	21.0	19.0	13.0	15.0	12.0
Marriage (F)	35.0	16.0	19.0	14.0	10.0	11.0

*Each number in the table stands for a number of individuals in the group indicating a mother preference. A score of .5 indicates a failure by an odd number of subjects to indicate a preference.

manner for various subgroups. Thus the highest possible score (unanimous mother preference) would be twenty-four for each of the sex groups, and sixteen for each of the age groups.

From Table 18–9 it can be seen that for the whole group the most extreme preferences for the other parent were given when either the mother or the father punished the child. Responses to these items are in the direction to be expected, and demonstrate the validity of the procedure. Mother preferences were shown for cooking, holding hands, having a bath, and reading by the mother. Father preferences were shown for playing with him and reading by him.

Sex differences were found on certain items. Greater overall mother preference is shown by girls and greater father preference by boys. The girls show a greater preference than the boys for having their mothers dress them, and in helping, sitting beside, and sleeping with them. The boys also show a much greater preference for playing with the father than do the girls. This would indicate that a considerable amount of "sex typing" has already taken place in preschool-age children, which seems partially to account for the difference in preference scores obtained in this study. Of note also is the fact that girls, much more than boys, show a reluctance to be reconciled with the father after he has punished them. The opposite trend is not shown in the boys' reconciliation with the mother.

In the analysis of age differences we find that the older the child the more he wants to be dressed and bathed by his mother. Three-year-olds are not as extreme in the preference for one parent after punishment by the other parent as are the four- and five-year olds. Four-year-olds show a decided difference from three- and five-year-olds in their preference for playing with the mother rather than with the father.

At the bottom of Table 18–9 are shown the responses to the "marriage" questions. Since these were not choice responses, the theoretical mean ("no preference") score cannot be used as a reference point. In general we see that a majority of all the Ss would like to marry either or both of their parents. There is a slight preference for marrying the mother over the father in the total of both groups and among the boys. The girls show no preference for marrying one parent rather than the other. The four-year-olds show the largest difference in marriage preference of the mother over the father. These results point to a "social" rather than a "sexual" concept of marriage as prevalent among preschool-age children.

Relation between Children's Expressed Preferences and Their Actual Experiences. At the beginning of this study it was thought that home experiences might well be related to the children's choices in doll-play. As outlined in the procedure section, parents were asked which parent most often carried out each of twelve activities with the child.

Table 18–10 presents the results of a comparison between doll-interview preferences and home experiences. For each group, percentage agreement was computed as follows: (1) a score of +1 was given for the item where home report and child's preference agreed (both "mother," both "father," both "either," both "neither"), (2) a score of +½ was given if either home report or child indicated "either" or "neither" and the other gave one of the parents, and (3) a score of zero was given where home report named one parent and the child the other. Thus maximum agreement would lead to a score of twelve, one point being given for each of the twelve items. Percentage agreement was calculated by dividing this score by twelve.

In order properly to evaluate the amount of agreement it was felt necessary to obtain an estimate of the amount of agreement which could be obtained by chance. With this in mind, all preference scores in both doll-interview sessions were reassigned at random to the 12 items of home experience and "agreement" was calculated as previously outlined. Inspection of the scores obtained through these chance pairings as given in Table 18–10 shows that there is apparently no more than chance agreement between doll-interview preferences and reported home experience. This could be due to at least two things: (1) lack of consistent effect of home experience on child's preference, (2) rather

TABLE 18-10

Percentage Agreement between Children's Expressed
Parental Preference in Both Doll-Interview Sessions and
Parent Reported as Most Often Carrying on the
Activity in Real Life for Twelve Situations*

| | Percentage Agreement | | | |
| | First Session | | Second Session | |
Group	Obtained	Chance†	Obtained	Chance†
3B	49	55	55	52
3G	46	51	39	49
4B	50	48	50	50
4G	51	57	60	61
5B	55	44	60	52
5G	55	55	59	60
3-year-olds	48	53	47	50
4-year-olds	50	53	55	55
5-year-olds	55	49	60	56
All girls	50	54	53	56
All boys	52	49	55	51
Total	51	51	54	54

*See procedure section for items used.
†See text for explanation of procedure.

complete unreliability of parental report. It was felt that parental reports were unreliable because of the large number of persons collecting them and because of the parents' reluctance in many cases to state which parent carried out the activity more frequently with the child.

Although children's preferences have been shown to be sufficiently stable for group comparisons, parental reports as obtained for this study were probably unreliable; consequently it is felt that no conclusions can be drawn as to the effects of children's home experiences on their preferences for parents.

DISCUSSION

From the results of this study it can be seen that what we defined as "unconscious preference" differs from "conscious preference." Whether or not the doll-play interview gave us truly "unconscious" attitudes and feelings could not be determined, but there is evidence from already available clinical and experimental data to show that doll-play, at least to some extent, reveals feelings of which the subject is "unaware." The fact that there was a considerable degree of consistency between the two doll-play sessions in five of the six groups and a median product-moment correlation of .61 for the whole group would indicate that the projected responses were not random and had some meaning to the Ss. The fact that there was less agreement between stated "conscious" and projected "unconscious" preference in the three-year-old groups than in the other groups points to the possibility that in the older groups projection is less "unconscious" than in three-year-olds and more like their conscious preferences. However, even in the older groups there is nothing approaching perfect agreement, so age differences may be due merely to an increasing reliability of the procedure.

Our findings very definitely contradict the theory of a generalized preference in children for the cross-sex parent. In fact, they seem to lend support to an opposite theory that children prefer the same-sex parent. The results do show a slight preference for the cross-sex parent in the case of three-year-old girls and five-year-old boys, but the differences from equal preference are not significant. Even though the three-year-old girls do prefer the father, this preference is not nearly so great as it is with three-year-old boys. The same is true in the opposite direction with five-year-old boys and girls.

It must be remembered that this study dealt with essentially "normal" children whereas many theories of Oedipal attraction have been based on clinical material. Perhaps a lack of a strongly functioning "Oedipus complex" is what makes the present Ss "normal." Or perhaps they are better able to take care of ("repress") their Oedipus feelings and are therefore "normal." Whatever the reasons for the results obtained, all we can say with certainty is that in our study, using a projective method, we obtained no clear-cut evidence for an important universal Oedipus complex. The children's preferences in certain situations fit in with what we already know about sex-typing and identification in our culture. It may well be that there are Oedipal feelings, but they are almost completely submerged by learned feelings with a cultural basis. That these findings fit in well with much current psychoanalytic thought on the subject should be apparent.

SUMMARY AND CONCLUSIONS

The present study was designed to investigate sex differences in parent preferences of preschool-age children, using doll-play interviews. Forty-eight children served as Ss, eight boys and eight girls each at the three-, four-, and five-year levels. The Ss were chosen to satisfy requirements of age, living with both natural parents, and "native white" cultural background.

Two methods were used to explore the children's preferences. One was a direct method of asking the child during free play at day care center or kindergarten which parent he liked better, and the other was to use two doll-play interviews in a prearranged situation to obtain responses to twenty specific situational questions concerning the preferences of the child doll.

Observer and scoring reliabilities were almost perfect. Session to session preference scores correlated .61 for the whole group, while median corrected odd-even reliabilities were .77 for the first session and .75 for the second.

Findings can be summarized as follows:

(1) There is some evidence from intersession score changes to indicate that there is less inhibition and a greater revelation of "true" feelings in the second session than in the first. These effects of repetition are not statistically significant.

(2) Only a 50% agreement was found between the "conscious" and "unconscious" preferences of these preschool children. This could be due to lack of reliability of the measures, or could be attributed to differential effects of repression.

(3) Three- and four-year-old boys showed a definite father preference while four- and five-year-old girls showed a definite mother preference. Three-year-old girls showed a slight father preference and five-year-old boys showed a very slight mother preference, although the scores of these two groups did not differ statistically significantly from equal preference.

(4) Statistically significant differences, in preference scores were found between three- and four-year-old girls; three- and five-year-old girls; and four-year-old boys and girls. Three-year-olds together differed significantly from both four- and five-year-olds. Taken together, boys differed significantly from girls. The first-mentioned group in each case showed a relatively greater father preference.

(5) From group responses to specific items on the scale it was found that the total group definitely preferred the father when the mother punished and the mother when the father punished. Mother preferences were shown also for situations involving cooking, holding hands, having a bath, and reading. The father was preferred for playing and reading, when he was already carrying on the activity.

(6) Sex differences were shown on specific items. The girls preferred more than the boys to have their mothers dress them, sit beside them, sleep with them, and were interested in helping their mothers rather than their fathers. An opposite trend was shown by the boys.

(7) Age differences were shown in that the older the child the more he wanted to be dressed and bathed by his mother. Three-year-olds in general were not as extreme in their preference for one parent after punishment by the other parent as were the four- and five-year-olds. This may be due to semantic difficulties associated with age.

(8) It seems highly significant that, although 87% of the boys and 79% of the girls would marry a cross-sex parent, 66% of the boys and 79% of the girls would marry the same-sex parent.

(9) An attempt to relate home experiences and parent preferences

was unsuccessful, apparently due to the unreliability of parental statements about the home situation.

It can be concluded that the doll-play interview provides a projective method of adequate reliability for investigating children's relatively unverbalized feelings. Application of this technique to the problem of cross-sex parent preferences gives no evidence for any extensive Oedipal feelings. On the contrary, theories based on the situational learning of preferences are given much indirect support. The willingness of three-to-five-year-old children to marry same-sex parents is not consistent with the idea that any extensive repressions have already developed. All the present findings emphasize the fact that the sources of parental preferences are many and are complexly interrelated.

REFERENCES

1. ADLER, A.   What life should mean to you. Boston: Little, Brown, 1931.
2. BACH, G. R.   Young children's play fantasies. Psychol. Monogr., 1945, 59, No. 2.
3. BUSEMANN, A.   Die Familie als Erlebnismilieu des Kindes. Z. Kinderforsch., 1930, 36, 17–83.
4. CONN, J. H.   The child reveals himself through play; the method of the play interview. Ment. Hyg., N. Y., 1939, 23, 49–70.
5. DESPERT, J. L.   A method for the study of personality reactions in preschool age children by means of analysis of their play. J. Psychol., 1940, 9, 17–29.
6. FREUD, S.   General introduction to psychoanalysis. New York: Boni and Liveright, 1920.
7. FREUD, S.   The passing of the Oedipus complex. In Collected papers. London: Hogarth, 1924. Vol. II.
8. FREUD, S.   Female sexuality. Int. J. Psychoanal., 1932, 13, 281–297.
9. HAMILTON, G. V.   A research in marriage. New York: A. and C. Boni, 1929.
10. HOMBURGER, A.   Vorlesungen über Psychopathologie des Kindesalters. Berlin: Springer, 1926.
11. JEFFRE, M. F.   Fantasied mother-child interaction in doll play. Unpublished PhD Dissertation, State University of Iowa, 1946.
12. KATZ, D., & KATZ, R.   Gespräche mit Kindern. Berlin: Springer, 1928.
13. LEVY, D. M.   Studies in sibling rivalry. Res. Monogr. Amer. Orthopsychiat. Ass., 1937, No. 2.
14. LINDQUIST, E. F.   Statistical analysis in educational research. New York: Houghton Mifflin, 1940.
15. MOLL, A.   The sexual life of the child. New York: Macmillan, 1924.
16. MURSELL, J .L.   Nutrition and the family. Psychol. Rev., 1925, 32, 457–71.
17. NEWELL, H. W.   Family attitudes as revealed by the psychiatric examination of 107 juvenile delinquents. Amer. J. Orthopsychiat., 1932, 2, 377–383.
18. PHILLIPS, R.   Doll play as a function of the realism of the materials and the length of the experimental session. Child Develpm., 1945, 16, 123–143.
19. PINTLER, M. H.   Doll play as a function of experimenter-child interaction and the initial organization of the materials. Child Develpm., 1945, 16, 145–166.
20. PINTLER, M. H., PHILLIPS, R., & SEARS, R. R.   Sex differences in the projective doll play of preschool children. J. Psychol., 1946, 21, 73–80.
21. ROBINSON, E. F.   Doll play as a function of the doll family constellation. Child Develpm., 1946, 17, 99–119.

22. SARGENT, H. Spontaneous doll play of a nine-year-old boy. *J. consult. Psychol.*, 1943, 7, 216–222.

23. SELIGMAN, B. Z. The incest barrier. *Brit. J. Psychol.*, 1932, 22, 250–276.

24. SIMPSON, M. *Parent preferences of young children.* New York: Teachers College, Columbia University, 1935.

25. WATSON, J. B. *Psychological care of infant and child.* New York: Norton, 1927.

26. WHITE, W. A. *The mental hygiene of childhood.* Boston: Little, Brown, 1920.

27. YARNELLE, E. C. The relation of children's preferences to the preferences and attitudes of their parents. *Smith Coll. Stud. soc. Wk,* 1932, 2, 376.

28. YARROW, L. J. *The effect of antecedent frustration on projective doll play.* Unpublished PhD Dissertation, State University of Iowa, 1946.

Thanks are due to Drs. C. E. Meyers and W. W. Grings of the University of Southern California for many valuable suggestions in connection with this study, to Mr. Daniel Brown of the University of Denver and to Dr. Jack Sparer of the University of Colorado for critical reading of the manuscript.

The authors wish to acknowledge the help of Miss Betty Johnson of the Denver Bureau of Public Welfare and Dr. W. D. Asfahl, principal of University Park School, Denver, Colorado, for assistance in obtaining children for this study; and Mr. Hans Kakies for aiding in the determination of observer reliability.

19

Mary M. Leichty

The Effect of Father-Absence During Early
Childhood Upon the Oedipal Situation
as Reflected in Young Adults

The experimental study of many psychoanalytic concepts has been difficult because the manipulation of the life experiences of human beings must of necessity be limited. To utilize human subjects under conditions as they occur in the natural course of events would be most satisfactory, but the occurrence of such usable conditions is rare. The present study is an attempt to take advantage of such a fortuitous combination of circumstances.

With the emergence and rapid growth of sociology and anthropology as independent disciplines, a number of followers of Freud, later identified as neo-Freudians, became dissatisfied with certain of his concepts. They attempted to understand the development of the child in terms of growth continuously affected by interpersonal relationships provided by the culture. In incorporating these sociological principles into the framework of psychoanalytic theory, the neo-Freudians rejected or minimized certain of the Freudian postulates, one of which is the role of the Oedipal complex in psychosexual development.

The Oedipal conflict is said by the Freudians to be resolved when the boy gives up his mother as object choice and identifies with his father. Various studies deal with the effects of father-absence on childhood development (4, 5, 6, 7), but none of these represents a systematic attempt to study the effects of the father's unavailability on the resolution of the Oedipal conflict.

During World War II, many fathers were called into the armed forces and were away during the period when their sons were, according to analytic theory, working through the Oedipal complex. With the father away from home, the boy was left in undisputed possession of the field so that his yearning for his mother could be indulged without experi-

Reprinted by permission of the publisher from *Merrill-Palmer Quarterly*, 1959–60, 6, 212–217.

encing the castration anxiety which he would have felt were his father present. Such an environment would be fertile ground for excessive gratification and overindulgence of the boy's desire for his mother—a situation which fulfills the criteria (3) for circumstances which may lead to fixation at a particular level of psychosexual development.

It can thus be hypothesized that if the father is not available to play his role at this time, there will be inadequate resolution of the conflict. The orthodox Freudians believe that an inadequately resolved Oedipal conflict will leave a permanent effect on adult personality. If this is valid, and the boys whose fathers were separated from them during the Oedipal period have been unsuccessful in resolving the Oedipal conflict, they should now, as young adults, show evidences of it.

SUBJECTS

The subjects for this study were Michigan State University freshmen. The experimental group consisted of thirty-eight male students whose fathers were overseas with the armed forces during World War II and were separated from their sons for at least the period when the subjects were between the ages of three and five. A group of twenty-nine male subjects whose fathers did not serve in the armed forces was chosen as a control group.

HYPOTHESES

Four hypotheses were formulated on the basis of psychoanalytic theory:

Hypothesis 1. More of the experimental subjects, as compared to the control subjects, will maintain a strong attachment to the mother.

In resolving the Oedipal conflict the boy renounces his mother as an object choice because of castration fear and identifies with his father. If the father is not present during the Oedipal period, the boy will have no need to renounce his mother as an object choice, and as an adult will still maintain her as an excessively cathected object.

Hypothesis 2. Fewer of the experimental subjects, as compared to the control subjects, will show strong castration anxiety.

The mother is said to be renounced as a love object because of threatened castration. If there is no father to act as a threat, the boy will not develop castration anxiety in relation to his Oedipal wishes.

Hypothesis 3. Fewer of the experimental subjects, as compared to the control subjects, will show strong identification with the father; and identification of the experimental subjects will be more diffuse than that of the control subjects.

The Oedipal conflict is resolved when the boy identifies with his father. If there is no father for the boy to identify with, his identification will be diffuse and extend to other significant figures, including feminine ones.

Hypothesis 4. Fewer of the experimental subjects, as compared to the control subjects, will choose their fathers for their ego-ideals. More of the experimental subjects, as compared to the control subjects, will feel that their fathers are inferior to their ego ideals.

If identification with the father has not taken place, a boy will choose some figure other than the father to represent his ego ideal. He will also feel that the ego ideal he has established is superior to the image he has created of his father.

METHOD

Because it was designed specifically to measure psychosexual development and object relationships, the Blacky Test (1) was chosen as the test instrument. This test consists of twelve cartoon drawings about a dog, Blacky, and his family, composed of Papa, Mama, and Tippy, a sibling. Spontaneous stories and responses to the standardized questions for each cartoon were obtained from each subject.

The test was scored, using Blum's scoring system (2). This yields a global score based on both the free association and the inquiry items. In addition to this global score, certain of the inquiry items were related to each hypothesis, and response to them examined individually. These specific items were chosen from the regular inquiry items because they were particularly pertinent to a hypothesis and/or because they were amenable to objective scoring and hence to statistical analysis. Thus there were two types of measurements obtained: a global one based on the free association plus all the objective responses, and a second measurement based on certain individual items. Chi-square was used as a test of significance of differences.

RESULTS

Hypothesis 1. The first hypothesis, that more separated subjects would maintain a closer attachment to the mother than would nonseparated subjects, had two aspects. First, more separated subjects would evidence strong Oedipal intensity as shown by their response to Cartoon IV, which pictures Papa and Mama together while Blacky watches from behind some bushes. This aspect of the hypothesis was supported by the global score at the .02 level of significance. It was in relation to the second aspect of Hypothesis 1, as tested by Cartoon XI, which shows Blacky dreaming about a dog with a ribbon on its neck, that unexpected and interesting data were obtained. It was expected that the experimental group would maintain the mother as an excessively cathected object. An examination of the responses to Cartoon XI showed that though both groups rejected the mother as love object, the control group, to a greater degree, gave responses indicating that the mother was the prototype of the love object. The experimental group, on the other hand, gave responses indicating the rejection of the mother both as love object and as prototype for the love object. For example, in question 1, Cartoon XI ("Who is the figure Blacky is dreaming about?"), instead of choosing the item response which says Blacky is dreaming of Mama, both groups said Blacky is dreaming of someone else. But in question 2 ("Whom does the figure remind Blacky of?"), the control group was evenly divided between saying that the dream figure reminds Blacky of Mama and saying that it reminds Blacky of someone else. On the other hand, the experimental group, almost three to one, said that the dream figure reminds Blacky of someone else. A similar situation existed in question 5 ("In Blacky's mind how does Mama stack up against the dream figure when he compares them?"). Two-thirds of the experimental group said she was not as good; the control group was again about evenly divided. There seemed to be represented in the experimental group something of a negative cathexis toward the mother.

Hypothesis 2. In no aspect was the second hypothesis, that more nonseparated subjects would show castration anxiety, supported by the data. The role of castration anxiety has been considered by some to be a weak point in Freudian theory, and the neo-Freudians, with their deemphasis of the Oedipal conflict, concern themselves very little with castration anxiety. The lack of discrimination, by means of the present techniques, between the experimental and control groups which was shown in relation to Hypothesis 2 would lend some support to the view that castration anxiety was not a relevant variable in relation to the total problem of this study.

Hypothesis 3. It was in terms of identification with the father that there appeared most clearly to be a difference between the experimental and control groups. Hypothesis 3 stated that the control group would feel a closer identification with the father than would the experimental group. Two out of three inquiry items on Cartoon VII, which shows Blacky shaking his paw at a toy dog, support this hypothesis at the .01 level of significance. To the item "Who talks like that to Blacky—Mama or Papa or Tippy?" significantly more of the separated boys said Mama or Tippy. To the item "Whom would Blacky rather pattern himself after —Mama or Papa or Tippy?" again more of the separated boys chose Mama or Tippy.

It was further hypothesized that more of the experimental, than the control, subjects would show diffusion of identification. Subjects who were ambivalent in responding to the inquiry items of Cartoon VII were considered to show diffuse identification. For example, if instead of choosing one of the item responses offered (Mama, Papa, or Tippy), a subject gave an answer referring to more than one individual (Mama and Papa, all of them), or, if he gave a response which indicated inability to make a choice (no one, no feeling, don't know), this was counted as an ambivalent response. Twenty-four of the experimental group as compared to three of the control group were ambivalent in their choice of response.

If one believes that the identification process has been affected by the father's absence, a natural question follows. What kind of identifications have these young men in the experimental group made? Though their fathers were absent, there were usually other adult males with whom the boys had close contacts. Many wives returned to their parents' home for the duration, in which case, the boy may have tended to identify with his grandfather. In many cases there were uncles or even older cousins, who could serve as a model. Sometimes the relationships available to the boy might be almost completely feminine, with no close male to whom he could relate. One might expect the most common pattern to be one of diffuse relationship, where there were several figures available to the boy, with no one individual in a very close association. But most important of all for the boy, none of these adult males would have, with his mother and himself, the same relationship as would his father.

Whether one accepts the Freudian concept of fixation at certain developmental levels or follows the neo-Freudian point of view in stressing the sum total of parent-child relationships, the implication of the data related to Hypothesis 3 is that the absence of the father during this period of the child's life has in some way affected the identification process.

Hypothesis 4. The present data lend only slight support to Hypothesis 4, that boys separated from their fathers during the Oedipal period will choose someone other than the father as their ego ideal. Both the experimental and control groups seemed to choose someone other than the father as an ego ideal, but a significantly greater number of the experimental group made such a choice.

CONCLUSIONS

The data presented in this study give some support to three of the four hypotheses formulated. More of the young male adults who were separated from their fathers during the Oedipal period showed strong

Oedipal intensity than did those in a similar group who were not separated. Fewer of the separated group felt a closer identification with the father than the nonseparated group. There was some evidence that the separated group tended to a greater degree to choose someone other than the father as their ego ideal. Castration anxiety was not a relevant variable in distinguishing the two groups.

That the absence of the father during the so-called Oedipal period has affected some aspects of personality development seems clear. Interpretation of these changes, however, is not so apparent. There appears to be the clearest difference between the two groups in terms of the boy's relationship with his father. But this difference need not be attributed solely to the absence of the father during a particular psychosexual period of development. Studies (7) have shown that the period of adjustment after the father's return is a difficult one. In this study, environmental factors after the father's return were not controlled as variables. It is possible that self-perpetuating patterns of relationship were established because of this difficult adjustment period, patterns which would not necessarily have appeared had the father been present continually. The question remains: What would have been the personality development in the experimental group if the father had returned to a warm, understanding relationship, without either father or child experiencing a difficult adjustment?

Future research controlling environmental differences after the father's return would limit experimental variables to the period of the father's absence. This would perhaps throw more light on the problem of finality of experience during certain psychosexual developmental periods.

REFERENCES

1. BLUM, G. S.   A study of the psychoanalytic theory of psychosexual development. *Genet. Psychol. Monogr.*, 1949, 39, 3–99.

2. BLUM, G. S.   *Revised scoring system for research use of the Blacky Pictures.* Ann Arbor: University of Michigan, Department of Psychology, 1951. (Mimeographed).

3. FENICHEL, O.   *The psychoanalytic theory of neurosis.* New York: W. W. Norton, 1945.

4. IRVINE, ELIZABETH.   Observations on the aims and methods of child-rearing in communal settlements in Israel. *Human Relat.*, 1953, 5, 247–275.

5. LYNN, D. G., and SAWREY, W. L.   The effects of father-absence on Norwegian boy and girls. *J. abnorm. soc. Psychol*, 1959, 59, 258–262.

6. RABIN, A. I.   Some psychosexual differences between Kibbutz and non-Kibbutz Israeli boys. *J. prof. Tech.*, 1958, 22, 328–332.

7. STOLZ, LOIS H.   *Father relations of war-born children: the effect of post-war adjustment of fathers on the behavior and personality of first children born while their fathers were overseas.* Stanford: Stanford University Press, 1954.

20

Paul Mussen & Luther Distler

Child-Rearing Antecedents of Masculine Identification in Kindergarten Boys

The concept of identification is undoubtedly one of the most prominent in the literature on personality development. Theoretical discussions of the concept are numerous (e.g., 2, 7, 8, 9, 12, 14, 17), and recently there have been a number of studies testing hypotheses derived from these theoretical writings (e.g., 13, 15, 18, 20).

Empirical investigations of the concept have customarily used, as operational indices of degree of identification with parents, measures of either (1) degree of "real" or "assumed" similarity between parent and child (4, 15, 24) or (2) personality characteristics or behavioral manifestations which are presumably consequents of the identification process, e.g., aggression (10), high conscience (20), use of the father doll in play (18).

Hypotheses about the antecedents and consequents of strong or weak identification with parents are tested by correlating an index of identification with measures of theoretically relevant variables. Thus, using the amount of use of the father doll as an index of identification with the father, Pauline Sears (18) showed that five-year-old boys with warm and affectionate fathers (as judged from interviews) identified with them more strongly. Similarly, it has been found that adolescent boys who respond to personality and attitude tests as their fathers do— a consequence of the boys' strong identifications with their fathers—are more likely, according to projective test responses, to view their fathers as highly nurturant and rewarding (15). According to another study, a high degree of conscience development in kindergarten children, presumably an index of parental identification, is related to the mother's warmth and acceptance and to her use of withdrawal of love as a method of control. For boys, acceptance by the father was also found to be related to this index (20).

Reprinted by permission of the publisher and the authors from *Child Development*, 1960, *31*, 89–100. Copyright 1960 by the Society for Research in Child Development, Inc.

Adequate sex-typing, or acquisition of the personality characteristics, behavior, and attitudes appropriate to the child's own sex, is generally considered to be a major consequent of strong identification with the like-sexed parent (12, 19). For this reason the present authors, in an earlier study, used a measure of sex-typing of interests in young boys as an index of identification with the father (13). In that study three hypotheses about the antecedents of identification were tested by comparing the responses of two groups of five-year-old boys—one group high and one group low in masculinity as measured by the IT Scale for children (ITSC) (3)—to nine semistructured familial doll play stories. Analyses of the doll play protocols indicated that highly masculine (i.e., highly father-identified) boys viewed their fathers as powerful sources of both reward and punishment. These data thus seemed to support both the developmental and defensive hypotheses of identification, i.e., boys highly identified with their fathers perceived them as more nurturant and rewarding (as the developmental identification hypothesis would predict) *and* as more threatening and punitive (in accordance with the defensive identification hypothesis). The authors concluded however, that "role theory with its explicit emphasis on the importance of both reward and punishment in role learning best integrates all these data" (13, p. 17).

It must be emphasized that these findings on correlates of masculinity were based only on the child's *perceptions* of his relationship with his parents, as these were reflected in his doll play. The present study, essentially an extension of the earlier one, is focused on the relationship between degree of sex-typing in young boys and their parents' child-rearing practices. Information on these practices was obtained from interviews with the mothers.

The purpose of the study was to test three major hypotheses (developmental, defensive, and role-taking) about the factors underlying the identification process—and thus to check the conclusions of earlier studies—with another, perhaps more objective, kind of data on family relations. More specifically, we wanted to evaluate the behavior of the fathers of the strongly father-identified (i.e., highly masculine) group toward their sons. Do they tend to act (1) warmly and affectionately, (2) punitively and threateningly, or (3) as powerful agents of both rewards and punishments?

Since the interview data of the present study are in many respects like those of the Sears et al. (20) study, including information on conscience development, we could also determine whether or not different presumed consequents of the identification process—high degree of sex-typing and conscience development—are related to each other and are associated with the same child-rearing variables.

PROCEDURE

The basic data about child-rearing practices were obtained from the mothers of the kindergarten boys who were subjects in the authors' earlier study of masculinity and identification (13). The boys had been selected from among thirty-eight white boys, pupils in two kindergarten classes of a predominantly middle-class public school, who had been given the IT Scale, a projective test of sex-role preference (3). Nine of the interviewees were the mothers of boys with the highest (most masculine) scores on the ITSC, and ten were the mothers of boys with the lowest (least masculine) scores. It must be emphasized that *all* the data, including those pertaining to fathers' attitudes and practices, are derived from mothers' reports.

For many reasons the interviews had to be limited to between one half-hour and one hour; hence the interview schedule was a relatively short one. It consisted of thirty-two open-ended questions, some of them with suggested probes taken from the interview schedule used by Sears et al. (20, Appendix A). Almost all the questions concerned the areas most directly relevant to theories of identification and to conscience development. They related to restrictions and demands on the child, use of praise in discipline, warmth, affection, and punitiveness of each parent, the child's dependence and his proneness to confess wrongdoing. The following two questions are illustrative:

How often do you spank X? [Probes: (1) How about your husband? How often does he spank him? (2) For instance, how often has X been spanked in the last two weeks?]

Now we'd like to talk awhile about X and his father. Will you tell me something about the way they act toward each other? [Probes: (1) For instance, when your husband comes home from work, when X is there, what happens? (2) How about after dinner? (3) What other kinds of things do they do together?]

All the interviews were conducted by a trained social worker who asked the questions in the prescribed order and using the exact wording given in the schedule. She took extensive notes on each interview, recording as much as possible verbatim.

After she had completed all the interviews, the social worker rated each of them on twenty-eight dimensions. The rating scales, taken from Appendix B of *Patterns of Child Rearing* (20), are listed in Table 20–1.

In order to eliminate any bias in her work, the social worker was not informed of the real purpose of the research until after she had finished all of her work. Therefore, neither her interviews nor her ratings could have been influenced by knowledge of the hypotheses or the method of selecting the interviewees.

TABLE 20-1

Differences Between High and Low Masculinity Groups on Rating Scales of Familial Variables and Conscience Development

Rating Scale	U	p	Direction of Differences Between Groups
Father-Son Relationships Variables			
Father's standard of obedience	35.0	ns	
Frequency with which *father* spanks	37.5	ns	
How child and father act toward each other	12.0	.001-.01	Highs have more affectionate relations
Amount of caretaking father does now	31.5	.14*	Highs = more caretaking by father
Affectional bond, father to child	13.5	.001-.01	Highs = fathers warmer
Strictness of father	40.5	ns	
Mother-Son Relationships Variables			
Mother's standard of obedience	34.5	ns	
Amount of mother's affectionate demonstration	43.5	ns	
Amount of time mother plays with child	33.0	ns	
Warmth, mother to child	33.0	ns	
Frequency with which *mother* spanks	32.0	.14*	Lows = spanked more frequently
Family Climate Variables			
Praise for good behavior at table	40.5	ns	
Strictness about bedtime	35.0	ns	
Strictness about noise	19.0	.025	Lows = parents more strict
Restrictions on physical mobility	40.5	ns	
Amount of praise for obedience	32.0	.14*	Highs = praised more
Amount of attention child wants	31.5	ns	
Sex role differentiation	45.0	ns	
Permissiveness for aggression toward parents	37.5	ns	
Punishment for aggression toward parents	36.5	ns	
Extent of use of tangible rewards	43.0	ns	
Extent of use of praise	18.0	.01-.025	Highs = praise used more often
Parents' agreement on child-rearing policies	33.0	ns	
Responsibility for child-rearing policies	30.5	.12*	Highs = father has more responsibility
Division of labor between husband and wife	23.0	.05	Highs = less division of labor
Conscience Development Variables			
Spontaneous telling of deviations	30.5	.12*	Highs = tell more often
Does child admit deviations when asked	12.5	.001-.01	Highs = admit to deviations
Evidence of conscience development	26.0	.05-.10	Highs = more evidence of conscience

*p values estimated by the Z transformation method (23).

RESULTS

Testing the hypotheses required determining the relationships between masculinity status, on the one hand, and child-rearing practices, the child's relationship with his parents, and conscience development, on the other. This was accomplished by comparing the low and high masculinity groups on each of the twenty-eight variables on which they had been rated.

Since the number of subjects in each group was small and the distributions of ratings were not normal, U tests (11) were used to compare rank transformation scores on all ratings of subjects in the two groups. The results of these tests and the significance levels, together with the meanings of the significant differences and trends in the data, are summarized in Table 20–1.

The two groups differed significantly or almost significantly in seven of the twenty-eight rated variables. There were some additional trends in the data; that is, there were five variables on which the two groups tended to be rated differently, although the differences were not statistically significant. In general, these trends are consistent with, and support, the statistically significant differences between the two groups.

The findings are particularly relevant to three broad areas—father-son relationships, family climate, and conscience development—and will therefore be presented in three sections.

Father-Son Relationships

As Table 20–1 indicates, the high and low masculinity groups differed in a number of familial variables. The data of the present study, like those of earlier ones (13, 15, 21), show that sex-typing of interests is more directly related to boys' interactions with their fathers than with their mothers. While none of the variables pertaining to mother-son relationships significantly differentiated the two groups, several of the variables of father-son interaction did. The differences were most clearcut in two variables: (1) the highly masculine boys and their fathers were rated as "acting more affectionately toward each other", and (2) the father-to-child affectional bonds are stronger in the case of the boys in this group.

These findings clearly lend support to the developmental identification hypothesis. They confirm the prediction, based on that hypothesis, that young boys are more likely to identify strongly with their fathers, and thus to acquire appropriately sex-typed responses, if their relationships with them are rewarding, warm, and affectionate.

Some additional trends in the data suggest that, if the father plays a very active role in his son's upbringing, the boy is more likely to develop strong masculine identification. Thus, compared with the fathers of the low masculine group, the fathers of highly masculine sons tended to take care of their sons more frequently and to have greater responsibility for the family's child-rearing policies. While these differences between the groups were not statistically significant, the findings suggest that the degree of the young boy's masculinity is related to the frequency and intensity of his contacts with his father and to the latter's influence in determining how the child is handled.

These trends, together with the significant findings about the warmth and affection of the fathers of highly masculine boys, may also be interpreted as evidence supportive of the role-taking hypothesis of identification. According to this hypothesis, a boy will be most strongly motivated to identify with his father, or, in role theory terms, to imitate him or take on his role, if he has intensive interactions with that parent and regards him as having a great deal of power. Predictions derived from this hypothesis appear to be confirmed by these data. Thus, it seems reasonable to infer that, since they are warm and affectionate, the fathers of highly masculine boys interact more frequently and more intensively with their sons. Therefore, these boys have more experience in practicing their appropriate sex roles. Moreover, since these fathers tend to take care of their sons often and, to a great extent, determine the techniques of disciplining the child, they do, in fact, have a great deal of power over the child, i.e., they can control his rewards and punishments. In short, these data seem to be consistent with the role-taking, as well as the developmental, hypothesis of identification.

None of the data of this study support the hypothesis of defensive identification, which maintains that high masculine identification is a consequence of the father being threatening and punitive. Ratings of the father's standards of obedience for the child, his frequency of spanking, and his strictness, based on the mothers' reports, did not significantly differentiate the high and low masculinity groups.

Family Climate

There is some evidence that, in addition to experiencing different kinds of father-son relationships, the two groups also encounter different general home atmospheres. Compared with the other group, the families of the highly masculine boys appeared to be more permissive, easygoing, more love-oriented, and less punitive in their disciplinary techniques. More specifically, as Table 20–1 indicates, the families of the highly masculine boys were less strict about noise in the home and more frequently used praise as a technique of discipline.

Other trends in the data give further support to these statistically significant findings. Highly masculine boys tended to be spanked less by their mothers and to get less praise for obedience. Since these boys' parents make more use of praise generally, their tendency to use less praise specifically for obedience may indicate that they place relatively less emphasis on this characteristic and thus maintain less strict, more permissive home atmospheres.

Moreover, the highly masculine boys tended to be less attention-seeking—and, by inference, less dependent—than their peers who were relatively low in masculinity. Interpreted in the light of findings of other studies, this may indicate that the high group experiences more maternal nurturance (22), less maternal rejection, and less punishment for dependency (20). While it must be emphasized that these last findings represent suggestive trends rather than statistically significant differences between groups, they give some further evidence that appropriate sex-typing is fostered by a warm and permissive familial milieu.

One other familial variable, division of labor between husband and wife, significantly differentiated the two groups. According to mothers' reports, the families of the highly masculine-identified boys are characterized by fewer specifically "mother" and "father" tasks and a greater tendency for each parent to help with all tasks. The relative paucity of rules regarding duties may be another reflection of the relaxed climate of the home of the highly identified child. It may also indicate a generally harmonious family situation in which the parents can depend on each other's assistance without regulations about assignments. As Mowrer (12) had suggested, in the harmonious family both parents are likely to reward the boy's imitation of his father. Thus, both encourage the boy to identify with his father and in this way promote the development of a high degree of masculinity.

Conscience Development

If, as is generally assumed, appropriate sex-typing and high conscience development are both products of the process of parental identification, it would be predicted that independent measures of these two variables would be related. The findings confirm this prediction and thus support the underlying assumption. As may be seen in Table 20–1, highly masculine boys were rated higher than boys low in masculinity in measures of conscience development. More specifically, the former group received higher ratings in the variables, "admitting deviations when asked" and "evidence of conscience development," an overall rating of superego. Moreover, there was a tendency for the highly masculine to be rated higher on the variable "tells about deviation," which referred to the child's proneness to confess wrongdoing spontaneously.

DISCUSSION

The interpretation of the findings is somewhat complicated by the fact that the data were derived exclusively from mothers' reports of their own and the fathers' behavior. The data on fathers' attitudes and general family climate may therefore be confounded. For example, reports that the fathers of highly masculine boys are affectionate might be a function of the mothers' view of the family climate as warm and permissive, rather than a specific commentary on the fathers' behavior. Nevertheless, the results of the present study are consistent with other empirical findings and with developmental and role theories of identification. The authors have previously reported that highly masculine kindergarten boys perceive their fathers as warm, nurturant, and rewarding (13), and the data of the present study suggest that, at least according to the mothers' replies, these fathers' overt behavior is characteristically affectionate. The consistency of the findings from two independently derived sets of data supports the validity of the developmental hypothesis of identification.

The present findings may also be interpreted as lending support to the role theory of identification. If the fathers of highly masculine boys are in fact more affectionate, they probably interact frequently and intensely with their sons. Furthermore, they tend to be influential in determining child-rearing policies and hence probably exercise considerable power over the boys. These two characteristics of the father— a high level of interaction with the son and great power over him—are, according to role theory, the primary prerequisites of the boy's strong identification with him.

The present data indicate that highly masculine boys live in relatively permissive, nonpunitive family climates. It seems plausible to infer that boys in such families are happier and more relaxed in their relationships with their parents than boys from stricter homes. Under these circumstances they are likely to seek frequent contact with their parents and to be relatively uninhibited in trying out many imitative responses in their presence. Responses that are appropriately sex-typed will be rewarded and hence will gain in habit strength, while inappropriate responses will not be rewarded and thus will be weakened or extinguished. In a stricter, more rigid home the child may tend to withdraw from his parents and, for this reason, will have less opportunity to learn which responses are most appropriate to his sex role.

While the findings based on mothers' reports of father-son relations and family climate were generally congruent with those discovered in the analysis of children's perceptions of their families, the two sets of data yielded different results for variables pertaining to father punishment and threat potential. Differences in the doll play responses of boys high and low in masculinity tended to support the defensive identification hypothesis, i.e., the former *perceived* their fathers as more punitive and threatening (13). According to the mothers' reports, however, the fathers of highly masculine boys did not *behave* more punitively or threateningly toward their sons than the fathers of boys low in masculinity. The data of the present study thus lend no support to the defensive identification hypothesis. There are no data that enable us to determine whether the child's or the mother's perceptions are more in accord with reality. The highly masculine boys' perceptions of their fathers may be related to the fact that these boys interact more with their fathers, and, consequently, in their doll play use the father dolls more prominently as agents of both nurturance and punishment. Thus, the threatening qualities attributed to the fathers in doll play may reflect, not their actual behavior, but their salience in the lives of their sons. On the other hand, it is equally possible that these fathers actually are, or have been, severe in their treatment of their sons. The mothers, however, viewing their husbands as affectionate toward their sons, may be unwilling or unable to admit the punitive aspects of the fathers' behavior. The problem can probably be solved only by systematic observations of father-son interactions among those high and low in masculinity.

Another finding of the study—the association between high degrees of masculinity in boys, assumed to be a manifestation of strong father identification and highly developed conscience, the index of identification used by Sears, Maccoby, and Levin (20)—merits discussion. Both measures have been found to be related to the high use of praise by parents and, more generally, to the use of love-oriented techniques of discipline. However, warmth and acceptance by the mother and acceptance by the father were found to be antecedents of a high degree of conscience development in kindergarten boys (20), while the father's warmth and affection, not the mother's, were found to be related to masculinity in boys this age. On theoretical and empirical grounds, it is reasonable to consider both conscience development and masculinity as signs of identification, but the two characteristics appear to have different correlates or antecedents.

In the process of ego and superego development the child undoubtedly has not one, but a number of identification models. Different aspects of his psychological structure become modeled after different identificands. Thus, for the five-year-old boy both parents probably serve as models for conscience development; that is, his moral values and ethical standards are products of identifications with his mother *and* father.* If this is true, then, according to the developmental identification hypothesis, a high degree of conscience development would depend upon positive affectional relationships between the child and *both* parents. Viewed in this way, association between the boy's high level of conscience and both his parents' acceptance and warmth (20) was to be anticipated. The same finding may also be interpreted as confirmation of a prediction

---

* It is, of course, possible that ultimately the boy's conscience will be modeled primarily after his father's, but during the preschool period his standards are more likely to be adopted from both parents.

based on role theory. Insofar as warm and affectionate parents interact more with their children, these children would be expected to identify strongly with them, to adopt more of their characteristics, and, consequently, to develop strong conscience.

The boy's adoption of masculine interests, on the other hand, must be almost exclusively the product of his identification with his father, for he is the parent who serves as the model for masculinity. Since the mother obviously cannot be the model for this, her role in her son's acquisition of masculine characteristics cannot be as vital as the father's. Therefore, according to the developmental identification hypothesis, appropriate sex-typing for the boy is a consequent of warm and affectionate interactions with his father, while his relationships with his mother are less important in this respect. Analogously, according to role theory, the amount and intensity of father-son, but not mother-son, interactions determine the masculinity of the boy's behavior and interests. The data of this study substantiate this reasoning. High degrees of masculinity were in fact fostered by affectionate—and, by inference, frequent and intense—father-son interactions, but were not significantly affected by mother-son relationships.

SUMMARY

The mothers of nineteen boys, nine of them high and ten of them low in masculinity as measured by the IT Scale, were interviewed about their own and their husbands' child-rearing practices and the boys' conscience development. On the basis of these interviews ratings were made on twenty-eight variables of father-son relationships, family climate, and conscience.

The major findings were as follows:

(1) The variables of father-son relationships are more directly associated with sex-typing than are those pertaining to mother-son relations.

(2) According to mothers' reports the fathers of the highly masculine group had stronger affectional bonds, and acted more affectionately, toward their sons than did the fathers of boys low in masculinity. These findings appear to support the developmental hypothesis of identification.

(3) There were trends in the data that suggest that the fathers of the highly masculine group play a greater role in their sons' upbringing, doing more of their sons' caretaking and having greater responsibility for child-rearing policies. These trends, together with the findings about the warmth and affection of the fathers of highly masculine boys, may be interpreted as supportive of the role theory of identification.

(4) The highly masculine boys appear to experience more per-

missive, easygoing familial climate and less punitive, more love-oriented techniques of discipline than their less masculine peers.

(5) Boys high in masculinity tend to be high in conscience development, too. The correlates of these two products of parental identification are quite different, however.

REFERENCES

1. BRIM, O. G., JR.   Family structure and sex-role learning by children: a further analysis of Helen Koch's data. *Sociometry*, 1958, 21, 1–16.
2. BRONFENBRENNER, U.   The study of identification through interpersonal perception. In R. Tagiuri & L. Petrullo (Eds.), *Person perception and interpersonal behavior*. Stanford Univer. Press, 1958. Pp. 110–130.
3. BROWN, D. G.   Sex-role preference in young children. *Psychol. Monogr.*, 1956, 70, No. 14 (Whole No. 421).
4. CAVA, E. L., & RAUSH, H. L.   Identification and the adolescent boy's perception of his father. *J. abnorm. soc. Psychol.*, 1952, 47, 855–856.
5. COTTRELL, L. S., JR.   The analysis of situational fields in social psychology. *Amer. sociol. Rev.*, 1942, 7, 370–383.
6. FREUD, ANNA.   *The ego and the mechanisms of defense*. London: Hogarth Press, 1937.
7. FREUD, S.   The passing of the Oedipus complex. In *Collected papers*, Vol. II. London: Hogarth Press, 1933. Pp. 269–282.
8. FREUD, S.   *The problem of anxiety*. New York: Norton, 1936.
9. FREUD, S.   *Group psychology and the analysis of the ego*. London: Hogarth Press, 1949.
10. LEVIN, H., & SEARS, R. R.   Identification with parents as a determinant of doll play aggression. *Child Develpm.*, 1956, 27, 135–153.
11. MANN, H. B., & WHITNEY, D. R.   On a test of whether one of two random variables is stochastically larger than the other. *Ann. math. Statist.*, 1947, 18, 50–60.
12. MOWRER, O. H.   *Learning theory and personality dynamics*. New York: Ronald, 1950.
13. MUSSEN, P., & DISTLER, L.   Masculinity, identification, and father-son relationships. *J. abnorm. soc. Psychol.*, 1959, 59, 350–356.
14. PARSONS, T.   Family structure and the socialization of the child. In T. Parsons & R. F. Bales, *Family, socialization, and interaction process*. Glencoe, Ill.: Free Press, 1955. Pp. 35–131.
15. PAYNE, D. E., & MUSSEN, P. H.   Parent-child relationships and father identification among adolescent boys. *J. abnorm. soc. Psychol.*, 1956, 52, 358–362.
16. RICHARDS, T. W., & SIMONS, MARJORIE.   Fels Child Behavior Scale. *Genet. Psychol. Monogr.*, 1941, 24, 259–309.
17. SANFORD, N.   The dynamics of identification. *Psychol. Rev.*, 1955, 62, 106–117.
18. SEARS, PAULINE.   Child-rearing factors related to playing of sex-typed roles. *Amer. Psychologist*, 1953, 8, 431. (Abstract)
19. SEARS, R. R.   A theoretical framework for personality and social behavior. *Amer. Psychologist*, 1951, 6, 476–482.
20. SEARS, R. R., MACCOBY, ELEANOR E., & LEVIN, H.   *Patterns of child-rearing*. Evanston, Ill.: Row, Peterson, 1957.
21. SEARS, R. R., PINTLER, M. H., & SEARS, PAULINE.   Effect of father separation on preschool children's doll-play aggression. *Child Develpm.*, 1946, 17, 219–243.
22. SEARS, R. R., WHITING, J. W. M., NOWLES, V., & SEARS, PAULINE.   Some

child-rearing antecedents of aggression and dependency in young children. *Genet. Psychol. Monogr.*, 1953, 47, 135–234.

23. SIEGEL, S. *Nonparametric statistics.* New York: McGraw-Hill, 1956.

24. SOPCHAK, A. Parental "identification" and "tendency toward disorders" as measured by the MMPI. *J. abnorm. soc. Psychol.*, 1952, 47, 159–165.

The authors wish to thank Mr. A. B. Campbell, Assistant Superintendent of Schools of Berkeley, Mr. C. B. Johnson, Principal of the Jefferson School, and Mrs. C. B. Holmes and Mrs. E. P. Light, kindergarten teachers, for their cooperation in this and the earlier study.

The authors are grateful to Mrs. Marie Mustache for her invaluable aid in conducting the interviews and making the ratings.

21

Irving Sarnoff & Seth M. Corwin

Castration Anxiety and the Fear of Death

Beginning with its formulation by Freud (4), the concept of castration anxiety has been widely invoked by psychoanalytically oriented therapists in their attempts to account for a variety of clinical phenomena (2, 3, 6, 7, 10). In recent years, several correlational studies have provided some empirical support for the concept of castration anxiety (5, 8, 9). The present experiment was undertaken to contribute further data to aid in the scientific evaluation of the usefulness of the concept. Specifically, this experiment concerns the relationship between castration anxiety and the fear of death.

The Concept of Castration Anxiety

Freud first put forward the concept of castration anxiety in connection with his theory of the Oedipal conflict and the psychological processes employed in its resolution. Briefly, Freud postulated that the male child becomes motivated, at one stage in his psychosexual development, to possess his mother sexually. However, such a desire cannot be countenanced by the child's father. Indeed, the latter threatens to castrate his son if he should persist in his illicit cravings. Presumably, this threat of castration may be made directly and literally, or it may be conveyed indirectly and symbolically. In any case, the threat is perceived by the child and it arouses his intense fear. To reduce this fear, the child must learn to behave in a way which will no longer provoke his father's jealous anger.

From the standpoint of the growing child, the effort to resolve the Oedipal conflict is an ongoing one whose outcome is not conclusively determined until after he has reached adolescence. In the course of this protracted effort, the child may draw upon a number of the mechanisms which are available in his repertoire of ego defense. According to psychoanalytic theory, however, the following three ego defenses are of principal importance in the child's struggle to attain mastery over the various facets of the Oedipal conflict: *identification, repression,* and *displacement.* Identification and repression are employed earlier than the mechanism of displacement. Nevertheless, after these ego defenses have been brought into play, they become part of the individual's habitual mode of coping with the Oedipal conflict.

When the conflict emerges during the phallic stage, the child, first of all, identifies with his threatening father. That is, the child adopts his father's sexual taboos and accepts the idea that it is wrong for a son to have sexual desires for his mother. Having internalized his father's prohibitions, the child then represses his sexual feelings for his mother. With this repression, the child ceases to be conscious of any sexual yearning for her.

The repression of sexual desire for the mother is followed by the latency period, a period of several years during which the child's sexual drive is relatively weak and quiescent. During this period, too, the child continues to cement his identification with his father. Hence, for a time, the child appears to be at peace with himself and the Oedipal conflict seems to have been mastered. Inevitably, however, the calm of the latency period is shattered by the onset of puberty. For the physiological changes of adolescence stir up imperative sexual tensions for which some outlet must be found, and sexual desires which had been dormant and unconscious throughout the latency period now tend to break through the barrier of repression which the child had built up against them.

In the throes of his reactivated sexuality, the adolescent may again be inclined to covet his mother. But any such inclination evokes the anticipation of castration which originally induced the child to renounce his mother as a sexual object. The adolescent is obliged to repress any newly awakened sexual desire for his mother, but must find some way of gratifying his urgent sexual cravings. Consequently, he is led to employ still another mechanism of ego defense, displacement. He diverts his sexual interest away from his mother and toward females whom he may consciously covet and pursue without arousing his castration anxiety. In effecting this displacement, the sexually mature male finally succeeds in establishing a lasting resolution of the Oedipal conflict.

Ideally, during the Oedipal period, the child is exposed only to that degree of castration threat which is sufficient to induce the repression of his sexual feelings for his mother alone. When the child attains adulthood, he should experience no anxiety when his heterosexual desires are aroused by any woman other than his mother, for he has learned to anticipate castration only when his mother is the object of his sexual desire. In actuality, however, children are exposed to varying degrees of castration threat; and if the amount of threat has been excessive, the individual may be led to repress his sexual feelings not only for his mother in particular, but also for women in general. In such cases the arousal of his repressed sexuality by *any* female may elicit the anxiety which has become associated with the incipient manifestation of a highly punishable motive. For a man who has suffered excessive threat of castration in childhood, therefore, sexual arousal, even by a female who is not his mother, is likely to evoke the anticipation of castration.

The Psychodynamic Relationship Between Castration Anxiety and the Fear of Death

Because men differ in respect to the degree of castration threat they have experienced in childhood, they may be expected to respond with differing degrees of castration anxiety to the same sexually arousing stimulus. Indeed, even in the absence of a particular external stimulus, men who, as children, were severely threatened with castration may be subject to chronic anxiety. This anxiety stems from the fact that their chronically repressed desires for sexual contact with women strive continually to break through into consciousness. Naturally, such individuals usually do not know that it is their own sexual motives which stimulate this anxiety, nor are they likely to be aware of the specific danger, castration, which they dread. Nevertheless, their underlying anxiety, as in the case of other strong unconscious affects, may be expected to color the content of their conscious thoughts, and they ought to become preoccupied with ideas which symbolically reflect the castration anxiety of which they are unaware. Hypochondria is an excellent clinical example of the way in which intense—but unconscious—castration anxiety may be indirectly expressed through a host of conscious fears concerning possible sources of infectious disease or bodily deterioration. Indeed, these hypochondriacal fears may, in some cases, actually focus on infections which could damage sexual organs. However, even in such instances, the individual is not likely to perceive the relationship between his conscious fear and the unconscious castration anxiety which it reflects. His concern tends to be outward rather than inward; and he spends his time and energy in attempts to escape infection.

Just as unconscious castration anxiety may be manifested in conscious fears of bodily injury, it may also manifest itself in a fear of the most extreme consequence of injury: death. Thus, it happens that individuals who are in the best of health and have never actually experienced any serious accident of illness may be obsessed by morbid and unremitting fears of dying or of being killed. These fears may become so acute that the individual is reluctant to go to sleep lest he should never again awaken.

Of course, the conscious fear of death may be developed for a variety of reasons, the most obvious of which concern the aftermath of traumatic events, such as military combat, which might have terminated the individual's existence. Still it would appear, in view of the preceding theoretical account, that an individual who has suffered intense castration threats should have a greater habitual fear of death than an individual who has been less severely threatened. Individuals who have severe castration anxiety ought also to show more fear of death after the arousal of that anxiety than individuals whose castration anxiety is less intense. In arriving at these deductions, we have assumed that people with different degrees of castration anxiety have experienced differential degrees of castration threat for the expression of their sexual feelings. However, we shall not address ourselves directly to an investigation of these presumed developmental differences in this experiment. Instead, we shall focus exclusively on the impact of castration anxiety on the conscious fear of death, after that anxiety has been stirred by the perception of sexually arousing stimuli.

In line with this reasoning, the central hypothesis of this experiment may be stated as follows: *Individuals who have a high degree of castration anxiety will show a greater fear of death after being exposed to sexually arousing stimuli than individuals who have a low degree of castration anxiety.*

METHOD

General Design

The experiment followed a "before-after" design which provided for the arousal of two levels of sexual feeling among subjects (Ss) possessing two degrees of castration anxiety. Castration anxiety was measured in pre-experimental sessions. Thus, the experiment studied the interaction of castration anxiety and sexual stimulation in determining the fear of death.

Subjects

Ss were fifty-six male undergraduates of Yale College. They were unpaid volunteers, recruited from among the general college population. Ss were run through the experiment one at a time in a dormitory room.

Rationale

This experiment was presented to the Ss as an investigation of some of the psychological factors which influence the appreciation of art. Ss were told that the investigators were interested in seeing how different individuals react to the same work of art, and how various attitudes and opinions are related to esthetic reactions. Ss were informed that they would first fill out a questionnaire which covered a number of opinions pertinent to our research objectives. After they had filled out this questionnaire, Ss were told that they would be shown several pictures about which they would be asked to write their esthetic reactions.

The Opinion Questionnaire

The first of the pre-experimental measures consisted of a twenty-two-item Likert-type scale. Included among these twenty-two items was a seven-item Fear of Death scale and a five-item Morality scale, both of which are described below. The ten remaining items in the questionnaire were interspersed among the items of these two scales. These ten "filler" items pertained to various aspects of esthetic preference. They were included for two reasons: (1) to inhibit the emergence of a response set to the other items and (2) to support the rationale of the experiment.

Ss indicated the extent of their agreement or disagreement with each item in the questionnaire. These responses were coded in terms of a six-point scale ranging from +3 (Strongly Agree) to −3 (Strongly Disagree). Ss were not permitted to take a midpoint on the scale; they were obliged to indicate some degree of agreement or disagreement with each statement.

The Fear of Death Scale (FDS). Since all the items in the questionnaire were devised on an a priori basis, and since the FDS measure was the basic dependent variable of the study, it was felt advisable to attempt to weed out those FDS items which were grossly nondiscriminating. Accordingly, after the "before" measures were collected, an item analysis was performed on the seven-item FDS. Two items failed to discriminate between the high and low scorers. Thus, the hypothesis was tested by using a summated score of the five items which were retained.

The following are the five items which comprised the final version of the FDS:

(1) I tend to worry about the death toll when I travel on highways.
(2) I find it difficult to face up to the ultimate fact of death.
(3) Many people become disturbed at the sight of a new grave, but it does not bother me. (reverse scores)
(4) I find the preoccupation with death at funerals upsetting.
(5) I am disturbed when I think of the shortness of life.

The Morality Scale (MS). The MS was included in the study in order to serve as an internal control for the plausible alternative hypothesis that a postexperimental increase in fear of death might be the result of an increase in guilt following contact with stimuli which violate one's moral values. Such a reaction following sexual arousal could induce an unconscious need for punishment in the guilty S and this need, in turn, might express itself in an increased fear of death. The MS consisted of five items dealing with attitudes toward sexual behavior. The MS items, constructed in the same a priori fashion as the FDS and contained in the same questionnaire as the FDS, were also subjected to an item analysis. Since the original MS items discriminated adequately between high and low scorers, they were all retained in the final version of the MS.

The following are the examples of items contained in the MS:

(1) Although many of my friends feel differently, I feel that one should wait until he is married to have intercourse.

(2) I am frequently disturbed by the complete lack of sexual control in the relationships of my friends and their dates.

The Measure of Castration Anxiety (CA)

After the administration of the scales described above, our measure of castration anxiety was obtained in the following way: Ss were presented with the so-called castration anxiety card of the Blacky Test (1). This card shows a cartoon depicting two dogs; one dog is standing blindfolded, and a large knife appears about to descend on his outstretched tail; the other dog is an onlooker to this event. Ss were asked to look at this card and then rank three summary statements which purported to summarize the situation which was depicted. Actually, each statement was composed, on an a priori basis, to express a different degree of anxiety, ranging from slight to intense. Thus, Ss attached a score of three to the statement they felt best reflected the emotions of the onlooking dog, a score of two to the statement they felt fit the situation second best, and a score of one for the statement they felt fit the situation least. The distribution of the scores turned out to be quite skewed: most Ss assigned a score of three to the low CA alternative, a score of two to the medium CA alternative, and a score of one to the high CA Alternative. The thirty-six Ss who showed this pattern of scores were placed in the Low CA group. The remaining twenty Ss were categorized in the High CA group. Below are the summaries used for the Blacky card. (L represents the Low castration anxiety statement, M, medium castration anxiety, and H, high castration anxiety)

L. The Black Dog appears to be experiencing some tension as he watches the scene in front of him. However, the sight of the amputation has little emotional significance for him, and he views the situation in a fairly detached manner.

M. The Black Dog is evidently quite frightened by what is going on in front of him. He is afraid that his tail might be next to be amputated. Nevertheless, he is able to bear up to the situation without becoming deeply upset or overwhelmed by anxiety.

H. The sight of the approaching amputation is a deeply upsetting experience for the Black Dog who is looking on. The possibility of losing his own tail and the thought of the pain involved overwhelm him with anxiety.

The Experimental Conditions

Approximately four weeks after they filled out the "before" measures, the Ss participated in the experiment. Since the experimental design called for variation in arousal of sexual stimulation, two experimental conditions were created: High and Low sexual arousal (HAS and

LAS). The experimental manipulations were administered individually, with twenty-nine Ss in the HAS condition and twenty-seven Ss in the LAS condition.*

It was decided that the easiest and most manageable arousal of sexual feelings would be by means of photographs of women. To produce the HAS condition, a series of four pictures of nude women were presented one at a time. These pictures were artistically mounted as if they were prints or lithographs. E said that these pictures were designed to study individual differences in esthetic reactions to the same work of art. To heighten the impact of the arousal, Ss were given four minutes to write down their reaction to each picture. According to the rationale of the study, this writing was done in order to provide a record of the Ss responses to the esthetic qualities of the picture.

In the LAS condition, the procedure was identical except for the fact that four pictures of fully clothed fashion models, taken from a magazine, were used instead of nudes.

After the experimental manipulations, Ss were required to fill out the following measures which are relevant to the data reported here: a rating scale designed to ascertain whether or not the HAS and LAS conditions succeeded in evoking different intensities of stimulation, the FDS scale, and the MS scale.

The postexperimental check on the sexually arousing quality of the manipulations indicated that the HAS pictures were clearly perceived as more sexually arousing than the LAS pictures. On a scale ranging from O (not at all arousing) to 100 (intensely arousing), the HAS Ss had an average score of 59, whereas the LAS Ss had an average score of 35. The difference between these means was well beyond the .001 level of significance. Thus, there can be little doubt concerning the difference in sexual stimulation of the two conditions of arousal.

It may also be relevant to note that, in postexperimental interviews, none of the Ss indicated that they had been suspicious about our stated research objective. Moreover, although some of the Ss in the HAS condition could not completely conceal their chagrin or embarrassment upon seeing the nudes, they did not doubt that we were interested in studying individual differences in reactions to the pictures.

RESULTS AND DISCUSSION

The hypothesis tested in this experiment holds that HCA Ss will become more afraid of death after exposure to the HAS condition than LCA Ss. To test this hypothesis, the change in the Ss' level of fear of death was

---

* To insure a sufficient number of HCA Ss within the HAS and LAS conditions, half of the Ss were randomly selected from the HCA and LCA Ss and assigned to the HAS condition. The other half were assigned to the LAS condition. Two Ss who had been assigned to the LAS condition failed to appear for the experimental session.

assessed by comparing their pre-experimental FDS scores with their postexperimental FDS scores. This comparison produced a "shift" score for each S, indicating by what amount and in which direction his "after" FDS score differed from his "before" FDS scores. A positive (+) shift score thus indicated that an S exhibited more fear of death, while a negative (−) shift score was indicative of a decrease in fear of death.

A t test showed that there was no difference between the high and low arousal groups in their initial level of fear of death. However, a strong relationship was found between fear of death and castration anxiety. The phi coefficient is .612, a figure which is significant at the .01 level. This result is in accordance with the anticipations previously stated in the theoretical section. As a result of this relationship, however, the HCA Ss tended to have higher pre-experimental FDS scores than the LCA Ss. Consequently, it is clear that HCA Ss entered the experimental conditions with less possibility for upward movement in the FDS than the LCA Ss. Conversely, the LCA Ss had less possibility for downward movement. Therefore, it was deemed advisable to test the hypothesis both with and without attention to the Ss' initial level of fear of death.

Table 21–1 presents the results pertinent to the basic test of our hypothesis. Without controlling for initial position on the FDS, the predicted difference between HCA and LCA Ss in mean FDS shift scores under the HAS condition is significant at the .03 level, whereas no statistically reliable difference between the HCA and LCA Ss is obtained under the LAS condition. A test of the difference between the differences in mean FDS scores (the difference between HCA and LCA Ss under the HAS condition compared with the difference between HCA and LCA Ss under the LAS condition) yields a t of 4.35. This result, which is statistically significant at beyond the .001 level, appears clearly to indicate that the arousal of sexual feeling interacted with level of castration anxiety in accord with our a priori predictions.

Mention ought, perhaps, to be made of the fact that both HCA and LCA Ss show a negative shift score, i.e., a decrease in the fear of death, under identical conditions. Thus when high and low levels of pre-experimental FDS are combined under the LAS condition, as in Table 21–1, HCA Ss get a mean negative shift score of −1.11 while the mean FDS shift score for LCA Ss is −.05. Similarly, it can be seen in Table 21–1 that, within the high level of pre-experimental FDS, but again under the LAS condition, HCA Ss obtained a mean FDS shift score of −2.00 as compared to −1.06 for LCA Ss. If we discount, as virtually negligible, the LCA shift score of −.05, the remaining three negative FDS shift scores seem best accounted for by the effects of statistical regression. Since the LAS condition arouses so little sexual feeling, it seems to permit the occurrence of the same sort of regression effects that are typically found among control groups: a drop in mean retest score for initially high-scoring Ss and a rise in mean retest score for initially low-scoring Ss. This is exactly what appears to have happened with initially high and low scoring HCA and LCA Ss under the LAS conditions. Thus, both HCA and LCA Ss who are high in pre-experimental

TABLE 21-1

Analysis of Mean FDS Shift Scores
(Differences Between HCA and LCA Ss Within High, Low, and Combined
Levels of Pre-experimental FDS Under HAS and LAS Conditions)

Strength of Sexual Arousal	Level of Pre-experimental FDS	Strength of Castration Anxiety					
		HCA		LCA		Difference Between Means	p
		N	Mean FDS Shift	N	Mean FDS Shift		
HAS	High and low	11	+3.36	18	+.45	+2.91	.03
LAS	High and low	9	−1.11	18	−.05	−1.06	n.s.
HAS	High	8	+1.88	6	+.33	+1.55	n.s.
	Low	3	+7.33	12	+.50	+6.83	.001
LAS	High	6	−2.00	7	−1.86	−.14	n.s.
	Low	3	+.67	11	+1.10	−.43	n.s.

FDS show negative mean FDS shift scores. On the other hand, both HCA and LCA Ss who are low in pre-experimental FDS show positive shift scores under LAS conditions. Finally, HCA Ss who tend, as we have indicated, to have high pre-experimental FDS scores as a consequence of the positive correlation between FDS and CA, also decrease in FDS under the LAS condition when the high and low levels of pre-experimental FDS are combined.

In order to test the possibility that results might be accounted for by a guilt reaction to infringement of moral values concerning the sexual feelings aroused by the HAS, the mean FDS shift scores of the high and low MS Ss were compared under both HAS and LAS conditions. The results of this analysis, presented in Table 21–2, indicate that, although there appears to be a slight tendency for Ss high in MS to show higher FDS shift scores than Ss low in MS, the difference is far from statistical significance. The possibility, then, that an infringement of moral values induced by the nudes caused an increase in fear of death is not supported.

It should be noted, finally, that our measure of the morality variable appears to be quite independent of the castration anxiety and fear of death measures. The product-moment correlation between pre-experimental FDS and pre-experimental MS was only −.034, while the correlation between CA and pre-experimental MS was also low and statistically insignificant (a phi coefficient of .105).

The results of the present experiment are interpreted as lending support to the validity of the Freudian concept of castration anxiety. Such an interpretation seems especially warranted since the plausible alternative explanation which we investigated failed to yield significant changes in the fear of death when Ss were categorized in terms of their

TABLE 21-2

*Differences Between HMS and LMS Ss in Mean FDS Shift Scores
Under HAS and LAS Conditions*

Strength of Sexual Arousal	Strength of Morality					
	HMS		LMS		Difference Between Means	p
	N	Mean FDS Shift	N	Mean FDS Shift		
HAS	15	+2.13	14	+.93	+1.20	n.s.
LAS	15	−1.08	14	+.22	−1.30	n.s.

moral scruples against sexual behavior. Since our pre-experimental measures of castration anxiety and morality were found to be quite independent of each other, we may conclude, with some confidence, that it was the arousal of castration anxiety rather than guilt feelings which produced the significant differences which we obtained.

Of course, nothing that was done here bears directly on the question of the etiology of castration anxiety. However, by demonstrating that sexually arousing stimuli exerted predicted and differential effects upon individuals with varying degrees of castration anxiety, we have provided circumstantial evidence which is consonant with Freud's emphasis on the significance of the sexual motive in the genesis of castration anxiety.

SUMMARY

The aim of this experiment was to test an hypothesis concerning the psychodynamic relationship between castration anxiety and the fear of death. Specifically, the hypothesis predicted that persons who have a high degree of castration anxiety (HCA) would show a greater increase in fear of death after the arousal of their sexual feelings than persons who have a low degree of castration anxiety (LCA).

Fifty-six male undergraduates of Yale College were assigned to two experimental conditions in a "before-after" design which permitted the manipulation of two levels of sexual arousal. Before being exposed to one or the other of these manipulations, Ss filled out booklets containing a scale designed to measure the fear of death (FDS), a questionnaire concerning moral standard of sexual behavior (MS), and a measure of castration anxiety (CA).

High arousal of sexual feeling (HAS) was induced by showing the Ss four pictures of nude females. The condition of low arousal of sexual feeling (LAS) consisted of showing Ss four pictures of fashion models.

Following the experimental manipulations, Ss again filled out the original FDS. In addition, Ss answered a questionnaire aimed at checking on the degree of sexual arousal which Ss perceived in the experimental manipulations.

The results clearly confirmed the hypothesis: HCA Ss showed a significantly greater increase in fear of death than LCA Ss after being exposed to the sexually arousing stimuli of the HAS condition. There were no significant differences in mean FDS shift scores between HCA and LCA Ss under the LAS condition. A postexperimental check of the difference in perceived arousal of sexual feelings revealed that Ss perceived the HAS condition as significantly more arousing than the LAS condition. A plausible alternative explanation of the obtained results was investigated and rejected. Thus, it was found that Ss who differed in the strength of their moral standards of sexual behavior did not differ significantly in their mean FDS scores after being exposed to the HAS condition.

REFERENCES

1. BLUM, G. S.   A study of the psychoanalytic theory of psychosexual development. *Genet. Psychol. Monogr.*, 1949, 39, 3–99.
2. ESMAN, A.   A case of self-castration. *J. nerv. ment. Dis.*, 1954, 120, 79–82.
3. FODOR, N.   Varieties of castration. *Amer. Imago.*, 1947, 2, 32–48.
4. FREUD, S.   Analysis of a phobia in a five-year-old boy. In S. Freud, *Collected Papers*. London: Hogarth Press, 1949. Vol. III, Pp. 149–295.
5. FRIEDMAN, S. M.   An empirical study of the castration and Oedipus complexes. *Genet. Psychol. Monogr.*, 1952, 2, 61–130.
6. KOBLER, F.   Description of an acute castration fear based on superstition. *Psychoanal. Rev.*, 1948, 35, 285–289.
7. ROTHENBERG, S., & BRENNER, A. B.   The number 13 as a castration fantasy. *Psychoanal. Quart.*, 1955, 24, 545–559.
8. SCHWARTZ, B. J.   Measurement of castration anxiety and anxiety over loss of love. *J. Pers.*, 1955, 24, 204–219.
9. SCHWARTZ, B. J.   An empirical test of two Freudian hypotheses concerning castration anxiety. *J. Pers.*, 1956, 24, 318–327.
10. STARCKE, A.   The castration complex. *Int. J. Psychoanal.*, 1921, 2, 179–201.

The authors wish to thank Professor Arthur R. Cohen for his helpful suggestions in regard to the preparation of this paper.

22

Rachel B. Levin

An Empirical Test of the Female Castration Complex

The female castration complex (also called, among other things, "penis envy" and the "masculinity complex") has been offered by psychoanalytic theorists as a major explanatory concept in the psychology of women. In general terms, the complex refers to the woman's presumed discontent with her femininity and her modes of reacting to this discontent. The complex is seen as occurring in varying degrees in most women, along a continuum from the normal to the abnormal; as being a conspicuous feature of feminine neuroses and pathological character formations; and as motivating a wide variety of behavioral manifestations. As an intervening variable, the female castration complex is supposedly related to observable clinical phenomena such as the feeling of having been castrated, envy of the penis, the desire to castrate men, or the wish-fulfilling fantasy of possessing a penis. In addition to or in place of, these sexual manifestations, the complex may also be related to more general social attitudes and behavior, such as a derogatory attitude toward women and their traditional social role, envious hostility toward men, and the attempt to emulate the masculine social role. Two frequently described clinical phenomena that cut across the sexual-nonsexual differentiation are wish-fulfillment" and "revenge" behavior; while both may occur in the same individual, one generally predominates. The wish-fulfillment type of behavior is illustrated by homosexuality, the pursuit of an intellectual or professional career, the avoidance of marriage and/or motherhood, hypomanic activity in any sphere, and gynecological disturbances of a functional nature. Some examples of the revenge type are frigidity, vaginismus, and prostitution (1, 5, 7, 11, 19, 22).

In spite of the broad agreement that psychoanalytic writers have shown as to these clinical or descriptive aspects of the complex, there have been many theoretical differences with regard to its genesis and basic nature. The complex is conceded by all theorists to be related to both sexual and nonsexual behavior, but there remains an unresolved

Reprinted by permission of the publisher and the author from *Journal of Abnormal Psychology*, 1966, *71*, 181–188. Copyright 1966 by the American Psychological Association.

issue as to which of these two is primary, and which is secondary or derived. According to the biological approach (1, 5, 9, 10, 11, 13), the origin of the complex is literal envy of the male anatomy. It is presumed that during the phallic stage every little girl falls victim to this envy, which in the course of normal feminine development is eventually resolved by being transformed into the wish for a child (equivalent to penis) from the father (the Oedipus complex). If, however, the girl's bisexual disposition is weighted in the direction of masculinity, her castration complex remains unresolved. In the adult woman the complex may take "rationalized" forms such as protests against the greater social freedom of men, or the pursuit of an intellectual or professional career, but its genetic roots and underlying motives are literally sexual and biological.

The culturally oriented theorists, on the other hand (14, 15, 21, 22), see the complex as stemming from social and family reactions to sexual differences. In the normal form in which it is believed to occur in most women in our culture, the complex is thought to represent a realistic wish for social equality with men. The complex may also be related to neurotic problems, such as deep feelings of inadequacy as a human being, which have become closely linked with the woman's sense of femininity. These problems arise from disturbed family relationships in which sexual differences play an important role, for example, the parents' preference for a male sibling. The complex may be symbolized in sexual forms such as literal penis envy, but its primary motives are nonsexual, for example, the needs for affection and self-esteem.

Notwithstanding the theoretical importance of the female castration complex, empirical studies of it have been few, both in the child and the adult (4, 6, 12, 16, 18, 20). Most of the research has been characterized by methodological inadequacies such as the use of direct questions or the failure to demonstrate scorer reliability; and/or by conceptual oversimplification, such as the tendency to equate the female castration complex with the male castration complex (both often vaguely defined as "castration anxiety"). Other relevant studies have focused on limited areas such as masculine identification (8), or have been more directly concerned with other topics (3).

In sum, there has been no systematic attempt to formulate a broad definition of the intervening variable of the female castration complex that would include its varied forms of expression in the adult woman; to design a reliable projective instrument for measuring these varied aspects or components; and, using this instrument, to test the validity of the construct by investigating its relationship to an independent, theoretically derived criterion. These were the general goals of the present research.

Since the complex has been assumed to be related to both literally sexual and more generalized nonsexual manifestations, it was decided to design a projective measure aimed at tapping both of these forms of expression. No hypothesis was formulated, however, with regard to the theoretical issue of the relative importance of the sexual as opposed to the nonsexual factors, since there was no way (evident to the author) of determining objectively which type of factor was basic and which was derived. In other words, sexual manifestations of the complex on the projective test might be symbolic expressions of generalized social attitudes (in the concrete language of the body), and conversely, nonsexual projective signs might be symbolic or derived representations of basically sexual factors. Our goal, then, was not to test the biological or cultural positions, but, very simply, to find out whether a group of women showing a type of overt behavior (the independent variable) theoretically related to the female castration complex, would show higher scores on a projective measure of the complex (the dependent variable) than a group of control women. The projective instrument was not designed to measure only the particular motivational factors that might be related to the specific behavioral criterion selected. It was devised with the more general aim of evoking as comprehensively as possible all the varied impulses and feelings, both sexual and nonsexual, both wish fulfillment and revenge, that are common to most of the accounts of the complex.

The specific behavioral criterion that was selected was masculinity of social role or style of life. In broad terms, analytic theory proposes that the intensity of the woman's castration complex, an intervening motivational variable, is related to the degree of masculinity of her social role, an overt behavioral variable. The research hypothesis, derived from this general proposition, was as follows: *Intensity of the female castration complex as measured by a projective test is significantly greater in women with a masculine social role than in women with a feminine social role.* Of course, masculinity of social role is only one of the many forms of behavior to which the complex has been theoretically related; this particular behavioral variable was selected on the basis of expediency, namely—the relative ease of obtaining research subjects. The hypothesis was not intended to imply that an overtly masculine style of life was the only way in which the castration complex expressed itself.

METHOD

Subjects

The research subjects consisted of fifty-one white, native-born, college-educated American women between the ages of thirty and fifty-five, in good physical health, and with no history of psychiatric treatment. These subjects were selected from a pool of 499 women, local alumnae of various colleges, who responded to an innocuous questionnaire entitled "A Sociopsychological Survey of American Women." The fifty-one women were divided into two groups: (1) twenty-six

career women, who represented a masculine social role, and (2) twenty-
five homemakers, who represented a feminine social role. Two criteria
were used in determining masculinity or femininity of social role: (1)
family status (marriage and children), and (2) occupation. The two
research groups contrasted clearly with respect to both of these criteria.
Thus, the career women were unmarried and employed in masculine
occupations, while the homemakers were married, living with their
husbands, mothers of two or more children, and not gainfully employed
outside the home. Masculine occupations were defined by a high ratio of
men to women in census statistics, or by a high level of status and
responsibility; using these definitions, two psychologists showed strong
agreement in assigning high ranks on masculinity of occupation to the
career women ($\rho = .92$, $p < .001$). They included lawyers, physicians,
research scientists, business executives, and university faculty members;
eighteen of them had higher degrees, including nine doctorates. The
homemakers had a median of four children each; none of them had
higher degrees, although they were all college graduates.

Later, the two groups were compared with respect to Vocabulary
subtest scores on the Wechsler Adult Intelligence Scale (WAIS); socio-
eonomic status of family of origin, as measured mainly by father's
education and occupation; and current socioeconomic status, as
measured by the education and occupation of the subject herself in the
case of the career women, and of the subject's husband in the case of
the homemakers. Comparison by means of the chi-square test showed
no significant differences between the two groups on any of these
variables. In both groups, the median age was in the range of 35–39,
and the majority were Protestant. The median Verbal IQ, as estimated
by the WAIS Vocabulary scores, was 129 for the career women and 132
for the homemakers.

Procedure. All subjects were tested by the investigator in individual
appointments that lasted about two hours each. Standard clinical procedures were used in administering first, the Rorschach test, and then,
the Vocabulary subtest of the WAIS. These were followed by two
especially designed instruments that the subjects filled out by themselves: an opinion questionnaire focusing on the social role of women
(not reported on here), and a biographical questionnaire (used in the
final equating of the groups). Cooperation by the subjects was excellent.

The female castration complex measure (FCCM). The first step in
constructing the measuring instrument was to delineate the major components (or modes of expression) of the female castration complex.
On the basis of a survey of the psychoanalytic literature, eight such
specific components were selected (see Table 22–1). While these eight
were not assumed to be a comprehensive list of "pure" factors, they
were felt to include most of the main features of the complex as described in the literature. The Rorschach was chosen as the most appropriate test upon which to base the measuring instrument. For each of
the eight components, a corresponding Rorschach measure consisting
of one or more signs was formulated (Table 22–1); the eight Rorschach

TABLE 22-1

*The Eight Components and Corresponding Rorschach Measures
of the Female Castration Complex*

Component	Rorschach Measure[a]
1. *Castration Anxiety:* The woman's fear and rejection of her femininity in a specifically genital sense. Conception of the female genitals as castrated, damaged, and inferior.	1. *Female Sexual Disturbance:* Disturbance of structure, theme, or style in female sex (genital) percepts or in responses to popular female sex areas. For example, "Blood stain" in II D3.
2. *Penis Envy:* The woman's envy of the male genitals, in a literal sense. Wish to castrate men in revenge for her own castration. Projection of her hostility with consequent fear of the penis.	2. *Male Sexual Disturbance:* Disturbance of structure, theme, or style in male sex (genital) percepts or in responses to popular male sex areas. For example, any percept scored F- in II D4.
3. *Confused Body Image:* The woman's confusion about the male and female body images, stemming from her own ambivalent sexual identification. Blurring or denial of the physical distinctions between the sexes.	3. *Difficulty in Assigning Sex:* Avoidance, confusion, or misperception in assigning sex to human or humanlike percepts For example, "Two people, I can't tell if they're men or women."
4. *Penis Fantasy:* The woman's defense against her castration by denial and the wish-fulfilling fantasy of possessing a penis, in a literal sense.	4. *Phallic Symbolism:* Explicit reference to phallic characteristics of percepts. For example, "Person with a very long nose."
5. *Rejection of Femininity:* The woman's fear and rejection of her femininity in a general (not specifically sexual) sense. Image of women as weak, inferior, and victimized, or defensive conception of them as powerful and dangerous.	5. *Female General Disturbance:* Disturbance of structure, theme, or style in female general (nonsexual) percepts or in responses to popular female general areas. For example, any percept scored F- in I D4.
6. *Envy of Men:* The woman's envy of men in a general (not specifically sexual) sense. Conception of men as superior and powerful, or defensive image of them as inferior and weak. Projection of her hostility with consequent fear of men.	6. *Male General Disturbance:* Disturbance of structure, theme, or style in male general (nonsexual) percepts or in responses to popular male general areas. For example, "Scowling man."
7. *High Activity:* The woman's identification with "masculine activity." An active, energetic orientation to the world, and strong needs for independence and self-assertion.	7. *Active Human Movement:* Perception of human or humanlike percepts in active kinds of movement. For example, "Clowns doing tricks."
8. *High Need for Achievement:* The woman's identification with "masculine striving." Competitiveness, ambition, and strong needs for status and achievement, especially in masculine fields.	8. *Achievement Content:* Responses with content reflecting strong drives for achievement and prestige, especially in masculine fields. For example, "An emblem."

*For the derivation of the popular areas of Measures 1, 2, 5, and 6, see Levin (17). Locations are those listed by Beck (2).

measures together formed the FCCM. The individual signs were derived from the Rorschach literature and from common clinical usage with this test. They included both traditional Rorschach scores (such as form level) and thematic and stylistic features of the protocols that conventionally do not receive formal scoring. While these signs might, of course, reflect factors other than the female castration complex, they were assumed to have some degree of face validity as indicators of the various aspects of the complex as they are described in Table 22–1. For a detailed description of the FCCM, including the rationale for each of the signs, see Levin (17).*

Since some of the FCCM signs consisted of conventional Rorschach scores, one person first scored the Rorschach protocols in the usual way. Then another person scored the protocols on the FCCM by deciding which, if any, FCCM signs were present in each Rorschach response. The FCCM scorer had first been trained in the application of the FCCM by the use of five protocols not included in the study. Neither of the two scorers had any knowledge of the design of the research. On ten protocols (five from each group of subjects) the first scorer (conventional Rorschach scores) showed percentages of agreement with another psychologist that ranged from eighty-four to ninety-one. The FCCM scorer's percentage of agreement with a second psychologist on twenty protocols (ten from each group) was ninety-one.

Nine main FCCM scores were computed for each subject: an overall FCCM score and eight specific measure scores. General Rorschach productivity (length of responses and total number of responses), was controlled in these main scores by counting each response a maximum of once for each FCCM measure (even if it contained more than one sign of that measure), and by expressing each FCCM score as a percentage of the subject's total number of responses (Total R). Thus, the subject's main overall FCCM score consisted of the number of her responses containing one or more FCCM signs, divided by her Total R, and multiplied by 100; and each of her eight main measure scores consisted of the number of her responses containing one or more signs of that measure, divided by Total R, and multiplied by 100. In addition, a second set of scores was computed for six measures, controlling productivity in the special categories of Rorschach responses that were pertinent to those measures, that is, the categories that were potential carriers of signs. For example, the pertinent category of responses for Measure 7, Active Human Movement (human or humanlike percepts in active kinds of movement), was the subject's total number of human movement (M) responses (both active and passive), since Measure 7 could occur only in M responses. Thus, the Measure-7 score controlling

---

* The complete manual of the Rorschach Female Castration Complex Measure, the instructions for its use, and the description of its rationale, have been deposited with the American Documentation Institute. Order Document No. 8532 from ADI Auxiliary Publications Project, Photoduplication Service, Library of Congress, Washington, D. C. 20540. Remit in advance $2.75 for microfilm or $7.50 for photocopies and make checks payable to: Chief, Photoduplication Service, Library of Congress.

for productivity in the pertinent category of Rorschach responses consisted of the number of responses containing active M, divided by the total number of responses scored M, and multiplied by 100; whereas in the main Measure-7 score, the number of active M was divided by Total R. Scores controlling for FCCM-pertinent productivity were not necessary in the case of Measures 4 and 8, since these measures could occur in any responses. For each FCCM measure, all scores (fifty-one subjects) were dichotomized at the median, and the chi-square value (corrected for continuity) of the difference between the groups was determined. For the sake of consistency, all tests of significance were one-tailed. In order to obtain a measure of the degree of relationship between the homemakers-career women dichotomy and the FCCM scores, Φ coefficients were computed for all chi-square values.

RESULTS

Main findings. The main findings were the results for the overall FCCM scores, the measure for the overall intensity of the female castration complex, taking all the specific scores into account. As Table 22–2 (scores controlling for Total R) indicates, the career women were significantly higher in overall FCCM scores ($p < .001$). A second analysis using the FCCM scores controlling productivity in FCCM-pertinent responses yielded similar results (see Table 22–3). The research hypothesis was thus supported.

Although both groups of subjects were psychologically "normal" as defined by the criterion of never having received psychiatric treatment, this was obviously a very crude criterion. It was possible, therefore, that the two groups differed widely in general disturbance or maladjustment, and that it was this difference that accounted for the overall FCCM difference (since many FCCM signs were by definition signs of disturbance). In order to investigate this possibility, a measure of general disturbance, or disturbance independent of the female castration complex, was derived by considering only those responses that did not contain any FCCM signs and/or were not in the categories of responses pertinent to the FCCM. The percentage of these non-FCCM-pertinent responses that contained the same structural signs of disturbance used in the FCCM (such as F-) was the score for general disturbance. Comparison of the two groups on these scores showed no significant difference ($x^2 = 1.62$, p *ns*). Also, the correlation between the overall FCCM scores and the general disturbance scores, although positive, was not significant ($x^2 = 2.38$, $\Phi = .22$, p *ns*). These findings do not exclude the possibility that disturbance of a general sort was manifesting itself only in the FCCM, especially since the measure of general disturbance, which included only structural signs, was probably not as sensitive as the FCCM, which contained also stylistic and thematic signs. Never-

TABLE 22-2

Relationship between the Homemakers-Career Women
Dichotomy and the Individual FCCM Measures:
Scores Controlling General Rorschach Productivity

| Measure | Median | | x^2 | ϕ | p[a] |
	Home-makers	Career Women			
1. Female sex disturbance	0	0	.04	.03	ns
2. Male sex disturbance	1.8	5.4	3.36	.26	< .05
3. Difficulty assigning sex	6.3	5.3	.02	.02	ns
4. Phallic symbolism	4.0	6.6	2.38	.22	ns
5. Female general disturbance	5.3	8.9	4.43	.30	< .05
6. Male general disturbance	9.1	13.0	.97	.14	ns
7. Active human movement	7.1	13.2	4.43	.30	< .05
8. Achievement content	3.2	8.9	7.10	.37	< .01
Overall FCCM	28.0	50.0	18.88	.61	< .001

[a]One-tailed tests.

TABLE 22-3

Relationship between the Homemakers-Career Women
Dichotomy and the Individual FCCM Measures:
Scores Controlling FCCM-Pertinent Rorschach Productivity

| Measure | Median | | x^2 | ϕ | p[a] |
	Home-makers	Career Women			
1. Female sex disturbance	0	0	.04	.03	ns
2. Male sex disturbance	25	100	5.66	.33	< .01
3. Difficulty assigning sex	50	32	.95	−.14	ns
4. Female general disturbance	67	93	2.38	.22	ns
5. Male general disturbance	75	100	2.38	.22	ns
6. Active human movement	50	75	8.93	.42	< .01
Overall FCCM	80	122	19.15	.61	< .001

Note.—Measures 4 and 8 were not affected by FCCM-pertinent productivity.
[a]One-tailed tests.

theless, the findings with regard to general disturbance do suggest that the significant differences between the two groups on the FCCM probably could not be attributed to differences in overall level of adjustment.

Analysis of specific measures. When the eight individual measures were intercorrelated, only one of the resulting twenty-eight intercorrelations (that between Difficulty in Assigning Sex and Male Sex Disturbance) was significant in the predicted (positive) direction ($\Phi = .25$, $p < .05$). Since one significant correlation out of a total of twenty-eight could be due to chance, it was concluded that the eight measures were independent of each other.

Of the eight individual measures, four were significantly higher in the career women when the main scores (controlling for Total R) were used (see Table 22–2). The results were essentially the same when scores controlling for productivity in FCCM-pertinent responses were analyzed, except that one significant measure no longer differentiated significantly between the groups, while the chi-square values of two other significant measures increased (see Table 22–3). If only the more conservative findings are selected from both analyses, these results may be summarized as follows: three measures differentiated significantly between the groups, one at the .01 level (Achievement Content) and two at the .05 level (Male Sex Disturbance and Active Human Movement); five measures failed to differentiate significantly between the groups (Female Sex Disturbance, Difficulty in Assigning Sex, Phallic Symbolism, Female General Disturbance, and Male General Disturbance).

Analysis of structural, thematic, and stylistic signs. Since thematic and stylistic types of signs might be assumed to be more amenable to conscious control than structural ones, it was important to determine whether all three types of signs contributed to the significant findings. Therefore, within each of Measures 1, 2, 5, and 6, the signs within each type (structural, thematic, and stylistic, respectively) were combined, and each combination (with Total R controlled) was correlated with the homemakers-career women dichotomy. The mean correlation of the structural combinations over all four measures was then computed, and similarly, the mean correlations of the thematic and stylistic combinations. For each of these three types of combinations, the mean correlation with the homemakers-career women dichotomy was significant ($p < .05$). All three types of signs, then, contributed significantly to the results.

DISCUSSION

The major finding of this study was that a group of career women (not married, and in masculine occupations) showed significantly higher scores than a comparable group of homemakers (married, with children, and not employed) on a Rorschach measure for intensity of the female castration complex. On the assumption that the two groups of subjects represented two contrasting social roles or general styles of life, the one more masculine and the other more feminine, the study provides some support for the hypothesis that intensity of the female castration complex is significantly greater in women with a masculine social role than in those with a feminine social role. Also, some evidence is furnished for the validity of the Rorschach-based instrument that was developed to measure the complex.

In addition to the overall Rorschach measure of the complex, three of the eight individual components were also significantly higher in the group of career women: Penis Envy (envious, hostile, and/or fearful reactions to the male genitals); High Activity (energy, independence, and self-assertion); and High Need for Achievement (ambition and drive for status). In other words, the career women relative to the home-makers were found to be more active and assertive, more oriented toward status and achievement, and more disturbed in their reactions to male sexuality. These motivational variables seem quite consistent, in a common sense way, with the careers these women were engaged in as well as with their failure to marry.

The findings do not imply, of course, that a masculine social role is the only possible mode of expression of the female castration complex, or conversely, that all career women necessarily have a high intensity of the complex. The latter becomes clearly more doubtful, for example, in the case of career women who are married and/or working in feminine types of occupations. The ambition and vitality inherent in the pursuit of a career might, of course, be found in conflict-free femininity. Also, the failure to marry might stem from factors other than the castration complex, for example, overdependence upon a parent, neurotic inhibition, or a philosophical objection to the institution of marriage. Nevertheless, the study suggests that there is a relationship between some motivational variables that have been included in descriptions of the female castration complex, and a social role that involves remaining single and pursuing a masculine type of career.

The question might be asked, do the significant Rorschach differences between the two groups reflect factors that contributed to the different role choices, or consequences of those different social roles? The available data do not provide an answer to this question. It is possible, to mention only one example, that the career women failed to marry because of reasons irrelevant to the castration complex (e.g., rejection by the men of their choice), and then reacted with negative feelings about sex and a compensatory channeling of their energies into their careers (particularly since they were faced with the necessity of supporting themselves). This study points only to a relationship between certain motivational variables as measured by the Rorschach and the overt behavior of the research subjects.

Why did five of the eight components of the complex fail to differentiate between the career women and the homemakers? First, it is possible that the Rorschach measures of these five components were not as sensitive as the others, even though all eight Rorschach measures were derived in the same fashion. It is also possible that all the Rorschach measures were equally valid, but that no real differences obtained between the two groups of women with respect to the five nonsignificant components. That is, one might conclude that the masculine role behavior of the career women of the study (both with respect to their choice of occupation and their failure to become wives or mothers) is related only to the three significant components. Other groups of women such as homosexuals, women with functional gynecological disorders, discontented housewives, career women who are married or in feminine types of occupations, and neurotic or psychotic patients, might show higher scores on other specific measures of the complex.

This raises the question of whether the female castration complex can be viewed as a unitary variable. The absence of significant intercorrelations among the specific measures would argue against the idea of a unitary variable. If different aspects of the complex do not "hang together," but are correlated with different types of behavior, then the phenomena under discussion may be unrelated to each other. The results of this study, for example, could be explained simply in terms of differences between the two groups of women in heterosexual adjustment, activity level, and achievement drive, without invoking the castration complex as an explanatory concept. It is possible, on the other hand, that the absence of significant intercorrelations among the specific Rorschach measures might be due to the lack of precision of some or all of the measures. Further research would be necessary in order to investigate more fully whether and to what extent the various factors of the complex covary, and in order to determine how useful or parsimonious the construct of the female castration complex might be.

REFERENCES

1. ABRAHAM, K. Manifestations of the female castration complex (1920). In *Selected papers of Karl Abraham*. New York: Basic Books, 1954. Pp. 338–369.

2. BECK, S. J. *Rorschach's Test*. Vol. I. New York: Grune & Stratton, 1944.

3. BLOOMINGDALE, E. C. *Psychological aspects of essential dysmenorrhea*. Unpublished doctoral dissertation, Radcliffe Graduate School, 1953.

4. BLUM, G. S. A study of the psychoanalytic theory of psychosexual development. *Genetic Psychology Monographs*, 1949, 39, 3–99.

5. DEUTSCH, H. *The psychology of women*. Vol. I. New York: Grune & Stratton, 1944.

6. EISENBUD, R.-J. *Factors influencing the repudiation of femininity: A comparison of professional and homemaking women*. Unpublished doctoral dissertation, Radcliffe Graduate School, 1951.

7. FENICHEL, O. *The psychoanalytic theory of neurosis*. New York: W. W. Norton, 1945.

8. FRANCK, K., & ROSEN, E.   A projective test of masculinity-femininity. *Journal of Consulting Psychology,* 1949, *13,* 247–256.

9. FREUD, S.   Some psychological consequences of the anatomical distinction between the sexes (1925). In *Collected papers.* Vol. V. New York: Basic Books, 1959, Pp. 186–197.

10. FREUD, S.   Female sexuality (1931). In *Collected papers.* Vol. V. New York: Basic Books, 1959. Pp. 252–272.

11. FREUD, S.   The psychology of women. In *New introductory lectures on psychoanalysis.* New York: W. W. Norton, 1933. Pp. 153–185.

12. FRIEDMAN, S.   An empirical study of the castration and Oedipus complexes. *Genetic Psychochology Monographs,* 1952, *46,* 61–130.

13. HAYWARD, E. P.   Types of female castration reaction. *Psychoanalytic Quarterly,* 1943, *12,* 45–66.

14. HORNEY, K.   *The neurotic personality of our times.* New York: Norton, 1937.

15. HORNEY, K.   Feminine psychology. In *New ways in psychoanalysis.* New York: W. W. Norton, 1939. Pp. 101–119.

16. LANDIS, C.   *Sex in development.* New York: P. B. Hoeber, 1940.

17. LEVIN, R. B.   *The psychology of women: An empirical test of a psycho-analytic construct.* Unpublished doctoral dissertation, Syracuse University, 1962.

18. LEVY, D. M.   "Control-situation" studies of children's responses to the differences in genitalia. *American Journal of Orthopsychiatry,* 1940, *10,* 755–762.

19. MENNINGER, K. A.   Somatic correlations with the unconscious repudiation of femininity in women. *Journal of Nervous and Mental Disease,* 1939, *89,* 514–527.

20. SCHWARTZ, B. J.   An empirical test of two Freudian hypotheses concerning castration anxiety. *Jonrnal of Personality,* 1956, *24,* 318–327.

21. THOMPSON, C.   Cultural pressures in the psychology of women. *Psychiatry,* 1942, *5,* 331–339.

22. THOMPSON, C.   "Penis envy" in women. *Psychiatry,* 1943, *6,* 123–135.

This article is based upon a dissertation submitted in partial fulfillment of the requirements for the PhD degree at Syracuse University. The author gratefully acknowledges the generous assistance of several members of the department, in particular Edward J. Murray, committee chairman, and Howard Friedman.

23

Paul Cameron

Confirmation of the Freudian Psychosexual Stages Utilizing Sexual Symbolism

Interest in Freud's (9) hypotheses that ". . . all elongated objects, sticks, tree trunks, umbrellas . . . represent the male member—small boxes, chests, cupboards and ovens correspond to the female organ" (p. 242), coupled with the contention of psychoanalysts (7, 26) that individuals tend to prefer shapes representative of the sexual organs of the opposite sex has recently provided the impetus for a number of investigations. One line of inquiry has attempted to establish the existence of the sexual referent in shape perception. Among adults the validity of the sexual referent in perception seems fairly well established (13, 24, 25, 27, 16), while Levy (17) and Acord (1) have found no evidence of a sexual referent in the shape perception of children. On a different tack, McElroy (18) and Jahoda (11) have exploited the assumed opposite-sex-shape preference to test the sexuality of preadolescents and adolescents.

The present study was undertaken to test the following psycho-analytic notions simultaneously: Hypothesis 1: Children under the age of four, being in the oral and anal stages, will evidence little or no preference for shapes representatives of either sex; children aged four to six (in the phallic stage) will prefer shapes representative of the opposite sex; children aged seven to eleven or twelve will be attracted to shapes representative of the same sex; and children over the age of twelve (genital stage) will prefer shapes representative of the opposite sex (derived from Freud, 8). Hypothesis 2: As the U. S. is a male-oriented culture (19) opposite-sex attraction will be evidenced by a greater preference by females for masculine shapes after the latency period. Further, assuming that children in the phallic stage are largely incapable of discerning ascendency of the male sex in our culture, their choice of shapes should be made according to opposite-sex-shape preference without interaction with the cultural norm of male-preference.

Reprinted with permission of author and publisher: Cameron, P. "Confirmation of the Freudian Psychosexual Stages Utilizing Sexual Symbolism." *Psychological Reports*, 1967, *21*, 33–39.

METHOD

The twelve pairs of sex-related shapes described by McElroy (18) were reproduced on one side of a 8½x11-in. sheet of paper. The letters "A" or "B" were not printed under each figure as in the McElroy (18) and Jahoda (11) studies to avoid grade connotation or symbol-letter interaction. Considerable care was exercised in preparing the drawings to assume symmetry and good form of each figure.

The subjects (Ss) were 2,336 children approximately evenly distributed between the ages of three and seventeen from western Wisconsin. Most of the Ss aged five or younger were obtained via an area sample of Menomonie and its environs. The area was divided into approximately equal sections and a random-like process determined the area that each of the forty-two interviewers would sample. Individual Ss were typically contacted in the yard or in the home of randomly-selected residences. Ss were given a sheet of the sex-related shapes and asked to chose the shape in each pair that they preferred or liked the best with the cover story that we were studying design preferences among children. Where possible, S drew a circle around or otherwise indicated his preferred shape for each pair, if the child was unable to mark his choice the interviewer marked it for him. Additional Ss were contacted in nursery schools. Most Ss aged six or older were sampled in class in one of three school systems. The cover story introduced the request for each pupil to indicate on his sheet of shapes the member of each pair S preferred; Ss were instructed to work alone and not to compare choices. For S above the second grade age was self-reported; most of the younger Ss' ages were reported by a teacher or parent.

RESULTS

Hypothesis 1, that the psychosexual stages would evidence themselves in the shape preferences of children, was confirmed. Table 23–1 presents the sexual attraction indexed by sexual symbolism for each age for the twelve McElroy and six Jahoda items which significantly differentiated beyond the .10 level. Although the values of χ^2 are typically small, they are generally in a direction consonant with the prediction. Table 23–2 groups the data by psychosexual stages with clear confirmation of the hypothesis.

Hypothesis 2, that as the U.S. is a male-oriented culture opposite-sex attraction would evidence itself by a greater preference by females for shapes representative of the male sex after the latency period, while in the phallic stage both females and males would prefer shapes representa-

multiplied by the percentage of the sample represented by the opposite sex. Their male choices were 1,573 [e.g., 1,391 (.54) + 1,790 (.46)] and female choices were 1,543 [e.g., 1,509 (.54) + 1,584 (.46)], yielding a χ^2 of .29 (NS) which suggests equal attraction to the opposite sex.

Items 5 and 7 do not separate males from females in the phallic and/or genital stages for our sample and were among Jahoda's three most weakly discriminating items. But these were among McElroy's seven most differentiating items, leading one to suspect that each item contains age- and culturally-linked attractants as well as the sexual referent [see Lessler (16) for an elaboration of this notion].

DISCUSSION

When one considers the rather small differences between the overall anatomy of males and females one must be struck with the audacity of psychoanalysts in magnifying this difference into one of the major factors in our artistic (10) and aesthetic (26) tastes. That adults might be influenced by opposite-sex-organ appeal has not been too strenuously questioned, but that "innocent children" should be so influenced has brought many a scornful smile to the faces of laymen and has encountered no little opposition among psychologists (17, 1). Three previous studies utilizing children reported mixed results regarding application of Freudian symbolism to children. Levy (17) had fifth graders (i.e., ten- to eleven-year-olds) match female and male names to sex-related shapes. Finding no correspondence between the shapes and the gender of names chosen, he concluded that he had found evidence weighing against the Freudian hypotheses. Acord (1) had his Ss (third, sixth, and ninth graders) create generic names for symbolic designs and also observed no correlation between their matches. Lessler (16) required fourth and ninth graders to sort symbolic shapes into piles labeled "masculine" or "feminine" and found the children did sort according to the Freudian hypothesis. These three studies required their Ss to *sort* according to gender, a regimen somewhat different from the choosing of "preferred" vs. "nonpreferred", e.g., Jahoda (11) found that Ss were largely incapable of verbalizing why they preferred one or the other of a pair of designs; attraction is often considerably less consciously rational than sorting seems to demand. It will be noted that Lessler's study, which appears to have required less rational judgment than the other two investigations, yielded results consonant with the Freudian paradigm.

A major problem in designing the hypotheses to be tested was that of tying the Freudian psychosexual stages to age periods. The phallic stage was defined by Freud rather loosely, e.g., ". . . between the ages of three and eight . . ." (8, p. 286), which could be construed as three- to eight-

years of age or from four to seven. Cameron (4) regards the lower limit
as three years of age, while Coleman (5), English and Pearson (6),
Johnson and Medinnus (12), and O'Connor and Franks (22) regard the
lower limit as four. We adopted four as representing the majority and
more mature psychoanalytic opinion. The upper limit of the phallic
stage is also difficult to tie down. Freud contended that from ". . . about
the sixth or eighth year onward a standstill or retrogression is observed
in the sexual development called a *latency period* (8, p. 286). Johnson
and Medinnus (12) regard latency as starting at about the age of six,
Cameron (4) at about the age five, English and Pearson (6) at the age
of seven. We decided to define the beginning of latency at the midpoint
of Freud's estimate (i.e., at seven years of age) and that left us with
six as the upper limit of the phallic stage. The upper age limit of the
latency period is defined as eleven or twelve by Cameron (4), at ten by
English and Pearson (6), at eleven by Jones (14), until "just before
adolescence" by Johnson and Medinnus (12). We included the twelve-
year-olds in the latency period analysis for statistical convenience; however, their absence would have in no way affected the results. Thirteen
was judged the clear onset of adolescence and the genital stage. We must
admit to a good deal of 'luck' that the data fell so neatly into our expectations. Obviously, if the data had shown the predicted pattern but
at different ages, e.g., as the phallic stage being evidenced as between
three and five years of age, the essential validity of this aspect of
Freudian formulation would not have been harmed thereby.

We further confess to almost complete surprise at the results. The
author has not regarded himself as a Freudian and, before these results,
had considered the psychosexual stages hypotheses with distrust. Our
results could not have fit the Freudian paradigm better if they had been
manufactured (although the strength of the relationship is small considering the large numbers of Ss employed and the relatively modest
probabilities associated with the results obtained). The present study
sought to 'kill' two birds—the validity of Freudian sexual symbolism
and the kind of psychosexual stages in children—but confirms both.

REFERENCES

1. ACORD, L. D. Sexual symbolism as a correlate of age. *J. consult. Psychol.*,
1962, 26, 279–281.
2. BUSIA, K. A. Agni. *Encyclopedia Britannica.* Vol. 1. Chicago: Benton, 1963.
P. 330.
3. BUSIA, K. A. Ashanti. *Encyclopedia Britannica.* Vol. 2. Chicago: Benton,
1963. P. 567.
4. CAMERON, N. *Personality development and psychopathology.* Boston: Houghton Mifflin, 1963.
5. COLEMAN, J. C. *Abnormal psychology and modern life.* (2nd ed.) Chicago:
Scott, Foresman, 1956.

6. ENGLISH, O. S., & PEARSON, G. H. J. *Emotional problems of living.* New York: Norton, 1945.

7. FENICHEL, O. *The psychoanalytic theory of neurosis.* New. York: Norton, 1945.

8. FREUD, S. *A general introduction to psychoanalysis.* New York: Garden City, 1943.

9. FREUD, S. *The interpretation of dreams.* New York: Random House, 1950.

10. GROTZ, B. Erotische Symbole. *Z. f. Sex.-wiss, u. Sex.-pol.,* 1930, *17,* 226–232.

11. JAHODA, G. Sex differences in preferences for shapes: a cross-cultural replication. *Brit. J. Psychol.,* 1956, *47,* 126–132.

12. JOHNSON, R. C., & MEDINNUS, G. R. *Child psychology: behavior and development.* New York: Wiley, 1965.

13. JONES, A. Sexual symbolism and the variables of sex and personality integration. *J. abnorm. soc. Psychol.,* 1956, *53,* 187–190.

14. JONES, E. *The life and work of Sigmund Freud.* New York: Basic Books, 1955.

15. LESSLER, K. Sexual symbols, structured and unstructured. *J. consult. Psychol.,* 1962, *26,* 44–49.

16. LESSLER, K. Cultural and Freudian dimensions of sexual symbols. *J. consult. Psychol.,* 1964, *28,* 46–53.

17. LEVY, L. H. Sexual symbolism: a validity study. *J. conult. Psychol.,* 1954, *18,* 43–46.

18. McELROY, W. A. A sex difference in preference for shapes. *Brit. J. Psychol.,* 1954, *45,* 209–216.

19. McKEE, J. P., & SHERIFFS, A. C. The differential evaluation of males and females. *J. Person.,* 1957, *25,* 356–371.

20. MURDOCK, G. P. *Africa: its people and their cultural history.* New York: McGraw-Hill, 1959.

21. MURDOCK, G. P., TUDEN, A., & HAMMOND, P. B. Africa peoples. *Collier's Encyclopedia.* Vol. I. New York: Crowell-Collier, 1962. Pp. 254–270.

22. O'CONNOR, N., & FRANKS, C. Childhood upbringing and other environmental factors. In H. J. Eysenck (Ed.), *Handbook of abnormal psychology.* New York: Basic Books, 1961. Pp. 393–416.

23. SMITH, S. Age and sex differences in children's opinions concerning sex differences. *J. genet. Psychol.,* 1939, *54,* 17–25.

24. STARER, E. Cultural symbolism: a validity study. *J. consult. Psychol.,* 1955, *19,* 453–454.

25. STENNETT, R. G., & THURLOW, M. Cultural symbolism: the age variable. *J. consult. Psychol.,* 1958, *22,* 496.

26. THOULESS, R. H. *General and social psychology.* (2nd ed.) London: Univer. Tutorial Press, 1947.

27. WINTER, W. D., & PRESCOTT, J. W. A cross-validation of Starer's test of cultural symbolism. *J. consult. Psychol.,* 1957, *21,* 22.

The author is grateful for the assistance of Catherine C. Alberg, Helen L. Barmore, Alice L. Beihl, Jeanne L. Bonnefoi, Barbara Burkel, Joyce A. Christensen, Barbara L. Dickmann, Lynnette M. Ellis, Gayleen L. Felland, Gail A. Glanzman, John M. Grgurich, Michele S. Groves, Joanne Hillman, Janet K. Holsten, Elizabeth R. Huegel, Janet P. Hughes, Jean L. Kaiser, Carla J. Keipe, Patricia R. Kirchherr, Mary M. Lowe, Rita M. Mellor, Virginia C. Meloche, Norma Milanovich, Karen S. Mitchell, Lynette Moberg, Julie M. Olson, Jeanne Petersen, Maureen A. Pierick, Donna M. Rice, Margelyn A. Richardson, Sylvia Ann Rundle, Sharon C. Ryan, Betty J. Schuerch, Marilyn E. Stremer, Mary E. Sutliff, Carola E. Taylor, Pamela J. Weaver, Sally L. White, Mary Jo Udovich, Jane M. Young, Judy L. Ziebell, and A. M. Zielanis.

PART V

ORIGINS OF

HOMOSEXUALITY

Homosexuality was attributed by Freud largely to the individual's inability to master problems associated with the Oedipal period. He did refer to other possible etiological influences, such as constitutional predisposition, but operationally he focused on difficulties growing out of intrafamily dynamics. He traced homosexuality in the male to conditions that result in an unusually intense erotic attachment to his mother and a particularly distant or hostile relationship with his father. These conditions were said to intensify the boy's Oedipal conflict with his father and consequently to maximize his fear of being attacked by him (castration anxiety). They presumably arouse strong concern about the possibility of penis loss. It is this concern, said Freud, which prevents the individual from taking a woman as a love object. He is unable to tolerate the sight of the female genital because it lacks a penis and therefore reminds him of what could happen to him. In addition, he unconsciously equates any female love object with his forbidden, erotically charged relationship with his mother; and so is likely to re-experience in every heterosexual contact the guilt surrounding his Oedipal attachment to her. Freud hypothesized that when the male who is to become homosexual discovers he cannot safely love his mother (or any woman) "he identifies with her" and chooses to love others as she would. Quite defensively, he shifts so that he plays her role instead of taking her as a love object. Freud added that the homosexual adopts himself as the model of the kind of object his mother would prefer, and he favors sexually males who resemble himself. What is particularly important to him is that the love object possess a penis whose presence will help to allay castration fears. Freud underscored the male homosexual's exaggerated overevaluation of the penis, and indicated that he was really seeking as a love object a "girl with a penis."

In the instance of the female homosexual, Freud sketched an etiological theory which is a mirror image of what he worked out for the male homosexual. He proposed that the potentially homosexual woman is one who, upon turning to her father for a relationship during the Oedipal phase, encounters an unusual amount of frustration. This frustration presumably causes her to give him up as a love object and defensively to identify with him instead. This, in turn, results in her regressively turning again to her mother (and other feminine figures) as love objects. She is comfortable only about sexual contacts that involve women. Freud suggested too that a contributing factor to the orientation of many homosexual women is a longstanding "pronounced envy of the penis." The homosexual identity might be said to provide illusory compensatory male attributes.

Most of the scientific studies that have examined the validity of Freud's homosexual constructs have concerned themselves with whether his concepts of the family patterns that foster homosexuality do actually appear in the backgrounds of homosexual persons. There has also been a good deal of interest in whether castration anxiety is as prominent in the male homosexual as Freud specified. The papers compiled in this section are primarily directed to evaluating whether homosexuals have had relatively unique patterns of relationships with their parents that would fit Freud's hypothesis.

Evans (Selection 24) undertook a study in which he compared homosexual and heterosexual men in their responses to a questionnaire dealing with multiple aspects of parent-child interactions. His findings confirmed Freud's view that the male homosexual grows up in a family setting in which the mother is close, binding, and seductive, and the father distant and unfriendly.

Thompson et al. (Selection 25) evaluated both male and female homosexuals. Their findings with regard to the males were quite similar to those reported by Evans in the study just cited. They also found certain distinct parent-child patterns in the female homosexual, but their interpretation was complicated by the fact that Freud's theories of homosexuality as they apply to the female are less clear and explicit than those for the male.

Snortum et al. (Selection 26) looked further at the differences between male homosexuals and heterosexuals as defined by their replies to a questionnaire concerned with their feelings about their parents. The material obtained pretty well confirmed once again Freud's portrayal of the male homosexual's original relationship to his mother and father.

Chang and Block (Selection 27) tried to test Freud's idea that homosexuality in the male is based upon overidentification with mother and underidentification with father. They had male homosexuals describe themselves and also their parents by means of a series of adjectives. As compared to a control group of nonhomosexual men, they proved to identify more with mother and less with father. This pattern of results conformed to theoretical expectation. The positive tenor of the studies presented here accurately reflects what holds true in the relevant empirical literature. Within the limits of existing research efforts, Freud's views concerning the etiology of homosexuality (especially in males) tend to be supported.

Childhood Parental Relationships of
Homosexual Men

A major conclusion of a study comparing homosexual and heterosexual men who were all in psychoanalytic therapy was that parental roles are paramount in the etiology of homosexuality (2). Those authors described the "classical" pattern as one where the mother is close-binding and intimate with her son and is dominant and minimizing toward her husband, who is a detached (particularly a hostile-detached) father to the son. They concluded that any son exposed to that parental combination will likely develop severe homosexual problems. The Bieber study was based on extensive questionnaires completed by the analysts for each patient; the patients themselves were not aware of the study. Two series of questions proved especially useful in differentiating the homosexual and heterosexual groups, a Developmental Six Score (concerning childhood fears and activities) and a Twenty Questions Score (relating to interparental and parent-child relationships).

There is an obvious risk in generalizing findings from patients in psychotherapy to a nonpatient population. The purpose of the present study was to determine whether questionnaire items adapted from Bieber et al. would differentiate samples of heterosexual and homosexual men who had never sought psychotherapy.

METHOD

Subjects

The sample consisted of 185 American-born, Caucasian men between the ages of twenty-two and forty-seven, who had at least a high school education, had never sought psychotherapy, and were living in the Los

Reprinted by permission of the publisher and the author from *Journal of Consulting and Clinical Psychology*, 1969, 33, 129–135. Copyright 1969 by the American Psychological Association.

Angeles metropolitan area. All subjects (Ss) were volunteers in a study of cardiovascular disease, but only the 43 homosexuals knew that aspects of homosexuality were also being studied. The latter volunteered, as homosexuals, through the cooperation of a Los Angeles-based organization; they did not constitute a representative group of homosexuals. The 142 "heterosexual" Ss volunteered for the cardiac study through a number of sources, and there was no opportunity to develop the kind of rapport needed to elicit information about their sexual preferences and behavior. For purposes of this study, it was assumed they were all heterosexual, though there may have been homosexuals among them, which would tend to attenuate group differences.

The homosexual men ranged in age from 22 to 46, with a mean of 33.8 years ($SD = 7.1$); the heterosexuals ranged from 25 to 47, with an average of 39.3 ($SD = 4.4$), and the difference was significant ($t = 4.84$, $p < .001$). They were reasonably similar to patients in the Bieber study, where the homosexuals averaged approximately 35 and the heterosexuals approximately 38 years of age.

In education, the homosexuals ranged from 12 to 19 years, with a mean of 14.4 ($SD = 2.2$); and the heterosexuals ranged from 12 to 20 years, with a mean of 15.1 ($SD = 2.1$), with the difference approaching statistical significance ($t = 1.87$, $p < .10$). Again, they were relatively similar to the Bieber patients, who averaged approximately 15 years of education.

There was an obvious and expected difference between the two groups in marital status. Among the heterosexuals, 5% were single, 87% married, and 8% separated or divorced; 86% of the homosexuals were single, 5% married, and 9% divorced. In the Bieber et al. study, 8% of the homosexuals and 51% of the heterosexuals were married.

As to sibling constellations, there were 12%, 35%, 14%, and 40%, respectively, only, oldest, middle, and youngest children among the homosexuals; comparable figures for the heterosexuals were 8%, 28%, 27%, and 37%. Those distributions were not significantly different. Bieber et al, reported 10% of their homosexuals and 22% of their heterosexuals were only children, which difference was significant at the .05 level.

Proportionately more of the homosexuals were employed in clerical work and in the arts, and fewer of them in other professions, management, and sales work. The difference in heterosexual-homosexual occupational distributions was significant ($x^2 = 42.88$, $df = 5$, $p < .001$). The occupational classifications of the present Ss and the Bieber patients were fairly comparable.

The homosexual volunteers rated their sexual experience on a seven-point scale adapted from Kinsey, Pomeroy, and Gebhard (3), which ranged from entirely heterosexual to entirely homosexual. Of the forty-three Ss, 58% described their experience as having been exclusively homosexual, 35% as predominantly homosexual with incidental heterosexual, and 7% as predominantly homosexual but more than incidental heterosexual experience. For their homosexual patients, Bieber et al.

reported 68% as exclusively homosexual, 28% as having some hetero-sexual experience, and 4% as inactive, so that the proportion of exclusive homosexuals in the two studies was similar ($x^2 = .89$, $p = .50$).

The homosexual Ss also completed an eleven-item questionnaire de-signed to determine their sexual identification. In their overall feelings, forty Ss (93%) considered themselves moderately or strongly masculine, and responses to the other ten items also indicated essentially masculine identification. Bieber et al. reported that approximately 2% of their homo-sexual patients were "markedly effeminate," so that seemingly Ss from the two studies were similar in this regard.

Procedure

Each S completed a twenty-seven-item questionnaire adapted from Bieber et al. so as to be as nearly comparable as possible. The essential content of the questionnaire appears in Table 24–1. Included were the Developmental Six (Items 2–7) and Twenty Questions (Items 8–27) scores, and one additional question regarding physical make-up in childhood (Item 1), which had also differentiated the Bieber groups. Four possible choices were provided for each item, whereas the Bieber study used a yes-no dichotomy for all except three items. Following is an example from Bieber et al. completed by the analysts: "Was patient excessively fearful of physical injury in childhood? (yes/no)." The corresponding item modified for the present study, for completion by S himself, was: "During childhood, were you fearful of physical injury? (seldom/sometimes/often/always)."

Questionnaires were used in the analysis only where all twenty-seven items had been answered, which eliminated eleven potential Ss, one homosexual and ten heterosexual. Differences between groups were calculated by means of chi-square, with twofold classifications corrected for continuity.

RESULTS

The content of each questionnaire item is given in Table 24–1, together with the proportion of Ss responding in each category, and the signifi-cance of differences between the homosexual and heterosexual groups. Comparable figures from the Bieber study are also included, with the significance values calculated from figures in Appendix A (2) using only Ss for whom definite response was available. Differences between the Bieber groups reached at least the .05 level of significance for twenty-four of the twenty-seven items, and the other three approached signifi-cance. (Bieber et al. reported all items significant, and the discrepancy

TABLE 24-1

Questionnaire Content and Item Responses

Questionnaire Item	Bieber Study				Present Study			
	Response	Homo-sexual	Hetero-sexual	p	Response	Homo-sexual	Hetero-sexual	p
Physical make-up as a child	Frail	50	17		Frail	37	11	
	Clumsy	24	08		Clumsy	14	06	
	Athletic	13	33		Athletic	05	45	
	Well coordinated	13	42	.001	Coordinated	44	38	.001
Fearful of physical injury as a child	Yes	75	46		Seldom	23	49	
	No	25	54	.001	Sometimes	51	46	
					Often	19	04	
					Always	07	01	.001
Avoided physical fights	Yes	90	56		Always	56	12	
	No	10	44	.001	Often	30	35	
					Sometimes	14	46	
					Never	00	07	.001
Played with girls before adolescence	Yes	34	10		Never	09	03	
	No	66	90	.001	Sometimes	49	83	
					Often	40	14	
					Always	02	00	.001
"Lone wolf" in childhood	Yes	61	27		Never	12	38	
	No	39	73	.001	Sometimes	35	51	
					Often	42	11	
					Always	12	01	.001
Played competitive group games	Yes	17	64		Never	09	01	
	No	83	36	.001	Sometimes	65	15	
					Often	23	52	
					Very often	02	32	.001
Played baseball	Yes	16	64		Never	19	05	
	No	84	36	.001	Sometimes	70	29	
					Often	09	35	
					Very often	02	32	.001
Father and mother spent time together	Great deal	01	13		Great deal	16	28	
	Average	42	50		Considerable	53	39	
	Little	36	24		Little	26	23	
	Very little	21	13	.002	Very little	05	09	.23
Parents shared similar interests	Yes	20	38		Great many	21	30	
	No	80	62	.01	Several	37	32	
					Few	35	33	
					None	07	05	.70
Mother insisted on being center of son's attention	Yes	64	36		Never	30	18	
	No	36	64	.001	Seldom	37	63	
					Often	16	17	
					Always	16	01	.001
Mother "seductive" toward son as a child	Yes	57	34		Highly	07	00	
	No	43	66	.002	Moderately	07	03	
					Slightly	09	13	
					No	77	85	.02
Mother discouraged masculine attitudes/activities	Yes	39	17		Often	05	02	
	No	61	83	.002	Sometimes	21	07	
					Seldom	30	14	
					Never	44	77	.001
Mother encouraged feminine attitudes/activities	Yes	36	12		Never	53	87	
	No	64	88	.001	Seldom	21	11	
					Sometimes	21	02	
					Often	05	01	.001

Note.—Significance levels based on chi-square, with twofold classifications corrected for continuity. Decimals omitted.

TABLE 24-1 (continued)

	Bieber Study				Present Study			
Questionnaire Item	Response	Homo-sexual	Hetero-sexual	p	Response	Homo-sexual	Hetero-sexual	p
Mother considered	Yes	67	51		Strongly	28	11	
puritanical	No	33	49	.05	Moderately	33	35	
					Mildly	23	23	
					No	16	30	.04
Mother's relation-	Frigid	72	56		Frigid	12	00	
ships with father/	Not frigid	28	44	.04	Cold	26	23	
other men					Warm	63	77	.10
Mother allied with	Yes	63	40		Often	33	06	
son against father	No	37	60	.002	Sometimes	21	18	
					Seldom	16	35	
					Never	30	42	.001
Mother openly pre-	Yes	59	38		Always	12	01	
ferred son to	No	41	62	.005	Often	14	06	
father					Seldom	21	31	
					Never	53	61	.004
Mother interfered	Yes	37	25		Often	12	00	
with heterosexual	No	63	75	.08	Sometimes	16	08	
activities					Seldom	19	20	
					Never	53	71	.004
Son was mother's	Yes	52	36		Never	30	27	
confidant	No	48	64	.03	Seldom	19	32	
					Sometimes	23	36	
					Often	28	05	.001
Son was father's	Yes	08	29		Strongly	09	09	
favorite	No	92	71	.001	Moderately	16	40	
					Mildly	40	37	
					No	35	14	.005
Felt accepted by	Yes	23	48		Strongly	23	42	
father	No	77	52	.001	Moderately	35	42	
					Mildly	23	11	
					No	19	06	.006
Son spent time	Great deal	03	03		Great deal	02	08	
with father	Average	12	39		Considerable	09	39	
	Little	37	31		Little	53	32	
	Very little	48	27	.001	Very little	35	21	.001
Father encouraged	Yes	48	61		Often	26	41	
masculine atti-	No	52	39	.07	Sometimes	26	32	
tudes/activities					Seldom	23	21	
					Never	26	06	.002
Aware of hating	Yes	61	37		Never	28	59	
father as a child	No	39	63	.002	Seldom	19	20	
					Sometimes	37	18	
					Often	16	03	.001
Afraid father might	Yes	57	43		Often	14	04	
physically harm	No	43	57	.06	Sometimes	19	23	
him					Seldom	30	13	
					Never	37	60	.003
Accepted father	Yes	21	51		Strongly	26	51	
	No	79	49	.001	Moderately	28	37	
					Mildly	33	09	
					No	14	03	.001
Respected father	Yes	30	49		Strongly	37	56	
	No	70	51	.01	Moderately	21	32	
					Mildly	21	08	
					No	21	03	.001

may be due to the method used here of ignoring "No Answer" and "Not Applicable" categories in the calculation of chi-square.)

In the present study, homosexual-heterosexual differences were significant at the .05 level or less for twenty-four items, one other approached significance, and for two items no difference was found. Thus, despite the very different method of collecting data, the nonpatient status of the Ss, and (perhaps minor) differences due to geographical location, the results were remarkably similar to those reported by Bieber et al.

Specifically, in retrospect, the homosexuals more often described themselves as frail or clumsy as children and less often as athletic. More of them were fearful of physical injury, avoided physical fights, played with girls, and were loners who seldom played baseball and other competitive games. Their mothers more often were considered puritanical, cold toward men, insisted on being the center of the son's attention, made him her confidant, were "seductive" toward him, allied with him against the father, openly preferred him to the father, interfered with his heterosexual activities during adolescence, discouraged masculine attitudes, and encouraged feminine ones. The fathers of the homosexuals were retrospectively considered as less likely to encourage masculine attitudes and activities, and Ss spent little time with their fathers, were more often aware of hating him and afraid he might physically harm them, less often were the father's favorite, felt less accepted by him, and in turn less frequently accepted or respected the father. Unlike Bieber's patients, these homosexuals were no different from the heterosexuals in amount of time they estimated their parents spent together or in the interests shared by their parents.

In addition, a total score on the twenty-seven-item questionnaire was obtained for each S by weighting each item from zero to three points, with the higher weighting at the "masculine" end, so there was a maximum possible score of eighty-one. The scores of the homosexuals ranged from 9 to 64, with a mean of 42.9 ($SD = 11.6$); those of the heterosexuals from 36 to 77, with a mean of 57.3 ($SD = 9.2$). Though there was considerable overlap in scores for the two groups, the difference was highly significant ($t = 7.50$, $p < .001$).

DISCUSSION

The results could not be accounted for on the basis of sample characteristics other than sexual orientation; no relationship was found between age and questionnaire scores, and the same was true of marital status, occupational classification, and sibling constellation. The fact that the homosexuals knew homosexuality was being studied might have affected the results, but if there was any tendency to distort in the direction of "normal," it was not sufficient to obscure group differences.

As to preponderance of homosexual experience, no relationship was observed between Kinsey-type ratings (completed only by homosexual Ss) and questionnaire scores ($x^2 = 0.0$), perhaps because of the limited variation in proportion of homosexual experience. However, a product-moment correlation of .47 ($t = 3.41$, $p < .01$) was found between the twenty-seven-item questionnaire and the eleven-item sexual identity questionnaire; the homosexuals with more "desirable" family backgrounds tended to consider themselves as more masculine.

It may be noteworthy that the present results were so similar to those obtained by the Bieber group despite a major difference in the level of observation. In the present study, the data were based on retrospective self-reports of how they now view their childhood, by Ss who had never been in psychotherapy. The Bieber data, on the other hand, were based on psychoanalysts' reconstructions of patients' early life circumstances, derived from impressions during psychotherapy. Arguments could be advanced for the superiority of one method over the other, and certainly both have limitations. The agreement in results could be interpreted as evidence of validity in both methods, or perhaps as an indication that the two methods are not essentially different.

The results strongly suggested poor parental relationships during childhood for the homosexual men, at least as seen in retrospect; however, the etiological significance of such relationships, or even the etiology of the relationships themselves, is another matter. Bieber et al. considered the chances high that any son exposed to the parental combination of maternal close-binding intimacy and paternal detachment-hostility will develop severe homosexual problems. Nevertheless, only 28% of their homosexual patients had such a parental combination, and the 11% of their control patients who had such parents did not become homosexual. Furthermore, Bieber et al. very much underemphasized one-third of the "triad," the son himself. They reported that "each parent had a specific type of relationship with the homosexual son which generally did not occur with other siblings," and that son was the "focal point for the most profound parental psychopathology." As to why a particular son is singled out, Bieber et al. proposed that son is unconsciously identified by the mother with her own father or brothers, and the son thereby becomes the recipient of sexual feelings carried over from the mother's own early life. Similarly, the father transfers to that son his unresolved hostility and rivalry with his own father/brothers. The above is an oversimplified summary of the Bieber formulation, but it does not exaggerate the neglect of the son's contribution to the triadic relationship, beyond eliciting parental transference feelings.

The personalities and behavior of parents undoubtedly affect a child's personality, but some consideration must be given to the notion that the child's innate characteristics at least partially determine parental reactions and attitudes toward him. For instance, that the father of a homosexual son becomes detached and/or hostile because he does not understand or is disappointed in the son is just as tenable as that the son becomes homosexual because of the father's rejection. Similarly, that a mother may be more intimate with and bind her homosexual son more closely because of the kind of person he is, is just as reasonable as the idea that he becomes homosexual because she is too binding and intimate. Bieber et al. did question whether paternal rejection and hostility were stimulated out of feelings of disappointment and failure because of the son's homosexuality, but concluded that was not likely since only 17% of the fathers were reported to have been aware of the son's homosexuality. Surely most parental reactions crucially affecting the child's personality occur when the child is far too young to be labeled homosexual or heterosexual. The Bieber group also concluded that the father's attitudes were not traceable to the fact that the sons were inadequate and unattractive children, since the mothers did not find them so. That the mothers did not find these sons unattractive is no indication the fathers did not; the evidence suggests the fathers did find them unappealing.

Judging from experience with adult homosexual males, O'Connor (4) also refuted the idea that lack of a good father relationship was a consequence rather than a cause of homosexuality, on the grounds that that would make it difficult to account for the many homosexuals whose fathers were physically absent. Bene (1) rejected the notion that the lack of a positive father relationship might be due to the son repulsing the father rather than the father repulsing the son, and she cited O'Connor's reasoning. That homosexuality occurs in sons whose fathers are physically absent is irrelevant to the fact that when the father is physically present the relationship with the homosexual son is often a poor one. Furthermore, that homosexuality occurs in the absence of a father not only detracts from the etiological significance of a poor paternal relationship but in fact supports the importance of other causal factors (possibly such as innate physical/personality characteristics of the son).

Information was obtained relevant to another conclusion of Bieber and colleagues, who stated: "We have come to the conclusion that a constructive, supportive, warmly related father *precludes* the possibility of a homosexual son; he acts as a neutralizing, protective agent should the mother make seductive or close-binding attempts" [p. 311]. The questionnaire responses gave no full and complete answer as to whether these fathers were constructive, supportive, and warmly related, but there was evidence that the father relationship of some homosexuals was as good as that of many heterosexuals. A score was calculated for each S based on Items 20–27 in Table 24–1, all of which concern the father-son relationship. With 0 to 3 points possible for each item, the total scores for the homosexuals ranged from 0 to 22, with a mean of 11.7; and scores for heterosexuals ranged from 3 to 23, with a mean of

16.5. While the difference was significant ($t = 5.95$, $p < .001$), 16% of the homosexuals scored above the heterosexual mean, and 16% of the heterosexuals scored below the homosexual mean. Therefore, it would seem that a moderately good relationship, at least as reflected in the above questionnaire items, does not preclude the appearance of homosexuality, even though it is well established that a poor father relationship is common among homosexual sons. The responses for the Bieber homosexuals on the corresponding questionnaire items suggested their father relationships were poorer than those of the present homosexual Ss, which could merely reflect methodological differences, but more likely is related to the fact that the Bieber Ss had all sought psychotherapy, whereas none of the present Ss had done so.

In a similar fashion, two other questionnaire scores were calculated, one regarding mother-son relationships (Items 10–19) and the other pertaining to development (Items 1–7). With a maximum score of 30 on the 10 mother items, the homosexuals ranged from 4 to 29, with a mean of 18.8; the heterosexuals ranged from 13 to 29, mean 22.9. Although the difference was significant ($t = 5.39$, $p < .001$), 30% of the homosexuals scored above the heterosexual mean, and 12% of the heterosexuals scored below the homosexual mean. As to the seven developmental items, with a possible score of 21, the homosexuals ranged from 1 to 15, with a mean of 8.9; and the heterosexuals ranged from 6 to 19, mean of 14.3. That difference was most significant ($t = 10.39$, $p < .001$), and only 2% of the homosexuals exceeded the heterosexual mean, with 4% of the heterosexuals scoring below the homosexual mean. Of the three content areas, then, the developmental items clearly differentiated Ss best, with the father and mother items similar in their differentiation. The childhood behavior reflected in some of the developmental items, of course, is not unaffected by parents, but the findings suggest the possibility of something more fundamental in homosexuality than a poor father relationship.

The results of the present study agreed closely with those obtained by Bieber et al. but they neither supported nor refuted the Bieber conclusions as to causal relationships. The complicated problem of the etiology of homosexuality probably could be more productively investigated with a prospective study.

REFERENCES

1. BENE, E. On the genesis of male homosexuality: An attempt at clarifying the role of the parents. *British Journal of Psychiatry*, 1965, *111*, 803–813.

2. BIEBER, I., DAIN, H. J., DINCE, P. R., DRELLICH, M. G., GRAND, H. G., GUND-LACH, R. H., KREMER, M. W., RIFKIN, A. H., WILBUR, C. B. & BIEBER, T. B. *Homosexuality: A psychoanalytic study.* New York: Basic Books, 1962.

3. KINSEY, A., POMEROY, W. B., & GEBHARD, P. H. *Sexual behavior in the human male.* Philadelphia: Saunders, 1948.
4. O'CONNOR, J. Aetiological factors in homosexuality as seen in Royal Air Force psychiatric practice. *British Journal of Psychiatry,* 1964, *110,* 381–399.

This study was supported in part by the California Foundation for Medical Research. Appreciation is extended to Jessie Marmorston for supplying the heterosexual Ss, and to One, Inc., for their cooperation in recruiting the homosexual Ss. Computational aid was furnished by the Loma Linda University Scientific Computation Facility, supported in part by Ntaional Institutes of Health Grant No. FR 00276.

25

Norman L. Thompson, Jr., David M. Schwartz,
Boyd R. McCandless, & David A. Edwards

Parent–Child Relationships and Sexual Identity in Male and Female Homosexuals and Heterosexuals

Considerable attention has been focused on the psychological factors involved in homosexuality. Today, most students in the area realize that a homosexual adjustment has exceptionally complex determining components, but they agree that one profitable approach is the study of the relationship between parents and the prehomosexual child, especially as this affects the child's sex-role identification.

Few research workers have studied female homosexuality. Thus, little is known about parent–child interactions among prehomosexual females and the relations of these interactions with later sexual identity; and the little research that has been conducted is inconsistent in its results.

Looking at homosexuals in Britain, Bene (3) found no differences between female homosexuals and the heterosexual controls in their reported feelings toward their mothers. In contrast, Gundlach and Riess (12) found that homosexual females more often reported feeling neglected and ignored by their mothers, who had treated the daughters impersonally and, in many instances, without love.

The fathers of the homosexual females are more consistently seen in an unfavorable manner. Bene's (3) homosexual subjects (Ss) were more hostile toward and afraid of their fathers than the heterosexual females. The homosexuals also saw their fathers as weak individuals. Gundlach and Reiss (12) found that lesbians reported their fathers as less warm and affectionate and more indifferent, acting like strangers toward their daughters.

In a study of females in extended psychoanalysis, Kaye et al. (15) found no differences between homosexuals and heterosexuals in their early relationships with their mothers. Findings from this study, in which the data were supplied by the therapist, indicated a negative relationship of homosexuals with their fathers. The father of the lesbian was seen as a superficially feared and puritanical person whó was overly possessive of his daughter. In addition, he was seen as attempting to discourage her development as a female.

Results from these studies suggest that the father may be centrally involved in the early interpersonal dynamics of the prehomosexual girl. The role of the mother is much less clear. Certainly, much more systematic research must be done in this area, using a more diverse group of lesbians than those who, for the most part, were members of a homophile organization (3, 12) or in psychoanalysis (15).

In studies of family backgrounds among males, Bieber et al. (2) and Evans (10) found that more homosexuals than controls had a mother who was close-binding and intimate with her son and minimizing toward her husband. The typical father of homosexuals was detached and hostile in his relations to his son. This is considered the "classical" pattern. Likewise, Bene (3) found that compared with her controls, more of the male homosexuals were hostile toward their fathers and saw their fathers as weak. However, Bene found no differences between experimentals and controls in their perception of their mothers. Apperson and McAdoo (1) also found that the reported relationship between male homosexuals and their fathers was quite negative.

Responsibility for appropriate sexual identification in males is thought to rest most heavily on the father (18). Evidence for this is relatively clear (5, 6). Therefore, based on the findings of Bieber et al. (2), Bene (3), Apperson and McAdoo (1), and Evans (10), it appears that homosexual males should exhibit a greater degree of inappropriate sex-role identification than heterosexual males. Moreover, the more closely the parental relationships for *any* male approximates the "classical" pattern, the more inappropriate in his sex-role identification.

Chang and Block (7) supplied evidence that supports the notion that male homosexuals have inappropriate identifications. They compared a group of adequately functioning male homosexuals with controls on a measure of parent identification. The homosexual group checked more of the same adjectives than the control group when asked to describe "yourself" and "your mother" and fewer of the same adjectives when asked to describe themselves and their fathers. Chang and Block concluded that these homosexuals more strongly identified with their mothers and more strongly disidentified with their fathers than the controls.

Authors of the previously mentioned studies have either explored parental factors or some aspect of sexual identity without looking directly at the relationship between the two. The present studies are further investigations of the reported parent–child interactions among adequately functioning female and male homosexuals (22) and heterosexuals, and the relationship between these early interactions and sexual identity.

METHOD

Subjects

The homosexual Ss were volunteers who were recruited through their friends. The friends ("tester") distributed the test packets that were eventually returned anonymously to the first author. Most of the Ss lived in Atlanta, but approximately one-third were from other eastern states. Heterosexual controls were recruited in the same manner, with almost half obtained by the same individuals who tested the homosexual Ss. These heterosexual controls were from about the same geographical distribution, although more of them came from universities in the Atlanta area.

A homosexual was defined as one who perceived himself as homosexual and was known to one of the testers as a homosexual. A heterosexual was defined as any individual not known to a tester as a homosexual. Three male control Ss originally tested as heterosexuals identified themselves as bisexual or predominantly homosexual in feelings, and were dropped from the study. However, heterosexual Ss who admitted to some homosexual experience and/or feelings (15% of the female and 22% of the male control group) but who stated that they were predominantly heterosexual in sexual feelings were kept in the sample.

In a study of this type, it is not possible to speak rigorously of refusals since one does not know whether failures to return test packets were a function of the testers or the Ss. However, in an anecdotal sense, the authors know of only three refusals from male homosexuals, each coming from a legally married man. There were many more refusals from female homosexuals, including sabotage of test packets that had been gathered in a group situation. In order of difficulty in filling out the samples, easiest were the female controls, the male homosexuals, the male controls, and the female homosexuals.

All Ss were American-born and white. Homosexual and heterosexual Ss (84 female homosexuals, 94 female controls, 127 male homosexuals, 123 male controls) were matched for age, sex, and education. Demographic data are given in Table 25–1. As can be seen, the Ss were young, well-educated, and predominantly Protestant in religion.

Instruments

Parent–child interactions. The items adapted by Evans (10) from the Bieber et al. (2) study were used to measure parent–child interactions. Several of the Evans items refer only to either mother–child or father–child interactions. Each of these questions was repeated to measure the individual's interactions with the parent of the opposite sex. Therefore, there were forty-six items in all, seven relating to develop-

TABLE 25-1

Age, Education, Marital Status, and Religion

Variable	Female Homo-sexuals ($n = 84$)	Female Hetero-sexuals ($n = 94$)	Male Homosexuals ($n = 127$)	Male Hetero-sexuals ($n = 113$)
Age (in years)				
Range	17-48	18-48	18-51	17-54
M	28.60	26.99	28.06	27.43
SD	6.04	6.21	7.11	8.27
Education (in years)				
Range	9-21	12-20	11-28	11-24
M	15.68	15.63	16.06	16.56
SD	2.48	1.97	2.69	2.81
Marital status (in %)				
Single	75.0	32.9	91.3	43.1
Married	4.8	60.6	3.2	52.0
Divorced or separated	19.0	2.1	5.5	3.3
Divorced remarried	1.3	3.2	.0	1.6
Widowed	.0	1.1	.0	.0
Religion (in %)				
Protestant	54.8	68.1	56.7	60.2
Roman Catholic	11.9	8.5	11.0	8.1
Jewish	2.4	12.9	4.7	11.4
Orthodox	.0	2.1	.8	.0
Other	1.2	.0	.0	.0
None	29.7	8.5	26.8	19.5

ment, thirty-eight pertaining to parent—child interactions, and one question regarding the S's physical make-up in childhood. In all, twenty-five (14% of the female and 12.8% of the male) Ss failed to answer one or more of the questions, while ten females and five males omitted three or more. There were no homosexual—control differences here. No Ss were dropped from the study due to the omission of items on the questionnaire.

Sexual identity. Three different instruments were used to measure sexual identity. The first of these was the semantic differential. This measure was employed to assess the individual's *perceived parental similarity* and *perceived sex-role similarity.* Osgood, Suci, and Tannenbaum (20) posited a three-dimensional semantic space composed of the evaluative, potency, and activity dimensions found through factor analysis. The meaning of a concept is learned through an individual's experience and thus lies at some point in the semantic space on these three dimensions. Two concepts lying near each other in the semantic space are assumed to have similar meanings. Therefore, if the meanings of the concepts "myself" and "my father" are similar and "myself" and "my mother" are dissimilar, it is assumed that this individual perceives himself as similar to his father. Lazowick (16) and Dignan (9) have found the semantic differential to be a useful measure of perceived similarity.

The nine concepts and nine scales in the present study were those used by Lazowick (16) and Dignan (9). The degree of perceived similarity was defined in terms of the D score described by Osgood et al. (20). D is the difference in the scale positions for each concept as rated by the S (e.g., myself/man), squared, summed, and the square root taken. The larger the D score, the farther apart the concepts are in meaning.

The Adjective Check List Masculinity–Femininity scale (13) was used as an objective measure of sexual identity. Each masculine adjective checked was given a score of 1. Feminine adjectives were each scored as -1. The total possible masculinity–femininity scores on the Adjective Check List ranged from 28 to -25.

The third measure of sexual identity was the Franck Drawing Completion Test (11). This projective instrument, which has differentiated between males and females in all societies in which it has been used, has been scored reliably and validated in a number of studies (8, 17, 19).

Eleven of the thirty-six Franck test stimuli were found to discriminate best between males and females by Strodtbeck, Bezdek, and Goldhamer (21). In the present study, responses to these eleven test stimuli were scored by two psychology graduate students trained in scoring according to the criteria set forth by Bezdek and Madsen (4). A score of one was given if a drawing corresponded to a masculine criterion response. Feminine drawings were scored as zero. The maximum possible score was eleven. Using the training manual, the two scorers attained a reliability of .90 and .95, respectively. They graded all protocols for both the female and the male studies without knowledge of the sex or sex orientation of the Ss. The reliability between the two scores, based on 200 protocols selected at random from the two studies, was .93.

RESULTS

From the forty-six-item Parent–Child Interactions Questionnaire, thirty items distinguished between the female homosexual and heterosexual groups at the .05 level or less, of which seven were at the .001 level or less. The seven best discriminators, from first to seventh, were: (1) played baseball (more homosexuals *often* or *very often*; more heterosexuals *sometimes*); (2) physical makeup as a child (more homosexuals *athletic*, more heterosexuals *coordinated*); (3) played with girls before adolescence (more homosexuals *sometimes*; more heterosexuals *often* or *always*); (4) avoided physical fights (more homosexuals *sometimes* or *never*; more heterosexuals *always* or *often*); (5) accepted father (more homosexuals *moderately* through *no*; more heterosexuals *strongly*); (6) felt accepted by mother (more homosexuals *moderately* through *not at all*; more heterosexuals *strongly*);

and (7) father openly preferred child to mother (more homosexuals *always* and *often*; more heterosexuals *seldom* or *never*).

These seven most significant chi-square differences clearly provide the flavor of the developmental and parent–child questionnaire results for the female samples.

For the male samples, the same forty-six-item questionnaire yielded thirty-two chi-squares significant at the .05 level or less, twenty-seven of them being at the .001 level or less. The seven most discriminating items in order from the highest were: (1) played baseball (note that this was also the most discriminating item for the women, with homosexuals concentrating on *never* or *sometimes*; heterosexuals, *often* or *very often*); (2) played competitive group games (homosexuals, *never* or *sometimes*; heterosexuals, *often* or *very often*); (3) child spent time with father (homosexuals, *very little*; heterosexuals, *considerable* and *a great deal*); (4) physical makeup as a child (homosexuals, *frail*, *clumsy*, or *co-ordinated*; heterosexuals, *athletic*); (5) felt accepted by father (homosexuals, *mildly* or *no*; heterosexuals, *strongly*); (6) played with boys before adolescence (homosexuals, *sometimes*; heterosexuals *often* or *always*); and (7) mother insisted on being center of child's attention (homosexuals, *often* or *always*; heterosexuals, *never* or *seldom*).

The other items significant for males at the .001 level or less, all in the predictable direction, were: fearful of physical injury as a child; avoided physical fights; played with girls before adolescence; parents share similar interests; mother "seductive" toward child; mother discouraged masculine attitudes/activities; mother's relationships with father/other men (homosexuals, *frigid* or *cold*; heterosexuals, *warm*); mother allied with child against father; mother openly preferred child to father; child was mother's confidant; child was mother's favorite; mother encouraged masculine attitudes/activities; aware of hating father as a child; afraid father might physically harm the child; accepted father; and respected father.

The pattern that emerged for females is one of tomboyishness and feelings of maternal rejection and father overacceptance with, at the same time, rejection of the father. The classic pattern of feminine play interests, doubts of (or a feeling of "grace" about) own body, mother seduction, feelings of rejection by father, and rejection of father emerged clearly for the male homosexual group.

Only seven of the forty-six items discriminated for neither sex. They were: mother and father spent time together; mother considered puritanical; aware of hating mother as a child; afraid mother might physically harm the child; father insisted on being center of attention; father discouraged masculine attitudes/activities; and father considered puritanical.

In order to obtain a clearer picture of the background patterns of the various groups and to be able to relate them to the measures of sexual identity, the items from the Parent–Child Interactions Questionnaire were combined into three scales similar to those used by Evans (10). These three scales (Developmental, Mother, Father) were composed of the items that Evans used, with the exception of the physical make-up questions. This question was omitted from the Developmental scale used in the present study, and the question concerning playing with boys as a child that was included in the present Developmental scale was not a part of the Evans scale.

A score was obtained for each S by weighting each item from 1 to 4 points, with the higher weighting in the direction of the "classical" male homosexual pattern (2). Any item omitted by an S was given a neutral score of 2.5. The total possible score was 40 for the mother scale, 32 for the father scale, and 28 for the developmental scale. We realize that this scale may be more suitable for the male than for the female sample, but since this is an exploratory study for females, it seems profitable to employ the same measures. Additionally, the work of Bene (3), Kaye et al. (15), and Gundlach and Riess (12) with female homosexuals suggested that their backgrounds may be similar to those of male homosexuals as far as father–child relations are concerned.

The results for these three scales are given in Table 25–2. As a group, the female homosexuals are more similar than the heterosexual control Ss to the "classical" male homosexual pattern in relation to their parents. In this pattern, the mother is close-binding and intimate with her child and dominant and minimizing toward her husband. The father is detached and hostile to the child. However, the lesbian is not similar to the "classical" male pattern in that the male homosexual describes himself as a lone wolf in childhood who played with girls, someone who was fearful of physical injuries and fights, and a nonparticipant in competitive games. The lesbian only fits this pattern in that she describes herself as a lone wolf.

TABLE 25-2

Means and Standard Deviations for the Ss for Mother, Father, and Developmental Scales from the Parent-Child Interactions Questionnaire

Variable	Female Homo-sexuals	Female Hetero-sexuals	t	Male Homo-sexuals	Male Hetero-sexuals	t
Mother						
M	21.99	19.95	3.19**	23.13	18.54	6.80***
SD	4.80	3.57		6.32	4.16	
Father						
M	16.80	15.14	2.43*	20.48	15.41	
SD	5.19	3.72		5.50	4.15	
Developmental						
M	14.10	16.56	5.21***	18.76	14.47	11.05***
SD	3.36	2.89		3.11	3.03	

*p < .05.
**p < .01.
***p < .001.

TABLE 25-3

Means and Standard Deviations for the Ss for Perceived Parental Role Similarity and Perceived Sex-Role Similarity

Variable	Female Homosexuals	Female Heterosexuals	t	Male Homosexuals	Male Heterosexuals	t
Mother						
M	4.90	4.52	3.82***	5.71	5.08	2.44*
SD	2.70	2.02		2.28	1.79	
Father						
M	6.28	5.25	2.69**	6.15	4.45	5.90***
SD	2.97	1.97		2.53	2.00	
Woman						
M	4.80	4.05	2.56*	5.97	4.97	3.65***
SD	2.11	1.76		2.55	1.71	
Man						
M	5.94	5.09	2.37*	5.14	4.15	3.51***
SD	2.49	2.26		2.56	1.85	

Note. High scores are less similar to the concept.
*p < .05.
**p < .01.
***p < .001.

Measures of Sexual Identity

Perceived similarity. Several measures of sexual identity were given in order to look at the Ss' present sexual identity. One of these was the semantic differential, which was used as a measure of perceived parental and sex-role similarity. The means and standard deviations of these measures are given in Table 25–3. They are expressed in terms of D scores (distance scores), so that the higher the score, the less similar the individual perceives herself or himself to that particular parent or sex role.

From Table 25–3, we can see that both female and male homosexuals are more distant from both parents, as well as from males and females in general, than are heterosexuals. In contrast the results of Chang and Block (7), who used a different measure of closeness to parent, the male homosexuals here did not see themselves as closer to one parent than to another ($t = 1.49$, $df = 252$) nor did the female homosexuals ($t = .36$, $df = 166$). As expected, heterosexual females perceived themselves as closer to their mothers than to their fathers ($t = 2.51$, $df = 186$, $p < .05$); and the heterosexual males perceived themselves as closer to their fathers than to their mothers ($t = 2.60$, $df = 244$, $p < .01$).

While both homosexual groups saw themselves as more distant from both sex roles than was true for the heterosexuals, homosexual and heterosexual females saw themselves as closer to the female than to the male role, and both groups of males saw themselves as closer to the male than to the female role (all $ts < .01$).

The picture that emerges for both homosexual males and females, then, is one of distance, perhaps alienation, from people in general. These females and males see themselves as equally distant from both their mothers and fathers. They perceive themselves to be closer to their biological sex in general than to the opposite sex. However, they are more distant from both than the same-sexed heterosexual groups.

Correlations between the Mother, Father, and Developmental scales from the Parent–Child Interactions Questionnaire and the perceived similarity scores are given in Table 25–4. Interestingly, there were no significant relationships among these variables for female heterosexuals. Female homosexuals who scored high on the Mother scale (assumed to indicate a close-binding, intimate mother) were more distant from men in general. Homosexual females who were high on the Father scale (presumably a hostile, detached father) were more distant from the concepts of father, women, and men. Lesbians who scored high on the Developmental scale (indicative of a passive, feminine, lone-wolf woman) saw themselves as more distant from both parents and males in general.

For the male groups, both homosexuals and heterosexuals who

TABLE 25-4

Correlations between the Mother, Father, and Developmental Scales from the Parent-Child Interactions Questionnaire and Perceived Similarity

Variable	Female Homo-sexuals	Female Hetero-sexuals	Male Homo-sexuals	Male Hetero-sexuals
Mother scale with				
Mother *D*	.04	.14	.17	.19*
Father *D*	.16	.09	.31**	.25**
Woman *D*	.01	−.12	.30	.01
Man *D*	.22*	−.03	.15	.12
Father scale with				
Mother *D*	.11	.01	.23**	.13
Father *D*	.41***	.20	.40***	.33***
Woman *D*	.25*	.11	.05	.11
Man *D*	.34**	.02	.19*	.15
Developmental scale with				
Mother *D*	.28*	.02	.13	.04
Father *D*	.35**	.07	.38***	.25**
Woman *D*	.17	.03	.00	−.05
Man *D*	.31**	.03	.38***	.23*

*$p < .05$.
**$p < .01$.
***$p < .001$.

scored high on the Mother scale were more distant from their fathers, and such heterosexuals were also distant from their mothers.

Homosexual and heterosexual males who scored high on the Father scale were more distant from their fathers, and the heterosexuals were also more distant from their mothers and from males in general. Although none of the correlations was very high, it is interesting that a reported negative relationship with either parent is related to perceiving the father as dissimilar from oneself for both groups of males.

Both male homosexuals and heterosexuals who did not engage in activities considered masculine in childhood were more distant from both their fathers and males in general. If this distance indicated alienation, such a relationship is reasonable given the American approval (especially by fathers) of boys who engage in competitive sports, with a resulting isolation of boys who do not.

Adjective Check List. The Adjective Check List Masculinity–Femininity scale was used as an objective measure of sexual identity. The female homosexuals scored more masculine than the heterosexuals (at $< .01$), and the male heterosexuals as more masculine than the homosexuals (at $< .05$). Correlations of Adjective Check List scores with other measures employed in these studies followed no consistent pattern, and were generally so low as not to be useful in predictive context.

Franck Drawing Completion Test. The Franck Drawing Completion Test was used as a projective measure of sexual identity. A score of zero is most feminine, a score of eleven is most masculine. There was no significant difference ($t = 1.42$, $df = 176$) between the female homosexuals' mean of 5.79 and the female heterosexuals' mean of 5.36. Male homosexuals scored 5.78, male heterosexuals 5.63. t for this difference was nonsignificant. The Franck test was not related to any other measure employed in these studies.

DISCUSSION

To the authors, the most striking features of the studies of male and female homosexuality reported here are (1) the prominent role played by weak and/or hostile fathers in the etiology of homosexuality for both women and men; (2) the lack of a clear role of mothers in female homosexual etiology but the striking role of mothers in the etiology of male homosexuals; (3) the clearer etiological pattern that emerges for male homosexuals; (4) the alienation from mothers, fathers, and "people" that characterized both female and male homosexuals; and (5) the extensive developmental and parent–child relations overlap between the homosexual and heterosexual sample of both sexes.

To us, these data suggest the need for a strong male figure to reinforce feminine-role adoption in the developing female child in our culture as it is now constituted. Our findings seem to support Johnson's (14) theory of sex-role development for females. As our culture is now arranged (or was for this young adult population), the mother as a female model "does not seem to be enough." An "instrumental father figure" also appears to be needed.

The picture for males seems quite clear from the present data and fits surprisingly well with data from two other very different populations (2, 10). From all three samples, we have the picture of a modal seductive mother working against maleness in her son, and a weak and/or rejecting and hostile father who discourages modeling on himself and who is also very likely consistently undercut by his wife as his son moves through childhood.

Alienation, lone-wolfishness, and a psychology of difference characterize both male and female homosexuals in this sample. This "difference" psychology may also play a part in determining their sex-role adjustment—given inadequate models (plus sabotage of the model for the modal male homosexual), do homosexuals simply move sexually in the direction of the most easily perceived similarity—biological similarity—so that the female homosexuals loves other females, the male homosexuals other males? Alienation from their peers may also have cut off influence by models who, for more socially involved children, powerfully reinforce heterosexual identification. Finally, it should be emphasized that there is much overlap in the sample: many female and male homosexuals come from backgrounds that seem ideally suited for heterosexual development, and vice versa.

REFERENCES

1. APPERSON, L. B., & McADOO, W. G., JR.   Parental factors in the childhood of homosexuals. *Journal of Abnormal Psychology,* 1968, 73, 201–206.
2. BIEBER, I., DAIN, H. J., DINCE, P. R., DRELLICH, M. G., GRAND, H. G., GUNDLACH, R. H., KREMER, M. W., RIFKIN, A. H., WILBUR, C. B., & BIEBER, T. B.   *Homosexuality: A psychoanalytical study.* New York: Basic Books, 1962.
3. BENE, E.   On the genesis of male homosexuality: An attempt at clarifying the role of the parents. *British Journal of Psychiatry,* 1965, 111, 803–813.
4. BEZDEK, W., & MADSEN, B. A guide for scoring sex-role identity from a brief version of the Franck Drawing Completion Test. Chicago: University of Chicago, Social Psychology Laboratory, 1970. (Mimeo)
5. BILLER, H. B.   Father absence and the personality development of the male child. *Developmental Psychology,* 1970, 2, 181–201.
6. BILLER, H. B. & BORSTELMANN, L. J.   Masculine development: An integrative review. *Merrill-Palmer Quarterly,* 1967, 13, 253–294.
7. CHANG, J., & BLOCK, J.   A study of identification in male homosexuals. *Journal of Consulting Psychology,* 1960, 24, 307–310.
8. COTTLE, T. J., EDWARD, C. N., & PLECK, J. The relationship of sex role identity and social and political attitudes. *Journal of Personality,* 1970, 38, 435–452.
9. DIGNAN, M. H.   Ego identity and maternal identification. *Journal of Personality and Social Psychology,* 1965, 1, 476–483.

10. EVANS, R. B.   Childhood parental relationships of homosexual men. *Journal of Consulting and Clinical Psychology*, 1969, *33*, 129–135.

11. FRANCK, K., & ROSEN, E. A.   A projecitve test of masculinity-femininity. *Journal of Consulting Psychology*, 1949, *13*, 247–256.

12. GUNDLACH, R. H., & RIESS, B. F.   Self- and sexual identity in the female: A study of female homosexuals. In B. F. Riess (Ed.), *New directions in mental health.* New York: Grune & Stratton, 1968.

13. HEILBRUN, A. B., JR.   Sex role, instrumental-expressive behavior, and psychopathology in females. *Journal of Abnormal Psychology*, 1968, *73*, 131–136.

14. JOHNSON, M.   Sex-role learning in the nuclear family. *Child Development*, 1963, *34*, 319–333.

15. KAYE, H. E., BERL, S., CLARE, J., ELESTON, M. R., GERSHWIN, B. S., GERSHWIN, P., KOGAN, L. S., TORDA, C., & WILBUR, C. B.   Homosexuality in women. *Archives of General Psychiatry*, 1967, *17*, 626–634.

16. LAZOWICK, L. M.   On the nature of identification. *Journal of Abnormal and Social Psychology*, 1955, *51*, 175–183.

17. LIPSITT, P. D., & STRODTBECK, F. L.   Defensiveness in decision making as a function of sex-role identification. *Journal of Personality and Social Psychology*, 1967, *8*, 10–15.

18. McCANDLESS, B. R.   *Adolescents: Behavior and development.* Hinsdale, Ill.: Dryden Press, 1970.

19. MILLER, D. R., & SWANSON, G. E.   *Inner conflict and defense.* New York: Holt, 1960.

20. OSGOOD, C. E., SUCI, G. J., & TANNENBAUM, P. H.   *The measurement of meaning.* Urbana: University of Illinois Press, 1957.

21. STRODTBECK, F. L., BEZDEK, W., & GOLDHAMER, D.   Male sex role and response to a community problem. *Sociological Quarterly*, 1970, *11*, 291–320.

22. THOMPSON, N. L., McCANDLESS, B. R., & STRICKLAND, B. R.   Personal adjustment of male and female homosexuals and heterosexuals. *Journal of Abnormal Psychology*, 1971, *78*, 237–240.

26

John R. Snortum, John E. Marshall, James F. Gillespie,
John P. McLaughlin, & Ludwig Mosberg

Family Dynamics and Homosexuality

On the basis of data from an interview questionnaire applied to patients in psychoanalytic treatment, Bieber et al. (1) delineated a characteristic pattern of family dynamics which distinguished homosexual male patients from a group of nonhomosexual patients. The investigators concluded that their data

. . . provide convincing evidence of the importance of the Oedipus Complex in the etiology of homosexuality. Our material highlights the parental distortions of this phase of child development, as noted in the overcloseness and seductiveness of the H-mother and the hostility of the H-father (Bieber et al., p. 308).

Churchill (2) noted several methodological weaknesses in the Bieber research and was particularly critical of the sampling bias. The subjects (Ss) were predominantly college graduates holding high-income, professional, and managerial positions in the New York City area. It was further suggested that Ss seeking treatment may manifest extremes of psychopathology that would not be typical of the general homosexual population. Two-thirds of the homosexual group were exclusively homosexual with no history of bisexuality, and the majority of Ss in the experimental and control groups carried additional psychiatric diagnoses such as psychoneurosis or schizophrenia.

The Bieber research is also vulnerable to the criticism of observer bias. While the use of an interview questionnaire by a skilled clinician interacting with a patient in analytic dialog may be valuable in elucidating deep, underlying dynamics, this procedure also engenders greater risk that S's responses may be inadvertently influenced by the theoretical commitments of the interviewer. In this regard, Churchill (2, p. 266) alluded to the possibility that the Bieber study might be accurately described as a "report on the attitudes of psychoanalysts toward homosexual patients."

Another problem in using depth interviews for data collection is

Reprinted with permission of authors and publisher: Snortum, J. R., Marshall, J. E., Gillespie, J. F., McLaughlin, M. P., & Mosberg, L. "Family dynamics and homosexuality." *Psychological Reports*, 1969, *24*, 763–770.

that it is an expensive and time-consuming process and, consequently, data from nonpatients are seldom obtained. In cautioning against over-simplified views of causality in homosexuality, Marmor (8) clearly implies the need for population base rates on family interaction patterns.

The simple fact is that dominating and seductive mothers; weak, hostile, or detached fathers; and the multiple variations on these themes that are so often suggested as being etiologically significant in homosexuality abound in the histories of countless heterosexual individuals also and cannot therefore be *in themselves* specific factors (Marmor, 8, p. 5).

The present investigation was an attempt to build upon the work of Bieber et al. (1) but introduced three important changes in method. First, a less select homosexual population was studied. Ss were males who were being evaluated for possible separation from military service because of reported homosexual incidents. Second, the questions were presented by means of a paper-and-pencil inventory, thereby permitting Ss to describe family dynamics more directly, without the mediating interpretations of an interviewer. Third, the homosexuals' responses were compared with those of a nonpatient control group. In this study, then, the investigators, the methods, and Ss were drawn from outside of the circle of psychoanalytic practice.

METHOD

The Inventory

The items for the test, hereafter called the Brooke Developmental Inventory (BDI), were derived by a conversion of some of the statistically significant questions in the Bieber interview questionnaire into a form suitable for a self-administering test. Four basic scales (MS, FT, SC and TS) and two validity scales (L and C) are described below.

Mother-son Relationship (MS scale)—Mother is described as a strong and controlling woman (eight items) who offers an exclusive kind of closeness and intimacy to her son (six items). She is seen as a feminizing agent who tries to counter any masculine identifications (twelve items). Although she is seen as sexually puritanical, she is seductive in subtle ways and jealously guards her son from other women (eight items).

Family Triangle (FT scale)—Father is seen as distant from his son and is described as a weak, rejected, and rejecting family figure (nine items). The relationship of the mother and father is depicted as full of discord and lacking in warmth (ten items).

Self-Concept (SC scale)—S recalls childhood fears of injury and other preoccupations with health and illness (seven items) and remembers feeling weak, effeminate, isolated, nonaggressive, and noncompetitive (fourteen items).

Total Score (TS scale)—A total score was found by summating the individual scales and reflects the degree to which S has answered items in the direction predicted for homosexuals (1).

Lie Score (L scale)—The MMPI L scale (6) was included by permission of the publishers to serve as a check upon the response set of Ss (fifteen items).

Consistency Score (C scale)—Response consistency was measured by repeating ten items from the basic scales (ten items).

The test title and written instructions were intended to present the BDI in neutral terms as a survey of developmental experiences. None of the test items made direct reference to homosexual practices. It was decided not to incorporate the F scale from the MMPI because this would increase the length of the test by 64%. In addition, it was feared that the bizarre content of the F scale might lend pathological overtones to the BDI which could stimulate defensiveness in responding to the basic scales.

Evidently the BDI is not inordinately transparent as a measure of homosexual dynamics. After fifty-five college males had completed the test (fifty-one of them, for the second time), they were asked to speculate about the clinical purpose of the test. It was found that 64% of the Ss had accepted the test at face value as a survey of parent-child relationships. The homosexual implications of the items were recognized by 24% of the Ss, and 13% detected items pertaining to masculinity-femininity.

Subjects

Army psychologists at twelve testing centers in the United States and Europe were asked to administer the BDI to "bona fide, acting-out, male homosexuals" who were being evaluated by a military board for possible separation from service. Eight psychologists responded and contributed an average of 5.8 Ss to the total homosexual sample of 46 enlisted men. The average age of experimental Ss was 23.85 years ($SD = 2.56$) and average education was 12.10 years ($SD = 2.29$). The military control group was composed of 21 enlisted men in training at Brooke Army Medical Center, with mean age of 21.14 years ($SD = 2.56$) and mean education of 12.52 years ($SD = 2.07$). There were no significant differences between groups in educational level, but a t test of the age difference was significant ($p = .05$).

The relationship of age and education to the TS scale was examined by a Pearson r. The r of educational level with TS was .02 for the control group and .20 for the experimental group. Age correlated $-.35$ with TS for the control group and $-.32$ for the homosexual group. Only the last r was significant ($p = .05$). There is, therefore, little likelihood that any group differences found on the BDI would occur as artifacts of the influence of age and education upon score, for the slight predominance of older and less educated Ss in the homosexual group would actually work against the probability of obtaining more deviant scores.

A second control group was added to provide a comparison sample from another social and educational population. These Ss were sixty-eight males enrolled in introductory psychology in a midwestern, liberal arts college.

RESULTS

A test and two-week retest of the BDI were administered to fifty-one of the college males. It appears that test stability is adequate, for reliability coefficients ranged from .88 on the SC scale to .95 on the TS scale.

Table 26–1 contains the group means, standard deviations and t test comparisons of mean difference on each of the scales. Since there was evidence of heterogeneity of variance and positive skewness of the distributions, two-tailed t tests were applied and a formula was employed which did not pool sums of squares for a common estimate of population variance (4, p. 253). It will be noted that all of the basic BDI scales sucessfully discriminated the homosexual group from the two comparison samples at the .01 level.

On the L and C validity scales there were no differences between the homosexual and military control groups. There was a significant difference between the homosexual Ss and the college control Ss on the L and C scales, but it should be noted that the college and military controls also differed significantly from each other on the L scale.

TABLE 26-1

Means, SDs, and t *Values for Homosexuals, Military Controls and College Controls*

Scale	Homosexual Group (H) N = 46		Military Controls (M) N = 21		College Controls (C) N = 68		t		
	M	SD	M	SD	M	SD	H/M	H/C	M/C
MS	12.00	6.09	8.14	2.52	8.63	3.50	3.68†	3.39†	.69
FT	9.17	4.49	4.86	2.71	4.71	2.95	4.84†	5.94†	.18
SC	8.83	4.75	4.57	2.56	4.40	2.61	4.73†	5.75†	.27
TS	30.00	13.06	17.57	5.82	17.74	6.97	5.38†	5.84†	.11
L	3.63	2.25	3.14	2.03	2.12	1.68	.88	3.89†	2.10*
C	.78	.87	.71	.90	.46	.70	.29	2.13*	1.21

*p = .05.
†p = .01.

Apparently then, social and educational variables may produce some differences on the validity scales, but it does not appear that the basic BDI scales, themselves, are seriously affected. For this reason, the college and military control groups were combined into a single control group for the remainder of the statistical analyses.

An item analysis of the seventy-four items entering into the basic scales yielded fifty-one phi coefficient comparisons which discriminated the control and the homosexual Ss in the predicted direction. Of these, forty were significant at the .01 point and eleven others were significant at the .05 point. Only the following item was significant ($p = .05$) in the reverse direction. "My mother encouraged me to hit back if people pushed me around." More control Ss (78%) than homosexual Ss (59%) checked the item as false. Table 26–2 contains the ten items, in rank order, which showed the largest absolute differences in percentage of homosexual and control Ss responding to the items.

For each of the basic BDI scales, the scores for all Ss were combined into a single distribution and the first (Q_1) and third (Q_3) quartiles were calculated. Table 26–3 shows the percentage of control and homosexual Ss placing below Q_1 and above Q_3.

TABLE 26-2

*Ten Items Showing the Largest Percentage Difference
between Homosexual and Control Groups*

Item Number and Content	% Controls $N = 89$	% Homosexuals $N = 46$
84. I never got along very well with my father. (T)	7	57
63. I was much closer to my mother than my father. (T)	28	76
53. My dad and I spent very little time together. (T)	27	74
38. My mother and dad were interested in the same things. (F)	17	61
77. My mother and dad were happily married. (F)	8	52
69. When my parents fought, I usually felt my mother was right. (T)	19	61
92. I rarely participated in competitive sports like baseball. (T)	12	52
94. As a child I usually watched rather than participated in group games. (T)	9	48
26. I believe I was a pretty good athlete. (F)	34	72
4. I had a strong fear of physical injury as a child. (T)	9	46

TABLE 26-3

Percentage of Homosexual and Control Ss Falling below Q_1
and Above Q_3 *on the BDI*

Group	N	Percentage Below Q_1				Percentage Above Q_3			
		MS	FT	SC	TS	MS	FT	SC	TS
Controls	89	29	32	31	30	14	11	7	6
Homosexuals	46	17	12	13	15	46	52	59	61

DISCUSSION

It appears that the family dynamics for homosexual patients described by Bieber et al. (1) were confirmed almost in toto. The pattern of MS scale items for the present homosexual group is consistent with the classical picture of the "close-binding-intimate" mother. The SC items reflect long-standing feelings of physical and social inadequacy and may demonstrate the debilitating effects of early maternal overprotection upon the developing self-concept.

Discriminating items from the FT scale suggest a characteristic mother-father relationship in which the mother's point of view seems to be the more persuasive and powerful, but in which neither partner obtains emotional or sexual satisfaction within the marriage. They present a negative model to their son of the gains that can accrue from establishing a heterosexual relationship. Furthermore, it can be inferred that they would fail to help him build an effective repertoire of responses to enable him to express heterosexual intimacy even if he should some-day desire it.

In assessing the role of the father, Bieber et al. (1) concluded that "a constructive, supportive, warmly related father *precludes* the possibility of a homosexual son; he acts as a neutralizing agent should the mother make seductive or close-binding attempts" (p. 311). In the present study, striking evidence of the pivotal importance of the father is illustrated by the item showing the clearest percentage differentiation of groups in Table 26–3, "I never got along very well with my father." The item was checked by 57% of the homosexual sample and by only 7% of the control Ss. The third ranked item was, "My dad and I spent very little time together." It is obvious that conditions for establishing masculine sexual identification are lacking here, for as Kagan (7) stated, "identification is facilitated when the model is seen as nurturant to the child and powerful vis-a-vis the mother" (p. 150).

The scales appear to provide clear discrimination between groups.

However, in any study which employs psychological tests, it is appropriate to raise the question whether some other variable, such as response set, may be determining the scores. The use of the L and C validity scales offers some protection in this regard. It will be recalled that both control groups differed significantly from the homosexual group on the basic BDI scales, but that both military groups (homosexuals and controls) differed from the college sample on the validity scales. This suggests that scores on the basic scales are independent of response sets for defensiveness or inconsistency.

Another possibility is a response set to feign psychopathology. Several auxiliary considerations serve to reduce the concern that the homosexual group might have been heavily weighted with combat malingerers or raw recruits evading the draft. None of the Ss had been stationed in a combat zone. Seventy-five percent of the homosexual Ss carried the "RA" serial number prefix which means that they were not two-year draftees, but had volunteered for a three-year tour. Furthermore, most Ss had accumulated sufficient military rank to suggest a degree of investment in the service. Only three Ss were ranked E-1 (less than four months of service) and ten held the rank of E-5 or above (sergeant).

Several months after the BDI was administered, an attempt was made to establish the judgmental disposition of each homosexual case by the military board. Of the original forty-six cases, forty-one case files were retrieved. It was found that thirty Ss were separated from service and that eleven Ss were permitted to return to duty. It is assumed that in these latter cases the homosexual behavior was judged to be situational, poorly documented, minimal in degree, or controllable. The mean TS score for those who were separated was 32.60 ($SD = 13.22$) and the mean for those retained was 23.54 ($SD = 7.13$). A t test of the difference between means was significant at the .01 level. This parallels the findings of Doidge and Holtzman (3) that Air Force trainees who were rated as being exclusively homosexual obtained significantly higher MMPI scores than Ss who were merely implicated in isolated occurrences or in homosexual activities while intoxicated. The data on quartile placements (Table 26–3) were reanalyzed after omitting Ss who were returned to duty. A slight improvement in discrimination was noted in that there were now 12% of the homosexual Ss below Q_1 on the TS scale and 71% who scored above Q_3.

That some form of pathology was present even in Ss retained for duty is suggested by the fact that their TS scores were significantly higher ($p = .05$) than the military controls. If it can be assumed that return to duty reflects S's motivation and if these Ss nevertheless had higher scores than the military controls, then an attempt to account for group differences solely in terms of a motivational response set seems less persuasive. An unequivocal statement could be offered, however, only if there were some control for the possibility that scores might be elevated simply because S is under the stress of evaluation by a military board.

In conclusion, the present findings lend strong support to the earlier results obtained by Bieber et al. (1). It appears that the pathological interplay between a close-binding, controlling mother and a rejecting and detached father is not unique to the subculture of sophisticated, upper-middle-class families who engage psychoanalysts, for this family pattern was also identified in a less select sample of homosexual Ss. At the same time, however, the low BDI scores of the military and college control groups suggest that this pattern of relationships is not so common in occurrence as to be typical of families in the general population. In further research, it would be interesting to apply the BDI to other diagnostic groups. It seems probable that such dynamics are not specific to homosexuality, for the characteristics presently ascribed to the parents of homosexuals bear a striking resemblance to those that have been attributed to parents of schizophrenic patients (5).

REFERENCES

1. BIEBER, I., DAIN, H. J., DINCE, P. R., DRELLICH, M. G., GRAND, H. G., GUNDLACH, R. H., KREMER, M. W., RIFKIN, A. H., WILBUR, C. B., & BIEBER, T. B. *Homosexuality: a psychoanalytic study.* New York: Basic Books, 1962.
2. CHURCHILL, W. *Homosexual behavior among males.* New York: Hawthorne Books, 1967.
3. DOIDGE, W. T., & HOLTZMAN, W. H. Implications of homosexuality among air force trainees. *J. consult. Psychol.,* 1960, *24,* 9–13.
4. EDWARDS, A. L. *Statistical methods for the behavioral sciences.* New York: Rinehart, 1954.
5. FRANK, G. H. The role of the family in the development of psychopathology. *Psychol. Bull.,* 1965, *64,* 191–205.
6. HATHAWAY, S. R., & McKINLEY, J. C. *The Minnesota Multiphasic Personality Inventory.* (Rev. ed.) New York: Psychological Corp., 1951.
7. KAGAN, J. Acquisition and significance of sex typing and sex role identity. In M. L. Hoffman & L. W. Hoffman (Eds.), *Review of child development research.* Vol. 1. New York: Russell Sage Foundation, 1964. Pp. 137–167.
8. MARMOR, J. (Ed.) *Sexual inversion: the multiple roots of homosexuality.* New York: Basic Books, 1965.

Appreciation is expressed to the various clinical psychologists who assisted in gathering these data, and to Lt. Col. James Hedlund for his aid in information retrieval.

27

Judy Chang & Jack Block

A Study of Identification in Male Homosexuals

In discussing the etiology of male homosexuality, Freud (3) has written:

> The typical process . . . [in homosexuality] is that a few years after the termination of puberty, the young man, who until this time has been strongly fixated to his mother, turns in his course, identifies himself with his mother, and looks about for love objects in whom he can rediscover himself, and whom he wishes to love as his mother loved him. (p. 240).

According to Freudian theory, therefore, homosexuality in males is a manifestation of an identification with the mother figure rather than the usual identification with a father figure. As a consequence of his twisted identification, the homosexual seeks narcissistic rather than anaclitic love objects.

The purpose of the present study is to test a consequence of this notion, namely, that male homosexuality involves both a turning *toward* the mother as a figure with which to identify *and* the turning *away* from the father as an identification figure. Specifically, the major hypothesis of this investigation was that frankly homosexual males have a pattern of parental identification such that they are more strongly identified with their mothers and, conjointly, more strongly disidentified with their fathers than are males in a relevant contrast group. This conjoint hypothesis of course can be further partitioned into two separate hypotheses of interest, permitting comparison of the homosexual and nonhomosexual subjects (Ss) with regard to their *absolute* degree of identification with mother and with father figures. The two subhypotheses that follow from the major hypothesis are: (1) overt homosexual males, when compared to nonhomosexuals, will show a stronger identification with their mothers, and (2) overt homosexual males will show less identification with their fathers than will members of the control group.

The meaning of the Freudian term identification has been the subject of some controversy (5, 6). For research purposes, various operational

Reprinted by permission of the publisher and the authors from *Journal of Consulting Psychology*, 1960, *24*, 307–310. Copyright 1960 by the American Psychological Association.

translations of the concept have been employed. The operational meaning of identification adopted for the purposes of the present study is based upon the following statement by Freud (2): ". . . when a boy identifies with his father he wants to *be like* his father" (p. 90). According to Freud, at least in this late statement by him on the matter, identification with an object is said to have occurred when an individual strives to take on attributes which are those of that object as the individual perceives that object; this object is no more and no less than one's ego ideal— the object ". . . towards which it . . . [the ego] strives" (2, p. 92). In this study, then, a measure of the extent of identification with one's mother or father following directly from this conceptual definition was derived by finding the degree of correspondence between the attributes of one's ideal self, i.e., the person one would like to be, and the attributes of one's mother or father, as described by the identifier. The higher the degree of correspondence between one's ego ideal and one's parent, the greater the identification with that parent.

METHOD

Two groups of Ss were used. One group, the experimental group, consisted of twenty overt homosexual males. These Ss were engaging in homosexual practices, i.e., most of them were involved in homosexual marriages. None of these Ss were receiving or, with the exception of one, had ever received psychotherapy. Thus, all of these Ss appeared to have accepted their homosexuality, a most important and perhaps unusual property of this sample. Their cooperation to serve as Ss was obtained through personal and necessarily confidential channels. These Ss were aware that they had been asked to participate in the experiment because of their homosexual practices but had not been informed of the purpose of the experiment. A second group of twenty males from the same urban community and equivalent with respect to age and education was used as a contrast group. Eight of these Ss were married, and twelve were still attending college. The mean age of the homosexual males was 31.9 years with a range from 22 to 39, that of the contrast group, 29.7 years with a range from 22 to 39. The mean educational level was 14.5 years for the homosexual group and 14.9 years for the contrast group.

The measure of identification with parent was obtained through the use of a list of seventy-nine adjectives selected to permit a comprehensive personality description.* Each S was instructed to describe his "ideal self" by the use of the adjectives, marking an X if he felt that the adjective was particularly characteristic of his ideal self or an O if it was particularly uncharacteristic. The S was allowed to make only and

* A copy of this list of adjectives is available by writing to the authors.

exactly thirty Xs and thirty Os in order to avoid the confusions engendered by response sets (1). Following this description, S was required to describe, in the same manner, "your mother," "your father," and "yourself (as you see yourself)." In order to facilitate independence of the several descriptions, each object description was made on a separate page of the experimental booklet.

Of thirty-five booklets circulated into the available homosexual population, only twenty-two were returned. Of these, only twenty were found to be usable in the sense of being complete or correctly filled out. Data for the contrast group then was collected by distributing booklets among individuals who were similar to the homosexual group with respect to age and educational level. Of thirty-one individuals requested to participate in the experiment, only twenty-one were willing to do so. One of these twenty-one control Ss was arbitrarily eliminated from the subsequent data analysis in order to equalize the sample size. In view of the fractional returns from the populations sampled, the possibility of some kind of selective bias in the results should, of course, be recognized.

For each S, a mother-identification score and a father-identification score was obtained by comparing his description of his ideal self with that of his mother and with that of his father, respectively. For a given adjective, a score of one was given if it was marked X, O, or left unmarked on both the ideal-self- and parent descriptions. An identification score was obtained by summing the number of these correspondences between the ideal-self-description and the parent description. The separate mother- and father-identification scores thus derived were used to test the two subhypotheses. For the major hypothesis, that male homosexuality represents simultaneously an idealization of mother together with a disparagement of father, a derived score was obtained by subtracting for each S his father-identification score from his mother-identification score. The score distributions for the mother-identification and father-identification variables had quite equivalent means and standard deviations (40.7 and 11.3; 41.0 and 11.5, respectively). Accordingly, it was legitimate to calculate the derived score from the original data distributions without going to the trouble of standardizing the separate score distributions. Thus, this derived score would be high if an S's mother-identification score was high and/or his father-identification score was low. In addition, a self-acceptance score was obtained by comparing the ideal-self-description with the self-description, scoring for correspondence in the manner described above. These four scores provided the basic data for analysis.

For each comparison of interest, the Mann-Whitney Test (4) was used to calculate the significance of the difference between the scores obtained by the experimental and control groups. With the exception of the analysis of self-acceptance scores, all the statistical results reported in this study are based on one-tailed tests of significance because the direction of difference was predicted in advance.

RESULTS

For the homosexual group, the derived scores expressing the primary variable, i.e., distance between mother and father on S's identification continuum, are significantly greater (.001) than the derived scores of the contrast group. Some indication of the separation between the two groups on this variable is provided by the finding that fourteen of the twenty homosexuals have positive scores where only four of the twenty nonhomosexuals are on the positive side of zero. The primary hypothesis, that overtly homosexual males are relatively more strongly identified with their mothers than with their fathers, is therefore supported by this finding.

When the primary variable is partitioned into its components (the mother-identification score and the father-identification score) and separately analyzed, a better perspective is gained on the nature of the preceding finding. When a comparison of the mother-identification scores of the two groups is made, the homosexual Ss show a significantly greater degree of identification with their mothers. The difference between the sums of ranks of mother-identification scores of the two groups of Ss is significant at the .03 level. An analysis of the father-identification scores of the two groups of Ss shows a not quite significant but still appreciable trend in the direction of less identification with father by the homosexual group. The one-tailed test results in a p value of .07, almost reaching the conventional level of significance. From these separate and rather equivalent findings, it is clear that the striking separation between the two groups in the test of the first hypothesis is a *joint* reflection of the two constituent scores rather than being dominated by but one of these. This kind of result is both a subtle and a more interesting one.

Self-Acceptance

The homosexual and control groups did not differ significantly in their extent of self-acceptance, where self-acceptance is defined as the degree of correspondence between the perceived self and ideal self. It should be especially noted that there is no perceptible trend for the contrast group to be relatively more self-accepting, as indicated by the two-tailed p value of .64 for the obtained difference between the sums of ranks. This finding is a rather interesting one for it calls attention to the special nature of this homosexual sample as one *not* psychiatrically disturbed and apparently well-accepting of their homosexual activities.

Analysis of Ideal-Self-Descriptions

The results in the preceding analyses might have been due to differences between the kinds of ego ideals of the homosexual and control groups. For this reason, an item analysis of the adjective descriptions of the ideal selves of the two groups of Ss was done. Only two of the seventy-nine adjectives discriminated (at the .05 level) between the ideal-self-descriptions of the two groups. The conclusion is made, therefore, that the differential valuations by the homosexual Ss and control Ss of their parents are *not* due to different ego ideals. For the sake of completeness, it may be recorded that nonhomosexual Ss considered "sympathetic" as an attribute of their ideal self more frequently than did homosexual Ss. Homosexual Ss, more than control Ss, tended to deny the characteristic "dependent" as an attribute of the ideal self. No additional adjectives were found to discriminate when the threshold of significance was lowered to the .10 level.

Analysis of Self-Descriptions

Since the homosexual and control Ss did not differ in their degree of self-acceptance and in their ideal-self-descriptions, one might expect that they would also not differ in their self-perceptions. But if this expectation were to be realized, then some of our preceding findings become questionable. The reasoning behind this remark is that homosexuals and normals are quite obviously rather different sorts of people and, consequently, these differences should, if only on a priori grounds, be manifest if a reasonably sensitive instrument is employed. Failure to find these differences would be presumptive evidence of the technique's inadequacy, a conclusion that might also explain away the failure to find differences with respect to self-acceptance and ego ideals. On the other hand, it is possible, despite the failure of the self-acceptance and ideal-self-analyses to show differences, for the self-description analyses to separate the groups. This possibility arises because the self-acceptance for neither group is so high as to require (because of equivalent ideal selves) that the content of the self-descriptions be equivalent. With moderate correlations of self- with ideal-self-descriptions, the different dimensions of self-description are free to operate and, hence, be seen.

Item analysis of the self-descriptions of homosexual and control Ss finds six adjectives discriminating at the .05 level, with an additional six adjectives meeting the .10 criterion—results not accountable by a proper statement of chance significance.* Moreover, the discriminating adjectives are consonant with the concept of the homosexual male. Compared to control Ss, the homosexual male sees himself as "affected, dependent, determined, personally charming, restless, and *not* tactless"

---

* By reference to "a proper statement of chance significance," we are alluding to a recently developed recognition that conventional expectations of chance significance have been appreciably wrong rather often. In the situation where the response distributions of both groups being compared are highly skewed (or in the dichotomous case, are extremely unbalanced as in the present study), at the, for example, .05 level, many less than 5% of the findings will be significant when chance alone is operating. The logic underlying this assertion and some empirical findings are detailed in a manuscript available from the second author.

(all of these significant at the .05 level). The picture can be extended by noting that the homosexual tends to see himself as "impulsive" but not "frank" or "easily embarrassed" or "ambitious." Our homosexual males are less often "friendless or introspective or self-aware" than the control Ss, all of these last differences reaching the .10 level.

Although the discriminating characteristics cluster and portray someone with the personality traits usually associated with homosexuality in this culture, it is especially noteworthy that such adjectives as "confident, psychologically secure, relaxed, dissatisfied, helpless, worried" and the like failed to discriminate between the self-perceptions of the two groups.

DISCUSSION

The major hypothesis of this study, that frankly homosexual males more than control males show a positive identification with their mothers together with a disidentification with their fathers, has been supported by the results of this study. Subsidiary hypotheses have also been supported. What now shall we make of this finding?

Clearly, no one study is able to test the Freudian hypothesis, in all its complexities, about homosexuality. The present research does, however, in its limited way, support the psychoanalytic position. Additional studies, by the present and alternative methods, are required to investigate the multifaceted Freudian theory that the relatively strong identification with mother found in homosexual males has been preceded by and is the result of a strong fixation upon the mother, that the starting point of homosexuality comes quite discretely in adolescence, and that homosexuality represents a narcissistic object choice. Such a research represents an undertaking of a much larger dimension than the present one.

With respect to the present study, the unusual nature of the experimental sample used—self-accepting homosexuals—should especially be noted. Our results may well be an expression of the special character of this group. In more conflicted homosexuals, where identifications have been less decisively made, the presently obtained relationships can be expected to exist less strongly. One should find, among individuals with more ambiguity of identification, that there is less self-acceptance and more personal despair than was observed among the effectively functioning and well-received homosexuals studied in the present research.

SUMMARY

The present study was concerned with a test of the Freudian notion that homosexuality in the male is based upon an overidentification with the mother figure together with an underidentification with the father figure. Two groups of Ss, equivalent with respect to age, education, and socio-economic level, were used: a group of twenty males engaging, apparently successfully, in homosexual practices, and a group of nonhomosexual males. Each S described his ideal self, his mother, his father, and himself, by the use of a list of adjectives. On the basis of an "ego-ideal" conception of identification, various identification scores and a self-acceptance score were obtained for each S, by comparing his description of his ideal self with that of the other individuals he described.

As tested, the hypothesis was supported for it was found that overt homosexual males were more identified with their mothers and more disidentified with their fathers than were the nonhomosexual males with whom they were compared. In addition, it was found that the two groups of Ss did not differ significantly in their degree of self-acceptance nor in regard to the kind of ego ideal toward which they aspired. The findings were briefly discussed.

REFERENCES

1. CRONBACH, L. J. Further evidence on response-sets and test design. *Educ. psychol. Measmt.*, 1950, *10*, 3–31.

2. FREUD, S. *New introductory lectures on psychoanalysis.* New York: Norton, 1933.

3. FREUD, S. *Collected papers.* Vol. 2. London: Hogarth, 1952.

4. MANN, H. B., & WHITNEY, D. R. On a test of whether one of two random variables is stochastically larger than the other. *Ann. math. Statist.*, 1947, *18*, 50–60.

5. SANFORD, N. The dynamics of identification. *Psychol. Rev.*, 1955, *62*, 106–118.

6. STOKE, S. M. An inquiry into the concept of identification. *J. genet. Psychol.*, 1950, *76*, 163–189.

This investigation, part of a larger research project, was supported by research grant M-1078 from the National Institute of Mental Health of the United States Public Health Service.

PART VI

PARANOID DELUSION

FORMATION

One of the boldest of Freud's theoretical forays is his attempt to explain the nature of the paranoid delusion. His work in this area crystallized after he had read the autobiography of a German jurist (Daniel Schreber), who described in great detail his feelings, images, and perceptual distortions during a period of psychosis characterized by gross paranoid delusions. Freud analyzed Schreber's life situation at the onset of his paranoid ideas and concluded that these ideas represented a desperate defense against unacceptable, unconscious homosexual wishes. More specifically, he considered that the paranoid development had been precipitated by an upsurge of homosexual feeling directed toward Schreber's psychiatrist, who had treated him earlier for neurotic symptoms. Furthermore, he interpreted Schreber's homosexual attraction to this psychiatrist as a "transference" of the feelings he had originally entertained toward his father. He concluded, in essence, that Schreber's "illness" represented a "means of warding off a homosexual wishful fantasy." In his analysis of the developmental conditions presumably fostering a paranoid orientation later in men, he emphasized the importance of a poor relationship with the father during the Oedipal period. An unusually intense Oedipal confrontation with the father was said to generate overwhelming castration anxiety and a parallel fear of heterosexuality, and to lead to fixation in a role of submission to the father. That is, the paranoid learns to be fearful of the consequences of relating sexually to a woman and retreats to his father as a love object. This attraction to the father, stated Freud, is unacceptable to the paranoid and he strongly represses it. But later stressful circumstances can cause regression and a revival of the need to submit (homosexually) to father. This upsurge of homosexual wishes can have such alarming significance that it must be denied at any cost—even to the extreme of a paranoid reconstruction of the world. Freud conceptualized the paranoid persecutory delusion, which usually conveys the theme "That man hates me and persecutes me," as a projection and complete inversion of the homosexual idea "I love that man." The "I love" gets converted into "I hate" and, for further defensive safety, is "projected" onto the homosexually tempting object and seen as an intent emanating from him. It should be noted that Freud's formulation concerning paranoid delusions in women was exactly parallel. He stated that the female paranoid was likewise defending herself against unconscious homosexual fantasies and projecting them onto a woman who, despite being cast in a persecutory role, represented a sexual temptation.

With few exceptions, those who have embarked on the scientific appraisal of Freud's theory of paranoid phenomena have taken the view that it stands or falls in terms of whether paranoid schizophrenics display an unusual amount of concern or defensiveness about homosexual themes. They have used a spectrum of procedures for bypassing the paranoid's surface defenses and probing his reactions to homosexual stimuli. It would be a fair statement to say that a majority of such studies have given results congruent with Freud's hypothesis.

The papers comprising this section illustrate the considerable ingenuity that has been exercised in validating the propositions concerning paranoid delusion formation. Zamansky (Selection 28) exposed paranoid and nonparanoid schizophrenics to pictures of men and women and measured the amount of time they spent looking at each. The paranoids, as predicted by Freud's theory, exceeded the nonparanoids in showing more interest in the male than female pictures. This finding, as well as others, confirmed the presence of a special homosexual sensitivity in the paranoids.

Watson (Selection 29) compared the reactions of paranoid and nonparanoid schizophrenics when they were asked to compose a story about a picture with homosexual connotations. Evidence emerged that the paranoids were relatively more disturbed by the homosexual theme.

Daston (Selection 30) focused on the differential ability of paranoid and nonparanoid schizophrenics to perceive briefly exposed homosexual vs. nonhomosexual words. The results indicated that the two groups did differ significantly in their recognition speed for the homosexual references. They did not differ in their ability to perceive nonhomosexual terms.

Klaf and Davis (Selection 31) tested several hypotheses concerning the presence of homosexual concern in the clinical records of paranoids, as contrasted to those of nonparanoids. They did observe a significant tendency for the paranoids to evidence an unusual preoccupation with homosexual thoughts and wishes.[1]

Zeichner (Selection 32) used the Rorschach Inkblot Test and the

Thematic Apperception Test to evaluate differences between paranoids and nonparanoids in psychosexual identification. The results were complex, but one finding was that the paranoids tended to exhibit more femininity in their imagery than did the nonparanoids.

NOTES

[1] As we indicated in our book, *The Scientific Credibility of Freud's Theories and Therapy* (New York: Basic Books, 1977), questions can be raised about whether such preoccupation is supportive of or contradicts Freud's formulations about paranoids.

28

Harold S. Zamansky

An Investigation of the Psychoanalytic
Theory of Paranoid Delusions

The purpose of the present study was to investigate, using an objective, partially validated technique, the psychoanalytic hypothesis that people who suffer from paranoid delusions have strong but unacceptable homosexual urges. In addition, an attempt was made to study the nature of these impulses and of the defenses erected against them.

The psychoanalytic explanation of the dynamics involved in the development of paranoid delusions is that these delusions serve as defensive measures to enable the patient to handle a strong conflict over powerful but unconscious homosexual strivings. What happens is that the proposition "I (a man) love him" is converted by reaction formation into "I hate him." As further insurance that the homosexual wish will not become conscious, this second proposition is transformed, by means of projection, into "He hates me" (5). One should find, then, that persons with paranoid delusions have strong homosexual wishes, but that these wishes are not permitted existence on a conscious level. Psychoanalysts generally (2, p. 435) have felt that this formulation applies not only to pure paranoia, but also to cases of the paranoid type of schizophrenia.

In the five decades since this formulation by Freud, his views have been supported by many psychoanalysts (3, 15, 16, 17). Other analysts, while agreeing that the paranoid individual is characterized by powerful but unconscious homosexual conflicts, have suggested that homosexuality itself serves a defensive function in the development of the psychosis and is not the primary etiological factor (7, 9, 14, 18). Knight (9), for example, pointed out that the strong homosexual wish of the male paranoid is, in actuality, a very intense and desperate attempt to neutralize and eroticize a tremendous unconscious hate directed toward the father. The very powerful need to keep the homosexual urges from awareness is based not on cultural pressures which prohibit the expression of these urges, but on the fact that the least approach to the object arouses intense anxieties that both the object and the patient will be destroyed by the hostility in the patient and the consequent hostility aroused in the object. These theoretical positions were based on and supported by observations made by psychoanalysts in the usual analytic situation with their patients. The question must be raised, however, as to whether the setting of analytic therapy constitutes an adequate observational situation for the testing of an hypothesis. Psychoanalysts have at times been accused of finding in their patients the material they set out to find. Few attempts, for example, have been made by psychoanalysts to compare their findings with a suitable control group.

On the other hand, other investigators have attempted to test the psychoanalytic hypothesis using techniques other than the usual analytic interview and have varied widely in the degree to which their findings supported Freud's conclusions. The studies of Aronson (1), Gardner (6), Musiker (12), and Norman (13) were generally supportive. On the other hand, investigations such as those of Klein and Horwitz (8) and Miller (10) indicated that an intimate relation between paranoid delusions and homosexuality could be demonstrated for only a relatively small percentage of the cases studied.

Because of the conflicting and sometimes ambiguous results of the studies in this area and because of the lack of proper controls in many of them, it seems that the psychoanalytic hypotheses concerning paranoid delusions have yet to be adequately confirmed.

THE PRESENT STUDY

The necessity for obtaining a measurable expression of a need despite powerful forces which act constantly to inhibit its manifestation presented the most difficult practical problem in this study. In developing the technique employed in the present investigation, we began with the assumption that homosexuality is a function of a greater than usual attraction toward members of one's own sex and/or an active rejection of members of the opposite sex. From this it follows that if an individual with strong homosexual urges is placed in a situation in which there is an equal opportunity for attraction to either a member of his own sex or of the opposite sex, he should manifest by his behavior (if the task is appropriately disguised) a greater attraction to the member of his own sex, and a lesser attraction to the opposite sex, than would the heterosexually oriented person.

More specifically, given an appropriately disguised task, it was expected that if a series of pairs of pictures, each pair consisting of a picture of a man and of a woman, were shown, one pair at a time, to a man with strong homosexual needs, he would spend a larger proportion of the total exposure time looking at the male member of the pairs than would a person with less or none of these needs.

Given the further assumption that paranoid individuals are characterized by strong homosexual needs, the following hypotheses seemed reasonable:

Hypothesis 1: Men with paranoid delusions, when compared to men without these delusions, will manifest a greater attraction to males than to females.

Hypothesis 2: Paranoid men will manifest a greater avoidance of homosexually threatening stimuli than will nonparanoid men.

Hypothesis 3: Paranoid men, when compared with nonparanoid men, will express a greater preference for women and a lesser one for men as this expression becomes more explicit or conscious.

Hypothesis 4: Paranoid men, when compared with nonparanoid men, will manifest a greater attraction to males than to neutral (nonhuman) objects.

Hypothesis 5: Paranoid men will manifest a greater avoidance of women than will nonparanoid men.

The picture-pairs technique employed in the present study to test these propositions is based on the assumption that a person will manifest a preference for (or a rejection of) a particular kind of erotic object by looking more (or less) at it than at another kind of object. An initial attempt to validate this technique (19), using groups of normal and overt-homosexual males, suggested that it may be considered a valid reflector of object choice.

METHOD

Subjects

In the present study, two groups of subjects (Ss), all patients at the Boston State Hospital, were used. The experimental group consisted of twenty males, most of whom were formally diagnosed as either paranoid condition or dementia praecox, paranoid type, in all of whom the dominant clinical symptom consisted of delusions of persecution, of reference, or of grandeur. These Ss (as well as the controls) were selected on the basis of their psychiatrist's recommendation and of a thorough study by the writer of the individual case histories. The experimental Ss ranged in age from twenty-three to forty-five years, with a mean of thirty years. The range of the duration of their present hospitalization was from one month to two years, seven months, and averaged thirteen months. Sixteen of the twenty Ss had had a formal education consisting of some years of high school or better; twelve were or had been married. Twelve Ss had been engaged in skilled or highly skilled occupations, while eight had been working at relatively nonskilled jobs such as shipper and shoe worker.

The twenty control patients were selected with a view to their being as similar to the experimental Ss as possible, with the exception of the presence of a dominant paranoid picture. All of the control patients were formally diagnosed as belonging to one of the subtypes of dementia praecox other than the paranoid type. Their age ranged from nineteen to forty-two years and averaged thirty-three years. They had been hospitalized from two months to two years, nine months, with a mean of eighteen months. Eighteen Ss had had some high school education or better; only two had ever been married. Thirteen had been engaged in skilled or highly skilled occupations.

Experimental Measure

In the measure of latent homosexuality, twenty-four pairs of cards, each 9x12 inches, were used. On each card was pasted a picture cut from a popular magazine. The pictures were exhibited, a pair at a time, in a specially designed tachistoscope-like viewing apparatus, which permitted the undetected observation of the S's eye movements by an E seated at the other end of the apparatus. Three push-button-controlled timers, operated by E, recorded the total exposure time as well as the S's male-side and female-side fixation times for each pair of cards. The observation and timing were done for all the Ss by the writer. To insure against the E's learning the location of any particular picture, the left-right order of the cards was randomly changed after every three or four Ss.

Psychoanalytic theory states that though strong homosexual impulses are present in people with persecutory delusions, there are also ego defenses to prevent the emergence of these impulses into awareness. Thus, it is necessary in a technique of this sort that the Ss be as unaware as possible of the fact that they are exercising some selection regarding which picture in each pair they look at for a longer period of time. For this reason, the instructions to the S indicated that the experiment was a study of the perception of differences in size. He was told that he was to look carefully at each pair of pictures in the viewing apparatus and tell the E which member of the pair was larger, that is, which picture had the greater overall surface area. In actuality, both pictures in any one pair, with the exception of three pairs of neutral pictures (i.e., pictures without people, usually landscapes of some sort), were identical in area, although their shapes usually differed. The S was allowed to look at each pair of pictures until he felt ready to make a judgment of size. Thus, the exposure time of each pair was left entirely up to the Ss.

As has been stated, twenty-four pairs of pictures were used in the experiment. Of these, six pairs consisted of a picture of a man and of a woman in ordinary dress and position, and three pairs of two or more men and two or more women. Since the task was disguised, it was expected that, if the psychoanalytic formulation is correct, the experimental Ss would spend a greater proportion of the exposure time looking at the male member of each pair of pictures than would the control Ss (*Hypothesis 1*).

In addition to testing for a preponderance of homosexual tendencies in paranoid over nonparanoid persons, an attempt was also made to obtain a manifestation of the strong defensive measures which are said to come into play whenever the emergence of these impulses into consciousness is threatened. For this purpose, two measures were used: (1) Included in the twenty-four pairs of pictures were four pairs of male-female pictures in which the men were pictured in poses which would appear threatening to a person attempting to ward off unconscious homosexual impulses (e.g., two men kissing, two men dressed in towels in a locker room with one man resting his hand upon the other's thigh). The pictures of the females in these pairs were in ordinary pose, not intended to be threatening. In the case of these four pairs of pictures, it was expected that the experimental Ss would fixate less on the male and longer on the female member of each pair in an effort to avoid the threatening male pictures (*Hypothesis 2*). (2) After all the pictures had been presented once, the entire series was shown again, and this time the S was asked to state which picture of each pair he found more appealing—which appeared to attract him more. It was expected in the case of the paranoid S that, since the matter of preference was now presented to him on a much more conscious level, his defenses would manifest themselves in such a way that he would select significantly fewer pictures of males than he had favored by his fixation in the first part of the experiment (*Hypothesis 3*).

Besides investigating the presence of homosexual urges and defenses against them in paranoid individuals, some attention was devoted to the question of whether this homosexuality consists primarily of an attraction to men or a rejection of women. For this purpose, four pairs were included in the twenty-four pairs of pictures which consisted of a picture of a man and a neutral picture (one without any people), as well as four pairs which consisted of a picture of a woman and a neutral picture. It was considered that an attraction to males would be implied if an S fixated longer than did the control Ss on the male cards of the male-neutral pairs. Similarly, an avoidance of women would be implied if he looked longer than the control Ss at the neutral pictures of the female-neutral pairs (*Hypotheses 4 and 5*).

Finally, three pairs were included in which both pictures were neutral ones. These were used to lessen the chance that the Ss would become suspicious that it was their reactions to people that E was primarily concerned with. The order of the five different kinds of pairs was systematically varied throughout the entire series of twenty-four. Table 28–1 summarizes the kinds of pictures used.

All the pictures of people (men, women, and threatening men) used

TABLE 28-1

Description of Picture-Pairs

Kinds of Pairs	Number of Such Pairs
Male-female	9
Male-neutral	4
Female-neutral	4
Threatening male-female	4
Neutral-neutral	3
Total	24

in this study were selected from a group of about 175 photographs. The final selections were made from the ratings of five judges (advanced graduate students in clinical psychology). These judges were asked to rate all the male pictures along a four-point scale, in terms of the amount of threat they would have for a person defending against latent homosexual tendencies if he were shown the pictures in the context of performing an intellectual task. The pictures of women were rated according to the degree of threat they would have for a male S who is severely threatened by women as sexual objects. From these ratings, only those pictures upon which all five judges agreed closely were selected for inclusion in the experiment. The threatening male pictures were selected from those given a high rating on the threat continuum. The ordinary-pose male pictures (used in the male-female and male-neutral pairs) were taken from those rated as low in threat value. All of the female pictures were taken from the low end of the threat scale. The agreement of the five judges with one another on the threat value of the pictures finally selected to be used in the test was better than 90%.

Scoring Procedure

In the case of the nine male-female pairs of pictures, all the scores were expressed as the number of seconds spent looking at the male pictures minus the number of seconds spent looking at the female pictures. Such a score was obtained for each S on each pair of pictures. Then these scores were averaged (divided by nine) for each S across all male-female pairs. Finally, these individual mean scores were averaged (divided by twenty) for each group of Ss. Thus the final score (Mean Attraction Score) expresses in seconds the mean excess amount of time spent looking at the male pictures in the nine male-female pairs by all twenty Ss in any one group. This same general procedure was also followed in arriving at the Mean Attraction Score for the other types of picture pairs. In the four threatening male-female pairs, the four male-neutral pairs, and the four female-neutral pairs, the original scores were expressed as the number of seconds spent looking at the threatening male, ordinary male, and female cards, respectively, minus the time devoted to the female, neutral, and neutral cards respectively.

Comparison of Groups

The performances of the experimental and control groups on any series of picture-pairs (such as male-female or female-neutral) were compared by calculating the significance of the difference between the Mean Attraction Score earned by each group for that particular set of cards. The usual formula for the significance of differences between the means of two independent samples was used. Since the direction of differences was predicted in advance in the hypotheses, all statistical results reported were based on one-tail tests of significance.

Since the individual Attraction Scores for the two groups of Ss were in some cases not normally distributed, the results yielded by the t tests were checked against comparisons of the experimental and control groups by means of the Mann-Whitney test (and, in the case of *Hypothesis* 3, the Wilcoxon matched pairs test), a nonparametric measure which is independent of assumptions about the shape of the population distribution (11, pp. 314–317).

RESULTS

Hypothesis 1: Men with paranoid delusions, when compared to men without these delusions, will manifest a greater attraction to males than to females. The results summarized in Table 28–2 reveal that the paranoid Ss tended, on the average, to look 1.49 seconds longer at pictures of men in the nine male-female pairs. The score of −.70 for the nonparanoid schizophrenics indicates that these Ss averaged .70 seconds longer looking at the pictures of women. The difference between these two scores is significant at beyond the .001 level. The corresponding median scores for experimental and control groups were 1.47 and −1.03 seconds respectively, and the Mann-Whitney test of the difference between the two groups was also significant at less than the .001 level ($z = 4.37$). These results lend strong experimental support to psychoanalytic formulations and to frequent clinical reports that paranoid delusions are usually accompanied by homosexual tendencies.

Hypothesis 2: Paranoid men will manifest a greater avoidance of homosexually threatening stimuli than will nonparanoid men. This is one of the two measures by which it was attempted to obtain a manifestation of the defensive mechanisms which are said to prevent the homosexual impulses from entering awareness. It was expected that in the case of the four pairs containing the threatening male pictures, the

TABLE 28-2

Mean Attraction Scores (M.A.S.) and Significance Levels

	Types of Picture-Pairs				
	Male-female	Threatening Male-female	Male-neutral	Female-neutral	Neutral-neutral
M.A.S.: Experimental group	1.49	1.41	.56	−2.02	−.28
M.A.S.: Control group	−.70	.85	−.90	−.88	−.88
t	5.34**	.98	2.18*	1.46	1.28

*$p < .05$
**$p < .001$

experimental Ss would look less at the male and longer at the female pictures than would the control Ss. The second column of Table 28–2 shows that there was no significant difference between the Mean Attraction Scores of the two groups, i.e., the two groups did not differ in the proportion of time spent looking at the threatening male cards; thus, the prediction was not supported. Two possible reasons for this are that, (1) contrary to analytic theory, the paranoid person does not have a strong need to keep homosexually threatening material from awareness and (2) the threatening stimuli used in the experiment were, in fact, not sufficiently threatening to call forth an explicit avoidance reaction. While the data provide no definitive basis for choosing between these hypotheses, it will be seen from the discussion of *Hypothesis 3*, which follows, that the first of these explanations is highly untenable.

Hypothesis 3: Paranoid men, when compared with nonparanoid men, will express a greater preference for women and a lesser one for men as this expression becomes more explicit or conscious. The second technique employed in attempting to obtain a manifestation of the paranoid's defenses against the awareness of homosexual impulses was to compare his selection of female pictures, as indicated by the amount of time he spent looking at them in preference to male pictures, with his selection when asked explicitly to specify "Which do you prefer?" The evaluation of *Hypothesis 3* was based on the nine pairs of male-female pictures. Table 28–3 reports the results of comparisons for the experimental and control Ss. The figures in the first two rows of this table are group means and are based on raw scores which indicate the number of female pictures preferred by each S (either by verbal selection or by a longer fixation time than for the corresponding male picture) in the nine male-female pairs. Since each group was compared with itself, the calculation of t was based on the usual formula for the significance of differences between the means of two equated samples.

As Table 28–3 indicates, when the paranoid Ss were asked to state which picture they preferred, they selected a significantly greater number

TABLE 28-3

Verbal Preference vs. *Preference by Fixation*

	Experimental Group	Control Group
Verbal Preference	5.75	5.80
Fixation Preference	2.80	5.60
t	4.40**	.27

**$p < .001$

of women (and so, of course, fewer men) than they did when their preference was assessed by determining which picture they tended to look at longer (a much less explicit process). As a matter of fact, the mean of their verbal choices was almost identical with that of the control group. On the other hand, the control Ss displayed no meaningful difference between the number of male and female pictures selected by verbal choice and by fixation preference. A nonparametric analysis of these data, using Wilcoxon's matched pairs test, yielded similar results.

These results support the hypothesis that, when measured by a disguised technique, men suffering from paranoid delusions indicate a higher preference for males than do men without paranoid delusions; however, when the question of their choice is made more explicit, and so more conscious, defensive forces are set into motion which lower the expressed preference for males and cause this preference to approximate that of persons who do not suffer from paranoid delusions.

Hypothesis 4: Paranoid men, when compared with nonparanoid men, will manifest a greater attraction to males than to neutral (nonhuman) objects.

Hypothesis 5: Paranoid men will manifest a greater avoidance of women than will nonparanoid men. The present study has corroborated the psychoanalytic contention that men with strong paranoid delusions may be characterized by more powerful homosexual urges than those who are relatively free of these delusions. One may ask further, however, whether this homosexuality is characterized by a primary attraction to men as sexual objects or whether it reflects principally a reaction to a rejection of women. As Knight pointed out (9, p. 150), Freud's theory did not attempt to analyze the forerunners of the proposition, "I love him." In the present experiment an attempt was made to explore this question by the inclusion of four pairs of male-neutral and female-neutral pictures in the series of stimulus cards. The third column of Table 28–2 indicates that the experimental Ss showed a preference for the pictures of males (in the male-neutral pairs) that was significantly greater than that of the control group. On the other hand (fourth column, Table 28–2), while there was some tendency ($t = 1.46$) for the experimental Ss to reject the female pictures (in the female-neutral pairs) more than did the controls, this difference was not statistically significant. Similar results were obtained from an analysis of these data by means of the Mann-Whitney test: a statistically significant ($z = 1.97$) preference by the experimental Ss for the male pictures and a trend ($z = -1.34$) toward avoidance of the female pictures. While these results fail to support *Hypothesis 5* at an adequate level of statistical significance, the trend noted in the data suggests that the null hypothesis should be accepted with caution.

With this caution in mind, the present evidence indicates that the male paranoid is characterized by a strong attraction to men, without necessarily rejecting women as sexual objects.

The Neutral-Neutral Picture Pairs

The last column of Table 28–2 indicates that the experimental and control groups were not significantly differentiated by the three pairs in which neither picture was of a person. Since these pairs were included only to prevent the Ss' guessing the central focus of the experiment, no significant difference between the two groups was expected here.

DISCUSSION

The present experiment has corroborated the hypothesis that men with paranoid delusions are characterized by stronger homosexual needs than men who do not suffer from these delusions. The results of the attempt to demonstrate the presence of defensive measures that function to prevent these needs from entering the persons' cognitive field have been somewhat more equivocal. A comparison between the experimental and control groups' performance on the threatening male-female pictures yielded nonsignificant differences.

More conclusive evidence comes from the second technique employed to demonstrate defenses against awareness of homosexuality. Here the results indicated that when the purpose of the test was disguised, the paranoid's choice of males was significantly greater than that of the nonparanoid, *but* when the matter of his selection was made more explicit and, presumably, more conscious, his choices of males approximated those of the nonparanoid in the same situation. From these results it appears that when homosexual impulses threaten to approach consciousness, the ego fulfils its protective function by bringing about a reorganization of cognitive forces so that, at least on a superficial level, the paranoid individual functions via-a-vis objects of opposite sex in a manner approximating that of the nonparanoid person. It may be that in this suggestion lies one explanation of the discrepant findings of investigators in this area, i.e., it is likely that researchers have varied in the extent to which their techniques have evoked a defensive reaction in their Ss which tended to obscure their results. It is, perhaps, no coincidence that the greatest experimental support of the psychoanalytic hypothesis has come from those studies which made use of projective techniques. These techniques have the advantage of permitting the S to give evidence of certain needs without his being aware that he is doing so.

Though the present experiment has demonstrated a greater degree of homosexuality in men with paranoid delusions than in nonparanoid individuals, these results tell us nothing about the role which homosexuality plays in the development of these delusions. Is it, as Freud believed, the primary etiological factor, or it is merely a link in a chain of psychodynamic factors leading eventually to the development of delusions? The present experiment was not designed to answer this question directly. Nevertheless, it is possible to make a number of inferences from the pattern of the results.

These inferences are based upon a consideration of the nature of the paranoid's homosexual attraction. The results of the present experiment indicated that the experimental Ss displayed a clear-cut preference for male figures (male-neutral pictures). On the other hand, the data did not demonstrate conclusively that the male paranoid tends to avoid female figures. If one assumes, then, that paranoid men are characterized by an attraction to males without necessarily expressing a rejection of women, the following reasoning seems appropriate:

Freud, in his discussion of homosexuality, listed a number of possible etiological factors (4, p. 241 ff). Most of these suggest that the (male) individual turns to men as sexual objects as the result of severe anxiety incurred at the idea of relations with women. For example, the individual may not be able to tolerate the absence of the penis in his love objects, or he may fear castration by the female sex organ, or he may feel required to reject women because of his father's wrath. In all of these cases a rejection of women as sexual objects precedes the development of an attraction to men.

In this same paper (4), however, Freud went on to mention yet another origin of homosexuality. He pointed out that powerful aggressive impulses that could culminate in death wishes directed against male siblings might, "under the influence of training," yield to repression and transformation, so that "the rivals of the earlier period became the first homosexual love objects." Here, then, is an instance in which homosexuality may involve an attraction to men without being based on a prior rejection of women. Freud commented (4, p. 243) that this pattern "led only to homosexual attitudes, which . . . did not involve a horror of women." He was, however, careful to emphasize that this pattern might be typical only of homosexuals; he felt that, ". . . it is a complete contrast to the development of persecutory paranoia, in which the person who has before been loved becomes the hated persecutor, whereas here [in homosexuality] the hated rivals are transformed into love objects" (4, p. 242).

Knight (9), however, suggested that the paranoid's homosexuality is actually a defense against powerful aggressive wishes toward male figures. In this, Knight has, in a sense, applied to the homosexuality of the paranoid one of Freud's explanations of general homosexuality and has thus presented an integrated theory of paranoid dynamics, one that takes into account more recent developments in psychoanalysis. It should be noted, however, that while both writers were dealing with the management of intense hostility toward male figures, Knight's focus was upon the figure of the father, while Freud's was upon male siblings.

If one considers, in the present experiment, that the paranoid patients were characterized by an attraction to males without at the same time manifesting a rejection of women, such a pattern would be consistent with what one would expect if the homosexual attraction were a function of intense hostile feelings directed toward male figures. It is suggested, therefore, that the results of the present experiment support the view of paranoia presented by Knight, namely, that the person with paranoid delusions is indeed characterized by strong homosexual impulses, but that these impulses themselves serve a defensive function, that of helping to neutralize and eroticize powerful hostile wishes against male figures.

It is of interest here that in another study by the writer (19) in which the performances of male overt homosexuals and normal controls were compared on the set of picture-pairs employed in the present experiment, the homosexuals manifested *both* an attraction to male figures and a rejection of female figures, although the latter was not so clearly demonstrated as the former. While a comparison of the two experiments is not entirely justifiable because the Ss in the present study were somewhat older and of lower educational and socioeconomic status than the overt homosexuals, it is, nevertheless, tempting to speculate that the homosexuality which is characteristic of the overt homosexual may, in some degree, be of a different psychodynamic origin than that involved in the development of paranoid delusions. In contrast to the paranoid individual, the overt homosexual's choice of male objects appears to be, at least in part, a function of his inability to tolerate the anxiety aroused by erotic relations with women.

This way of accounting for the data is highly speculative and needs testing by further experiments. It does, however, lead to hypotheses that might serve as the basis for these experiments. One would expect, for example, that overt homosexuals would have less unconscious hostility toward men, or would be better able to handle their conscious aggressive feelings toward them, than would people with paranoid delusions. Again, one would expect overt homosexuals to be more sensitive to anxieties of castration by women and to regard them more as threatening figures.

The question of "choice of symptom" has always baffled students of psychopathology. In the area of the present experiment, theorists have been embarrassed by the question of why, given strong homosexual impulses, one person develops paranoid delusions and another becomes an overt homosexual. Perhaps the answer lies in different origins of the homosexual attraction. The person whose homosexuality serves as a defense against strong hostile wishes dares not risk intimate contact with other men. Therefore, there is a great need for him to develop a means of avoiding this, such as projecting his homosexual impulses away from himself or transforming them into another emotional guise. The person, however, in whose homosexuality a hatred for members of the same sex plays a less important role has less of an intrapsychic need to deny it and can afford to give direct expression to his homosexual impulses in his behavior.

SUMMARY

In this study an attempt was made to investigate the psychoanalytic theory that paranoid delusions are developed in an attempt to cope with powerful but unconscious homosexual urges. In addition, some aspects of the nature of these urges and of the defenses erected against them were studied. Two matched groups of Ss were used: a group of twenty hospitalized psychotic males (mostly diagnosed dementia praecox, paranoid type) in whom paranoid delusions were a dominant symptom, and twenty hospitalized schizophrenic males in whom paranoid symptoms were absent. The experimental technique provided for a measure of object choice as the difference in time spent looking at pictures of different kinds of (human) objects.

The following hypotheses were tested:

(1) Men with paranoid delusions, when compared to men without these delusions, will manifest a greater attraction to males than to females.

(2) Paranoid men will manifest a greater avoidance of homosexually threatening stimuli than will nonparanoid men.

(3) Paranoid men, when compared with nonparanoid men, will express a greater preference for women and a lesser one for men as this expression becomes more explicit or conscious.

(4) Paranoid men, when compared with nonparanoid men, will manifest a greater attraction to males than to neutral (nonhuman) objects.

(5) Paranoid men will manifest a greater avoidance of women than will nonparanoid men.

The results of the experiment supported the first, third, and fourth hypotheses at a statistically significant level. The paranoid Ss spent a significantly greater amount of time than did the nonparanoids in looking at the pictures of men in the male-female pairs and in the male-neutral pairs. When asked to express verbally their preference for pictures of men or of women, the paranoid Ss selected significantly fewer men than they had chosen by the less explicit fixation-time technique. A similar difference was not manifested by the control Ss.

These findings support the following conclusions:

(1) Men with paranoid delusions tend to have stronger homosexual impulses than male psychotics who are relatively free from these delusions.

(2) Men with paranoid delusions tend to avoid explicit or direct manifestations of homosexual object preference.

(3) The homosexuality of paranoid men tends to be characterized by a primary attraction toward men as sexual objects, and not necessarily by an avoidance of women.

The results of the present experiment also permit the following inferences which are, however, merely speculations at the present stage of investigation:

(1) The homosexuality of the male paranoid appears as an intermediary process in the development of his delusions, rather than being the primary etiological agent.

(2) One of the defensive functions which the homosexuality of the male paranoid serves is to help neutralize and eroticize powerful aggressive wishes directed toward male figures.

REFERENCES

1. ARONSON, M. L.   A study of the Freudian theory of paranoia by means of the Blacky Pictures. *J. proj. Tech.*, 1953, *17*, 3–19.

2. FENICHEL, O.   *The psychoanalytic theory of neurosis.* New York: W. W. Norton and Co., 1945.

3. FERENCZI, S.   On the part played by homosexuality in the pathogenesis of paranoia. In *Sex in psychoanalysis.* New York: Basic Books, Inc., 1950.

4. FREUD, S.   Certain neurotic mechanisms in jealousy, paranoia and homosexuality. In *Collected papers*, Vol. II. London: Hogarth Press, 1950.

5. FREUD, S.   Psychoanalytic notes upon an autobiographical account of a case of paranoia (dementia paranoides). In *Collected papers*, Vol. III. London: Hogarth Press, 1950.

6. GARDNER, G. E.   Evidence of homosexuality in one hundred and twenty unanalyzed cases with paranoid content. *Psychoanal. Rev.*, 1931, *18*, 57–62.

7. HENDRICK, I.   The contributions of psychoanalyisis to the study of psychoses. *J. Amer. med. Ass.*, 1939, *113*, 918–924.

8. KLEIN, HENRIETTE R., & HORWITZ, W. A.   Psychosexual factors in the paranoid phenomena. *Amer. J. Psychiat.*, 1949, *105*, 697–701.

9. KNIGHT, R. P.   The relationship of latent homosexuality to the mechanism of paranoid delusions. *Bull. Menninger Clin.*, 1940, *4*, 149–159.

10. MILLER, C. W.   The paranoid syndrome. *Arch. Neurol. Psychiat.*, 1941, *45*, 953–963.

11. MOSTELLER, F., & BUSH, R. R.   Selected quantitative techniques. In G. Lindzey (Ed.), *Handbook of social psychology.* Cambridge, Mass.: Addison-Wesley, 1954, 289–334.

12. MUSIKER, H. R.   *Sex identification and other aspects of the personality of the male paranoid schizophrenic.* Unpublished doctoral dissertation, Boston Univer., 1952.

13. NORMAN, J. P.   Evidence and clinical significance of homosexuality in 100 unanalyzed cases of dementia praecox. *J. nerv. ment. Dis.*, 1948, *107*, 484–489.

14. NUNBERG, H.   Homosexuality, magic and aggression. *Int. J. Psychoanal.*, 1938, *19*, 1–16.

15. PAYNE, C. R.   Some Freudian contributions to the paranoia problem. *Psychoanal. Rev.*, 1913–14, *1*, 76–93, 187–202, 308–321, 445–451.

16. PAYNE, C. R.   Some Freudian contributions to the paranoia problem (continued). *Psychoanal. Rev.*, 1915, *2*, 93–101, 200–202.

17. SHOCKLEY, F. M.   The role of homosexuality in the genesis of paranoid conditions. *Psychoanal. Rev.*, 1913–14, *1*, 431–438.

18. THORNER, H. A.   Notes on a case of male homosexuality. *Int. J. Psychoanal.*, 1949, *30*, 31–47.

19. ZAMANSKY, H. S.   A technique for assessing homosexual tendencies. *J. Pers.*, 1956, *24*, 436–448.

This paper is based upon a portion of a dissertation submitted to the Department of Social Relations, Harvard University, in partial fulfilment of the requirements for the degree of Doctor of Philosophy in Clinical Psychology. The writer is greatly indebted to Dr. Gardner Lindzey, who was principal advisor for this study and who was always liberal with advice, suggestions, and encouragement. In addition, the writer is grateful to Professor Henry A. Murray, who helped clarify a number of theoretical aspects of this experiment, and to Dr. Norman Livson, University of California at Berkeley, who was especially helpful during the developmental phases of the study.

29

Charles G. Watson

A Test of the Relationship Between Repressed
Homosexuality and Paranoid Mechanisms

PROBLEM

Freud (2) theorized that the etiology of paranoia begins with the presence of repressed homosexual tendencies, i.e., repression is strengthened by the use of one or more of four secondary defense mechanisms (projection, erotomania, megalomania, and delusions of jealousy) which produce the overt symptomatology of paranoid schizophrenia.

Several studies of Freud's theory have appeared in the literature. Gardner (3), Norman (10), and Klaf and Davis (7) have found evidences of homosexuality strikingly common among paranoid groups. Aronson (1) found higher incidences of Wheeler's (12) homosexual signs in the Rorschach protocols of paranoid schizophrenics than among normal or psychotic control groups. Grauer (4), after criticizing Aronson's method of selecting paranoids, compared the latter's control psychotics to a new group of paranoid schizophrenics and found differences between the means of the two groups on the three measures used by Aronson significant at the .20 level. However, Klein and Horwitz's (8) findings of reported homosexual behavior or cravings in only 20% of the clinical files of their paranoid population casts some doubt on Freud's contention.

Although several studies have suggested that paranoids show more homosexual tendencies of some sort than normal or psychotic controls, none have tested predictions derived from Freud's original contention that *repressed* homosexuality is the etiological variable behind most, if not all, paranoid schizophrenia. It was the purpose of the present project to test three hypotheses derived from this theory.

Because of their presumed repression of homosexual thoughts and wishes, it was hypothesized that paranoid schizophrenics would obtain

Reprinted by permission of the publisher from *Journal of Clinical Psychology*, 1965, 21, 380–384.

a lower mean score than nonparanoid schizophrenic controls on an objective, true-false scale of awareness of homosexual tendencies.

Secondly, it follows from his theory that homosexual stimuli are more threatening to paranoids than to nonparanoids. Therefore, it appeared that the response latencies of paranoids to Thematic Apperception Test (TAT)-type pictures with and without obvious homosexual content would differ from those of nonparanoid schizophrenics. It was expected that the former subjects would take a relatively longer time to respond to a homosexual picture than would members of the latter group and that the mean response latency ratio of homosexual to neutral cards would be greater among paranoids than among controls.

Thirdly, it was hypothesized that the paranoids, as a function of homosexuality-related tendencies toward feminine identification and interests, would produce a higher mean raw score on the relatively unthreatening Minnesota Multiphasic Personality Inventory (MMPI) Masculinity-Femininity (MF) scale than nonparanoid schizophrenics.

PROCEDURE

Subjects. All Ss were male schizophrenics under the age of fifty from the Veterans Administration Hospitals, Knoxville, Iowa, and St. Cloud, Minnesota. The experimental group consisted of twenty-seven patients diagnosed Schizophrenic Reaction, Paranoid type who had never carried another schizophrenic diagnosis, while controls were twenty-three schizophrenics who had never been diagnosed paranoid. Patients with history of lobotomy, other evidences of organicity, or more than twenty-five electroshock treatments were excluded from the study. Furthermore, no subject producing a raw score of more than seven on the MMPI L scale or more than sixteen on the F scale (both of which were administered as part of an inventory to be described below) was included because of the presumed relationship of higher scores on these variables to the invalidity of self-report scales. As a part of the inventory, the K scale of the MMPI was also administered as a measure of test-taking defensiveness. On this variable, the paranoids scored a mean of 15.26 while that for the controls was 12.00 ($t = 2.29$; $p < .05$). Since results of the study might be attributed to defensiveness, the data were analyzed with modified groups not differing in mean K scores. To this end, the four remaining paranoids with the highest K scores were eliminated. After this had been accomplished, the mean paranoid score was 14.13, which did not significantly differ from that of the control schizophrenics ($t = .94$, $.3 < p < .4$). At this point, there were twenty-three subjects in each group. These groups did not differ significantly (at the .05 level) with respect to mean age (37.13 years), education (10.73 years), total length of neuropsychiatric hospitalization(s) (36.83 months), Revised Beta IQ (100.15), or associated variances.

Tests. Homosexuality awareness scale (HA): The HA scale is a rationally-derived, locally constructed scale of twenty-three items, the content of which concerns the presence of homosexual thoughts and feelings. After its items had been chosen, it was administered to the groups as part of a mimeographed true-false inventory which also included the K, L, F, and MF scales, as well as twenty-seven filler items, from the MMPI.

Thematic pictures. Two pictures, one with a high level of homosexual content (homosexual card) and one with less rated homosexual content (neutral card) were employed in the study. These two cards had been selected from a set of fifteen plates, thirteen of which were taken from Murray's Thematic Apperception Test and two of which were especially drawn for possible use in this project. The fifteen cards had been presented to five student nurses who had had no previous experience with psychological tests and who had been asked to rate each plate on a nine-point scale of apparent homosexual content. The card with the highest mean rating (one of the custom-made cards) was designated as the "homosexual" card. Since general anxiety proneness is also a determinant of latency time, an attempt was made to choose a neutral card differing from the homosexual plate in homosexuality

TABLE 29-1

Ha Scale Items with Significant Scoring

1. I guess I am more attracted to men than most people. (T)
2. Sometimes I think I am physically attracted to other men. (T)
3. Sometimes I have sexual thoughts about boys and men. (T)
4. I have felt a great deal of affection for a man at one time or another. (T)
5. I once had some sexual relations with another person of my own sex. (T)
6. There is nothing unattractive about the bodies of men. (T)
7. I am very strongly attracted by members of my own sex. (T)
8. Sometimes I think I am a little bit homosexual. (T)
9. I sort of like to think about men in a sexual way. (T)
10. Physically, women are more attractive than men. (F)
11. I particularly like to take showers in large rooms with other men. (T)
12. Young boys are more attractive than young girls. (T)
13. I once was in love with another man. (T)
14. Homosexual thoughts sometimes come to my mind. (T)
15. Anyone who says I am homosexual in any way is wrong. (F)
16. I like to be with handsome men. (T)
17. I agree with some of the great artists who say that nothing is more beautiful than the male body. (T)
18. I would like to have sexual relations with another man. (T)
19. Sometimes I notice that I get sexually excited when I am with boys or men. (T)
20. I think young boys are better-looking than young girls. (T)
21. Sexually, I am more interested in women than men. (F)
22. I would like to feel a man's tail end. (T)
23. I refuse to have anything to do with homosexuality. (F)

rating but not with respect to the rated likelihood of evoking an anxiety response. To this end the judges had also been asked to rate each plate on another nine-point scale for the amount of anxiety likely to be aroused in a psychiatric patient presented the pictures. The mean anxiety rating of the homosexual card was compared to those of all other cards. It was noted that several of the *t*'s, including that for the comparison of the means of two especially-drawn cards, were non-significant ($p > .05$). Because these two pictures differed in mean homosexuality rating but were similar in several other respects (drawing style, sex, and number of the characters), the second custom-drawn card was chosen as the "neutral" plate. The difference between the mean homosexuality ratings of these two pictures was significant at the .005 level ($t = 6.50$) while the *t* for the difference between mean anxiety ratings was a nonsignificant 1.06 ($p > .20$).

Procedure. The Ss were administered the Revised Beta Examination, the above described inventory, and three thematic picture cards—a warm-up card (TAT plate 2), the neutral plate and the homosexual card, in that order. The number of seconds elapsing between the presentation of each card to the S and the onset of verbal production was recorded and the difference between the mean ratios of homosexual to neutral plate latencies analyzed by *t* tests.

RESULTS AND DISCUSSION

Table 29–2 presents the mean HA, latency ratio, and MF scores of the two groups, and *t*'s for the two groups. The paranoids produced a lower mean HA score and higher mean latency ratio than did the controls. The difference between the mean MF scores was not significant.

The results were partially consistent with Freud's paranoia-repressed homosexuality hypothesis. The significantly higher mean latency ratio of the paranoid group suggests that they are made more anxious by

TABLE 29-2

Means and SD's of Ha, Latency Ratio, and Mf Scores of Modified Samples of Paranoid (N = 23) and Control (N = 23) Schizophrenics, and t Ratios

	Paranoid		Control		
	M	SD	M	SD	*t*
Ha	1.30	1.34	3.35	3.17	2.85**
Latency Ratio	1.66	.56	1.03	1.20	2.28*
Mf	22.57	5.24	25.48	5.17	1.90

*Significant at .05 level.
**Significant at .01 level.

FIGURE 29-1
Neutral Card

FIGURE 29-2
Homosexual Card

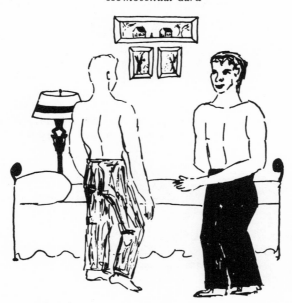

homosexual stimuli than nonparanoid schizophrenics. Likewise, the significantly lower mean HA score of the former group supports the contention that paranoids are less aware of homosexual feelings or needs than nonparanoid schizophrenics and is consistent with the repression hypothesis. To this extent our data were predictable from Freudian theory.

The MF finding seems to run counter to psychoanalytic prediction, suggesting that high feminine interests are not peculiar to the paranoid subclassification of schizophrenics and/or that repressed homosexual wishes do not manifest themselves in feminine interest patterns. This finding complements that of Page and Warkentin (11), who found the Terman M–F scores of their paranoids markedly different from those of either active or passive homosexuals.

As is the case with any result, the above differences could be explained by a myriad of other theories and the present results cannot be considered conclusive. Although it is a theory's ability to predict, rather than explain, data that is the most fruitful yardstick of its worth, one alternate explanation deserves mention here. It would seem possible that the present differences resulted from a higher level of test-taking defensiveness and suspicion among paranoids than among controls. Such a defensiveness hypothesis could explain the lower HA scores and higher mean latency ratio of paranoids in comparison to the nonparanoid schizophrenics. However, if such defensiveness is highly related to K (9, 5, 6), a consideration of the differences found in the two groups, whose mean K scores did not differ significantly, at least casts doubts on this particular explanation.

It is also important to realize that the necessity of eliminating Ss with high K, L, and F scale scores and conflicting diagnoses restricted the samples to certain subgroups of patients; therefore, the present groups cannot be considered random samples of paranoid or nonparanoid schizophrenics in general. The reader should also be aware that the present findings do not necessarily indicate that high homosexual needs are more characteristic of paranoid than nonparanoid schizophrenia. For example, in considering the present findings, one could argue that the important difference between paranoids and nonparanoids might lie in their methods of handling homosexual drives rather than in the quantity of drive present. Whether results of the sort described here are products of differences in homosexual needs or differences in defense mechanisms must remain a topic for future research.

SUMMARY

Three hypotheses derived from Freud's paranoia-homosexuality theory were tested in a comparison of the behavior of twenty-three paranoid and twenty-three nonparanoid schizophrenics. Two hypotheses were that (1) on an objective awareness-of-homosexuality scale, paranoids would produce a lower mean score than nonparanoids and that (2) the mean response latency ratio of homosexual to neutral pictures in a story-telling task would be greater among paranoids than in a control schizophrenic group. Both of these hypotheses were supported. However, a third prediction, that the mean MMPI MF score of the paranoids would be higher than that of the nonparanoids, went uncorroborated. The data suggest that repression of homosexual feelings and anxiety in the face of homosexual stimuli are more typical of paranoid than nonparanoid schizophrenics, but that members of these two groups do not differ with respect to the amount of feminine interest.

REFERENCES

1. ARONSON, M. L.   A study of the Freudian theory of paranoia by means of Rorschach's test. *J. proj. Tech.*, 1952, *16*, 397–411.

2. FREUD, S.   Psychoanalytic notes upon an autobiographical account of a case of paranoia (dementia paranoides). *Collected Papers*, Volume III. London: Hogarth Press, 1949.

3. GARDNER, G. D.   Evidences of homosexuality in 120 unanalyzed cases with paranoid content. *Psychoanal. Rev.*, 1931, *18*, 57–62.

4. GRAUER, D.   Homosexuality in paranoid schizophrenics as revealed by the Rorschach test. *J. consult. Psychol.*, 1954, *18*, 459–462.

5. GRAYSON, H. M. and OLINGER, L. B.   Simulation of "normalcy" by psychiatric patients on the MMPI. *J. consult. Psychol.*, 1957, *21*, 73–77.

6. HANLEY, C. H.   Deriving a measure of test-taking defensiveness. *J. consult. Psychol.*, 1957, *21*, 391–397.

7. KLAF, F. S. and DAVIS, C. A.   Homosexuality and paranoid schizophrenia: a survey of 150 cases and controls. *Amer. J. Psychiat.*, 1960, *116*, 1070–1075.

8. KLEIN, HENRIETTE R., and HORWITZ, W. A.   Psychosexual factors in the paranoid phenomena. *Amer. J. Psychiat.* 1949, *105*, 697–701.

9. McKINLEY, J. C., HATHAWAY, S. R. and MEEHL, P. E.   The Minnesota Multiphasic Personality Inventory: VI. The K scale. *J. consult. Psychol.*, 1948, *12*, 20–31.

10. NORMAN, J. P.   Evidence and clinical significance of homosexuality in 100 unanalyzed cases of dementia praecox. *J. nerv. ment. Dis.*, 1948, *107*, 484–489.

11. PAGE, J. and WARRENTIN, J.   Masculinity and paranoia. *J. abnorm. soc. Psychol.*, 1938, *33*, 527–351.

12. WHEELER, W. M.   An analysis of Rorschach indices of male homosexuality. *J. proj. Tech. Rorschach Res. Exch.*, 1949, *13*, 97–126.

The assistance of Nancy D. Watson, Mary B. King, Rowena M. Rash., Betty Alvord, Pamela J. Lunsford and Dr. D. D. Cahoon in this project is very gratefully acknowledged. This was an individual study of the V. A. Psychiatric Evaluation Project, Dr. Lee Gurel, Director.

30

Paul G. Daston

Perception of Homosexual Words in
Paranoid Schizophrenia

This study was undertaken to investigate the relationship postulated in psychoanalytic theory between paranoid schizophrenia and homosexuality. The methodological orientation was derived from research in the general area of selective perception.

Psychoanalytic theory. On the basis of his study of the Schreber case, Freud (8) postulated that the major factor in all the paranoid disorders was a conflict over inadequately repressed homosexual impulses. The paranoid male unconsciously desires to be the passive recipient of sexual advances from other males. In order to cope with these unacceptable motives which threaten to be expressed at a conscious level, he utilizes the mechanisms of denial and projection. Recognizing that schizophrenic and paranoid phenomena can be combined in any proportion, Freud emphasized that it was the paranoid component which was related to homosexual impulses. In schizophrenia uncolored by paranoid mechanisms, he felt it was extremely unlikely that homosexuality played an equally important etiological role.

Research evidence has not provided consistent support for this psychoanalytic interpretation. Observational studies (1, 9, 14) have indicated some relationship between paranoid mechanisms and homosexual impulses, but the findings have been more suggestive than decisive. Correlating response times to a word-association test with recognition times of tachistoscopically presented pictures, Ericksen (6) found little evidence for homosexual motives with paranoid or other subjects (Ss). More recently, Aronson (2), using paper and pencil tests as well as projective techniques, found evidence supportive of the Freudian hypothesis. In general, paranoid psychotics gave more homosexually indicative responses than did either nonparanoid psychotics or normal control Ss. However, Aronson concluded that faulty ego controls

Reprinted with permission of the next of kin of author and publisher: Daston, P. G. "Perception of homosexual words in paranoid schizophrenia." *Perceptual and Motor Skills*, 1956, *6*, 45–55.

as a function of psychosis may also have been instrumental in eliciting a greater number of these responses from both his clinical populations.

Perceptual theory. The finding that individuals are selectively sensitive in their reactions to various types of environmental stimuli has been accounted for by the postulation of an interaction between perceptual and personality variables (3, 4, 7). Various experiments have tended to show that past experience and current motives influence the S's perception (3, 4, 6, 13). The time required for correct verbal recognition of tachistoscopically presented stimuli has commonly been used as a measure of selective perception. Using recognition times to "neutral" stimuli as a baseline, it has been found that relatively fast recognition times characterize responses to stimuli which are congruent with the S's areas of concern (e.g., values, needs, motives, etc.). This more rapid recognition can be interpreted as a function of greater familiarity with stimuli pertaining to areas of interest or concern for the individual. Conversely, slower recognition times would be related to stimuli reflecting areas of less individual concern or a lesser degree of familiarity. Time required for correct identification was felt to be at least partly determined by response availability.

From the psychoanalytic point of view, the projective defense system and frontal attack on perceived threat by the paranoid is directly related to his underlying concern with homosexual impulses. There is supposedly a greater awareness of and sensitivity toward homosexually connotative stimuli. Within the perceptual methodology, it was reasoned, this sensitivity should reflect itself in time required for correct recognition of tachistoscopically presented words connoting homosexuality. For reasons of availability paranoid schizophrenics were employed as the paranoid population, and hypotheses were formulated following these considerations. In the major hypothesis it was predicted that paranoid schizophrenics would verbally identify words with a homosexual meaning relatively more rapidly than would either normal control or nonparanoid schizophrenic Ss. There were also several corollary control hypotheses dealing with recognition times to words other than homosexual, i.e., neutral words and heterosexual words.

METHODOLOGY

Subjects. The Ss consisted of twenty-five paranoid schizophrenics, twenty-five unclassified (nonparanoid) schizophrenics, and twenty-five normals. All were white, American-born, male war veterans, under forty-five years of age. None had visual or intellectual deficiencies marked enough to cause undue difficulty in identifying or reporting tachistoscopically presented words. Each S was required to read above the sixth-grade level on the Jastak-Bijou *Wide Range Achievement Test* (10) to minimize the possible effect of reading ability on performance.

The diagnosis of each S in the two schizophrenic groups was established by a staff of hospital psychiatrists and was arrived at by an evaluation of the presenting symptom picture. Differential diagnosis depended almost completely on descriptive nosological features. In addition, information derived from personal interviews and clinical records was examined for corroborative descriptive evidence in each case. The possibility of psychoanalytic considerations having influenced diagnosis and having contaminated the sample was minimal. There were evidences of concern over homosexuality in a number of records, but these appeared in both schizophrenic groups. Apparently in no case had homosexual ideation been a criterion for diagnosis. All Ss were cooperative and showed reality contact good enough to allow them to be tested. The normal group was composed mainly of patients in a general hospital with various medical conditions. None of the latter reported ever having any emotional difficulties severe enough to require either psychiatric consultation or treatment.

Table 30–1 presents a comparison of the groups in terms of age, education, and reading ability. Only in age are there any differences between the groups; the unclassified schizophrenics are slightly, but significantly, younger than the other two groups. The point could be raised that the younger unclassified schizophrenics might develop paranoid symptomatology as they grew older. Such a radical shift in defense systems in a short time interval was deemed unlikely, and the age differences were not considered important.

Stimulus words. Such extraneous variables as word length, familiarity, and affective value were controlled in the selection of stimulus words. First, a tachistoscopic study was conducted with ten Ss, using thirty five- and six-letter words equated for usage frequency according to the Thorndike-Lorge word counts (15). Time for correct verbal identification was noted. When the standard error of differences between means was calculated, the t value was 0.76. This difference was not significant and indicated five- and six-letter words could be considered equivalent for purposes of the study.

TABLE 30-1

Comparison of Experimental Ss as to Age,
Education, and Reading Ability

	Age		Education		Reading Ability	
	Mean	t Value	Mean	t Value	Mean	t Value
1. Normals	33.32	$t_{12} = 2.91^*$	11.04	$t_{12} = 0.4$	9.52	$t_{12} = 0.82$
2. Unclassified Schizophrenics	28.52	$t_{13} = 0.09$	11.32	$t_{13} = 0.7$	10.02	$t_{13} = 1.71$
3. Paranoid Schizophrenics	33.48	$t_{23} = 3.10^*$	11.56	$t_{23} = 0.3$	10.65	$t_{23} = 0.88$

*Significant at beyond the .01 level of confidence.

Following this, a preliminary list of 200 five- and six-letter words was constructed. Forty words considered to have homosexual connotation, forty purportedly heterosexual, and 120 words probably nonsexual in meaning were used. Two forms of this list were presented to forty judges, a peer group of the experimental populations.

On the first form of the list, judges rated the words on the dimension of affectivity, indicating the emotional value each word had for them. Following this, a rearranged list of the same words was presented them with instructions to classify only those words with which they were familiar* as being homosexual, heterosexual, or nonsexual in meaning. A "Don't Know" category was also provided, in which they placed words with which they had some familiarity but about whose meaning they were unsure. Any word omitted or placed in the "Don't Know" category by five raters was considered to be too obscure to be of value and was discarded.

The affective ratings were converted into McCall T scores, and interquartile ranges were computed. Percentages of agreement were calculated for words in the sexual categories, and the results of both sets of judgments were combined. A list of thirty-six test words was then selected, made up of those nine words in each sexual category and those eighteen words in the nonsexual category most clearly differentiated by the judges for both sexuality and affectivity. This was the list of words used in the study (see Table 30–2).

It can be seen in Table 30–2 that the judges were less consistent with both affective and sexual ratings for homosexual words than with others, perhaps because few, if any, of these words had an exclusively homosexual meaning. The inclusion of those nine words in the homosexual category was dictated by practical considerations, although it was recognized that their lack of denotative meaning might work against the principal hypothesis of the study. That is, if words purportedly homosexual were familiar to the experimental populations in contexts other than a homosexual one, then they should be recognized more rapidly by all groups than would be the case if they were related exclusively to homosexuality as an area of concern. It was felt this limiting factor might reduce the size of the hypothesized differences.

Procedure. Each S was tested individually. In a Gerbrands tachistoscope, he was shown a group of nine pretest words to familiarize him with the apparatus and procedure. Then he was shown the list of test words. Both pretest and test words were capitalized and double spaced, electrically typed on individual sheets of white paper.

Each word was presented once at each timer setting; and, wherever possible, the first exposure time for any of the test words was .05 faster

---

* It was felt no available frequency of word usage tables would give as adequate a measure of a word's familiarity as would a peer group. This writer felt, with McGinnies (11), that frequency of usage tables derived from popular periodicals do not list socially taboo words in the frequency with which they are actually used in written and spoken language.

TABLE 30-2

Words Used as Stimulus Variable Along with Judges' Ratings

Word	Affective Rating M_T	Q_1-Q_3	% Agreement on Sexual Meaning	Word	Affective Rating M_T	Q_1-Q_3	% Agreement on Sexual Meaning
	Homosexual				*Nonsexual*		
Pleasant				*Pleasant*			
Fruit	42.9	39-46	70	Jolly	40.1	37-41	90
Fairy	50.6	44-58	85	Alert	41.0	36-46	97.5
Pansy	52.0	45-60	50	Prize	41.2	38-43	90
				Church	38.1	35-40	97.5
Neutral				Famous	40.0	37-42	92.5
Homos	55.5	51-60	82.4	Wealth	41.2	38-44	95
Blown	53.6	49-59	71.1				
Rectum	56.6	53-61	52.5	*Neutral*			
				Cellar	52.1	45-60	90
Unpleasant				Turtle	48.8	46-51	100
Sissy	59.9	47-63	52.6	Tablet	49.2	46-51	100
Sucked	59.0	53-63	72.5	Swish	50.4	46-52	90
Queer	60.4	58-63	94.9	Yeast	49.8	47-51	97.4
				Ounce	49.0	46-51	95
	Heterosexual			*Unpleasant*			
Pleasant				Murder	61.9	61-66	90
Caress	40.4	35-43	100	Nausea	63.1	60-66	90
Bosom	42.4	38-45	90	Lynch	61.9	59-67	92.5
Breast	43.0	39-47	92.5	Death	63.3	61-68	97.5
				Vomit	63.6	62-67	95
Neutral				Agony	64.5	61-68	89.7
Piece	49.1	46-51	97.5				
Pickup	49.8	46-52	95				
Screw	51.4	49-55	97.4				
Unpleasant							
Fucked	57.9	51-66	100				
Whore	60.1	57-64	100				
Rapist	62.4	61-66	92.5				

than S's quickest recognition time to any of the pretest words.* Exposure time was lengthened in even steps of .01 sec. until correct recognition occurred. If, after twenty-five successive exposures to the same word, S was still unable to recognize it correctly, step-intervals were increased to .05 sec. This was done primarily to reduce feelings of frustration in S. When a word was correctly recognized, the setting of the timer was recorded, and the next word was presented. The procedure was the same for all words with all Ss.

Words were presented in a random order, no two Ss being shown the words in the same order. Participants were requested to maintain silence about the procedure, and there was no evidence to indicate they did otherwise.

* The method was essentially that of a reaction time experiment. The terms "reaction time" and "time for correct recognition" were considered synonymous for the present study.

RESULTS

In designing the experiment, it was felt the analysis of variance technique would provide a meaningful statistical treatment. Of the requirements to be met for analysis of variance, that of homogeneity of variance in the experimental population was determined by Bartlett's test of homogeneity of variance, as suggested by Edwards (5). The derived chi-square was 0.537. With a chi-square this small, the null hypothesis could not be rejected. A second requirement, normality of distribution in the experimental population for the variables considered, was assumed. Also, the independence of individual measurements was favored by random presentation of words in the list to each S in the experiment (see *Procedure*). The particular analysis of variance technique used was a modification of one found in Edwards (5, p. 295) for analysis of data involving successive trials. It was chosen because it tended to minimize the effect of practice upon recognition times of Ss to words presented successively in the test list and because it allowed a sharper test of variance between groups of Ss to be made (see Table 30–3).

From the table it can be seen that there were differences between words, significant at the .01 level of confidence. This finding, that individual Ss reacted differentially to words in the test list, was essential to the proposition that the perceptual technique used in the experiment could yield differences among groups of Ss. Without this finding, further examination of the data would have been superfluous.

Affective connotation of the words did not differentiate. By itself, the emotional quality of the words did not appear to be an important variable. An extremely important item for the hypothesis under test concerned the interaction term, Groups x Sexuality, which was significant at beyond the .05 level of confidence. When this interaction was examined, it was found that the two schizophrenic populations behaved alike with both heterosexual and nonsexual words, having slower recognition times to these than did the normal population. On the other hand, with the homosexual words, paranoid schizophrenics and normals behaved alike, both having significantly faster recognition times to these words than did the unclassified schizophrenics.

It had been planned to use reaction times to nonsexual words as a common baseline from which to make comparisons among the groups of Ss to homosexual and heterosexual words. The finding that statistically significant differences existed among groups in their recognition times to nonsexual words necessitated statistical treatment of the data beyond that which had been provided for in the original design.

It seemed likely that unknown, uncontrolled variables had affected the groups of Ss differently in terms of their word recognition times. One possible explanation for this disparity may have been lack of concentrative ability on the part of the clinical populations. It is well known that

TABLE 30-3

*Results of the Analysis of Variance of Times
Required for Correct Recognition of Words*

Source of Variance	df	Mean Square	F	p
Total Variance	2699			
A. *Between Subjects*	74			
1. Between Groups of Subjects	2	229.4	< 1	N.S.
2. Residual (within) Variance	72	427.9		
B. *Within Subjects*	2625			
1. Between Words	35	113.0	9.28	.01
2. Between Affective Categories				
(Holding Subjects and				
Sexuality Constant)	2*	24.01	1.97	N.S.
3. Between Sexual Categories				
(Holding Subjects and				
Affectivity Constant)	2*	367.8	30.2	.01
C. *Interaction Terms*	2590			
Words x Groups**	70	14.5	1.19	N.S.
Affectivity x Sexuality x Groups	8*	10.9	< 1	N.S.
Groups x Affectivity				
(Sexuality Held Constant)	4*	3.3	< 1	N.S.
Affectivity x Sexuality				
(Groups Held Constant)	4*	256.9	21.09	.01
Groups x Sexuality				
(Affectivity Held Constant)	4*	32.15	2.64	.05
Residual (Pooled Subjects x Groups				
Interaction) Variance	2520	12.18		

*Degrees of freedom for these variables are from the 70 *df* in the overall interaction term, Words x Groups.

**"Groups," where used in this table, refers to groups of *S*s.

the concentrative attention span of psychotics is limited, and this factor may have operated generally to increase their reaction times to all classes of words. Whatever the explanation, it was necessary to transform the data statistically in such a way as to equate the experimental groups for recognition times to nonsexual words. Analysis of covariance, following McNemar (12), appeared to be a method of considerable promise for eliminating the effect of these uncontrolled variables on differential word recognition times.

It was also found that differences in recognition times for the various affective categories in the nonsexual words had been well below statistical significance for each experimental group. However, in cognizance of previous research in the area of selective perception, it was decided to use recognition times to nonsexual neutral words as the common baseline from which to examine reactions of each experimental group to heterosexual and homosexual words. Two separate analyses of covariance were done: the first comparing experimental groups on reac-

TABLE 30-4

*t Tests for Significance of Differences Between Means of
Total Recognition Times for all Homosexual Words
Following Analysis of Covariance Transformation*

Subjects	Adjusted Mean for Total in Hundredths of a Second	t	df	p
Paranoid	40.30			
versus Normal		3.10	71	.01
versus Unclassified		2.21	71	.05
Normal	52.65			
versus Unclassified		0.90	71	N.S.
Unclassified	49.08			

σDifference = $\sqrt{\text{(Residual Variance)} \ (1/n + 1/n)}$

σDifference = $\sqrt{197.802 \ (1/25 + 1/25)}$

σDifference = 3.98

tion times to heterosexual words, the second comparing reaction times to homosexual words. In both analyses, recognition times for nonsexual neutral words were held constant.

In the analysis with heterosexual words the derived F with untransformed data was not significant, nor did it attain significance following the covariance transformation. This lack of significance indicated there were no appreciable differences among the groups of Ss in their reactions to the heterosexual words in the study, when groups were equated for reactions to nonsexual neutral words.

The second analysis of covariance, with homosexual words, provided definite evidence upholding the major hypothesis of the study. The results of this comparison indicated that, with corrections made for differential reactions to nonsexual neutral words, there was a statistically significant difference among the experimental groups in their reaction times to homosexual words. The derived F with untransformed data was not significant; but with the covariance transformation the F became 4.984, significant at the .01 level of confidence. The means of reaction times were then adjusted, following McNemar (12, pp. 323–329), and the standard error of the difference calculated. Following this, t tests were applied to determine the sources of the difference implied in the F ratio.

Thse comparisons, shown in Table 30–4, demonstrated that the paranoid group differed considerably from the normal group. They reacted more rapidly to homosexual words, the difference being significant at the .01 level of confidence. When the two psychotic groups were compared, the difference was significant at the .05 level, with paranoids reacting faster than unclassifieds. The last comparison, normals vs.

unclassifieds, was well below statistical significance. It would appear then, from the results of these analyses of covariance, that the major hypothesis was supported.

DISCUSSION

Within the limitations of this study, the results demonstrated a relationship between paranoid schizophrenia and homosexual impulses, as was hypothesized. These findings supported the psychoanalytic proposition. Furthermore, the finding that paranoid schizophrenics correctly recognized homosexual words more rapidly than did unclassified schizophrenics, coupled with the finding that unclassified schizophrenics did not differ from normals in recognition times for homosexual words, indicated that sensitivity to homosexual stimuli was more a function of the paranoid components involved than of schizophrenia itself. This also supported Freud's contention.

Homosexuality appeared to be an area of greater concern for paranoid schizophrenics than for either unclassified or normal Ss. Regardless of their willingness or ability to verbalize overtly their concern with homosexuality, the greater relative sensitivity of paranoid Ss to homosexual words indicated they had more familiarity with these words. Had it been possible to employ words more denotatively homosexual, rather than words with other meanings in addition to a homosexual one, greater sensitivity of paranoid Ss to these stimuli might have been even more clearly demonstrated. Despite this limiting factor, there was fairly clear-cut evidence that it was the paranoid component involved in paranoid schizophrenia which was related to concern regarding homosexuality.

There was also some interesting qualitative information. For example, a number of paranoid Ss reacted to the word "queer" with a great deal of feeling, stating how much they hated "queers." One S, a chronic paranoid, recognized the tachistoscopically presented word "homos" and commented it must be a Latin word, although new to him. Shortly thereafter, he told the examiner about the female psychologist who works with the FBI and who keeps calling him a "homo" over the radio. There were several other indications of high idiosyncratic familiarity with homosexual words among paranoid Ss which undoubtedly influenced time for correct recognition. On the other hand, none of the unclassified schizophrenics gave any overt sign noted by E of overconcern with homosexual words, despite the fact a number of them had histories indicating that homosexuality was an area of conflict. These qualitative findings may be interpreted as indicating that to be "concerned with" or in conflict over homosexual impulses or any other impulses may be important but not sufficient in and of itself in the determination of perceptual response. In fact, the bulk of presently available evidence points up the likelihood of perceptual response reflecting the complex interaction of many stimuli and intraorganismic determinants.

Whether homosexuality is a *major* area of concern for paranoid individuals, or whether it alone is causative of behavior diagnosed as paranoid, could not be determined from the present findings. There was a relationship demonstrated between paranoid mechanisms and homosexual impulses, and it would appear reasonable to infer that homosexuality, as an area of concern, is involved in the determination of paranoid personality components. However, there may well be other areas of concern that serve to differentiate paranoid from other individuals. How and to what degree homosexuality or other areas of concern are related to paranoid aspects of personality functioning is a possible subject for further studies. The perceptual technique used in this research may also be of value in future research of a more general nature. Perceptual tests of hypotheses derived from personality theory might well contribute to existing knowledge in this area.

The findings in the present study agree in general with other findings, with the exception of the experiment by Ericksen (6). The more direct test of the psychoanalytic postulate in the work reported here may have accounted for the difference in results. Because there were fewer variables extraneous to the psychoanalytic proposition to be considered, these results may be somewhat more indicative than were those of Ericksen.

SUMMARY

The present study was undertaken to investigate the relationship postulated in psychoanalytic theory between paranoid schizophrenia and homosexual impulses. The methodological orientation was derived from research in the area of selective perception. Time required for correct verbal recognition of various classes of tachistoscopically presented words was used, previous research having indicated that stimuli pertaining to areas of individual concern are recognized more rapidly than "neutral" stimuli, presumably as a function of greater individual familiarity. It was held that motivational variables were involved in the determination of areas of individual concern and that the interaction of motivational with perceptual variables would affect perceptually mediated response. If homosexuality were an area of concern for paranoid individuals, words reflecting homosexuality would be recognized relatively more rapidly by them than by individuals less concerned with homosexuality. Three groups of Ss were employed: paranoid schizophrenics, unclassified schizophrenics, and normals. Each S's time for correct verbal recognition of tachistoscopically presented words from a test list was recorded. This test list was composed of words which had been previously judged on the dimensions of affectivity, sexuality, and familiarity. Word length was controlled. It was found that: (1) affective value of the words had little effect on time required for correct verbal recognition (2) paranoid Ss recognized homosexual words significantly faster than did the other two groups of Ss, and (3) normals and unclassified schizophrenics did not differ significantly in recognition times to homosexual words. In addition, differences in recognition times to heterosexual words were not significant among the groups. These findings supported the psychoanalytic proposition, in that there was a relationship demonstrated between paranoid aspects of personality functioning and homosexuality. Whether homosexuality was a major area of concern for paranoid individuals was not determined.

REFERENCES

1. ALEXANDER, F., & MENNINGER, W. C.   The relation of persecutory delusions to the functioning of the gastrointestinal tract. In S. S. Tomkins (Ed.), *Contemporary psychopathology*. Cambridge, Mass.: Harvard Univer. Press, 1946. Pp. 381–393.

2. ARONSON, M. L.   *A study of the Freudian theory of paranoia by means of a group of psychological tests*. Unpublished Ph.D. dissertation, Univer. of Michigan, 1950.

3. BRUNER, J. S.   Personality dynamics and the process of perceiving. In R. R. Blake, and G. V. Ramsey (Eds.), *Perception: an approach to personality*. New York: Ronald, 1951, Pp. 121–147.

4. BRUNER, J. S., & POSTMAN, L.   An approach to social perception. In W. Dennis (Ed.), *Current trends in social psychology*. Pittsburgh: Univer. of Pittsburgh Press, 1948. Pp. 71–118.

5. EDWARDS, A. L.   *Experimental design in psychological research*. New York: Rinehart, 1950.

6. ERICKSEN, C. W.   Perceptual defense as a function of unacceptable needs. *J. abnorm. soc. Psychol.*, 1951, 46, 557–564.

7. FRENKEL-BRUNSWICK, E.   *Personality theory and perception*. In R. R. Blake, and G. V. Ramsey (Eds.), *Perception: an approach to personality*. New York: Ronald, 1951. Pp. 356–420.

8. FREUD, S.   Psycho-analytic notes upon an autobiographical account of a case of paranoia. *Collected Papers*, Vol. III. London: Hogarth, 1948. Pp. 387–470.

9. GARDNER, G. E.   Evidence of homosexuality in one hundred and twenty unanalyzed cases with paranoid content. In S. S. Tomkins (Ed.), *Contemporary psychopathology*. Cambridge, Mass.: Harvard Univer. Press, 1946. Pp. 394–397.

10. JASTAK, J.   *Wide Range Achievement Test*. Wilmington, Del.: Story, 1946.

11. McGinnies, E.   Discussion of Howes' and Solomon's "Note on emotionality and perceptual defense." *Psychol Rev.*, 1950, 57, 235–240.

12. McNemar, Q.   *Psychological statistics.* New York: Wiley, 1949.

13. Postman, L., Bruner, J. S., & McGinnies, E.   Personal values as selective factors in perception. *J. abnorm. soc. Psychol.*, 1948, 43, 142–154.

14. Sears, R. R.   *Survey of objective studies of psychoanalytic concepts.* New York: Social Science Res. Council, Bulletin 51, 1943.

15. Thorndike, E. L., & Lorge, I.   *The teacher's wordbook of 30,000 words.* New York: Teachers College, Columbia Univer., 1944.

31

Franklin S. Klaf, M.D. & Charles A. Davis, M.D.

Homosexuality and Paranoid Schizophrenia:
A Survey of 150 Cases and Controls

In his analysis of Dr. Schreber's autobiography, Freud suggested that paranoid psychotic symptoms develop as a defense against emerging unconscious homosexual wishes. This hypothesis has generally been regarded as proven, but few scientific studies have been done to verify it.

Modern logic has taught us that, as Morris R. Cohen (2) puts it, "Those who begin with absolute truth cannot improve upon it." Unfortunately, on the basis of a few noncontrolled observations, Freud's paranoia hypothesis was accepted as absolute truth, although Freud himself (4) cautioned against this, writing skeptically,

It remains for the future to decide whether there is more delusion in my theory than I should like to admit, or whether there is more truth in Schreber's delusion than other people are as yet prepared to believe.

Modern logic has also taught us three important principles about hypotheses like Freud's. First, scientific investigation cannot prove such an hypothesis to be absolutely true, but only to be better than others in the field. Second, the real meaning of any hypothesis resides in its consequences. Third, the implications of an hypothesis should be considered independently of the question of whether it is in fact true. That is to say, although an hypothesis may be false, it may have useful determinate consequences.

Applying these principles to Freud's hypothesis, we see, first, that it would be impossible to design a study the results of which would prove the hypothesis to be absolutely true. According to the third principle, it really makes little difference whether the original hypothesis is true, since, even if it is not true, we still may obtain useful data by investigating its consequences. Therefore, we shall follow the second

Reprinted by permission of the publisher and the authors from *American Journal of Psychiatry*. 1960, *116*, 1070–1075. Copyright 1960 by the American Psychiatric Association.

principle and investigate the meaning of Freud's hypothesis in its implications and consequences.

The process of investigating the consequences of an hypothesis is termed "verification." This process requires: first, that we deduce the consequences of the hypothesis; and second, that we examine these deduced consequences to see whether they agree with the hypothesis. Freud's hypothesis states that during an acute paranoid psychotic illness, a relative failure of repression occurs and repressed material comes closer to consciousness; paranoid symptoms develop as a defense against the emergence of unconscious homosexual wishes.

The first consequence deduced from Freud's hypothesis is as follows: Since unconscious homosexual wishes are emerging during the acute illness, we should expect to find such patients preoccupied with homosexual thoughts and wishes. With failing repression the histories obtained from these patients might more frequently contain evidence of previous homosexual experiences.

A second consequence of the Freudian hypothesis concerns the content of the paranoid delusions and hallucinations. Since the sexual problem is theorized to be of paramount importance as the basis of paranoia, we should expect the delusions and hallucinations to have prominent sexual content.

A third consequence concerns the sex of the persecutor. Freud states (4),

The person who is now hated and feared as a persecutor was at one time loved and honored. . . . It is a remarkable fact that the familiar principal forms of paranoia can all be represented as contradictions of the single proposition "I (a man) love him (a man)."

Since the persecutor was previously the homosexual love object, we should expect the sex of the persecutor to be the same as that of the patient.

A fourth consequence requires clarification. Modern concepts of logic and operationalism have shown that facts and theories are meaningless except as parts of a system. Thus, Freud's paranoia hypothesis is an integral part of his entire system explaining psychodynamic development and functioning. In the Schreber analysis, Freud relates Dr. Schreber's religious preoccupation to Schreber's disturbed relationship with his famous and punitive father. Freud discusses elsewhere (5) the relationship between the domineering ego ideal and the development of a pathological propensity for religious belief. Thus, the role of the strict father in the development of pathological religious ideas and in the determination of actual and fantasied homosexual object choice is constantly stressed. Consequently, we should expect religious preoccupation to be close to the surface and freely expressed by many acutely ill patients, especially those whose premorbid religion was characterized by strong repression.

We shall examine the above deduced consequences to see whether they agree with or contradict Freud's basic hypothesis, and his hypothesis as expressed in his system.

MATERIAL

The material is derived from the 1943–57 psychiatric case records of the U. S. Public Health Service Hospital, Ft. Worth, Texas. During and after World War II, the hospital was a center for the treatment of servicemen (Navy, Marine Corps, Coast Guardsmen, and Veterans) suffering from the major mental illnesses. Most of the patients were seen in the acute stage of their first episode of mental illness.

METHOD

From these psychiatric case records, 150 male cases diagnosed paranoid schizophrenia, and a control group of 150 male nonpsychotic cases of other miscellaneous diagnoses (Table 31–1) were selected. In selecting the cases, the entire chart of each patient was reviewed. If there was any doubt concerning the diagnosis, the case was excluded from the study. Only patients conforming to the criteria of the American Psychiatric Association Diagnostic and Statistical Manual of Mental Disorders for the diagnosis of paranoid schizophrenia were included in the paranoid group. The nonpsychotic cases were scattered among the three diagnostic categories listed in table 31–1. The main selection factor used for both groups was the presence in each record of an "adequate sexual history." By "adequate sexual history" we mean the notation in the psychiatric evaluation of each patient of a heterosexual and homosexual history. A definite recorded statement by the patient of the presence or absence of previous homosexual experiences was required for both groups in the study. Records containing only opinions of the examiner regarding the presence of latent homosexuality or the patient's inability to express concern about homosexuality were discarded. Many of the records, complete in other respects, did not meet these specifications and could not be included. An observation made during the perusal of the records was that the various examiners seemed to be divided into two main groups, the first seemingly trained to seek out homosexuality as the underlying factor in the paranoid schizophrenic process, and the second group, who seemed reluctant to take a complete sexual history on acutely ill psychotic patients. A typical comment of the second type of examiner was, "The patient was not questioned in this sphere (homosexuality) for fear of further shattering his defenses."

The following factors were selected for statistical evaluation:

(1) *Age.*

(2) *Marital Status.* The patient was placed in the married group if

TABLE 31-1

Diagnostic Categories in Control Group

Psychoneurotic Disorders (includes former category "Mixed Psychoneurosis")	Personality Disorders (Includes former category "Psychopathic Personality." Paranoid Personalities were excluded.)	Transient Situational Personality Disorders
$\frac{101}{67.3\%}$	$\frac{42}{28\%}$	$\frac{7}{4.7\%}$

he had ever been married. No distinction was made for divorced or separated patients.

(3) *Religion.*

(4) *Previous Homosexual Experiences*—by which we mean the report of one or more overt homosexual experiences after puberty, i.e., oral or anal sexual relations between individuals of the same sex, or mutual masturbation between individuals of the same sex.

(5) *Presence of Homosexual Preoccupations During the Illness*—were recorded as present if homosexuality was reported as the predominant concern of the patient's verbalizations.

(6) *Presence of Delusions or Hallucinations of Sexual Content During the Illness.* It is to be noted that this category is termed "Sexual," rather than "Homosexual," as it includes delusions and hallucinations regarding infidelity.

(7) *Presence of Religious Preoccupations During the Illness*—recorded as present, if concern with religion was emphasized by the patient in his verbalizations.

(8) *Sex of the Persecutor.* Often the patient's persecutor was not a specific individual, but was stated to be a group, e.g., the officers in the Navy or the Communist Party. In such cases, the patient's persecutor is listed as male.

DISCUSSION

No comparison of the results of this study with those of previous studies will be attempted because of differing criteria used to define homosexuality and homosexual experiences and the absence of control groups in most other papers. The data compiled from this case are summarized in Tables 31–2, 31–3, and 31–4. Tables 31–2 and 31–3 show comparisons of the collected data of the control and paranoid schizophrenic groups. Table 31–4 includes data on the persecutor within the paranoid schizophrenic group.

TABLE 31-2

	Paranoid Schizophrenic	Controls
Previous Homosexual Experiences*	55 / 36.7%	28 / 18.7%
Homosexual Preoccupations	46 / 30.7%	9 / 6%
Delusions or Hallucinations of Sexual Content	40 / 26.7%	0
Religious Preoccupations	33 / 22%	4 / 2.7%

*Within the Paranoid Schizophrenic Group.

1. 40% of those who had delusions or hallucinations of sexual content had previous homosexual experience.

2. 50% of those who had homosexual preoccupations had previous homosexual experience.

TABLE 31-4

Data on Persecutor in Paranoid Schizophrenia Group
(None in Controls)

Persecutor	Total Number and Percent	Married	Single	Previous Homosexual Experiences	Homosexual Preoccupations	Delusions and Hallucinations	Religious Preoccupations
Female Only	8 / 5.3%	8 / 100%	0	3 / 5.4%	2 / 4.3%	3 / 7.5%	1 / 3.0%
Male and Female	15 / 10%	6 / 40%	9 / 60%	5 / 9.1%	5 / 10.9%	6 / 15%	3 / 10%
Male Only	127 / 84.7%	56 / 44.1%	71 / 55.9%	47 / 85.5%	39 / 84.8%	31 / 77.5%	29 / 87.0%

TABLE 31-3

	Controls							Paranoid Schizophrenia						
	Age (Avg.)	Marital Status	Religion	Prev. Homosexual Experiences	Homosexual Preoccupations	Delusions or Hallucinations	Religious Preoccupations	Age (Avg.)	Marital Status	Religion	Prev. Homosexual Experiences	Homosexual Preoccupations	Delusions or Hallucinations	Religious Preoccupations
Age	31.8				27.3		24.7	32.4				31.9	32.7	32.0
Married		89 / 59%		12 / 13.5%	4 / 4.5%	0	1 / 1.2%		71 / 47%		23 / 32.4%	20 / 28.2%	15 / 21.1%	17 / 23.9%
Single		61 / 41%		16 / 26.2%	6 / 9.8%		3 / 4.9%		79 / 53%		32 / 40.5%	26 / 32.7%	25 / 31.6%	16 / 20.3%
Catholic			15 / 10%	5 / 33.3%	3 / 20%		1 / 6.7%			34 / 22.7%	16 / 47.1%	10 / 29.4%	13 / 32.5%	8 / 23.5%
Protestant			126 / 84%	21 / 16.7%	6 / 4.8%		3 / 2.4%			116 / 77.3%	39 / 33.6%	36 / 31.1%	27 / 67.5%	25 / 21.6%
Jewish			2 / 1.3%	0	0		0			0				
No religion			7 / 4.6%	2 / 28.6%	1 / 14.3%		0			0				

ADVANTAGES OF THE STUDY

(1) The material was drawn from psychiatric reports that were not specifically designed for this study, thus reducing bias. The presence of an "adequate sexual history" was the main selection factor used. (2) Only paranoid schizophrenic cases conforming to the official diagnostic criteria were used. All of these patients had delusions of persecution. (3) This study, with the exception of two small Rorschach studies by Chapman and Reese (3) and Aronson (1), represents the first psychiatric study on this subject to include a control group. (4) The scope of recorded data in the various categories of the study is specifically defined. This is in marked contrast to previous studies, such as Gardner's (6), where a broad criterion like "Symbolism in action or words" is recorded as evidence of homosexuality, and Norman's (7), where fear of sexual relations with women is taken as evidence of conscious homosexuality.

LIMITATIONS OF THE STUDY

(1) The material is secondary source material. Further verification of Freud's theory and its consequences would require study of a large sample of primary source material. (2) The material used was obtained by several physicians with varying degrees of psychiatric experience, under the supervision of more experienced psychiatrists. This has been compensated for by a clear definition of terms and a careful review of the case protocols. (3) As is true in all psychiatric case studies, certain data may be influenced by the impressions of the examiner. In this paper, the recording of the presence or absence of homosexual or religious preocupations may, to some extent, be so determined.

RESULTS AND THEIR RELATIONSHIP TO THE HYPOTHESIS

The first consequence of Freud's hypothesis was that we should expect to find acutely ill psychotic patients preoccupied with homosexual thoughts and wishes. In the paranoid schizophrenic group, twenty-three (41.8%) had homosexual preoccupations during the illness, as compared with nine (6%) in the control group. This difference was found to be very significant using the Chi-square Test of significance. (A divergence as large as the one noted could have happened by chance alone less than one time in a hundred.) The first consequence was thus verified, since homosexual preoccupations during the illness were recorded approximately seven times as frequently in the paranoid psychotic group as in the control group. It was also proposed that, as a result of shattered defenses, it might be easier to obtain a history of previous homosexual experiences from the psychotic group. This was found to be the case. Previous homosexual experiences were recorded 1.96 times, or nearly twice as frequently in the paranoid psychotic group as in the control group. This difference was also found to be very significant using the Chi-square Test.

The second consequence noted was that we should expect the delusions and hallucinations of the paranoid group to have prominent sexual content. No comparison is possible with the control group, since nonpsychotics do not have delusions and hallucinations. Within the paranoid group, only forty or 26.7% had delusions and hallucinations of sexual content, including delusions of infidelity. Thus, the second consequence was not found to be verified by the study.

The third consequence of Freud's hypothesis was that since the persecutor was supposedly the homosexual love object, we should expect the sex of the persecutor to be the same as that of the patient. This was found to be as predicted. With the paranoid group, 127 (84.7%) had male persecutors, 8 (5.3%) had female persecutors, and 15 (10%) had persecutors of both sexes.

The fourth consequence was that we should expect religious preoccupations to be expressed by many acutely ill psychotic patients. This was verified by the study. In the paranoid schizophrenic group, thirty-three (22%) had religious preoccupations during the illness, as compared with four (2%) in the control group. Thus, religious preoccupations during the illness were recorded approximately eight times as frequently in the paranoid as in the control group. This difference was found to be very significant using the Chi-square Test.

SUMMARY

In this paper, the data obtained from a study of the records of 150 paranoid schizophrenic patients and a control group of 150 nonpsychotic patients were presented and discussed in relation to Freud's hypothesis concerning the development of paranoid symptoms. Four consequences of Freud's hypothesis were deduced. Three of the deduced consequences received strong verification from the study, the differences between the paranoid psychotic and control groups being found very significant. The fourth consequence, that we should expect the final delusions and hallucinations of the paranoid group to have prominent sexual content, did not receive verification from the study. Comparison with the control group here was impossible due to the absence of delusions in the control group.

Another point needs to be mentioned concerning the present study. This is the fact that two trends may exist together in a personality and yet not necessarily be related. Bleuler originally brought up this point in commenting that homosexuality was very prominent in Schreber's case history, but may not have been the determining factor in the paranoid illness. While the present study, within its limits, lends strong verification to three consequences of Freud's theory, it is possible that future investigation may show the coexistence of the two trends of paranoia and homosexuality to be a coincidental finding.

Few psychiatrists dispute that Freud's fecund intelligence was productive of many theories that have deepened our knowledge of psychological functioning. But, it is also a logical fallacy to argue that a theory is verified because it explains certain facts.

The process of verification, as utilized in this paper, is the same method used by the vast majority of scientific investigators.

We feel that the following studies of this important subject are needed:

(1) Studies of the relationship of homosexuality to paranoid schizophrenia in female groups, as compared with control groups. As noted in the literature review, there are only two nonpsychoanalytic case reports dealing with homosexuality and paranoid schizophrenia in females.

(2) Studies on this subject utilizing primary source material. A protocol should be drawn up in advance, including definition of terms and categories to be recorded. This protocol should be used in interviewing a random sampling of paranoid schizophrenic patients, and a similar group of nonpsychotic patients of varying diagnoses. Other control groups may also be used. The examiners should be free of preconceived opinions regarding the relationship of homosexuality to the paranoid schizophrenic process.

Until more scientific studies are made and analyzed, the hypothesis that paranoid psychotic symptoms develop as a defense against emerging unconscious homosexual wishes cannot be regarded as verified.

REFERENCES

1. ARONSON, M. L.:   *J. Proj. Tech., 16:* 397, 1952.
2. COHEN, M. R.:   *A Preface to Logic.* New York: Meridian, 1957.
3. CHAPMAN, A. H., and REESE, D. B.:   *J. Clin. Psychol., 9:* 30, 1953.

4. FREUD, S.:   Collected Papers, Vol. 3. London: Hogarth Press, 1925.
5. FREUD, S.:   The Future of an Illusion. New York: Doubleday Anchor, 1957.
6. GARDNER, G. E.:   Psychoanal. Rev., 18: 57, 1931.
7. NORMAN, J. P.:   J. Nerv. and Ment. Dis., 107: 484, 1948.

The authors wish to express their appreciation to Drs. James F. Maddux, Jr. and Robert N. Rasor for their invaluable assistance in the revision of this paper.

32

Abraham M. Zeichner

Psychosexual Identification in Paranoid Schizophrenia

The etiology of paranoid schizophrenia has, as a result of psychoanalytic theory and practice, been linked to the psychosexual development of the individual involving specifically latent homosexuality or conflicts over homosexual wishes. Adherents to this point of view have posited a causal relationship between the homosexual components and the paranoid syndrome (4, 15, 5, pp. 387–470). Some writers have been more guarded in considering the relationship between homosexual conflicts and paranoid syndromes as involving causality in most, let alone all, cases manifesting paranoid defense patterns. Deficiencies in role taking and impaired social growth (3, pp. 442–443), disturbances of security such as early traumata, impaired self-esteem, frustrated ambitions, feelings of inadequacy, etc. (21, p. 401) have been cited as dynamic factors in the development of paranoid reactions.

Norman, who concluded in his study that there is much evidence for ascribing strong conscious and unconscious homosexual trends to paranoid patients, expressed the view that, "There is no proof, however, that these homosexual tendencies are a primarily etiologic factor in the schizophrenic process" (20, p. 489). Aronson (1), who studied the occurrence of "homosexual signs" on the Rorschach in paranoid patients, also concluded that although the results supported the Freudian hypothesis, they did not prove an etiological relationship between homosexual conflicts and paranoia.

The question may be raised whether the attempts to demonstrate the occurrence of homosexual trends in paranoid subjects at the descriptive level can lead to conclusions concerning etiology. Perhaps, it is necessary, rather, to investigate the dynamic aspects of psychosexual development so that a clear understanding of the etiology of specific variations within the broad range of patterns of human adjustment may eventually emerge through research.

Upon examining the fundamental elements in the emergence of personality, particularly with respect to the development of the individual's social role, the process of identification may be found to play a

Reprinted by permission of the publisher and the author from *Journal of Projective Techniques*, 1955, 19, 67-77.

major part. Homoeroticism and its variations in all aspects of behavior in males have been analyzed in terms of the identifications experienced by the individual in the process of psychosexual development, specifically identification with the mother (2, 6, 8, 10). Thompson (24) observed that the one ubiquitous feature in homosexuality, whether it be passive or active types, is the identification with the mother and the consequent adoption of love attachments consonant with a feminine role.

Specifically with respect to schizophrenia, Gerard and Siegel (7, p. 67) reported that confusion of sexual identification constitutes one of a number of characteristics in the family background of schizophrenics that are contributory to their pathological personality development. Reichard and Tillman (23) found that in 76% of seventy-nine male schizophrenics the mother was the dominant parent. Klein and Horwitz (13, p. 700) reported that for 75% of the forty male paranoid cases they studied, the mother was the prime love object. Kasanin et al. (12) reported overprotection as a characteristic pattern among the mothers of schizophrenic individuals, and concluded that this interfered with the child's emancipation from the mother and prevented the emergence into a mature psychosexual role.

STATEMENT OF THE PROBLEM

Consideration of the literature concerning the relationship between psychosexual identification and homoeroticism, and the implications of this relationship to the development of paranoid patterns of adjustment, gives rise to a specific problem. How will a group of paranoid schizophrenics resemble or differ from a group of "nonparanoid" schizophrenics and a group of normals with respect to psychosexual identification? It is hypothesized that:

(1) The paranoid schizophrenic group will show more confusion with regard to psychosexual identification, and will tend to identify more with the female figure, than the normal group.

(2) Whereas both the paranoid schizophrenic group and the nonparanoid schizophrenic group may exhibit confusion with regard to psychosexual identification, the paranoid group will show greater tendencies toward feminine identification.

SUBJECTS

The thirty schizophrenic subjects of this investigation were male veterans of World War II, selected from patients hospitalized in Veterans Administration Hospitals. The diagnostic categories accepted were determined by the final psychiatric staff diagnosis, in turn based upon a psychiatric mental status examination, psychological testing, and a social history of the individual and his family background. Patients with complicating diagnostic features, such as epilepsy, alcoholism, or neuropathy, were not utilized. Patients with history of overt homosexuality were also not included, in order to keep from introducing the very variable being searched for, i.e., feminine identification, into the data. The fifteen normal subjects were selected from the surgery wards of Veterans Administration Hospitals. They were screened for neuropsychiatric involvement with the Cornell Index (25). Their hospital records were inspected in order to ascertain the nature of their hospitalization. Finally, they were interviewed to rule out a history of neuropsychiatric disorder.

The fifteen patients comprising the experimental group consisted of individuals who were diagnosed schizophrenic reaction, paranoid type. The "nonparanoid" control group consisted of eight catatonics and seven hebephrenics. The normal controls consisted of six patients with pilonidal cyst, and nine with hernia. All of the normal subjects were post-operative. The mean ages were: paranoids 32.60 years, nonparanoids 30.20, and normals 31.27. The three groups did not differ significantly in statistical comparisons with respect to age. The groups were equivalent also in terms of the highest school grade completed. The means were: paranoids, 11.40, nonparanoids 11.43, and normals 11.87.

PROCEDURE

The tests used for this study were the Rorschach Psychodiagnostic Test and the Thematic Apperception Test.

(1) Rorschach Psychodiagnostic Test

The administration of the Rorschach was oriented toward obtaining content and human movement responses in order to make it possible to examine the subjects' attitudes as they pertain to psychosexual identification and concept of sexual role.* The first step was the administering of the Rorschach Test in the manner prescribed by Klopfer and Kelley (14). The second step consisted of Testing the Limits for Sex as described by Pascal et al. (22). The third step was Testing the Limits of Movement, a modification of Testing the Limits for Sex, and designed to elicit additional movement responses with inquiry as to the type of movement and sex of the person or persons perceived. Human movement responses and

---

* The present report is concerned with psychosexual identification. The data involving concept of sexual role will be reported separately.

content pertaining to humans and sex relevant to this report were classified as follows and a tally made to obtain frequency of occurrence.

(1) Male Percepts
   (a) Figures: human, mythological, animal, caricature, anatomy;
   (b) Objects: clothing, ornaments.
(2) Female Percepts
   (a) Figures: human, mythological, animal, caricature, anatomy;
   (b) Objects: clothing, ornaments.
(3) Ambiguous Percepts
   (a) Symmetrical figures, one of which is seen as male and the other as female;
   (b) Figures seen as capable of being either male or female;
   (c) Unspecified.
(4) Testing the Limits for Sex
   (a) Male organs;
   (b) Female organs;
   (c) Male and/or female organs.*
(5) Movement Responses in Male Figures
   (a) Homosexual movement;
   (b) Heterosexual movement.
(6) Movement Responses in Female Figures
   (a) Homosexual movement;
   (b) Heterosexual movement.

In order to test the reliability of the investigator's classification of the responses, a qualified clinical psychologist was asked to classify the responses independently. There was complete agreement on the straightforward content categories, sex responses, and the homosexual and heterosexual movement responses.

The following specific predictions were derived from the basic hypotheses with regard to the Rorschach findings:

(1) The paranoid group will produce more responses relating to feminine content, in proportion to responses dealing with masculine content, than either the normal or nonparanoid groups.

(2) The paranoid and nonparanoid groups will produce more ambiguous content responses, in proportion to specific male and female content responses, than the normal group.

(3) The paranoid group will produce more female sexual responses, in proportion to male sexual responses, than either the normal or nonparanoid groups.

(4) The paranoid and nonparanoid groups will produce more ambiguous sexual responses, in proportion to specific male and female sexual responses, than the normal group.

---

* The responses: "Buttocks, could be man's or woman's"; "This looks like a man's (penis) also a woman's (vagina)."

(5) The paranoid group will produce significantly more homosexual human movement responses than either the normal or nonparanoid groups.

(2) Thematic Apperception Test

Thirteen cards were selected, because of the variety of figures and situations they portray. These cards were: 1, 2, 3BM, 4, 6BM, 7BM, 8BM, 10, 12M, 13MF, 18BM, 18GF, and 20. The contents of the stories obtained from the subjects were organized for analysis in the following manner:

(1) Designation of the Sex of Figures
    (a) Accurate designation of the sex of figures;
    (b) Uncertainty as to the designation of the sex of figures;
    (c) Misidentifying the sex of figures.
(2) Sexual Attitudes of Male Toward Male
    (a) Guilt over homosexuality;
    (b) Ambivalence toward homosexuality;
    (c) Positive attitude toward homosexuality.
(3) Sexual Attitudes of Male Toward Female
    (a) Guilt over heterosexuality;
    (b) Ambivalence toward heterosexuality;
    (c) Positive attitude toward heterosexuality.
(4) Sexual Attitudes of Female Toward Male
    (a) Guilt over heterosexuality;
    (b) Ambivalence toward heterosexuality;
    (c) Positive attitude toward heterosexuality.
(5) Sexual Attitudes of Female Toward Female
    (a) Guilt over homosexuality;
    (b) Ambivalence toward homosexuality;
    (c) Positive attitude toward homosexuality.

As on the Rorschach, an independent judge was employed to test the reliability of the investigator's classification of the Thematic Apperception Test data. There was complete agreement in scoring the stories for Designation of Sex. Reliability between judgments was determined by calculating coefficients of contingency based upon chi-square determinations. The latter were set up to check the null hypothesis that the agreement between the judges could have occurred by chance. The reliability coefficients were .83 for Homosexual Attitudes and .80 for Heterosexual Attitudes. Disagreements were settled by submitting the data to a third judge. The two scores out of the three which concurred were accepted as the final criteria for classifying the items in question.

The following specific predictions were derived from the basic hypotheses with regard to the Thematic Apperception Test results:

(1) The paranoid group will make more misidentifications, in relation to accurate designations, than either the normal or nonparanoid groups.

(2) The paranoid and nonparanoid groups will show greater uncer-

tainty in the designation of sex of figures, in relation to accurate designations, than the normal group.

(3) The paranoid and nonparanoid groups will depict guilt and ambivalence over heterosexual interest or activity, in relation to positive attitudes, to a greater extent than the normal group.

(4) The paranoid group will produce more themes dealing with homosexual activity or interest than either the normal or nonparanoid groups.

RESULTS

1. Rorschach Psychodiagnostic Test

The groups did not differ significantly from each other with respect to the ratio of male to female responses (Table 32–1, Comparison A).

The nonparanoid group produced a significantly greater number of the combined sexually ambiguous responses, as compared with the total specific responses, than either the paranoid or normal groups; in both instances, at better than the .01 per cent level of significance (Table 32–1, Comparison B). The paranoid group, however, was not significantly differentiated from the normal group with respect to this comparison. The male and/or female responses were combined with the male-female-symmetry responses for this analysis because of the very low frequency of responses in the latter category. For the comparison in question, this combination constitutes no injustice to the data. The psychological significance of the two categories in question is essentially the same, since they both represent responses in which identical areas on the Rorschach plate are seen as capable of being either male or female.

The paranoid group was differentiated from the normal group at the .06 level of significance, in the direction of a greater proportion of unspecified responses over total specific male and female percepts (Table 32–1, Comparison C). The nonparanoid group produced a significantly greater number of unspecified responses as compared with total specific percepts than did the paranoid group, at better than the .01 level. The nonparanoid group, though not decisively differentiated from the normal group, showed a trend toward a greater proportion of unspecified responses between .10 and .20 levels of significance.

The preponderance of female over male sex percepts which differentiates the paranoid group from the normal group is significant at the .02 level (Table 32–1, Comparison D). The paranoid group was differentiated from the nonparanoid group, toward predominance of female sex responses over male sex responses, at the .06 level of significance. The nonparanoid group did not differ significantly from the normal group with respect to this comparison.

The paranoid and nonparanoid groups differed significantly from

TABLE 32-1

Comparisons of Paranoid, Nonparanoid and Normal Groups
on Content of Rorschach Responses

Comparison A. Total Male to Total Responses

Groups	Male	Female	Chi Square	Level of Significance
Paranoid	118	89	.21	.50-.70
Normal	58	39		
Paranoid	118	89	1.04	.30-.50
Nonparanoid	35	35		
Nonparanoid	35	35	1.58	.20-.30
Normal	58	39		

Comparison B. Male and/or Female Combined with Male-Female-Symmetry Responses to Total Specific Responses

	Male and/or Female and Male-Female-Symmetry	Specific	Chi Square	Level of Significance
Paranoid	20	207	1.02	.30-.50
Normal	5	97		
Paranoid	20	207	21.25	< .01
Nonparanoid	28	70		
Nonparanoid	28	70	20.32	< .01
Normal	5	97		

Comparison C. Unspecified Responses to Total Specific Responses

	Unspecified	Specific	Chi Square	Level of Significance
Paranoid	37	207	3.49	.06
Normal	29	97		
Paranoid	37	207	13.79	.01
Nonparanoid	34	70		
Nonparanoid	34	70	2.68	.10-.20
Normal	29	97		

Comparison D. Male Sex Responses to Female Sex Responses

	Male	Female	Chi Square	Level of Significance
Paranoid	40	81	5.37	.02
Normal	31	30		
Paranoid	40	81	3.73	.06
Nonparanoid	36	41		
Nonparanoid	36	41	.22	.50-.70
Normal	31	30		

Comparison E. Male and/or Female Sex Responses to Male Sex Responses

	Male and/or Female	Male	Chi Square	Level of Significance
Paranoid	11	40	4.03	.02-.05
Normal	1	31		
Paranoid	11	40	.34	.50-.70
Nonparanoid	13	36		
Nonparanoid	13	36	7.42	< .01
Normal	1	31		

the normal group, with a greater proportion of male and/or female sex responses; the former at the .02–.05 level of significance, and the latter at better than the .01 level (Table 32–1, Comparison E). The paranoid group was not differentiated significantly from the nonparanoid group with respect to this comparison.

The low frequency with which the groups produced homosexual human movement responses does not permit meaningful statistical comparison. The paranoid group, however, was responsible for all of the frank homosexual movement responses, a total of five. Neither the normal nor the nonparanoid group produced any homosexual movement responses.

2. Thematic Apperception Test

The question of identification of the sex of figures is applicable to those figures on the Thematic Apperception Test cards which lend themselves to uncertainty or misidentification. The criterion for accurate identification used in this study was the description of the figure concerned given in the TAT manual. Six of the cards used in this study contain figures which lend themselves to uncertain designation or misidentification of the sex of the figures: 3BM, 8BM, 10MF, 12M, 18GF, 20. If the figures on these cards were identified in accordance with the manual, the subject was credited with six accurate identifications. Each group, consequently, could have obtained a maximum of ninety accurate identifications.

Comparison A, Table 32–2 compares the groups with respect to the uncertain designations of sex in relation to accurate identifications. None of the determinations indicates significant differentiations. The same is true for the comparison of misidentification of sex in relation to accurate identification, as shown in Comparison B, Table 32–2. However, in the former instance, the nonparanoid group was differentiated from the normal group at the .10–.20 level of significance, suggesting a trend toward greater production of uncertain designations, in proportion to accurate designations, by the nonparanoid group.

The paranoid and nonparanoid groups are each significantly differentiated from the normal group, at better than the .01 level, in the direction of greater frequency of themes involving guilt concerning heterosexuality over responses of positive attitudes (Table 32–2, Comparison C). The paranoid group is not differentiated significantly from the nonparanoid group with respect to this comparison.

The paranoid and nonparanoid groups were differentiated significantly from the normal group, at better than the .01 level, in the direction of greater ambivalence with respect to heterosexuality over positive attitudes (Table 32–2, Comparison D). The paranoid group did not differ significantly from the nonparanoid group with respect to this comparison.

Stories involving homosexual themes occurred primarily on cards depicting male figures. There were relatively few stories concerning

TABLE 32-2

Comparisons of the Paranoid, Nonparanoid and Normal Groups on Designation of Sex and Heterosexual Themes on Thematic Apperception Test

Comparison A. Uncertain Designation of Sex to Accurate Designation of Sex

	Uncertain	Accurate	Chi Square	Level of Significance
Paranoid	8	73	1.50	.20-.30
Normal	4	78		
Paranoid	8	73	.01	.90-.95
Nonparanoid	8	70		
Nonparanoid	8	70	1.66	.10-.20
Normal	4	78		

Comparison B. Misidentification of Sex to Accurate Designation of Sex

	Misidenti- fication	Accurate	Chi Square	Level of Significance
Paranoid	9	73	.13	.70-.80
Normal	8	78		
Paranoid	9	73	.49	.30-.50
Nonparanoid	12	70		
Nonparanoid	12	70	1.14	.20-.30
Normal	8	78		

Comparison C. Responses of Positive Attitude Toward Heterosexuality to Responses of Guilt Toward Heterosexuality

	Positive	Guilt	Chi Square	Level of Significance
Paranoid	20	41	15.18	.01
Normal	48	24		
Paranoid	20	41	.02	.80-.90
Nonparanoid	16	31		
Nonparanoid	16	31	12.18	.01
Normal	48	24		

Comparison D. Responses of Positive Attitude Toward Heterosexuality to Responses of Ambivalence Toward Heterosexuality

	Positive	Ambivalent	Chi Square	Level of Significance
Paranoid	20	30	14.27	< .01
Normal	48	16		
Paranoid	20	30	.13	.70-.80
Nonparanoid	16	28		
Nonparanoid	16	28	16.11	< .01
Normal	48	16		

homosexuality in which female figures were the principals. Comparison A, Table 32–3 compares the groups for total number of homosexual themes (guilt, ambivalence, and positive attitudes combined). The paranoid and nonparanoid groups produced significantly more homosexual themes than the normal group, being differentiated at better than the .01 level of significance, whereas the paranoid group did not differ significantly from the nonparanoid group. If the groups are compared on the basis of responses involving homosexuality in males, as in Comparison B, Table 32–3, then the paranoid group may be seen to differ significantly from the normal and the nonparanoid groups, in case of the normal group at better than the .01 level, in case of the nonparanoid group, at the .02–.05 level. The nonparanoid group differed significantly from the normal group at better than the .01 level. Evidently, the data relevant to homosexuality in female figures when com-

TABLE 32-3

Comparison of Paranoid, Nonparanoid and Normal Groups on Homosexual Themes on Thematic Apperception Test

Comparison A. Total Homosexual Themes			
	Total Homosexual Themes	Chi Square	Level of Significance
Paranoid	34	21.56	< .01
Normal	5		
Paranoid	34	1.38	.20-.30
Nonparanoid	25		
Nonparanoid	25	13.34	< .01
Normal	5		

Comparison B. Male Homosexual Themes			
	No. of Responses	Chi Square	Level of Significance
Paranoid	31	19.78	< .01
Normal	5		
Paranoid	31	4.08	.02-.05
Nonparanoid	17		
Nonparanoid	17	8.00	< .01
Normal	5		

Comparison C. Ratio of Male Homosexual Responses to Female Homosexual Responses in Paranoid and Nonparanoid Groups

	Male	Female	Chi Square	Level of Significance
Paranoid	31	3	3.69	.06
Nonparanoid	17	8		

bined with the data concerning homosexuality in male figures change the picture with respect to the paranoid and nonparanoid groups. Comparison C, Table 32–3 compares the ratio of male homosexual responses to female homosexual responses that prevails between the paranoid and nonparanoid groups. The paranoid group produced a greater proportion of homosexual themes involving male figures, in contrast to the tendency on part of the nonparanoid group to produce themes involving homosexuality in female figures, at the .06 level of significance.

INTERPRETATION AND DISCUSSION OF RESULTS

In comparing the paranoid with the normal group with respect to the data pertaining to confusion in psychosexual identification, four out of seven determinations yielded statistically significant results ($P = .05$ or better). The nonparanoid group was differentiated in a like manner, four out of seven determinations being conclusively significant ($P = .05$ or better) with two of the seven indicative of trends in the predicted direction ($P = .10–.20$). In addition, the nonparanoid group was significantly differentiated from the paranoid group in two out of seven determinations ($P = .05$ or better). On the basis of these results, it may be concluded that the schizophrenic groups exhibited significantly greater psychosexual confusion than the normal group. In addition, though it was not initially postulated, the nonparanoid group revealed significantly greater confusion in psychosexual identification than the paranoid group.

With respect to feminine identification, the paranoid group was differentiated significantly from the normal group in three out of six determinations, ($P = .05$ or better) and also from the nonparanoid group in three out of six determinations ($P = .06$ or better). In addition, the nonparanoid group was differentiated significantly from the normal group, in the direction of greater feminine identification, in two out of six determinations ($P = .01$ or better).

Evidently, the hypothesis that the paranoid group would show significantly greater feminine identification than the normal and nonparanoid groups is decisively demonstrated in relation to the paranoid and normal groups. The two schizophrenic groups, however, pose some problems. There is evidence to indicate that the nonparanoid group, as well as the paranoid group, reveals significantly greater feminine identification than the normal group. Then too, there is evidence to indicate that the paranoid group is more preoccupied with homosexuality in male figures than the nonparanoid group. Some order may be established if the total picture pertaining to psychosexual identification is integrated, and the issues of confused identification and feminine identification viewed as related aspects of sexual adjustment. London (17) observed that the schizophrenic individual has never reached the heterosexual level of development. Many schizophrenics are fixated at a psychosexual level that is more primitive than the homosexual one, whereas some schizophrenics attain the homosexual level. Since the results of this investigation reveal that the nonparanoid schizophrenic group exhibits greater tendencies toward confused psychosexual identification than the paranoid group, it may be postulated that the trend toward feminine identification represents an attempt at resolving the confusion on the part of the paranoid individual, through a more clearly defined attempt at structuring his sexual role.

The presence of trends toward feminine identification in the nonparanoid group may be understood in the light of the conception of psychopathology which denies that an all or none principle applies either to the symptomatology or the dynamics of the various schizophrenic syndromes. As has been made clear in the literature (11, 19), the schizophrenic subtypes are not hard and fast delineations; rather, they are characterized by considerable overlapping of defenses and symptoms. From this standpoint, a paranoid schizophrenic may be viewed as an individual who utilizes certain defense mechanisms and adaptive patterns to a greater extent than a catatonic schizophrenic, but there may be an overlapping in this respect which would result in some similarities in personality, including psychopathology. Consequently, as the results of this study indicate, the paranoid group shows greater trends toward feminine identification than the nonparanoid group, but both the paranoid and nonparanoid groups reveal these trends to a significantly greater degree than the normal group.

One of the specific areas, regarding feminine identification, in which the paranoid group was not decisively distinguished from the nonparanoid group, occurred on the Thematic Apperception Test. The paranoid group did not differ significantly from the nonparanoid group with respect to the total number of homosexual themes, involving female as well as male figures. It was determined, however, that the paranoid group was relatively more concerned with male homosexuality, and the nonparanoid group more concerned with female homosexuality. Lazell (16) observed that homoerotic trends occur in hebephrenic as well as in paranoid schizophrenics. He differentiated the homoeroticism that occurs in the two groups by postulating that the hebephrenic reaction represents incestuous wishes toward the mother, whereas the paranoid reaction constitutes a defense against the father. Extending this observation, it may be surmised that the hebephrenic might view homosexuality between females as one way of gratifying the wish for incestuous contact with the mother. It is noteworthy that four of the six nonparanoid subjects who produced homosexual responses involving female figures were hebephrenic. Research may further elucidate these matters.

A broader issue may be evoked by calling attention to the fact that, though there were significant differences between the schizophrenic groups and the normal group, the latter, nevertheless, produced responses involving psychosexual confusion and feminine identification. Also, there were paranoid subjects who failed to produce responses relevant to psychosexual confusion or feminine identification. With regard to the incidence of psychosexual confusion and feminine identification among the normal subjects, it may be postulated that the concept of the person encompasses virtually all roles, attitudes, and identifications, that in the normal individual the multiple trends are integrated into a more or less smoothly functioning organization. In the psychotic individual, various facets of the personality appear exaggerted in comparison with the rest of the person. In response to conflict, various aspects of identification, or other dynamisms, assume dominance and make excessive demands upon the individual's total energy distribution, thereby effecting an imbalance in the individual's adjustive capacities.

SUMMARY

The problem of this study was to compare a group of fifteen paranoid schizophrenics with a group of fifteen nonparanoid schizophrenics and fifteen normals with respect to psychosexual identification. It was hypothesized that the paranoid schizophrenic group would show more confusion with regard to psychosexual identification, and will tend to identify more with the female figure, than the normal group. It was also hypothesized that whereas the paranoid schizophrenic group and the nonparanoid schizophrenic group may exhibit confusion in psychosexual identification, the paranoid group would show greater tendencies toward feminine identification. The Rorschach and selected cards of the Thematic Apperception Test were used.

The evidence indicates that the paranoid group displayed greater confusion in psychosexual identification than the normal group, four out of seven chi-square determinations yielding results significant at the .05 level or better and one at the .06 level. The nonparanoid group likewise displayed significantly greater psychosexual confusion than the normal group, four chi-square determinations out of seven yielding results significant at the .05 level or better and two determinations out of the seven indicating trends at the .10–.20 level of confidence. In addition, the nonparanoid group differed at the .05 level or better from the paranoid group in two out of seven determinations, indicating greater psychosexual confusion on the part of the former.

The direction of identification of the paranoid group in comparison with the normal group was significantly more feminine, three out of six chi-square determinations yielding results significant at the .05 level of confidence. The paranoid group differed significantly, at the .06 level of confidence or better, from the nonparanoid group in three out of six chi-square determinations in the direction of greater feminine identification. In addition, the nonparanoid group differed significantly from the normal group, at better than the .01 level, in two out of six chi-square determinations in the direction of greater feminine identification. The implications of the results were discussed.

REFERENCES

1. ARONSON, M. L. A study of the Freudian theory of paranoia by means of the Rorschach test. *J. proj. Tech.*, 1952, *16*, 397–411.

2. BURROW, T. The genesis and meaning of homosexuality and its relation to the problem of introverted mental states. *Psychoanal. Rev.*, 1917, *4*, 219–233.

3. CAMERON, N. *The psychology of behavior disorders.* New York: Houghton Mifflin Co., 1947.

4. FERENCZI, S. *Sex in psychoanalysis.* New York: Robert Brunner, 1950.

5. FREUD, S. *Collected papers,* Vol. III. London: Hogarth Press, 1948.

6. FREUD, S. *Group psychology and the analysis of the ego.* London: Hogarth Press, 1948.

7. GERARD, D. L. and SIEGEL, J. The family background of schizophrenia. *Psychiat. Quart.* 1950, *24*, 47–73.

8. HART, H. H. Problems of Identification. *Psychiat. Quart.*, 1947, *21*, 274–293.

9. HENDERSON, D. K. and GILLESPIE, R. D. *A textbook of psychiatry.* New York: Oxford University Press, 1947.

10. HENDRICK, I. *Facts and theories of psychoanalysis.* New York: Alfred A. Knopf, 1939.

11. JENKINS, R. L. Nature of the schizophrenic process. *Arch. Neurol. Psychiat.*, 1950, *64*, 243–262.

12. KASANIN, J., KNIGHT, E., and SAGE, P. The parent-child relationship in schizophrenia: I. overprotection-rejection. *J. nerv. ment. Dis.*, 1934, *79*, 249–263.

13. KLEIN, H. R. and HORWITZ, W. A. Psychosexual factors in the paranoid phenomena. *Amer. J. Psychiat.*, 1949, *105*, 697–701.

14. KLOPFER, B. and KELLEY, D. M. *The Rorschach technique.* New York: World Book Co., 1946.

15. KNIGHT, R. P. The relationship of latent homosexuality to the mechanism of paranoid delusions. *Bull. Menninger Clin.*, 1940, *4*, 149–159.

16. LAZELL, E. W. The group treatment of dementia praecox. *Psychoanal. Rev.*, 1921, *8*, 168–179.

17. LONDON, L. S. *Libido and delusion.* Washington, D.D.: Mental Therapy Publications, 1946.

18. MARCONDES, D. Relaciones de objeto en la paranoia masculina y feminina. *Rev. Psicoanal.*, B. Aires, 1947, *4*, 492–507.

19. MUNCIE, W. *Psychobiology and psychiatry,* St. Louis: C. V. Mosby Co., 1939.

20. NORMAN, J. P. Evidence and clinical significance of homosexuality in 100 unanalyzed cases of dementia praecox. *J. nerv. ment. Dis.* 1948, *107*, 484–489.

21. NOYES, A. *Modern clinical psychiatry.* Philadelphia: W. B. Saunders Co., 1948.

22. PASCAL, G. R., RUESCH, H. A., DEVINE, C. A., and SUTTELL, B. J. A study of genital symbols on the Rorschach test. *J. abnorm. soc. Psychol.*, 1950, *45*, 286–295.

23. REICHARD, S. and TILLMAN, C. Patterns of parent-child relationships in schizophrenia. *Psychiatry*, 1950, *13*, 247–258.

24. THOMPSON, C. Changing concepts of homosexuality in psychoanalysis. *Psychiatry*, 1947, *10*, 183–189.

25. WEIDER, A., WOLFF, H. G., BRODMAN, K., MITTELMANN, B., and WECHSLER, D. *Cornell Index*, Form N–2, Manual, 1949, p. 8.

This article is based on a dissertation submitted in partial fulfillment of the requirements for the degree of Doctor of Philosophy in the School of Education of New York University. Grateful acknowledgments are due to the Chairman of the sponsoring committee, Professor Brian E. Tomlinson, and to the other committee members, Professors Bernard N. Kalinkowitz and Frederic M. Thrasher.

Acknowledgments for their generous cooperation are due to Dr. Jules D. Holzberg, Director, and Professor Murray Wexler, Department of Psychology, State University of New York; Professor Robert H. Knapp, Wesleyan University; Drs. Robert S. Morrow and Seymour G. Klebanoff, of the Veterans Administration.

PART VII

PSYCHOANALYTIC

PSYCHOTHERAPY

Freud emphasized that psychoanalysis, in addition to being a procedure for the investigation of mental processes, was also a method of treatment for neurotic disorders. The history of Freud's psychoanalytic therapy reveals a shift in focus from the treatment of symptoms to the gaining of insights concerning underlying causes and their role in symptom formation. In a parallel way, the treatment technique shifted from the patient's recalling hypnotically and affectively the pathogenic traumatic events thought to underlie his neurosis, to recovering significant forgotten memories and reconstructing the past accurately through free associations, analyses of dreams, and slips of the tongue. Emphasis also changed from mere recall of memories to an exploration of how the past unnecessarily repeats itself in the patient's relationships to others and to the psychoanalyst (transference). Through the use of interpretations, the analyst helps the patient overcome resistances to revealing links between past and present. The idea implicit in the treatment was that the patient would benefit by knowing, understanding, and experiencing his deepest thoughts, motivations, and emotions. While Freud presented a rough outline of his treatment, he was hesitant to detail the technique of psychoanalysis. He concluded that we know only some of the opening and closing moves, and left the rest to intuitively applied guidelines.

The papers presented in this section touch briefly on a number of issues explored extensively in our review of the empirical literature for psychoanalytic therapy. Brody (Selection 33) in presenting a detailed analysis of Freud's case load, helped to clarify the nature of the sample from which Freud's therapeutic and theoretical conclusions were drawn. This analysis revealed the highly select nature of Freud's reported case load in terms of sex, age, social class, and diagnosis.

In contrast, a series of three papers by Aronson and Weintraub (Selections 34, 35, and 36) offered a look at the modern analytic patient through a survey of the full case loads of thirty American analysts. Again, the highly select nature of the majority of analytic patients in terms of such factors as age, race, religion, education, and social status is apparent. The third report in this series investigated patient changes during private classical psychoanalytic treatment. It is included, not because it is a model study of therapy outcome, but because it provides another view of the patients described in the previous two papers and because it demonstrates some of the problems and drawbacks evident in much of the psychoanalytic literature dealing with outcome. In particular we might point to the total reliance, in assessing treatment outcome, on nonsubstantiated judgments made by reporting analysts (without reliability or validity checks), and the lack of either a non-treated control group or a similar group of patients treated with another approach. Without an appropriate control group, there is no way of confidently attributing any of the potential changes found to the treatment. The study also highlights some differences involved in trying to gauge personality change as opposed to symptomatic change.

Studying experimentally a therapy labeled "psychoanalysis" implies that the approach is reliably applied by different practitioners and that analysts as a group are more alike than different in their practices. In fact, studies based on individual analyst ratings, such as the treatment outcome report by Aronson and Weintraub noted earlier, would necessitate that analysts be in significant agreement with each other in their perceptions and judgments. A review of the empirical literature, however, reveals that analysts are extremely variable in their concept of analytic therapy, their therapeutic practices, and their manner of interpreting the same clinical material. Such an observation, drawn from a number of investigations, leads to the conclusion that, as currently practiced, a single, unified approach to patients that can be designated "psychoanalysis" does not exist.

Two studies pertinent to this conclusion are presented in this section. Lakin and Lebovits (Selection 37) investigated the influence of theoretical orientation on conceptualization of a patient. Responses of psychoanalytically trained psychiatrists were compared with client-centered therapists and eclectic psychiatrists in terms of mode of speculation and selective emphasis. The freedom of analyst speculation, on the basis of minimal data, and the willingness to tolerate even "mutually contradictory" conclusions is noted.

Cutler et al. (Selection 38) compared experienced and inexperienced psychoanalysts with clinical psychologists in rating depth of interpretations from both typescript and tape-recorded interviews. It was anticipated that there would be progressively greater sensitivity and rater reliability with increasing analytic training. While the differences are small, the findings are opposite to the prediction, with the psychologists showing consistently higher agreement than the analytic groups. Moreover, providing additional information lowered agreement among the analysts.

Looking at the scientific studies that have ignored the possible heterogeneity of psychoanalytic therapy and examined the outcome of a treatment labeled "psychoanalysis" leads to two general conclusions: There is some evidence that psychoanalysis is more effective with chronic neurotic patients than no treatment. There is presently no basis for assuming that a therapy called "psychoanalysis" results in a greater degree of improvement with any type of patient than approaches given other labels. Related to these conclusions are the three last papers presented in this section.

Heine (Selection 39) compared reports of changes from patients seen in psychoanalytic, nondirective, and Adlerian therapy. While there were some differences in the factors to which patients attributed change, there were no differences in the types of actual changes reported by patients treated with the various approaches.

Heilbrunn (Selection 40) reported in a personal way on the results he obtained over a seventeen-year period of treating patients by means of what he felt were three different treatment classifications: psychoanalysis, extended psychoanalytic therapy, and brief psychoanalytic psychotherapy. To his surprise he found his improvement rates to be comparable no matter what his presumed approach. The paper represents a clinician's attempts to confront his own biases and open the door to viewing data objectively. The fact that he emphasized the potential role of neurochemical and neurobiologic data should not distract from the major point of the paper—the need to remain critical and questioning about what we do.

The paper by Sloane et al. (Selection 41) was a carefully controlled attempt to compare the outcome of an analytically oriented psychotherapy with the outcome of a behavioral treatment. The study is unusual in its utilization of "real" patients as well as experienced psychoanalysts and behavior therapists. Results indicated that neither form of treatment proved superior to the other, although both were superior to no treatment. This conclusion parallels our overall review findings concerning the comparative effectiveness of psychoanalysis, as generally practiced, and other treatment approaches.

33

Benjamin Brody

Freud's Case Load

Probably more than most other sciences, psychoanalysis is the creation of a single man. The clinical experience, social ideology, and perhaps even personal idiosyncrasies of Sigmund Freud are still the cornerstones of analytic practice and theory some sixty years after his initial observations. Regardless of the fervor of their orthodoxy or the exact nature of their heresies, it seems clear that most analysts are still following, sifting over, or rejecting some phase of Freud's work.

Under these circumstances, a careful examination of the cultural, psychological, and clinical bases of Freud's thinking seems imperative for an evaluation of the validity and limitations of his conclusions. Thus, Fromm and Horney, reconsidering Freud's biological orientation, concluded that it is theoretically cumbersome and therapeutically superfluous in the light of the newer knowledge of culture and Freud's milieu. In a more personal vein, through a critical study of his writings, David Riesman (15, 16) examined the influences of Freud's attitudes to work, play, authority, and liberty. There is a growing realization that Freud himself, as a human being with personal and clinical assets and limitations, must be considered in any evaluation of psychoanalysis.

Through an analysis of his clinical writings, this study will estimate the nature of Freud's clinical experience in terms of the characteristics of the population of patients with which he dealt.

METHOD

The writings alone probably give only a small and highly selected sample of Freud's total case load. However, until his files and clinical notes become available for analysis—if they exist—his published works remain the best approximation. In spite of their lack of completeness, they

Reprinted by permission of the publisher and the author from *Psychotherapy: Theory, Research and Practice*, 1970, 7, 8-12.

possess a unique value; it seems reasonable to assume that they represent those cases which stimulated Freud sufficiently to motivate him to a full report or passing reference and, accordingly, formed the important raw material for both his own conclusions and the studies of his disciples.

The case reports themselves range from full clinical histories containing a relatively complete anamnesis, some record of the therapeutic process, and a theoretical discussion to the barest mention of a patient in connection with a single point. However, even in the most detailed account it is frequently difficult to ascertain the kind of vital statistic in which we are interested, perhaps because of the need for professional discretion as well as a certain literary predilection that frequently obscures the presence of factual life-history material. Thus, in the famous Wolf-Man (Freud, 9) case, some rather involved calculation is necessary to establish that the patient was about twenty-three years old when he first came for treatment. Freud frequently conducted armchair analyses of literary and historical characters he had never seen or of incidents and personalities outside the confines of his consulting room, utilized case material offered by colleagues or from his personal life and nonclinical observations, and, on at least one occasion, constructed an ideal-type case (Freud, 5) for illustrative purposes. To further complicate the data, a favorite case is frequently utilized in several different papers; references to the Wolf-Man case, for example, appear in at least four different sources.

To obviate these difficulties, only patients whom Freud personally treated are considered in this study. In all instances, the criterion of inclusion is categorical evidence that Freud himself actually saw the patient in clinical contact. Insofar as identification is possible, a case is cited only once at the date of its earliest publication.

Obviously, a full clinical report of several hundred pages resulting in important theoretical and therapeutic considerations demands quite different treatment than a passing reference of a few lines. Not only is the former more important from an historical point of view, but our confidence in the reliability and completeness of the data is proportionately greater. Accordingly, the case material is divided into major and minor categories and treated separately. The major category is composed of those cases that are at least several pages in length, include some statement of the patient's life circumstances, and serve as the vehicle for a theoretical discussion; the minor cases are simply the remaining ones. This definition of the major case, it should be noted, has some claim to operational validity; with only a few additions, it includes all the case presentations in Freud's two clinical volumes: the *Studies in Hysteria* and Volume III of the *Collected Papers*.

Both major and minor cases were analyzed in terms of sex, age, marital state, diagnosis and social class. Especially in his fuller presentations, Freud himself provides fairly accurate information on the first four of these variables though, as we have noted, it is frequently incomplete and occasionally requires reconstruction from the available evidence. Within these limitations, we can be certain that whatever information does exist is valid. As Freud (8) says: ". . . I have altered the *milieu* . . . in order to preserve the incognito of those concerned, but . . . I have altered nothing else. I consider it an undesirable practice, however excellent the motive may be, to alter any detail in the presentation of a case. One can never tell which aspect . . . may be picked out by a reader of independent judgment, and one runs the risk of giving the latter a false impression."

The situation is somewhat different in relation to social class. Though clearly realizing the fact of social stratification, Freud rarely explicitly identified his patients as belonging to one or another status hierarchy; indeed, it is probable that such a task was beyond the state of sociological knowledge during most of his working lifetime. However, W. Lloyd Warner and associates (19) at the University of Chicago evolved a group of indices which are closely associated with actual levels of social participation. By a systematic, empirical evaluation of such information as occupation, source of income, education, religion, and ethnic origin, a statistically valid estimate of social status can be computed. Although complete calculation of the index is rarely possible with our data. Warner's scales can be utilized toward a reasonably accurate estimation of social class. Thus, we can be certain that the Wolf-Man was of at least middle class status because of the references to his family estates, nurse, and English governess. Similarly, Dora's (Freud, 7) extensive education and her father's position as "a large manufacturer in very comfortable circumstances" place her in the middle class group. Warner's three primary class divisions have been consolidated into two groups; our "upper" class is equivalent to his upper and middle classes, and our "lower" class is identical with his lower class. Because of the incompleteness of our data, any attempt at precise class placement is avoided by this technique and the effect of changes in class identification from Freud's time to our own is minimized.

RESULTS

With the exception of a few obituaries, prefaces, and minor papers, Freud's complete works were analyzed as cited in Strachey's (17) bibliography of Freud's writings in English translation. A total of 114 papers were searched for major and minor cases and all of Freud's twenty-two books were examined in terms of the major category alone. Table 33–1 summarizes the results for the twelve major cases and Table 33–2 for the 133 minor cases.

It is interesting to note that about half of both the major and minor cases were published from 1889 to 1900, a period that is equivalent to the first stage of psychoanalytical development according to Thompson (18), and that ended with Freud's growing involvement in the intricacies

TABLE 33-1

Major Cases

No.	Period	Date	Name	Sex	Age	Marital State	Social Class	Diagnosis
1	I	1893	—	Female	20-30	Married	Upper	Hysteria
2	1889-1900[2]	1893	Lucie R.	Female	Young Lady	Single	Upper	Hysteria
3		1895	Emmy Von N.	Female	About 40	Married	Upper	Hysterical Delirium
4		1895	Katherina	Female	About 18	Single	Upper	Hysteria
5		1895	Elizabeth R.	Female	24	Single	Upper	Hysteria
6		1899	—	Male	38	—	Upper	Phobia
7	II	1905	Dora	Female	18	Single	Upper	Hysteria
8[1]	1901-1912[2]	1909	Hans[1]	Male	5	Single	Upper	Phobia
9		1909	"Rat-Man"	Male	Youngish Man	Single	Upper	Obsessional Neurosis
10	III	1915	—	Female	30	Single	Upper	Paranoia
11	1913-1924[2]	1918	"Wolf-Man"	Male	23 (c.)	Married[3]	Upper	Post Obsessional Neurotic Condition
12		1920	—	Female	18	Single	Upper	Homosexuality

[1] Freud actually saw this patient personally only once.
[2] Periods of psychoanalytical development according to Thompson (18).
[3] Information from R. Brunswick (3).

of instinct psychology. As Thompson says: "This was a time of great discovery gleaned from clinical observation . . . the period of Freud's greatest creativeness. No theories he later developed can compare with the brilliance of the early discoveries." The sharp decrement in the number of case presentations after 1900 is thus closely associated with the development of the libido theory. It seems clear that Freud's interest in people and their relationships diminished around 1900 in favor of constitutional factors. To quote Thompson once more: ". . . he came to minimize what actually happens between people, failed to take into consideration . . . that it is the dynamic interaction between people which provides the locus of functional mental illness." In the 1920s, during the period of pessimism about the efficacy of psychoanalytical therapy and the first experiments with therapeutic technique, Freud published no major cases and comparatively few minor cases.

Sex

Tables 33-1 and 33-2 reveal that women composed about two-thirds of Freud's published cases. Though such a preponderance is

TABLE 33-2
Minor Cases

	Sex			Marital State			Age					Diagnosis						Social Class			Total
	Male	Female	No data	Single	Married	No data	Children: Under 12	Adolescents: 12-20	Young Adults: 21-30	Adults 30+	No data	Primary Dx: Obsessional Neurosis	Primary Dx: Anxiety Neurosis	Primary Dx: Hysteria	Unclassified Neurosis	Primary Dx: Psychosis	No data	Upper Class	Lower Class	No data	Total
Period I[2] 1889-1900	14	34	22[1]	9	19	42[1]	1	4	9	34	22[1]	21	13	31	2	2	1[1]	9	0	61[1]	70
Period II[2] 1901-1912	4	9	0	0	3	10	0	1	0	10	2	5	1	0	0	1	6	3	0	10	13
Period III[2] 1913-1924	15	21	4	0	8	32	0	3	10	23	4	5	2	2	4	7	20	10	0	30	40
Period IV[2] 1925-1938	8	2	0	0	2	8	0	1	3	6	0	1	0	1	4	0	4	4	0	6	10
Total	41	66	26	9	32	92	1	9	22	73	28	32	16	34	10	10	31	26	0	107	133

[1] Does not include a reference (Freud, 1898) to "over 200 patients" but with no other information given.
[2] Periods of psychoanalytical development according to Thompson (1950).

understandable because of the limited outlets and opportunities available to women during most of Freud's time, it is noteworthy for the light it casts on his own cultural ideology. In spite of the composition of his case load, Freud, like many contemporary classical analysts, confessed comparative difficulty in formulating the psychology of women. As late as 1924, for example, in discussing the psychosexual development of girls, he (8) says: "Here our material—for some reason we do not understand—becomes far more shadowy and incomplete." Similarly, Hendrick (12) writes: "The psychology of the female has proved to be no simple problem for Freud and other analysts. She has remained an enigma. . . . Few doubted that she existed; no one seemed able to prove with certainty how she got that way." "Incomplete" as Freud's formulation of female psychology may be, critics such as Horney and Thompson have felt that Freud's formulation of female psychology reflected Victorian attitudes and, in effect, discriminated against women. From our data, on the basis of a clinical practice largely devoted to women, Freud derived a male psychology. The limitations of Freud's culture affected and perhaps outweighed the influence of his clinical experience.

Diagnosis

Freud diagnosed half of his twelve major cases as hysteria, two as obsessional neurosis and phobia, and one each as homosexuality and paranoia. In general, these proportions are maintained in the minor group; about 65% have as their primary diagnosis hysteria and obsessional neurosis, 15% anxiety neurosis, and the remainder are divided equally between unclassified neurotic conditions and psychoses. Freud's limited and, from our tables, relatively late experience with psychotic patients may be reflected in his belief that they are incapable of transference and hence not amenable to analytical therapy. His extensive experience with hysteria and obsessions may have resulted in the belief, still held by many analysts according to Thompson, that "only hysteria, obsessions, and phobias are suitable cases for analysis." Although it is difficult to be certain of the exact causal relationships, the inference is strong that a limitation of Freud's clinical experience has been elevated to the dignity of a therapeutic principle.

Age

Nine of Freud's major cases were between eighteen and twenty years of age, only two were older than thirty, and only one was a child. These trends are maintained by the minor cases as well. Only one patient is under twelve, nine are between twelve and twenty, and only two are over forty-five. About 90% of the total patient group is between twenty and forty-four. Freud's cases, then, were derived almost exclusively from the adult and young adult groups; he had very few adolescents and practically no children as patients. One wonders to what extent his limited experience with older patients is responsible for the dictum that psychoanalysis is not indicated with older people.

Social Class

The data on the social class affiliations of the major cases is definitive. Every one of these patients is a member of the upper class as we have defined it. As a matter of fact, it is our impression that probably only a minority are as low in status as middle class by Warner's more detailed divisions. Freud provides less data permitting class identification for the minor cases than with any of our other variables indicating, perhaps, a relatively limited realization of the importance of social affiliation. In any case, the data are consistent here as well; all twenty-six minor cases are upper class. It is clear that Freud's patients were drawn exclusively from the upper and middle class. Wassermann (20; Ansbacher, 1), working in Poland, has corroborated these findings to a remarkable extent in spite of the incomplete nature of his data and a somewhat impressionistic technique of arriving at class affiliation. The insistence of the cultural school of analysis that Freud's conclusions were derived from a limited social group is confirmed.

In all probability, this is true of present-day American analysis as well. The extensive occupational data on patients treated at the Institute for Psyhoanalysis in Chicago (*Ten Year Report*, 21) and Kubie's (14) statistics on the scale of analytical fees makes it highly unlikely that more than a few lower class patients have been analyzed. Crowley (4) has called attention to the comparatively small numbers of lower class patients even in the Low Cost Psychoanalytical Service of the William Alanson White Institute where financial inability presumably represents no objection. Brody (2) and Grey (11) in the Middle West and afterwards Hollingshead and Redlich (13) in New England found a similar situation in psychiatric clinics and hospitals where the treatment is not strictly psychoanalytic but psychoanalytically oriented. Is it possible that something in the ideology and technique of analysis makes it difficult for lower class people to use successfully? The class origins of both analytical patients and practitioners seem to make this a likely hypothesis.

Marital State

Seven of the ten adult major cases were single in contrast to only 22% of the minor ones. The significance of this difference, however, should not be overestimated because of the small number of cases in the major category. In the minor group, however, about 85% of the female patients were married while about 55% of the males were. Though the evidence is not clear, it seems probable that a majority of Freud's patients were married.

REFERENCES

1. ANSBACHER, H. L.   The significance of the socio-economic status of the patients of Freud and of Adler. *Amer. J. Psychotherapy,* 1959, *13,* 378–383.

2. BRODY, B.   *Relationships between Slavic ethnicity and psychological characteristics of psychiatric patients.* Ph.D. thesis, U. of Chicago, 1949.

3. BRUNSWICK, R. M.   A supplement to Freud's History of an infantile neurosis. *Int. J. Psycho-Anal.,* 1928, *9,* 439–476.

4. CROWLEY, R. M.   A low-cost psychoanalytical service: first year. *Psychiat. Quart.* 1950, *24,* 462–482.

5. FREUD, S.   The aetiology of hysteria; 1896. In *Collected papers,* Volume I. London: Hogarth Press, 1924. Pp. 183–219.

6. FREUD, S.   Sexuality in the aetiology of the neuroses; 1898. In *Collected papers,* Volume I. London: Hogarth Press, 1924. Pp. 220–248.

7. FREUD, S.   Fragment of an analysis of a case of hysteria; 1905. In *Collected papers,* Volume III. London: Hogarth Press, 1924. Pp. 13–148.

8. FREUD, S.   A case of paranoia running counter to the psycho-analytical theory of the disease; 1915. In *Collected papers,* Volume II. London: Hogarth Press, 1924. Pp. 150–161.

9. FREUD, S.   From the history of an infantile neurosis: 1918. In *Collected papers,* Volume III. London: Hogarth Press. Pp. 473–605.

10. FREUD, S.   The passing of the Oedipus-complex; 1924. In *Collected papers,* Volume II. London: Hogarth Press, 1924. Pp. 269–276.

11. GREY, A.   *Relationships between social class and psychological characteristics of psychiatric patients.* Ph.D. thesis, U. of Chicago, 1940.

12. HENDRICK, I.   *Facts and theories of psychoanalysis.* New York: Knopf, 1941.

13. HOLLINGSHEAD, A., & REDLICH, F.   *Social class and mental illness.* New York: Wiley, 1958.

14. KUBIE, L. S.   A pilot study of psychoanalytical practice in the United States. *Psychiartry,* 1950, *13,* 227–246.

15. RIESMAN, D.   The themes of work and play in the structure of Freud's thought. *Psychiatry,* 1950, *13,* 1-16 (a).

16. RIESMAN, D.   Authority and liberty in the structure of Freud's thought. *Psychiatry,* 1950, *13,* 167–187 (b).

17. STRACHEY, J.   Bibliography: list of English translation of Freud's works. *Psychoanalyt. Quart.* 1946, *15,* 207–225.

18. THOMPSON, C.   *Psychoanalysis: evolution and development.* New York: Hermitage House, 1950.

19. WARNER, W. L.   *Social class in America.* Chicago: Science Research Associates, 1949.

20. WASSERMANN, I.   Letter to the editor. *Amer. J. Psychotherapy,* 1958, *12,* 623–627.

21. *Ten Year Report. Institute for psychoanalysis,* Chicago, 1942.

34

Walter Weintraub, M.D. & H. Aronson, Ph.D.

A Survey of Patients in Classical Psychoanalysis:
Some Vital Statistics

The criticism has been made by both partisans and detractors of psycho-analysis that analysts have been slow to collect and to publish certain data relevant to the practice of their art (4). Nowhere in the literature is there to be found a systematic report describing the background of the typical analytic patient, his reasons for seeking help, and his progress in therapy. During the past fifty years, only a few statistical studies of this kind have been published, and, in almost all instances, the patients reported on were treated by inexperienced candidates (3).

Responding to the need for basic statistics, a Central Fact-Gathering Committee was established by the American Psychoanalytic Association in 1952 for the purpose of collecting and processing the data of psycho-analytic practice. Hundreds of analysts filled out a series of question-naires for thousands of patients in analysis and psychotherapy. Because of methodological difficulties, interest in the project declined, and, in 1957, the Central Fact-Gathering Committee was discharged. Although a final summary of the Committee's findings was distributed to members of the American Psychoanalytic Association in 1958, a full report was not issued until February, 1967 (2).

Convinced that an objective study of psychoanalytic practice can best be carried out by investigators not subject to the direction of any psychoanalytic organization, we decided to study the question inde-pendently. The senior author, a graduate of the Baltimore Psychoanalytic Institute and a member of the American Psychoanalytic Association, requested the cooperation of his local institute in order to complete a survey of analytic patients in the Baltimore area. When this proposal met with energetic opposition, the project was abandoned. The study was opposed for four principal reasons: (1) A number of analysts felt that confidentiality could not be maintained in a study limited to the Baltimore area. (2) The opinion was expressed that information

Reprinted by permission of the publisher and the authors from *Journal of Nervous and Mental Disease*, 1968, *146*, 98–102. Copyright 1968, The Williams & Wilkins Co.

gathered by means of a questionnaire would inevitably be superficial and misleading. (3) Perhaps most important of all, it was feared that opponents of psychoanalysis would be provided additional ammunition with which to attack the analytic movement. (4) Another source of opposition to the study was the understandable reluctance of many Baltimore analysts to repeat on the local scene the unfortunate experience of the Central Fact-Gathering Committee.

In 1963, when it became clear that a survey of the Baltimore area was not feasible, we decided to collect data from psychoanalysts practicing in several East Coast communities. Extensive questionnaires were sent out to a number of analyst friends and acquaintances of the senior author. Respondents were asked to complete a questionnaire for each analytic patient seen during the year September 1, 1962 to August 31, 1963. Thirty analysts reported on a total of 144 patients. Most of the analysts are members of the American Psychoanalytic Association, and all are associated with member societies or institutes.

The questionnaire consisted of a number of multiple choice items through which the participating analysts supplied considerable background information about their patients as well as data relating to the practice of psychoanalysis. A number of items were devoted to an assessment of therapeutic results.

Analysis of the data has been proceeding for some time. This paper will be limited to a survey of some of the descriptive statistics of the 44 analytic patients.

RESULTS

Thirty analysts participated in the study. Ten had been graduated from psychoanalytic institutes for more than five years; eight had been graduated for a period of less than five years; and twelve were still candidates.

Table 34–1 categorizes the number of cases reported on according to length of experience. It shows that the median number of patients for whom the respondents contributed data is 6.50 for the more senior analysts, 6.25 for the recent graduates, and 2.42 for the candidates.

Sex: Of the 144 patients, 90 or 62.5% were male and 54 or 37.5% were female (Table 34–2).

Race: All 144 patients were white. This finding is particularly significant in view of the fact that many of the analysts who participated in the study are practicing in communities having large Negro populations and at least a moderate number of Orientals.

Age: Table 34–3 describes the patient population with respect to age as of September 1, 1963. Ninety-three were in the twenty- to fifty-

TABLE 34-1

Case Load and Status of Reporting Analysts*

Analyst's Status	No. of Analysts	No. of Cases†	No. of Cases per Analyst	
			Mean	Range
Candidate	12	29	2.42	1-4
Graduate with less than 5 years of experience	8	50	6.25	2-10
Graduate with more than 5 years of experience	10	65	6.50	2-12

*Several graduate analysts began treating survey patients at a point when their experience was in a lower category than that given here. This table refers to the status of the analyst in 1962-1963.

†While for most of the analysts these figures represent a full report of their patients, the number is reduced somewhat for the more senior analysts since two senior analysts did not return information on patients where confidentiality might be in doubt.

year-old range. A majority, 53% were in the fourth decade of life. Only 4% of the patients were under twenty and 3% had reached the age of fifty.

Marital status: At the onset of treatments, 87 or 60% of the patients were married; 48 or 33% were single; 9 or 7% were divorced, separated or widowed. Of the eighty-seven married patients, four had been married twice; 37.8% of the male patients and 23.3% of the female patients were single. For patients over thirty at the time of the survey, 31.5% of the men and 17.6% of the women had begun their analyses when still single.

Number of children: At the onset of analytic treatment, 96 of the 144 patients were or had been previously married. Information on the number of children was provided for 86 of these patients. The mean number of children per married patient was 1.87.

TABLE 34-2

Distribution of Analytic Patients by Sex of Patient and by Seniority of Analyst at Initiation of Analysis

Sex of Patient	Status of Analyst When Analysis Began			Total
	Candidate	Graduate with < 10 Years of Experience	Graduate with > 10 Years of Experience	
Male	25 (52%)	30 (60%)	35 (76%)	90 (62.5%)*
Female	23 (48%)	20 (40%)	11 (24%)	54 (37.5%)
Total	48	50	46	144

*$\chi^2 = 5.98$, $p < .05$, one-tailed test of significance.

TABLE 34-3

Age of Patient at Time of Survey

Age of Patient	No. of Males	No. of Females	Total	Percentage
yrs				
Under 10	4	2	2	1
10-15			4	3
16-19	—	—	—	—
20-29	13	18	31	22
30-39	54	22	76	53
40-49	18	8	26	18
50-59	1	4	5	3
Over 59	—	—	—	—

TABLE 34-4

Marital Status of Analytic Patients
at the Time of Initiation of Treatment

	Male	Female	Total	Percentage
Marital status				
Single	34	14	48	33
Married	50	37	87	60
Separated			4	3
Divorced	6	3	4	3
Widowed			1	1
Total	90	60		144
Number of times married				
0			48	36
1			83	61
2			4	3
3 or more			—	—
Total				135
Data not given				9
Number of children				
0			57	46
1			18	15
2			31	25
3			11	9
4			6	5
5			1	1
More than 5			—	—
Total				124
Data not given				
Single				10
Married				10

TABLE 34-5

*Religious Affiliation of the
Analytic Patients*

Affiliation	No. of Patients
Protestant	48 (33%)
Catholic	19 (13%)
Jewish	58 (40%)
Other	2 (1%)
None	17 (12%)
Total	144

Data on the number of children were given for thirty-eight of the forty-eight single analysands. None of these patients was reported as having any offspring.

Religion: Table 34–5 delineates the religious affiliation of the 144 patients at the start of therapy. It shows that fifty-eight or 40% of the group were Jewish, forty-eight or 33% were Protestant, and nineteen or 13% were Catholic. Seventeen or 12% were reported as having no religious affiliation and two or 2% belonged to other religious denominations. Compared with the religious distribution of the several communities in which the patients lived, the patient sample contained a greatly disproportionate share of Jews and a gross underrepresentation of Catholics.

DISCUSSION

As indicated above, there is a scarcity of data concerning the background of the typical analytic patient. The project of the Central Fact-Gathering Committee (2) and a recent report by Siegel (5) deal with some of the areas investigated in our study.

The Central Fact-Gathering Committee's data are derived from responses to a two-part questionnaire. Participating analysts and senior candidates filled out and returned part I for each patient in analysis or therapy. Part II was returned at the termination of treatment. Part I forms were submitted for approximately 10,000 patients by 800 analysts whereas only about 3,000 part II forms were submitted. Because the part I questionnaires were not preserved, certain data were lost and information for the 10,000 patients is not available for all items of the questionnaire. Thus, for those aspects of analytic patients' background considered in this paper, the Central Fact-Gathering Committee's data are complete for age, sex, and race. With respect to religion and marital status, only the part II figures are available. A more important point is the fact that for all these categories, the Central Fact-Gathering Committee's figures combine psychoanalytic and psychotherapy patients.

Siegel circulated a seven-item questionnaire among a sample of 100 active members of the American Psychoanalytic Association requesting certain background information for patients they were analyzing. Fifty-two analysts returned questionnaires for 476 patients.

With respect to color and age, our results closely parallel those of the two studies referred to above. The Central Fact-Gathering Committee's data for 10,000 patients in analysis and psychotherapy placed 89% between ages nineteen and forty-five; 99% of the patient population were white. All 476 patients reported on in Siegel's study were white and the mean age for both sexes was between thirty-four and thirty-five years.

Because of slight differences in category construction, it is not possible directly to compare the Central Fact-Gathering Committee's or Siegel's data on the marital status of analytic patients with ours. Patients in analysis do appear, in all three studies, to be a late-marrying group. This is, perhaps, due partly to the fact that they are from a well educated, middle class population (1) and partly to the likelihood that many come for treatment of sexual difficulties.

With regard to sex, both the data of the Central Fact-Gathering Committee and Siegel's indicate an approximately 50–50 male-female ratio whereas our group contains a significantly greater number of men. Although the reasons for this difference are not clear, Table 34–2 indicates that as analysts gain more experience, they tend to see a greater proportion of male patients. Kubie (4) reported a similar phenomenon when he compared analytic candidates' patients with those of graduate psychoanalysts. This is undoubtedly due to the fact that candidates and other mental health professionals, the majority of whom are male (1), tend to be analyzed by more experienced analysts. Our respondents may have contained a higher proportion of more experienced analysts than the Fact-Gathering Committee or the Siegel surveys.

In the "religion" category, our findings are comparable to those of the Central Fact-Gathering Committee in that their sample also contains a large percentage of Jewish patients (45.2) and a relatively small number of Catholics (approximately 10%).

Our population of analytic patients can be described as white, between the ages of thirty and fifty, largely of Jewish or Protestant background, and containing more men than women. Although a majority have married, the percentage of single patients of marriageable age is high. Our analytic patients seem to marry late and have few children. The percentage of divorce or separated patients is relatively low. It is likely that many of these characteristics can be accounted for by assuming that we are dealing largely with a group of conservative, white, middle class professionals.

SUMMARY

This is the first of a series of reports describing characteristics of patients in classical psychoanalysis. Thirty analysts, practicing in several East Coast communities, contributed data for 144 patients treated between September 1, 1962 and August 31, 1963. This report has considered the vital statistics of age, race, sex, religion, marital status, and size of family. We found that our population was entirely white, largely of Jewish and Protestant background, and contained a significantly greater number of males. A majority of the patients were in their thirties. Compared with the general population, the group appeared to be a late-marrying one with relatively few children.

REFERENCES

1. ARONSON, H. and WEINTRAUB, W.   Social background of the patient in classical psychoanalysis. *J. Nerv. Ment. Dis., 146,* 91–97, 1968.

2. HAMBURG, D. A.   *Report of Ad Hoc Committee on Central Fact-Gathering Data.* American Psychoanalytic Association, New York, 1967.

3. KNIGHT, R. P.   Evaluation of the results of psychoanalytic therapy. *Amer. J. Psychiat., 98:* 434–446, 1941.

4. KUBIE, L. S.   A pilot study of psychoanalytic practice in the United States. *Psychiatry, 13:* 227–245, 1950.

5. SIEGEL, N. H.   Characteristics of patients in psychoanalysis. *J. Nerv. Ment. Dis. 135:* 155–158, 1962.

This investigation was supported in part by the U. S. Public Health Service Award K3–MH–19393 and Grant MH–07434 from the National Institutes of Health.

35

H. Aronson, Ph.D. & Walter Weintraub, M.D.

Social Background of the Patient
in Classical Psychoanalysis

More than in the case of physical illnesses, the treatment of emotional disorders may be heavily influenced by the social setting in which the disturbances take place. Those who are close to the psychoanalytic movement are aware of the fact that analytic patients comprise a selected segment of our society. Relatively few studies, however, are available with data to demonstrate this phenomenon. Hollingshead and Redlich (5) have described analytic patients as coming almost exclusively from the higher social classes. Since they studied fewer than twenty patients undergoing analysis, however, they could say relatively little about analytic patients as a group.

The present study is based upon a survey of 144 patients who were undergoing psychoanalysis from 1962 to 1963. A general description of the procedure by which our data were collected is reported elsewhere (10). The data, some of which will be given below, comprise the full case loads of a group of analysts.

In the paper referred to above, the authors outlined an analytic patient group in terms of broad descriptive categories, i.e., age, sex, race, religion, etc. This paper will deal primarily with social status: education; income; sources from which such income is derived; and geographic mobility.

Several writers have suggested that the similarity in social background between patient and therapist is an important variable in determining the course of therapy (5, 8). Since 43 (30%) of our 144 patients were engaged in professions pertaining to mental health, it became possible to compare subsets of our group, based upon occupation. That comparison will also be reported here.

Reprinted by permission of the publisher and the authors from *Journal of Nervous and Mental Disease*, 1968, *146*, 91–97. Copyright 1968, The Williams & Wilkins Co.

RESULTS

Total Patient Population

Education: Table 35–1 gives the level of education reached by the patient, his spouse, and his parents. It indicates that 50% of the patients had completed postgraduate training and only 7% had not had some instruction beyond the high school level. Their spouses were also relatively well educated, more than half being college graduates. The patients' parents were also better educated than is usual for their age groups. In all, 22% of the fathers had postgraduate training and only 26% did not complete high school. Only 27% of their mothers did not complete high school.

As shown in Table 35–2, the proportion of the U.S. population with at least college training, at all age and sex levels, is less than 20%. For the age range in which the patients' parents are likely to be found, less than 40% of the U.S. population are high school graduates.

Occupation: Table 35–3 indicates the patients' occupations upon entering treatment. Only 9% of the patients were engaged in occupations involving business or physical labor, skilled or unskilled. The majority were professionals in medical and other fields. Half their spouses were either housewives or professionals with a similar dearth of businessmen and laborers. The patients' fathers did follow occupations in business, government and labor, although, here too, professional fields are highly represented (22%). Few of the patients' mothers could be considered regular wage earners (22%). Those who did work were most often teachers, nurses or technicians (9%).

Social status: The occupation and education of each patient and that of his spouse were translated into scores of Hollingshead Two Factor

TABLE 35-1

Education of Patient, His Spouse and Parents

Total Responses	Patient (N = 144)	Spouse (N = 76)	Father (N = 124)	Mother (N = 116)
Graduate professional training completed	72 (50%)	24 (32%)	27 (22%)	5 (4%)
Graduate professional training incomplete	17 (12%)	8 (10%)	2 (2%)	1 (1%)
College or university graduate	30 (21%)	22 (29%)	22 (18%)	14 (12%)
Partial college or technical training (1 year or more)	13 (9%)	11 (14%)	4 (3%)	11 (9%)
High school or trade school graduate	5 (3%)	10 (13%)	37 (30%)	53 (46%)
Partial high school (grades 10-11)	2 (1%)	1 (1%)	16 (13%)	19 (16%)
Junior high school (grades 7-9)	0 (0%)	0 (0%)	4 (3%)	3 (2%)
Less than 7 years schooling	5 (3%)	0 (0%)	12 (10%)	10 (9%)
Unknown	0	20	20	28
Does not apply	0	48	0	0

TABLE 35-2

1960 Census Report of Highest School Grade Completed by White Population*

							Schooling					
	None		1-7		7-11		High School		Partial College		College, 4 Years or More	
ge	M	F	M	F	M	F	M	F	M	F	M	F
rs	%	%	%	%	%	%	%	%	%	%	%	%
-29	0.7	0.5	8.3	6.1	28.3	28.6	33.5	45.0	13.6	11.7	15.6	8.1
-34	0.7	0.5	10.1	7.5	33.0	30.9	29.2	42.5	11.2	11.0	15.8	7.6
-39	0.7	0.6	10.9	8.4	32.6	31.2	31.2	42.5	10.6	10.8	14.0	6.5
-44	0.7	0.6	13.0	10.4	36.4	36.2	29.3	36.5	9.9	9.8	10.7	6.5
-49	0.9	0.8	17.1	13.9	40.6	40.2	23.4	28.9	8.8	9.7	9.2	6.5
-54	1.2	1.1	20.9	17.2	43.2	42.2	17.6	22.6	8.3	10.1	8.8	6.8
-59	1.8	1.8	26.2	21.8	44.2	43.7	13.1	17.9	7.2	9.1	7.5	5.7
-64	2.9	3.2	29.9	25.5	43.4	43.5	11.2	15.3	6.6	8.0	6.0	4.5
-69	5.2	5.3	34.7	28.6	41.1	42.4	9.2	12.8	5.7	7.1	5.1	3.8

*Derived from Table 174, U.S. Census, 1960 (Ref. 1).

Index of Social Position (4). For ease of computation each patient was assigned whichever of the two scores indicated the higher social level. Next, where sufficient data were available ($N = 120$), similar transformations were made on the occupational and educational standing of the patients' parents.

Hollingshead has divided the total range of scores into five arbitrary classes. About 10 to 12% of the general population should be expected to fall into the first two classes, 17 to 21% into the third, and the remaining 65 to 75% into the two lowest groupings. Of the patient group, 72.8% fall into the highest social level, 21.6% into the second, 4.8% into the third, and less than 1% into the fourth. The patients' parents do not place quite so high on the social ladder. Here only 29.2% are in the highest category, 21.7% in the second, 34.2% in the third, and 15% in the two lowest social groupings.

Nuclear income: The incomes of analytic patients are shown in Table 35–4. Only 2% of the patients earned or received less than $5,000 per year. Their median income level lay between $10,000 and $14,999 per year and 22% had yearly incomes of $20,000 or more. The Bureau of the Census found the median U.S. familial income in 1963 to be $6,249 (2).

Derivation of income: Only 68% of the analysands depended totally upon salary, self-employment, aid from relatives, or some combination of the three for their support. A total of 32% obtained part (30%) or all (2%) of their income from inherited wealth or personal investment.

Geographic mobility: The birthplace of each patient and his parents was obtained. Table 35–5 details this information, indicating that 95% of the patients were native Americans and 26% were still living in the

TABLE 35-3

Occupation of Patient at Initiation of Treatment

Occupation	No. of Patients (*N* = 143)
None	2 (1%)
Student	16 (11%)
Housewife	18 (12%)
Physician (nonpsychiatric)	10 (7%)
Psychiatrist or psychiatric resident (noncandidate)	21 (15%)
Clinical psychologist	4 (3%)
Psychiatrist or psychiatric resident (candidate)	4 (3%)
Social worker, psychiatric nurse	14 (10%)
Minister	2 (1%)
Academic professional (*e.g.*, lawyer, engineer, architect)	25 (17%)
Artistic professional (*e.g.*, writer, musician, artist)	4 (3%)
Technician (*e.g.*, teacher, nurse, lab assistant)	10 (7%)
Clerical worker, sales worker	5 (3%)
Manager, large business, major public official (*e.g.*, Federal judge Major)	3 (2%)
Manager, moderate business, moderate public official (*e.g.*, Captain)	3 (2%)
Owner, moderate business (*i.e.*, value $25,000-$100,000)	1 (1%)
Owner, large business (*i.e.*, value over $100,000)	1 (1%)
Unknown	1

general area of their birthplace. The parents of the patients have a higher proportion of immigrants, 27% of the fathers and 22% of the mothers being foreign, largely European-born.

Mental Health Professions

Descriptive statistics: The forty-three patients who were members of the mental health professions—psychiatrists, psychologists, psychiatric social workers and psychiatric nurses (hereafter called MHP)—were compared to the 101 patients who worked in other fields (non-MHP) or were unemployed. There were few notable differences in descriptive statistics between the two subgroups. The proportion of single, married, etc., were almost identical, as were the number of times married, number of children and category of religious affiliation. When the patients are divided into those at or below twenty-nine years verses those thirty and above, a χ^2 shows the MHP group to be significantly ($p < .05$) older than the non-MHP group.

TABLE 35-4

Gross Annual Nuclear Family Income

Total Responses	Mental Health Profession?*		Combined (N = 121)
	No (N = 87)	Yes (N = 34)	
Less than $5,000	3 (3%)	0 (0%)	3 (2%)
$5,000-$9,999	23 (26%)	5 (15%)	28 (23%)
$10,000-$14,999	30 (34%)	15 (44%)	45 (37%)
$15,000-$19,999	15 (17%)	3 (9%)	18 (15%)
$20,000-$24,999	7 (8%)	2 (6%)	9 (7%)
$25,000-$50,000	6 (7%)	5 (15%)	11 (9%)
More than $50,000	3 (3%)	4 (12%)	7 (6%)
Unknown	14	9	23

*The χ^2 of MHP *vs.* non-MHP, when bracketed categories are combined, is significant ($p < .02$).

Education: A χ^2 which divides the patients into those with professional training completed verses all other educational levels shows the MHP group to have considerably ($p < .001$) more members with professional training completed than the non-MHP group. There is a tendency for the spouses, fathers, and mothers of the MHP group to be less represented at the lowest scholastic levels. However, this reaches significance only for the fathers.

Social status: The Hollingshead Two Factor scores of the eighty-two scorable non-MHP patients were compared with those of the forty-three MHP patients. The mean score of the non-MHP group was 16.22 as compared with 13.44 for the MHP patients. A Mann-Whitney U test used to test this difference indicated that the MHP group had significantly higher ($p < .05$) status.

TABLE 35-5

Place of Birth of Patient and His Parents

Total Responses	Patient (N = 144)	Father (N = 140)	Mother (N = 140)
General area of patient's present residence	38 (26%)	23 (16%)	28 (20%)
U.S., other than patient's present area of residence	98 (68%)	79 (56%)	81 (58%)
Europe	3 (2%)	34 (24%)	27 (19%)
Foreign, other than Europe	5 (3%)	4 (3%)	4 (3%)
Unknown	0	4	4

Similar comparisons of parental social position gave Two Factor means of 28.56 for the non-MHP and 27.69 for the MHP parents. The *t* test performed on this difference was not significant.

The above data would place both patient subgroup means in the highest social position. The means of both parental subgroups fall at the demarcation point between the second and third levels of a possible five.

Geographic mobility: A greater proportion ($p < .05$) of non-MHPs remained in the area of their birthplace while MHPs more often moved to the place of their analysis from other points. Fathers of MHP patients were more often ($p < .05$) foreign-born and less often born in the immediate vicinity in which treatment was obtained. Mothers of MHP patients tended ($p < .10$) to follow a similar pattern when compared to non-MHP mothers.

Helping Professions

Dichotomizing patients into MHP verses non-MHP does not fully reflect the special social function performed by a great proportion of the analytic patients and their families. The data were, therefore, reclassified for a second dichotomy encompassing social function rather than specific occupation. That function, for descriptive purposes, will be called "helping." The "helping" classification was obtained by combining the linear and nuclear families of the following professional groups: all physicians, clinical psychologists, social workers, psychiatric nurses, and the clergy. The MHP group is a subset of these "helping" patients.

"Helpers" encompass a full half (51.4%) of the total patient group, an increase of about 70% over the original MHP proportion. Close family members of "helping" professionals were included in this category since their social roles may be strongly determined by their ties. It should be noted, for example, that 11% of the non-MHP married patients and 43% of the MHP married patients have MHP spouses.

Table 35–6 gives the distribution of "helpers" and MHP obtained in terms of the seniority of the analyst at the time treatment was initiated. A relationship can be seen between the relative number of patients in the "helping" category and the extent of experience of the treating analysts. The proportion of MHP patients in the analyst's case load increases with the seniority of the analyst. Others in the "helping" category, who are more peripherally related to mental health (i.e., "Helping" but not MHP), show the opposite progression. Although the progression is not as striking as that above, there is a steady decrease in the relative number of non-MHP "helping" patients as the seniority of the analyst increases.

TABLE 35-6

Proximity to Mental Health Professions of Analytic Patients
in Terms of the Seniority of Their Analysts

Profession	Analyst Experience*			
	Candidate	Graduate	Senior	Combined
MHP patient	4 (8%)	11 (22%)	28 (61%)	43 (30%)
All other "helping"	13 (27%)	10 (20%)	8 (17%)	31 (22%)
Total "helping"	17 (35%)	21 (42%)	36 (78%)	74 (51%)
Total not helping†	31 (65%)	21 (58%)	10 (22%)	70 (49%)
Total	48	50	46	144

*Candidate refers to the fact that analysis began with an analytic candidate in training; a graduate analyst is one who had passed his candidacy but had less than ten years of experience at the initiation of treatment; a senior analyst is one who was ten or more years beyond his analytic training at the time the patient entered his current treatment.

†Nonpsychiatric nurses are incorrectly included here. The method of data collection does not allow the differentiation of nonpsychiatric nurses from the general category of technicians.

DISCUSSION

Patient variables: The above results form a composite description of a typical analysand. On the surface this composite describes a person who has an established and secure place in society. However, the great proportion of patients have not remained in the geographic area of their birth, where their families might have established an acknowledged role for them to take in the local society. Again, since almost a third are children of at least one foreign-born parent and since a large group were Jewish, their early years may have involved uncertain social position.

If a member of one of the mental health professions, the patient is somewhat older and more likely to have had greater education. He has, more likely, moved from his area of origin, probably in order to obtain his training. Otherwise, his social standing does not especially single him out as different from the other analytic patients his analyst sees.

One study which tapped many of the variables reported here is that of the American Psychoanalytic Association's Ad Hoc Committee on Central Fact-Gathering Data (3). Unfortunately, much of the information given combines patients in both analysis and psychotherapy and cannot, undifferentiated, be immediately compared with these results. Data on income, which was compiled separately for analytic and non-analytic patients, would place the Fact-Gathering patients at approximately the same median income as that reported here with considerably larger numbers falling in the $1,000 to $5,000 per year category and somewhat fewer in the over-$20,000 group. This may be partially understood in terms of inflation since the data reported there were obtained approximately ten years prior to our own.

In terms of occupation, statistics reported by Siegel (9) are closely similar in the proportion of physicians, business and sales people, and students. Of that group, 21% were housewives as compared to 12% here, and a smaller proportion of nonphysician professionals and subprofessionals were reported by Siegel. This difference may be due to the greater proportion of females in the Siegel patient population than in that reported here.

Knapp et al. (6) reviewed 10 cases who applied, but were not necessarily accepted, for control psychoanalysis with candidates in analytic training. Their applicants numbered a greater proportion of professionals (72%) and also a larger percentage of workers in mental health areas ("approximately half") than found here. Unfortunately, their report does not indicate the occupational percentages for those potential patients who did initiate analysis.

Our patient statistics agree with those reported by Hollingshead and Redlich (5) as to the kind of patient who is found in dynamic as opposed to directive therapy. It would be of interest, here, to conjecture the rationale for these patients choosing, or being chosen for, analysis rather than other dynamic treatment forms.

One very striking consideration is the need for a relatively high income in order to afford the more frequent number of treatment hours that analysis requires. Again, the fact that an analytic patient requires three to five regular appointments each week, usually during business hours, would tend to bar even highly paid laborers and a variety of business executives and office workers. Analysis would, realistically, be more within the reach of someone who was either a housewife, a self-employed professional, or a member of an occupational group in which such leave-taking was considered justified. These occupations are highly represented in our sample.

Is, all other considerations being equal, a housewife who falls within the limits described as being important for successful analysis and who can afford analysis more likely to be directed toward it than toward some other dynamic form of treatment? We suspect that her disposition would depend at last partially upon the bias of the referring agent.

Function of psychoanalysis: Our finding that over half our patients served, or were closely related to those who served in a helping capacity, appears to be a conservative one. Knapp et al. reported half their potential patients as being in mental health areas alone. This abundance of patients who perform a general social role highlights the dual function served by psychoanalysis in the American culture. It is difficult to assess the extent to which analysis is a form of treatment and the degree to which it is an educational tool. Analysis is openly considered an educational process as well as a therapeutic technique for candidates in analytic training. The same can undoubtedly be said of other patients/ students who may use their analytic discoveries in their work. To a great extent, therefore, the analytic session is a tutorial encounter. The senior faculty teaches "graduates" while the candidates carry much of the "undergraduate" load.

Menninger (7) suggested that education is the proper function of analysis:

> Freud warned us against the emphasis on the therapeutic effect. Now I know he was right; therapeutic effect it does have, but, in my opinion were this its chief or only value, psychoanalysis would be doomed. . . . The educational value of psycho-analysis grows, in my mind. It is an intensive post-academic education, albeit an expensive one. . . . The greatest good for the greatest number depends upon the appli-cation of the principles and knowledge gained from the science of psychoanalysis rather than upon its therapeutic applications in particular instances.

To the extent that the case loads found here represent actual clinical practice, it may be that analysis is quietly following the suggested path. It is likely that, as each analytic institute introduced analysis to another section of the country, its first task was to train future members. Perhaps it is only in the older, more established areas of analytic work that the proportion of "helpers" is this low and that of the general public this high. The high proportion of patients in "helping" areas may partially explain the fact that the knowledge and popularity of analysis is much broader in modern psychiatry than the actual number of practitioners would warrant.

Thus far, we have considered analysis as an educational process for those with a general social function. However, almost half the patients seen do not fall into such a category. What social function might analysis serve which would direct those patients to this specific form of treat-ment?

There is a parameter involved which is more often referred to in-directly than openly when the choice of alternative treatment form is considered. That is the attitude of the patient and those with whom the patient relates as to the value, worth, or importance of therapy. Among the dynamic therapies analysis ranks high in prestige for the analysand.

A possession gains in prestige value when it is more fashionable or timely, functions more efficiently, or is in short supply. While we shall leave to the reader the ranking of analysis on the first two of these three criteria, the third is obvious. The number of analysts as compared to other therapists is small. Since the nature of analysis prevents the individual analyst from treating large numbers of patients, the shortage is made even greater. A patient who "possesses" an analyst is much in the position of the man who owns a handmade violin in comparison with a neighbor with a factory model. If his analyst can trace his treatment back to Freud through only one generation, he gains in social position much as does the man who purchases a Stradivarius.

The social status of the typical analytic patient may be rising above that of his parents. He is likely to be a newcomer in a community. He may belong to a religious minority as well. The prestige level of alternative treatments may take on major importance to such a person when he makes his choice.

SUMMARY

A group of 144 patients seen in analysis from 1962 to 1963 was described along a number of social parameters. These findings were then discussed in terms of social factors related to the selection of analysis as an alternative among dynamic therapies.

REFERENCES

1. Bureau of the Census. Level of school completed by persons 14 years old and over, by age, color and sex for the United States, 1960, and for conterminous United States, 1940 to 1960 (Table 174). In *Characteristics of the Population*, vol. 1, part 1, pp. 419–421. U. S. Government Printing Office, Washington D. C. 1960.

2. Bureau of the Census. *Current Population Reports*, Series P–60, No. 47. Income in 1964 of Families and Persons in the United States, p. 3. U. S. Government Printing Office, Washington, D. C. 1965.

3. HAMBURG, D. A.   *Report of Ad Hoc Committee on Central Fact-Gathering Data.* American Psychoanalytic Association, New York, 1967.

4. HOLLINGSHEAD, A. B.   *Two Factor Index of Social Position, United States, 1957.* [Available in mimeograph form from author]. Yale Univ., New Haven, Conn. 06511.

5. HOLLINGSHEAD, A. B. and REDLICH, F. C.   *Social Class and Mental Illness.* Wiley, New York, 1958.

6. KNAPP, P. H., LEVIN, S., McCARTER, R. H., WERMER, H. and ZETZEL, E. Suitability for psychoanalysis: A review of one hundred supervised analytic cases. *Psychoanal. Quart.*, 29: 459–477, 1960.

7. MENNINGER, K.   *Theory of Psychoanalytic Technique*, pp. 11–12. Basic Books, New York, 1958.

8. ROBINSON, H. A., REDLICH, F. C. and MYERS, J. K.   Social structure and psychiatric treatment. *Amer. J. Orthopsychiat.* 24: 307–316, 1954.

9. SIEGEL, N. H.   Characteristics of patients in psychoanalysis. *J. Nerv. Ment. Dis.* 135: 155–158, 1962.

10. WEINTRAUB, W. and ARONSON, H.   A survey of patients in classical psychoanalysis: Some vital statistics. *J. Nerv. Ment. Dis.*, 146: 98–102, 1968.

This investigation was supported in part by U. S. Public Health Service Award K3–MH–19393 and Grant MH–07434 from the National Institutes of Health.

36

H. Aronson, Ph.D. & Walter Weintraub, M.D.

Patient Changes During Classical Psychoanalysis as a Function of Initial Status and Duration of Treatment

Psychoanalysis differs from nondynamic forms of therapy not only in theory and technique but also in duration. Treatment in psychoanalysis is probably longer than that in any of the other widely utilized therapies. The great period of time spent in treatment may result, in part, from the fact that the goals of analysis go beyond the amelioration of symptoms—that is, analysis works toward the achievement of personality changes. While treatment forms derived from analytic theory share many of its goals and can also be lengthy, analysis can be considered as dynamic psychotherapy in its purest form. What is true for analysis can easily be generalized as relevant to other dynamic therapies. An examination of the changes which come about in the course of psychoanalysis and the factors which may enter into such modifications was one goal of a survey carried out by the authors. In two other studies we presented descriptive data for a group of patients who were in psychoanalysis.* This paper focuses upon the kinds of changes which occurred during analysis of these patients and relates these changes to two major variables: initial status and duration of treatment.

In undertaking this study we did not pose any specific hypotheses. Instead we examined the following questions:

(1) Psychoanalysis was developed by Freud for the treatment of neurotic disorders. Analysts continue to consider neurosis the chief indication for analytic therapy. Is there a relationship between diagnostic status and change during analysis?

Reprinted by special permission of the William Alanson White Psychiatric Foundation, Inc. and the authors from *Psychiatry: Journal for the Study of Interpersonal Processes*, 1968, *31*, 369–379. Copyright for this article is held by the Foundation.

* H. Aronson and Walter Weintraub, "Social Background of the Patient in Classical Psychoanalysis," *J. Nervous and Mental Diseases* (1968) 146:91–97. Walter Weintraub and H. Aronson, "A Survey of Patients in Classical Psychoanalysis—Some Vital Statistics," *J. Nervous and Mental Diseases* (1968) 146:98–102.

(2) Analysis is said to require considerable ego-strength and may, therefore, be more appropriate for the less incapacitated patient. Is there a relationship between degree of initial dysfunction and change with analysis?

(3) If improvement is associated with the development of insight, this could imply that some changes might come relatively late in analytic treatment. How does the length of time spent in analysis relate to the changes which occur?

(4) If some changes are more difficult to accomplish than others, certain changes might occur more rapidly while others might take place relatively late in treatment. Are there regular steps in the changes which come with analysis?

(5) Cartwright has suggested that there are critical durational periods in client-centered therapy.* Can the same be said for analytic treatment?

PROCEDURE

Subjects

The data reported here were collected during the course of a survey of patients undergoing analysis from September, 1962, through September, 1963. Thirty analysts, all of whom were either members of the American Psychoanalytic Association or candidates in psychoanalytic training in affiliated institutes, agreed to supply information on *all* patients they had seen in classical analysis during the year studied.

Our sample, thus, covers the total analytic case loads of a group of analysis,† with the following exceptions: (1) several patients known by their analysts to be personally acquainted with the authors were excluded, and (2) two analysts with a combined total of seventeen patients responded to a shorter set of selected questions for their entire case loads. The questions studied here were not covered in the information these analysts provided.

The final sample for this report, then, includes a total of 127 cases reported upon by twenty-eight analysts. The information collected relates to both the initial status of the 127 patients and to their status during the surveyed period. Deriving from a prevalence study, the information obtained represents patients seen at all points in their analyses, from initiation to either completion or discontinuation of treatment.

The two patient variables reported upon here, diagnosis and dura-

---

* Desmond S. Cartwright, "Success in Psychotherapy as a Function of Certain Actuarial Variables," *J. Consulting Psychology* (1955) 19:357–363.

† See Weintraub and Aronson in footnote on p. 375.

tion, were defined as follows: (1) diagnosis—all patients were divided into three major categories: neurotic, character disorder, and borderline; no psychotics were treated by the reporting analysts during the period studied; (2) duration—treatment was classified into four intervals: less than one year, one through two years, three through four years, and five or more years.

Measure of Initial Level of Functioning and of Change

Due to the nature of our survey all measures were limited to judgments of the reporting analysts. Whenever a single judge is required to give his opinion on a number of cases, it is possible to utilize a unidimensional scale or a numerical continuum including such terms as "worse," "much improved," and so on. When, however, many judges are asked to make comparable judgments, their interpretations can easily range so widely that a patient whom Judge A considers much improved might be considered only slightly improved by Judge B. Therefore, it was decided to use, wherever possible, fixed points which describe what is meant for each step of our scales. Unfortunately, with the many and varied initial symptoms which may be presented by a patient, we were not able to formulate a fixed-point scale of symptomatic change. Instead, the judges were asked to rate symptomatic change for each patient in terms of the following:

Present status of symptoms. (1) complete remission or greatly improved, (2) moderately improved, (3) minimal improvement, and (4) exacerbation of symptoms.

These data were then reduced so that a rating of either "1" or "2" was considered as improvement, "3" was considered as no change, and "4" was considered as worse. While this kind of scale has been used frequently and allows some comparison to be made with other results, it retains the difficulty of questionable interjudge reliability.

Symptomatic change is of interest no matter what form of therapy is studied. However, analysis has the goal of the achievement of personality change. While personality change is difficult to define objectively, it should manifest itself in functional modifications which might be more readily measured and should be observable in most major areas of life. Three target areas were selected, therefore, in which a change of personality might be expected to operate: (1) ability to function vocationally, (2) ability to form healthy relationships with others, and (3) capacity to enjoy life.

In these three areas fixed points could be established. The points were calculated both to cover a wide range and to indicate a sufficiently large difference between steps, so that any change, either for better or worse, could be considered meaningful.

Additionally, with fixed points, it was possible for each judge to use the same criteria to rate his patients both at initiation of analysis and in September, 1963—or at the time of termination if this occurred during the survey period. The points used for each initial scale are given

below. The alternative forms, used to measure status in 1963, cover the
same points with appropriate changes in headings and verb tense.

Initial vocational adjustment. (1) patient unable to find work or
keep a job (for housewife: unable to perform responsibilities of wife
and mother; for student: unable to make passing grades); (2) patient
able to keep position but not at a level appropriate to his intelligence,
training, and experience (for housewife: able to perform responsibilities
of wife and mother, but at a low level of efficiency; for student: able to
make passing grades, but not performing up to potential); (3) patient
able to work at level appropriate to intelligence, training, and experience (for housewife: carries out responsibilities of wife and mother
efficiently; for student; performance in school is up to potential).

Initial object relations. (1) patient had no close ties, (2) patient had
some close ties, but they were all grossly pathological, (3) patient had
one or two solid, healthy relationships, and (4) patient had several or
more solid, healthy relationships.

Initial capacity of patient to experience pleasure. (1) patient experienced little or no pleasure in work and/or recreation, (2) patient was
able to experience some pleasure in work and/or recreation, but relatively infrequently, (3) patient could experience some pleasure in work
and/or recreation fairly frequently, and (4) patient derived a great deal
of pleasure from most of his usual work and recreational activities.

The two scores, that on initial functioning and that on present
status, were compared for changes. If the second rating was different,
a meaningful change was considered to have occurred. Any change
toward greater functioning was considered as improvement, regardless
of the number of scale steps involved. Any change toward decreased
functioning was considered as showing deterioration, again regardless
of degree.

It is important to note that a patient initially rated at the extreme
of a fixed-point scale cannot be seen as having changed in the direction
of his extreme rating. Our results, therefore, relate changes found only
with those patients who were potentially changeable in terms of each
measure of initial status.

Researchers have utilized numerous measures of improvement with
therapy. Some use a rough scale not dissimilar to our own measure of
symptomatic improvement. Client-centered therapy patients are occasionally measured in terms of increased self-awareness or acceptance
of self. Since these are the goals of such treatment, it is reasonable to
measure the therapy's effectiveness accordingly. Our own measures reflect other goals. Without correlational studies between criteria of
change, little can be said of actual differences or similarities between
them.

Research Design

It is important to note that our work has been based upon the
assumption that groups of patients, each group studied at a different

durational period in relation to their psychoanalysis, would provide approximately the same information that we might otherwise have obtained by repeatedly measuring a single group of patients as they proceeded through the same time periods. The use of different groups to accomplish the same end, while not too common to the study of psychotherapy, has been used quite profitably in fields such as learning and memory. This approach eliminates the effects of a series of evaluative intrusions upon the judge and the treatment. There is, however, one drawback to such a design. Since patients may leave analysis at different times, dependent upon personality or treatment variables and other extraneous events, it is important to include an examination of patients present at one durational period who do not remain for a later-in-analysis investigation. For this reason, as well as for an interest in dropouts as such, we have included information on attrition of patients at each durational level.

Dropouts. There is some confusion in the analytic literature concerning patients who do not remain in analysis until there is mutual agreement between patient and analyst that the analysis has had its maximum benefit. These patients are generally not included in discussions of treatment effects. Patients may leave analysis because the analyst believes that an analytic form of treatment is no longer feasible or has even harmed the patient, because the patient made a similar decision, or because external events—such as moving away from the locale of the analyst—force a premature disruption upon both participants.

In order to identify the patient groups, we have designated those patients who, at the time of the survey, were continuing in analysis or had ended ("completed," in analytical terminology) an analysis during the surveyed year, as the "core" group. Those who left analysis during the surveyed period for any reason other than the mutually agreed-upon completion of treatment are referred to as the "attrition" group. Whenever patients in general are referred to, we mean both the "core" and "attrition" patients, or all patients within the category named, regardless of status at the end of the surveyed period.

RESULTS

The data reported upon below are based upon the distribution of patients shown in Table 36–1. The majority of patients, sixty-nine, were considered character disorders by their reporting analysts. Only fifteen cases considered to be borderline were seen, while forty-two were classified as neurotic. The reporting analyst was unwilling to diagnose one patient who had been in analysis for less than a year. Of those patients for whom data were available, twenty-nine were in analysis less than one year, forty-eight from one through two years, thirty-two for three through four years, and seventeen for five or more years.

TABLE 36-1

Number of Patients, by Diagnosis and Length of Treatment*

Diagnosis	Years in Treatment					Total No.
	< 1	1-2	3-4	5 or More	Unknown	
Neurotic	12	13	10	6	1	42
Character disorder	13	30	18	8	—	69
Borderline	3	5	4	3	—	15
Unknown	1	—	—	—	—	1
Total No.	29	48	32	17	1	127

*The number of patients reported upon within this study varies from 125 to 127 depending upon the completeness of information obtained for each area.

Question 1: Diagnosis and Change

Our four measures of improvement showed no significant difference on chi-square tests between neurotic, character disorder, and borderline patients. This lack of differentiation of change among diagnostic categories does not appear to be a function of grossly different distributions in terms of time in analysis. Neurotics, patients with character disorders, and borderline patients who had less than three years of treatment comprised 61%, 62%, and 53% of their respective groups. On all four measures, the proportion of borderline patients who became worse with psychoanalysis was greater than that in either of the other diagnostic classifications. However, there were insufficient cases to establish this difference statistically.

As with all our ratings, the diagnostic information was obtained in the midst of rather than at the initiation of therapy. Thus, the categorization of a patient as borderline was made after the fact of deterioration. It is possible, for example, that the reporting analysts utilized a theory of personality which precluded using the classification "neurotic" for anyone showing psychotic signs. They might easily have assigned to a borderline category, therefore, a patient who presented himself originally as an obvious neurotic but later took on psychotic symptoms. With further information as to the presenting symptoms, and so forth, we might be able to make a more definitive statement on this question. In any case, we were not able to establish that a different rate of improvement exists in cases considered borderline in comparison with cases categorized under other major classifications.

Question 2: Original Dysfunction

Luborsky has suggested that analytic patients are less incapacitated than others and may achieve less improvement than other patient groups since amelioration becomes increasingly difficult as the condition of the entering patient approaches an optimal level initially.* However, Strupp and his colleagues reported a nonsignificant relationship between the therapist's estimate of initial adjustment and his rating of overall success for patients in varying degrees of depth of analytic psycho-therapy.†

Our data were examined, therefore, to determine whether those who were initially more incapacitated showed greater or lesser change, and to try to determine whether the relationship was a function of analysis or an artifact of our measuring system. Table 36–2 provides this in-formation for the three measures for which initial status was available. It indicates that vocational functioning and capacity for pleasure do show greater improvement for those more incapacitated initially, the latter to a significant degree (x^2, $p < .001$).

Table 36–2 also indicates that 36.5% of this analytic population began treatment while functioning at an appropriate occupational level. In fact, only 8% were severely incapacitated in terms of their initial ability to work.

TABLE 36-2

Change in Vocational Functioning, Object Relationships, and Capacity for Pleasure, as Related to Initial Status

Measure	Initial Status	N (126)	Improved %	No Change %	Worsened %
Vocational Functioning	Low	10	80	20	*
	Moderate	70	39	60	1
	High	46	*	100	0
Object Relationships	Low	10	30	70	*
	Minimal	77	40	56	4
	Moderate	30	23	73	3
	High	9	*	100	0
Capacity for Pleasure**	Low	18	89	11	*
	Minimal	79	51	49	0
	Moderate	26	23	73	4
	High	3	*	100	0

*Already at limit of range. Further changes not measurable by methods utilized.
**x^2, $p < .001$, for relationship of greater initial incapacity and greater improvement.

* Lester L. Luborsky, "A Note on Eysenck's Article, 'The Effects of Psychotherapy; an Evaluation,'" *British J. Psychology* (1954) 45: 129–131.
† Hans H. Strupp, Martin S. Wallach, and Michael M. Wogan, "Psychotherapy Experi-ences in Retrospect: Questionnaire Survey of Former Patients and Their Therapists," *Psychol. Monographs* (1954) 78:Whole No. 588.

Question 3: Duration and Change

Figure 36–1 demonstrates a steady increase of improvement the longer patients remain in analysis. A chi-square of the differences in improvement between durational periods is highly significant ($p < .001$) for each of the four measures of change. However, an increase in improvement with time might simply be due to attrition of patients who do not improve. To check for such an effect, the data were reexamined by dividing the patients into a "core" group (those who remained in analysis up to and including completion) and an "attrition" group (those who terminated their treatment short of completion during the survey year).

The results of that examination are shown in Table 36–3. It demonstrates that those in the attrition group were not generally early dropouts who had not improved. In fact, the earlier attrition patients showed

FIGURE 36-1

Percent of Change in Symptomatic Status, Vocational Functioning, Object Relationships, and the Capacity to Experience Pleasure by Diagnosis and by the Length of Time in Analysis

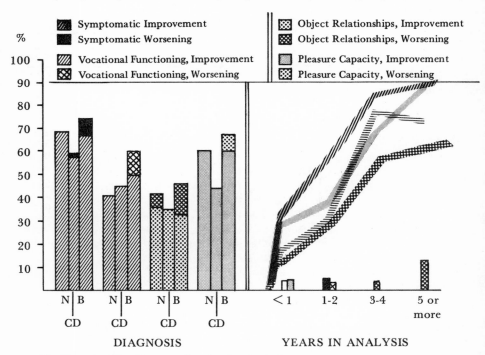

N = Neurotic; CD = Character disorder; B = Borderline

TABLE 36-3

Changes in Symptomatic Status (S), Vocational Functioning (V),
Object Relationships (O), and the Capacity for Pleasure (P), by Diagnosis,
by Years in Analysis, and by Continuation of Treatment

	N	Percent of Patients Who Improved*				Percent of Patients Who Worsened*			
	(126)	S	V	O	P	S	V	O	P
Diagnosis: "core" group									
Neurotic	34	65	40	38	61	0	0	6	0
Character disorder	63	57	43	33	44	2	0	0	0
Borderline	12	67	50	42	67	0	0	0	10
Diagnosis unknown	1	0	0	0	0	0	0	0	0
Diagnosis: "attrition" group									
Neurotic	7	86	50	33	57	0	0	0	0
Character disorder	6	67	67	50	33	0	0	0	0
Borderline	3	67	50	—	33	33	50	67	0
Years in analysis: "core" group									
< 1	26	27	18	12	27	0	0	4	5
1-2	43	56	29	28	40	2	0	0	0
3-4	26	85	78	54	79	0	0	0	0
5 or more	15	87	71	62	86	0	0	7	0
Years in analysis: "attrition" group									
< 1	3	67	0	0	33	0	0	0	0
1-2	5	60	50	20	20	20	20	0	0
3-4	6	83	75	60	50	0	0	17	0
5 or more	2	100	—	50	100	0	0	50	0

*Percentages were determined on the basis of patients with an initial potential to either improve or become worse in terms of our scales. The greatest drop in the number of patients with potential to change was found for the vocational functioning scale.

greater symptomatic improvement than did core patients of the same treatment duration (67% as opposed to 27%). However, their improvement on the variables we have chosen to represent personality modifications was not quite so great as was their symptomatic change. Again, the numbers are too small to be statistically significant.

It is important to note that the attrition group contains half of the patients who were rated as deteriorated. Two of the three patients who became worse and left analysis did not do so until the third or fourth years of treatment. These cases tended to reduce the proportion of cases showing improvement in the later years and cannot explain the overall steady rise in improvement as analytic time increases.

What has been found here is dependent on the assumption that analysts are able to make accurate retrospective judgments concerning the initial status of their patients. Cartwright found that there was a difference between therapist ratings of initial status made after the first interview and ratings of initial status made at the conclusion of treatment.* If one used the latter ratings rather than the former, one would find a stronger relationship between time in client-centered therapy and improvement. This was taken to indicate that memory plays tricks on the therapist in that he underrates the early condition of patients after seeing them for long periods of time. However, it is equally probable that an accurate estimate of a patient's functioning is not possible at the onset of treatment. Since these alternative interpretations have not been fully examined, either may be valid.

We again examined our data to see if they revealed that patients who had spent longer periods of time in therapy were considered worse on entrance into therapy (see Table 36-4). No significant differences were

TABLE 36-4

*Comparison of Initial Status of Patients in
Analysis for Briefer and Longer Periods*

Measure of Initial Status	Years in Analysis			
	Less than 3		3 or more	
	N	%	N	%
Vocational Adjustment				
Poor or moderate	51	66	29	59
Good	26	34	20	41
Object Relations				
Bad or poor	53	69	34	69
Moderate or good	24	31	15	31
Capacity for Pleasure				
Bad or poor	56	73	41	84
Moderate or good	21	27	8	16

found. Patients seen for longer periods were sometimes judged as more and sometimes judged as less well-adjusted originally than those seen for shorter durations.

The above argument does not eliminate the possibility that after having treated a patient for a longer period, an analyst may see improvement where none exists. Fixed-point scales, which describe the behavior of the patient for each evaluation, would make such a bias more difficult to apply. However, we cannot claim to have eliminated it entirely.

Question 4: Relationship of Changes

The figure demonstrates that the changes which arose within each of the four measures closely paralleled each other. The similarity in the slopes of the three curves measuring personality change and in the slope of the curve measuring symptomatic change is remarkable, especially

* Desmond S. Cartwright et al., "Length of Therapy in Relation to Outcome and Change in Personal Integration," *J. Consulting Psychology* (1961) 25:84–88.

since our measures were so roughly constructed. As a test of contingency, phi coefficients were determined for each of the possible combinations of our four measures of change. Here the cases were regarded as either improved or unimproved, and only those patients were included whose initial ratings showed potential for improvement in both measures being correlated. The resulting phis range from .42 to .58 and all were highly significant (x^2 range, 13.8 to 39.4; $p < .001$).

We are not able to demonstrate any regular steps in which one function routinely improves prior to another. In fact, our data suggest that a change for the better would be reflected in most areas of a patient's life.

Question 5: Critical Periods

While there are insufficient cases to provide statistical evidence of the relationship, there seem to be several critical periods for attrition. The patients in the early attrition group were largely neurotics who improved rapidly in their symptomatic conditions and were somewhat better able to enjoy life. Their relationship with others did not show a similar improvement, which could indicate that they did not undergo a comparable modification in personality structure. This may be a quantitative way of describing the patient qualitatively seen as having taken a "flight into health." Another critical point was in the durational period of three to four years, at which time attrition reached its highest.

A small group of attrition patients, borderline in diagnosis, dropped out after having deteriorated. Unfortunately, with our method of sampling different groups at varying times in analysis, we were not able to delineate attrition patients who may have been undergoing a short period of regression in overall functioning from which they later easily recovered and after which they continued treatment, perhaps even benefiting from an understanding of their regressed status.

In general, when patients were scored as having regressed, regressions may have been the result of the breaking down of previously rigid but functioning defenses. Some patients who became worse may have been unable to integrate the growing self-awareness accompanying the analysis, and may have become symptomatic in order to avoid further confrontation. They may have reacted to the advent of completion of treatment, and to concomitant separation problems, with anxiety and regression. It is even possible that changes occurred which have no correlation with their status as analytic patients.* We cannot differentiate among any of the above. We can say that deterioration was scored very seldom by our reporting analysts, and, by definition, any period in which deterioration occurs is a critical one.

For patients diagnosed as having a character disorder, there is, on

---

* For a recent discussion of regression, see John Frosch, "Severe Regressive States During Analysis: Introduction," *J. Amer. Psychoanal. Assn.* (1967) 15:491–507.

inspection, very little difference in terms of improvement rate between core patients and attrition patients.

For the core patients, who have gone through the regular steps of analysis, we find a modest initial change followed by a rapidly accelerating rate of improvement up to the last years of treatment. It is, perhaps, at that time that the analytic process focuses upon the maintenance of achieved insight and the prevention of the deterioration seen in some of the later attrition patients.

It is relevant to note here that during the course of analysis relatively few of our patients became measurably less able to function in the major areas of their lives. It has been postulated that in order to achieve major reorganization of personality, some degree of regression or disorganization must occur. These patients, seen at varying periods during their treatment, do not appear to demonstrate any regularity of deterioration, at least not to the extent that their day-to-day lives are measurably affected.

It may be the case that our scales are simply too insensitive to describe such changes. Another interpretation, and one which the authors are more prone to suggest, is that those who have reached a relatively high level of functioning prior to treatment may not be subject to the same degree of regression in response to the stress of analysis as are more disturbed patients.

Combined Changes

Our results have, thus far, been concerned with specified differences, along single measures, in those patients who showed initial potential for change. Here we will attempt a reply to the more general question: What proportion of people who enter into analysis are changed in any discernible therapeutic way? To do so, we will consider differences in any of our four measures as showing some evidence of change concurrent with analytic treatment. Since we have found that patients who were in treatment longer showed greater change within the individual measures, we have divided the cases into two groups: those in analysis for less than three years and those whose analyses had been in progress for three years or more at the time of the survey.

For those seventy-seven patients in analysis less than three years, 57% showed at least one positive change; 5%, at least one negative change; and 38%, no change on any of our measures. None showed any mixture of positive and negative changes. For those forty-nine patients in analysis for three years or longer, 84% showed at least one positive change; none showed at least one negative change; 6%, any mixture of positive and negative changes; and 10%, no differences from an initial status.

Within the second durational group were nine patients who completed their analyses during the survey year. Of those patients, seven changed positively on one or more of our measures; none changed negatively; one had a mixture of positive and negative changes; and one could not, by the methods employed here, be differentiated from his initial state.

DISCUSSION

It is difficult to compare these findings on patients examined at various points within treatment with the results of other studies. Most such studies concern changes found upon conclusion of treatment or at follow-up. We have, instead, concerned ourselves with intra-analysis changes, under the assumption that gross changes between groups will reflect individual changes in the course of treatment. Since there is no control group, we are not able to state whether the changes found here differ from changes which might arise during the general course of unanalyzed living. Nor can we guarantee that the patient groups which entered analysis at different points in time were equivalent.

If our results are compared to those provided by the American Psychoanalytic Association's Central Fact-Gathering report,* our improvement rate for those in the last years of their analysis is quite modest. However, the APA's statistics on patients completing analysis do not include a large attrition group. Such a sample eliminates a number of bona fide patients from improvement statistics and tends to overstate the case for the effectiveness of analysis.

On the other hand, when we examine the statistics summarized by Eysenck,† we find that our results suggest considerably greater improvement than that cited for both analytic and eclectic groups. Here, we have included results on patients who dropped out prior to the third year, while Eysenck routinely considered such patients as treatment failures. Our data on the attrition group indicate that such a reduction is misleadingly large, since these patients are, in fact, often symptomatically improved.

For many therapies reported upon, patients who are seen for longer than six months are considered long-term. When our results on the early—that is, occurring in less than one year—changes during analysis are compared with the improvement ratings on shorter therapies,** it would appear that either analysis has relatively little effect or our criteria

---

* David A. Hamburg, *Report of Ad Hoc Committee on Central Fact-Gathering Data;* New York, Amer. Psychoanal. Assn., 1967.

† Hans J. Eysenck, "The Effects of Psychotherapy," in *Handbook of Abnormal Psychology,* edited by H. J. Eysenck; New York, Basic Books, 1961; p. 712.

** Joseph Wolpe, *Psychotherapy by Reciprocal Inhibition;* Stanford Univ. Press, 1958.

for change are considerably more stringent than those employed by other investigators. It is also true that early symptomatic improvement is not a primary goal of analysis. The data suggest that those who drop out early, who are often considered analytic failures, show rapid symptomatic improvement.

The fact that only 8% of our patients were vocationally incapacitated and that 36.5% were already operating optimally in their work at the initiation of therapy would place in doubt any comparison of therapies—for example, Eysenck's use of the Denker findings—which stressed vocational adjustment as its major criterion for improvement. Such a criterion is simply not as appropriate for analytic patients as it is for other patient groups.*

Our finding of no significant differences in improvement between patients diagnosed as neurotic, character disorder, and borderline may be due to the fact that analytic patients are carefully screened and only those with high improvement potential are accepted. There is considerable indication that a nonneurotic diagnosis is not necessarily a deterrent to successful analytic treatment. In fact, if the proportions of diagnostic categories found in this survey hold for analysis in general, it is the character disorder rather than the neurotic who comprises the bulk of today's analytic case load.

Early attrition, which is common in a great proportion of clinic patients,† is relatively infrequent in psychoanalysis. Reports of dropouts within the first five interviews often range as high as 40 to 50% in public clinics, whereas the rate of attrition found here ranges from 10 to 19% for each rather broad durational level, with the peak of the attrition coming during the third through fourth years. The small number of early dropouts may, again, be due to extensive screening and the fact that considerably greater commitment on the patient's part is required to enter analysis than to enter other, less intensive treatments. Commitment would be especially high in those patients whose analysis entered into their professional training. It is likely that mental health professionals comprise a larger proportion of analytic patients than of any other therapeutic group.**

Our major finding is more relevant to the process of psychoanalysis than to the questions of initial selection or of the efficacy of analysis as a treatment form. Our results indicate that a typical analytic patient

---

* For corroborative findings in a low-income analytic population, see Henriette R. Klein, "A Study of Changes Occurring in Patients During and After Psychoanalytic Treatment," in *Current Approaches to Psychoanalysis,* edited by Paul H. Hoch and Joseph Zubin; New York, Grune & Stratton, 1960.

† Betty Overall and H. Aronson, "Expectations of Psychotherapy in Patients of Lower Socioeconomic Class," *Amer. J. Orthopsychiatry* (1963) 33:421–430. Jerome D. Frank, et al., "Why Patients Leave Psychotherapy," *AMA Arch. Neurology and Psychiatry* (1957) 77:283–299.

**See Aronson and Weintraub in footnote on p. 375.

shows relatively little change during the early stage of treatment. Early symptomatic improvement does not necessarily indicate that improvement in character structure is likely to occur. Change, when it begins, is relatively rapid and covers a number of essential areas of life. The few occasions when patients regress or decompensate tend to come relatively late rather than quite early in treatment.

This investigation was supported in part by Public Health Service Award K3–MH–19393, and Grant HM–07434, from the National Institutes of Health, USPHS.

37

Martin Lakin, Ph.D. & Binyamin Lebovits, Ph.D.

Bias in Psychotherapists of Different
Orientations: An Exploratory Study

Investigation of the role of the therapist in the treament process has repeatedly encountered the issue of the influence of school orientation or bias upon treatment. One point of view is that regardless of orientation, psychotherapists operate according to certain principles held in common (9). A recent study appeared to indicate that experienced practitioners of markedly divergent orientations are, in fact, closer to one another in treatment operations than are the novices and the experts of a homogenous theoretical persuasion (4).

Other studies have emphasized the significance of differences in theoretical orientation for treatment. By way of illustration, we may cite one study in which it was found that group therapy time spent in discussion of sexual material varied with the interests of the therapists involved (1). Yet another investigation has indicated that selectivity is inherent in the operations of the therapist. It was suggested that facts and feelings introduced by the patient may be ignored or utilized depending upon the orientation of the therapist (7).

Until now, relevant research has been centered upon general characteristics of the therapeutic atmosphere. Study of the therapist has been by and large limited to assessment of the kind of climate provided for the patient, i.e., directive or nondirective, permissive or authoritarian, reflective or interpretative. There is, however, growing concern with the differing "conceptualizing sets" which may obtain among therapists of diverse orientations and which may play an important part in determining the character of the therapeutic atmosphere.

In the present experiment, it was intended to focus upon such "sets" and upon their operations in the very initial phase of treatment —that of conceptualization of the patient by the therapist and the "formulation" of his problem. In the present study, our central concern might be put thusly: What are the ways in which psychotherapists of diverse orientations are *prepared* to see a patient?

Reprinted by permission of the publisher and the authors from *American Journal of Psycotherapy*, 1958, 12, 79–86.

METHOD

Minimal identifying information concerning a patient in the initial phase of treatment was given to seventeen psychotherapists. Nine of these individuals were *psychoanalytically trained* psychiatrists. Five were *eclectic psychiatrists*. Three were *client-centered* (nondirective) therapists. The eclectic were the most experienced, averaging six years of therapeutic work, while the client-centered therapists were the least, averaging four years of such activity. All the subjects were similarly instructed: "We would like to know how therapists go about thinking about a patient when they have gotten only a referral—with only a few scanty facts." Following this introduction to the study, they were allowed to view the material reproduced below, were assured that it related to a bona fide patient, and were asked to "free-associate" to the question raised at the close of the identifying information. "As a psychotherapist, how would you think about this person?" They were then left alone to utilize the recording apparatus for a ten-min. period.*

Stimulus Material

Vivian Salisbury,† thirty, is a white American-born housewife and graduate student with an M.A. in political science. She lives with her husband and two children, both girls, ages five-and-a-half and four. Their first child, a boy, died of cancer when six months old. Her parents, father, sixty-two, mother, sixty, are living together. She has two siblings, a brother, twenty-five and a sister, twenty-four. As a psychotherapist, how would you think about this person?

RESULTS

Table 37–1 shows the average number of associations for each of the groups of therapists.

It was found possible to classify associations into several categories and to subdivide these as follows:

---

* The method outlined a laboratory, not a clinical situation. However, it was felt that this approach permits study of conceptualizing processes and of the influence of bias without the contaminating influences of other factors such as may be involved in transference and countertransference phenomena .

† The patient, listed here under a false name, had requested psychiatric help because of "panic in public places" and "frequent depressions." Intake psychiatric diagnosis was, "Borderline state with phobic and repressive features." The subsequent psycho-diagnostic evaluation characterized the patient as showing "repression, withdrawal, and regressive tendencies."

TABLE 37-1

Number of Associations for
Three Groups of Psychotherapists

Therapists	Average Number of Associations	Range
Analysts ($N = 9$)	34.3	20-49
Eclectics ($N = 5$)	10.2	8-14
Client centered ($N = 3$)	13.6	12-14

(*1*) *Speculations about etiologic factors:*
   (a) "Dynamic," early childhood experiences, early primary relationships; (b) "Experiential," adult trauma, role conflict, marital tension.
(*2*) *Speculations about diagnostic issues:*
   (a) Degree of illness or health (ego integration level); (b) Mention of specific nosology.
(*3*) *Speculations about therapeutic issues:*
   (a) Ideational content; (b) Transference and countertransference phenomena; (c) Therapeutic goals.

Table 37–2 shows the percent of associations falling into each of the three main categories for the three groups of therapists.

Table 37–3 shows the varying degrees of interest manifested in the one traumatic incident listed in the material provided—the death of the first child from cancer as compared with interest in early primary relationships.

DISCUSSION AND CONCLUSIONS

Virtually, all the therapists, regardless of school affiliation, evaluate the patient similarly (positively) in terms of potential for recovery. This evaluation appeared to be based upon the level of education achieved and upon the facts of marriage and children. This is the major point of concurrence of the subjects. Beyond this general agreement, background factors unique to each orientation appear to determine a selective emphasis as well as a mode of approach.

The psychoanalysts are the most "productive" in associations. They appear to speculate more freely as if many more avenues of formulation were open to them. They were also less concerned about the possibility of being grossly in error and seemed to tolerate even mutually contradictory associations. This may be contrasted with a cautious, more or less noncommittal approach on the part of the eclectic psychiatrists.

TABLE 37-2

A Comparison of Percents of Associations
Devoted to Three Categories of Speculation

Therapists	Etiological Factors	Diagnostic Speculations	Therapy Speculations
Analysts	64	20	15
Eclectics	76	23	0
Client centered	70	6	23

The phrase, "We have insufficient evidence" was most frequently observed in the protocols of these individuals. The client-centered therapists, on the other hand, revealed a basic disinclination to speculate and appeared to have difficulty in overcoming their reluctance to do so. The following excerpt from one of their protocols illustrates this attitude. "If the question had read . . . as a diagnostician, I could do this more easily . . . but as a therapist—well—I just feel I want to be as naive as possible regarding the client . . . I don't feel very comfortable doing this sort of thing."

It is interesting that the client-centered individuals do proceed to evaluate and to formulate, despite the protest. Nonetheless, it is clear that to be "naive" as regards the patient or to be nonjudgmental and try to remain "within the client's frame of reference" is a central aim of the client-centered therapist. By contrast, the psychoanalyst is certainly encouraged to formulate, sometimes on the basis of even meager material. Clearly personal experience in a training or therapeutic analysis would do much to reinforce a formulating tendency. Of the three, the eclectic is most wary. His protocol abounds with the demand for more extensive case material before he will venture an "opinion." His empirical "set" is more evidenced in the attitudes of strict reliance upon the given factual material.

TABLE 37-3

A Comparison of Percent of Associations
Devoted to Death of First Child and
Percent of Associations Devoted to
Developmental Problems with Own Parents

Therapists	Child's Death	Early Parent-Child Relationships
Analysts	5	12
Eclectics	14	8
Client centered	49	3

Etiologic Factors

The analysts reveal greater concern with etiological factors than do the other therapist groups. Their concerns in this area center about possible early childhood experiences and, among these, certain aspects of early primary relations. There is much speculation, for example, concerning "early deprivation," "a hostile and rejecting mother," as well as "a distant and nonsupporting father." Client-centered and eclectic therapists seem more inclined to deal with more recent experiential and/or situational factors. A partial demonstration of the differences in emphasis is reflected in the varying degrees of concern with etiologic significance of the death of the patient's first child. As shown in Table 37-3, the analysts are relatively unconcerned with this factor; the eclectic therapist considers it a bit more extensively; the client-centered therapist focuses upon it.

It might be that this finding illustrates the effort of the latter individuals to achieve a state of empathic responsiveness with what they regard as the most painful elements in the individual's background. As has been indicated, the analysts are more concerned with developmental problems. Where, in certain of their protocols, this occurrence is noted, it usually elaborated in terms of a possible reactivation of earlier aggressive and guilty feelings toward the male sibling.

Diagnostic Speculations

Although client-centered therapists refrain from formal diagnosis, they do engage in some form of patient assessment but in highly self-conscious terms. "I could work with this kind of person."; "This is the kind of person I think my therapy would work well with." The eclectic therapists voiced the impression "on the basis of the available evidence" that the individual was "rather well integrated." The analysts, on the other hand, showed considerable inter-individual variability in their assessments of the patient. They ventured nosological classifications in contrast to the other therapists. Examples of the range and variability were specific "diagnoses" of obsessive personality, character neurosis, reactive depression, psychosis, and phobic reaction.

It is somewhat surprising to find this relatively strong classificatory tendency among the more "dynamic" psychiatrists instead of among the eclectic therapists. This question needs further study. On the other hand, the abstention of the client-centered individuals from diagnostic activity comes as no surprise. Their performance, in this regard, reflects a theoretical position which eschews conventional psychiatric nosology.

Speculations About Therapy

Associations relating to this area occurred only among the analytically oriented and among the client-centered therapists. Proportionately, the client centered therapists appear to give more attention to this area. We may infer that both these groups are more therapy-oriented in their associations than are the eclectic psychiatrists. The latter individuals, consistent with their empirical approach, choose to defer the question of treatment. It is also possible, of course, that they are less frequently committed in advance to a preference for psychotherapy as the treatment of choice than are the other therapists. Also, analysts and client-centered therapists appear to share the assumption that psychotherapy may nearly always be helpful regardless of the nature of the illness.

Associations to this area of the analysts and client-centered therapists differed markedly from the point of view of focal concern. The latter individuals appear to emphasize therapist responsiveness rather than patient behavior and the satisfactory abreaction of feelings rather than the achievement of therapeutic goals. The former individuals tend to presume an adequate therapist responsiveness and articulate therapeutic goals more fully. Therapeutic process is speculated about in terms of the patient's resistiveness, defenses, and possible transference reactions.

The limitations of the present study because of the inadequate representativeness of the various therapeutic orientations necessitate caution in interpretation of the findings. This has been only an exploratory step in delineation of a large problem. The present data do clearly emphasize, however, the factor of selectiveness based upon therapist orientation.

Clinicians' predispositions have been studied as an important variable in the related area of diagnostic assessment (2, 5, 8). From these studies and from the data presented here, it seems possible to conclude that clinicians attend to different aspects of even the most minimal information. Clinicians differ as to which aspects of any given situation will be prepotent for them. Likewise, the individual therapist apparently has a set to perceive in a certain fashion and will unconsciously or consciously accept, reject, and reorganize material presented in terms of this set.

It would be important to discover whether and how these therapists respond to additional material. How does the prepotent bias affect the utilization of added diagnostic or historical material? Two studies (10, 3) seem to suggest that such sets may remain constant even in the face of regular increments of data. Another, perhaps even more significant, question involves assessment of whether and to what extent predisposing sets or biases determine the datum of therapy and the interpretation of its results.

It seems to the authors that investigation of these questions is basic to scientific study of the role of the therapist and, ultimately, to the study of psychotherapy. The present paper has merely indicated the area and scope of the problem. That these differing conceptual approaches will determine an initial therapeutic atmosphere seems likely. They appear to be relatively independent of factors in the patient and are determined by factors in the therapist's background. Further study in this area should help bring greater understanding of the dimensions of psychotherapeutic activity.

SUMMARY

An experiment was designed to study the influence of orientation upon conceptualization of a patient when only minimal identifying information was provided. Seventeen psychotherapists, representing three different "schools," served as subjects for the study and "free-associated" to the question: "As a psychotherapist, how would you think about this person?" Therapists' associations were compared and discussed in terms of mode of speculation and selective emphasis. Further comparative investigation of changes in predisposing sets or biases in the face of added information was suggested. Study of these factors was regarded as necessary to an understanding of the psychotherapeutic process.

REFERENCES

1. BRENMAN, MARGARET (Chairman): "Research in Psychotherapy," Round Table, 1947, *Amer. J. Orthopsychiat.*, 1948, *18*, 92–118.

2. DAILEY, C. A.: "The Effects of Premature Conclusions upon the Acquisition of Understanding of a Person," *J. Psychol.*, 1952, *33*, 133–152.

3. KELLY, E. L.; and FISKE, D. W.: *The Prediction of Performance in Clinical Psychology.* The University of Michigan Press, Ann Arbor, 1951.

4. FIEDLER, F. E.: "A Comparison of Therapeutic Relationships in Psychoanalytic, Nondirective and Adlerian Therapy," *J. Consult Psychol.*, 1950, *14*, 436–445.

5. LUFT, J.: "Implicit Hypotheses and Clinical Predictions," *J. Abnorm. Soc. Psychol.*, 1950, *45*, 756–759.

6. MANN, S.; MENZER, D.; and STANDISH, C.: "Psychotherapy of Psychoses— Some Attitudes in the Therapist Influencing the Course of Treatment," *Psychiatry*, 1950, *13*, 17–23.

7. POWDERMAKER, FLORENCE; and FRANK, J. D.: *Group Psychotherapy.* Harvard University Press, Cambridge, 1953.

8. SARASON, S. B.: *The Clinical Interaction.* Harper and Brothers, New York, 1954.

9. SHOBEN, E. J. JR.: "Toward a Theory of Therapy." In Mowrer, O. H. (Ed.): *Psychotherapy Theory and Research.* Ronald Press Company, New York, 1953.

10. SOSKIN, W. F.: "Bias in Postdiction from Projective Tests," *J. Abnorm. Soc. Psychol.*, 1954, *49*, 69–74.

11. WOLF, W.: "Fact and Value in Psychotherapy," *Amer. J. Psychotherapy*, 1954, *8*, 466–486.

38

Richard L. Cutler, Edward S. Bordin,
Joan Williams, & David Rigler

Psychoanalysts as Expert Observers of

the Therapy Process

Our research group has as its major interest the study of the process of psychotherapy, that is, the analysis of the interaction between patient and therapist (2, 3, 6). One immediate goal is the testing of several specific hypotheses concerning the relationship of the therapist's interpretive activity to the manifestation of resistance in the patient. Due to the relative recency with which interest in this area of therapy research has developed, however, we have found it necessary to digress in order to solve some of the measurement and methodological problems involved in operationalizing our variables (1, 5). This paper reports a further research concerned with the effects of varying conditions of rating and classes of raters upon one of our key variables, Depth of Interpretation.

In a previous study clinical psychologists made ratings of therapy interviews on Depth of Interpretation under varying conditions of presentation, context, and unit size. In that study, as in the present one, interpretation was defined as "any behavior on the part of the therapist that is an expression of his view of the patient's emotions and motivations . . ." (4, p. 247). The greater the disparity between the view expressed by the therapist, and the patient's awareness of these emotions and motivations, the deeper the interpretation. A seven-point scale for rating Depth of Interpretation was developed by the Method of Equal Appearing Intervals from seventy statements descriptive of therapist behavior. An analysis of variance revealed: (1) raters were able to apply this particular scale so as to distinguish between interviews, (2) a single, overall rating of an interview led to a deeper rating than that obtained from the mean of response-by-response ratings, and (3)

ratings made from typescripts did not differ from those based upon
tape recordings.

All of these findings supported our expectations. Contrary to what
we anticipated, however, there were no differences ascribable to varying
amounts of context. That is, it made no difference whether the raters
were given the immediately preceding interview in its entirety before
rating the crucial interview, or whether they made their ratings using
only the therapist's responses, with all patient material deleted.

It was primarily because we were concerned about this inability
of our raters to utilize increasing amounts of contextual information to
increase their interjudge agreement that the present study was designed.
We first sought logically to identify those elements in the stimulus
material which were potential contributors to the variance in rating
Depth of Interpretation. The first of these hypothetical contributors,
Element A, may be thought of as consisting of valid clues from the
stimulus material which provide evidence as to the level of the patient's
awareness of his emotions and motivations, as to the therapist's expression of *his* view of the patient's emotions and motivations, and, hence,
as to the disparity between them. Thus, Element A represents the "true"
variance of Depth of Interpretation. The second, Element B, consists of
a set of cues which lead to reliable judgments based upon some implicit,
absolute conception of what constitutes a deep or shallow interpretation.
The third, Element C, consists of irrelevant or interfering cues from
either the patient's or the therapist's comments, which serve to mis-
lead or confuse the raters. A fourth element, which is relatively independent of the stimulus material, but which interacts with Elements A,
B, and C in the total rating process, is the sensitivity to the various
proportions of A, B, and C in the stimulus material which is available in
the particular judge population.

It is immediately apparent that Element A should be present to a
greater degree in a situation where stimulus material is presented with
more, rather than less, context. Element B may or may not be increased
by increasing the amount of contextual material available to the judges
during the rating process. Element C is almost certainly increased, since
the judges are asked to maintain an awareness of considerable additional material, and must, in addition, decide whether a given bit of
stimulus material is valid and relevant (Element A) or irrelevant (Element C).

We were thus led to consider the possibility that the judge population was crucial in this particular rating process, and that a particular
kind of sensitivity to the nuances of therapeutic interaction was
necessary to enable judges to capitalize upon the additional contextual
material to increase their interjudge reliability. Given adequate training
in the perception of cues in the patient's and therapist's responses
relevant to the rating of Depth of Interpretation, and in the disregarding
of irrelevant or confusing cues, our judges should demonstrate more
convincing interjudge agreement than had been found in the earlier
study.

PROCEDURES

Accordingly, we enlisted as expert judges in this study four psychoanalysts and four psychiatrists who had completed their personal analyses and were undergoing control training in psychoanalysis, but who had not yet been admitted to full standing in either the local or national analytic societies. The former group are hereafter called analysts; the latter, for want of a better term, fledglings.

Our rationale for the selection of this particular judge population was as follows: even though our clinical psychologist judges had had experience as psychotherapists, only a few had completed a personal analysis, and none had had the benefit of psychoanalytic training. We felt that the emphasis in analytic training upon the development of an acute self-awareness, with its consequent increased perceptual and interpersonal sensitivity and objectivity, might better enable the analysts to judge the degree of the patient's awareness of his emotions and motivations, to assess the therapist's statements concerning his view of the patient's emotions and motivations, and hence more reliably to rate Depth of Interpretation. These judges should also be better equipped to weed out irrelevant cues, and perhaps to be less led astray by invalid cues of Element B. In short, we hoped that the analysts and fledglings would be better able to capitalize upon increased amounts of contextual information to increase their interjudge agreement by making maximal use of Element A and by limiting the distracting effects of Element C.

In addition, by including the fledglings, we hoped to assess the effects of varying amounts of training and experience within the group which had had the benefit of formal analytic training.

A modified latin-square design was projected which was essentially a replication of the design of our earlier study. It permitted the systematic variation or control of two levels of context (therapist responses only vs. preceding interview) and two methods of presentation (typescript vs. tape recording). It also enabled us to assess the effects of practice, order of presentation of the interviews, judges, and differences due to the interviews themselves. In addition, it was possible to obtain a rough estimate of the effect of experience within this judge population (analysts vs. fledglings) by means of a t test, although this difference is confounded with order and conditions. In the actual process of rating, each judge rated each of the four interviews response-by-response on the seven-point Depth of Interpretation rating scale (Table 38–1).

TABLE 38-1

Assignment of Raters to Experimental Conditions[a]

Typescript (TY)		Recording (RE)	
Therapist Only (TO)	Preceding Interview (PI)	Therapist Only (TO)	Preceding Interview (PI)
A[b], I, 4, 1	A, I, 2, 2	A, I, 3, 4	A, I, 1, 3
A, II, 4, 1	A, II, 2, 2	A, II, 3, 4	A, II, 1, 3
A, III, 2, 4	A, III, 4, 3	A, III, 1, 1	A, III, 3, 2
F, IV, 2, 4	F, IV, 4, 3	F, IV, 1, 1	F, IV, 3, 2
F, V, 3, 3	F, V, 1, 4	F, V, 4, 2	F, V, 2, 1
F, VI, 3, 3	F, VI, 1, 4	F, VI, 4, 2	F, VI, 2, 1
A, VII, 1, 2	A, VII, 3, 1	A, VII, 2, 3	A, VII, 4, 4
F, VIII, 1, 2	F, VIII, 3, 1	F, VIII, 2, 3	F, VIII, 4, 4

Note.—The latin square was originally designed to pair one analyst and one fledgling in each of the four order-condition-case sequences. However, due to difficulties in obtaining qualified raters, it was necessary to modify the design as above.

[a]This table may be recomposed into a modified latin-square design.

[b]Key to notation. Capital letters refer to Analyst (A) or Fledgling (F). Roman numerals indicate judges' identifying numbers. First arabic numeral in sequence indicates interview number. Second arabic numeral in sequence indicates order in which the particular judge performed this segment of his rating task.

RESULTS

The results of the analysis of variance are presented in Table 38–2. A word should be said at this point about this analysis. We were concerned with the effect of the varying conditions of rating upon the means of the response-by-response ratings in an interview. These means are extremely stable, and thus the total sum of squares is extremely small. In order to be conservative, we included the second and third order interactions in the error term.

The analysis of variance showed that, as in the previous study, this second judge population was able to apply the Depth of Interpretation rating scale to differentiate between interviews. By far the greatest amount of the total variance was contributed by the judges; neither order of presentation nor varying amounts of context contributed significantly to the variance. However, the context by presentation interaction approached the .05 level of significance.

TABLE 38-2

Breakdown of Sums of Squares and F Tests for Analysis of Variance

Source of Variation	Sum of Squares		df	Mean Square		F	
Sequences	4.26		3	1.420		33.02**	
Raters within sequences	5.46		4	1.365		31.74**	
Total between raters	9.72		7				
Order	.05		3	.017		—	
Interviews	1.93		3	.643		14.95**	
Experimental conditions	.28		3	.093		2.16	
Presentation		.08	1		.080		1.86
Context		.01	1		.010		—
Presentation × Context		.19	1		.190		4.42
Pooled error	.65		15	.043			
Total within raters	2.91		24				
Grand total	12.63		31				

**Significant at the .01 level.

A second portion of our data analysis was directed toward the inter-judge agreement or rating reliability across and within the varying conditions. A summary of the interjudge reliabilities by cases is presented in Table 38–3. The product-moment correlations are remarkably constant across Cases I, II, and III, but in Case IV there is a significant drop in interjudge reliability.* A possible explanation for this difference lies in the fact that while Cases I, II, and III are counseling or psychotherapy sessions with normal or neurotic subjects, Case IV is from a series of interviews between a schizophrenic patient under insulin treatment and an inexperienced psychotherapist.

In Table 38–4 are presented the interjudge reliability coefficients by conditions of presentation and context. Significantly higher interjudge agreement is found when the analyst-fledgling judges rate under identical conditions of presentation and context than when ratings are made under totally different conditions. However, the rather startling result is revealed that when this group of judges had additional contextual material at its disposal, the interjudge reliabilities were significantly lower than when they made their ratings on the basis of information from the therapist's responses alone. When the results for the analysts and fledglings are viewed separately, the number of correlations becomes so small that statistical significance is not obtained, but the trend is equally apparent in both the analysts and the fledglings and

* Significance of difference between ranges of correlations was assessed in every case by the Median test, a nonparametric statistic which does not require the assumption of underlying normality in the population of correlations (7).

TABLE 38-3

Interjudge Reliabilities by Cases
(Analyst-Fledgling group)

Case	Range	Median
I	−.03 to .56	.34
II	−.05 to .65	.31
III	.09 to .53	.32
IV	−.15 to .48	.16

Note.—Cases I, II, and III show significantly ($p <$ .05) higher interjudge agreement than Case IV. Cases I, II, and III do not differ significantly.

cannot be considered to be the result of the difference in experience. In addition, agreement was slightly, although not significantly, better when the ratings were based upon typescripts rather than upon tape recordings.

Data from the earlier study with the psychologists were further analyzed to permit the assessment of the effects of varying cases and conditions of presentation and context upon their ratings. The results of these analyses are presented in Tables 38–5 and 38–6. Once again, Case IV is seen to yield consistently lower interjudge agreement, although the Median test reveals only the difference between Cases III and IV to be significant. There is no significant difference in interjudge agreement which can be attributed to different methods of presentation, and while ratings made under the preceding interview context condition yield slightly higher interjudge agreement than those made under the "therapist only" condition, the difference is not significant. Additionally, identical conditions of presentation and context produce no higher agreements among the psychologists than do totally different conditions.

Finally, comparisons were made of the interjudge reliabilities within and among the psychologist, analyst, and fledgling groups. In general, we find higher interjudge agreement among the psychologists than among either the analysts or fledglings. When ratings are made under identical conditions of presentation and context, the psychologists yield a range of interjudge reliabilities from .04 to .58, with a median of .42, while the comparable figures for the analyst group are −.01 to .56, median .22; and for the fledglings, .09 to .25, median .14. These differences among the groups, due to the small numbers of cases involved, are not significant.

A comparison of the interjudge reliabilities within each of the three groups' ratings made under entirely different conditions of presentation and context reveals a range of .07 to .62 for the psychologists, with a median of .42; range, .35 to .42, median .36 for the analysts; range −.02 to .43, median .31 for the fledglings. Once again, these differences

TABLE 38-4

Interjudge Reliabilities by Conditions of
Presentation and Context
(Analyst-Fledgling group)

Conditions	Range	Median
Identical[a]	.01 to .56	.37
Totally different[b]	−.05 to .58	.26
Identical context (TO)[c]	.05 to .65	.32
Identical context (PI)[d]	.00 to .46	.25
Identical presentation (RE)[e]	−.15 to .53	.25
Identical presentation (TY)[f]	.03 to .53	.31

Note.—Identical vs. totally different—$p < .05$.
    Therapist Only context vs. Preceding Interview context—$p < .01$.

[a]Includes only those correlations between raters operating under the same conditions of context and presentation.
[b]Includes only those correlations between raters operating under both different context and presentation conditions.
[c]Includes those correlations between raters operating under the Therapist Only context condition, irrespective of method of presentation.
[d]Includes those correlations between rater operating under the Preceding Interview context condition, irrespective of method of presentation.
[e]Includes those correlations between raters rating recordings, irrespective of context condition.
[f]Includes those correlations between raters rating typescripts, irrespective of context conditions.

fail to reach statistical significance, probably because of the small number of correlations involved.

The amount of agreement among the three groups was determined by a series of cross-correlations. That is, the ratings of the analyst group were correlated with the ratings of the psychologist group, the analysts with the fledglings, etc. These results may be summarized by saying that in general, the psychologists agreed more with both the analysts and fledgling groups than the latter agreed with each other.

DISCUSSION

This study supports our earlier evidence that raters are able to apply the Depth of Interpretation scale so as to differentiate between interviews, and indicates further that levels of experience and exposure to

TABLE 38-5

Interjudge Reliabilities by Cases
(Psychologist group)

Case	Range	Median
I	−.04 to .62	.37
II	.13 to .63	.37
III	.31 to .64	.48
IV	−.05 to .73	.26

Note.—Significant difference between III and IV, $p < .01$.

TABLE 38-6

Interjudge Reliabilities by Conditions of
Presentation and Context
(Psychologist group)

Conditions	Range	Median
Identical[a]	.04 to .58	.42
Totally different[b]	.07 to .62	.42
Identical context (TO)[c]	.09 to .63	.35
Identical context (PI)[d]	−.05 to .64	.43
Identical presentation (RE)[e]	.04 to .59	.41
Identical presentation (PI)[f]	.03 to .73	.37

Note.—None of the three comparisons reveals a significant difference.

[a]Includes only those correlations between raters operating under the same conditions of context and presentation.

[b]Includes only those correlations between raters operating under both different context and presentation conditions.

[c]Includes those correlations between raters operating under the Therapist Only context condition, irrespective of method of presentation.

[d]Includes those correlations between raters operating under the Preceding Interview context condition, irrespective of method of presentation.

[e]Includes those correlations between raters rating recordings, irrespective of context condition.

[f]Includes those correlations between raters rating typescripts, irrespective of context conditions.

formal analytic training do not substantially modify this ability. There is consistent evidence that the method of presentation of the interview material (typescript vs. recording) has no effect either upon mean level of rating or interjudge agreement. While the differences in level of interjudge agreement among the three groups are small, thre is a consistent tendency for the psychologist group to agree among themselves to a slightly greater extent than either the analysts or fledglings. In addition, we find that our hypothesis concerning the effect of the increased sensitivity resultant from analytic training upon the perception of cues provided by additional contextual information is not confirmed. Instead, we find the paradoxical result that among the analyst-fledgling group, additional context results in a significant decline in interjudge agreement.

It may be possible to acount for the generally higher interjudge agreement among psychologists in terms of their greater familiarity with rating tasks of the sort demanded by these studies. This does not, however, explain why the analyst group was handicapped by the additional context. It is possible that when this group was faced only with the therapist responses, it was able to impose a generally more meaningful rationale upon the data than when the additional context provided a much larger number of alternative hypotheses. Perhaps with the fuller context of having reviewed *all* of the preceding interviews, the analyst group would tend to converge on a more unanimous judgment. The possibility that analytic training leads to a somewhat greater ability to entertain multiple alternative hypotheses in the face of larger amounts of contextual information should not be overlooked.

Whatever may account for the few differences between psychoanalysts and clinical psychologists in rating Depth of Interpretation, it seems very clear that the two groups are essentially interchangeable as observers in studies which use this method of rating. Even though some may question the validity of this particular method of differentiating Depth of Interpretation, it is fairly representative of the commonly used methods. Therefore, one may proceed with the confidence that choice within this particular range of observers will not have profound influences on the results obtained.

We continue to be troubled by the generally low reliability of the Depth of Interpretation scale, although we have previously demonstrated the possibility of increasing interrater agreement by means of specific instruction in the application of the scale, and by using ratings of somewhat larger segments of the interview. We continue to feel that the approach to psychotherapy research by means of response-by-response analysis is the most promising of several alternatives, and are convinced that the variable Depth of Interpretation is a meaningful and useful one in psychotherapy research. A recent study by Speisman (8) lends support to this contention.

SUMMARY

In order to explore the possibility that increased perceptual sensitivity to the subtleties of the therapy relationship would allow raters to increase their interjudge agreement in rating Depth of Interpretation, four psychoanalysts and four analysts in training were enlisted as expert judges. These judges rated four therapy interviews under different condition of presentation and context.

An analysis of variance carried out on a modified latin-square design revealed that these raters could distinguish between interviews, but that neither the method of presentation of the interviews nor the amount of contextual information available to the judges had any systematic effect upon the means of response-by-response ratings.

A correlation analysis revealed that this group of raters had generally lower interjudge reliabilities than a group of psychologists who had previously rated the same interviews under the same conditions. The analyst-fledgling group among themselves showed significantly better interjudge agreement when their ratings were made under conditions of minimal context (therapist only condition) than when increasing amounts of context were available (preceding interview condition).

These results were discussed in terms of the greater familiarity of psychologists with rating tasks of the sort used, and the possibility was raised that analytic training made it possible to entertain a greater number of alternative hypotheses (and thus to decrease rating reliability) in the face of added contextual information. The essential identity of the two populations of judges was pointed out, and it was suggested that one may proceed with the confidence that choice within this particular range of observers will not have profound influences on the results obtained in studies in which this and similar rating scales are used.

The implications of the study for the continued application of the Depth of Interpretation rating scale to the process analysis of psychotherapy were discussed.

REFERENCES

1. BORDIN, E. S., CUTLER, R. L., DITTMANN, A. T., HARWAY, N. I., RAUSH, H. L., & RIGLER, D.   Measurement problems in process research on psychotherapy. *J. consult. Psychol.,* 1954, *18,* 79–82.

2. CUTLER, R. L.   *The relationship between the therapist's personality and certain aspects of psychotherapy.* Unpublished doctoral dissertation, Univer. of Michigan, 1953.

3. DIBNER, A. S. *The relationship between ambiguity and anxiety in a clinical interview.* Unpublished doctoral dissertation, Univer. of Michigan, 1953.

4. HARWAY, N. I., DITTMANN, A. T., RAUSH, H. L., BORDIN, E. S., & RIGLER, D. The measurement of depth of interpretation. *J. consult. Psychol.,* 1955, *19,* 247–253.

5. RAUSH, H. L., SPERBER, Z., RIGLER, D., WILLIAMS, JOAN V., HARWAY, N. I., BORDIN, E. S., DITTMANN, A. T., & HAYS, W. A dimensional analysis of depth of interpretation. *J. consult. Psychol.,* 1956, *20,* 43–48.

6. RIGLER, D. *Some determinants of therapist behavior.* Unpublished doctoral dissertation, Univer. of Michigan, 1956.

7. SIEGEL, S. *Nonparametric statistics.* New York: McGraw-Hilil, 1956.

8. SPEISMAN, J. C. *The relationship between depth of interpretation and verbal expressions of resistance in psychotherapy.* Unpublished doctoral dissertation, Univer. of Michigan, 1956.

This study was carried out under the auspices of United States Public Health Service Grant M–516, "Analyses of Therapeutic Interaction," E. S. Bordin and R. L. Cutler, Principal Investigators.

39

Ralph W. Heine, Ph.D.

A Comparison of Patients' Reports on Psychotherapeutic Experience with Psychoanalytic, Nondirective, and Adlerian Therapists

INTRODUCTION

Although there is a voluminous and growing body of literature devoted to psychotherapy, rarely have the questions implicit in the existence of various conflicting theoretical positions been explored experimentally. The only real precedent from an experimental point of view to the study reported here is the work of Fiedler (3) who demonstrated that capacity to form a salutory treatment relationship is more a function of expertness of the therapist than of school affiliation.

In theory, this investigation took as its point of departure some of the questions raised by Rosenzweig (5, 6) and more recently by Shoben (7). It was designed to test the hypothesis that patients associated with various schools of psychotherapy when asked to describe changes they have experienced and the factors in the psychotherapeutic experience which they feel produced the changes do not necessarily group themselves according to the school in which they obtained their therapy. Further, the experiment was designed to test the hypothesis that changes and factors seen as responsible for changes are related regardless of the type of therapy involved.

PROCEDURE

Twenty-four subjects, of whom eight had been treated in each of three schools of psychotherapy—psychoanalytic, nondirective, and Adlerian—were provided with 120 prepared statements descriptive of

Reprinted by permission of the publisher and the author from *American Journal of Psychotherapy*, 1953, 7, 16–23.

many possible changes resulting from psychotherapy. These subjects were asked to sort these statements in such a way as to distinguish between those changes which applied to them and those which did not. Similarly, they were provided with a set of prepared statements describing some of the events which might occur in the course of a therapeutic relationship and which might presumably be responsible for the changes experienced. They were asked to distribute these "factors" so as to indicate the extent to which each was responsible for the changes they had experienced.

The statements describing changes were divided in two ways. First, among the 120 there were 60 favorable changes and 60 unfavorable changes (based on the unanimous decision of three expert judges.) Second, 60 items described generalized trait changes while the other 60 described what the writer has called interrelated changes. The former were stated simply in terms of the subject having more or less of a particular trait, such as modesty, tolerance, honesty, independence, prudishness or alertness. The latter were stated in such a way as to indicate that change in the manner in which a subject viewed himself or the people around him had the effect of freeing him to make other changes.

The factors were also divided into those judged favorable to salutory change and those judged unfavorable. Further, the 120 statements contained 60 descriptive of technique and 60 descriptive of what the writer has called the therapeutic atmosphere. The items describing technique included references to interpretation, reassurance, suggestion, persuasion, questioning, structuring, reflection, etc. Those describing atmosphere referred to status, attention, ease of communication, degree of collaboration, mutual trust, friendliness, warmth, etc.

The subjects, in addition to sorting the two arrays of statements described above, were asked to check a questionnaire describing the amount of change experienced (quantitatively), their reason for considering and entering treatment, their reason for selecting their therapist as they had, their attitude toward psychotherapy prior to entry, and their reason for terminating therapy. In addition, they were asked for certain descriptive data including age, occupation, education, and the number of hours of therapy experienced.

RESULTS AND CONCLUSIONS

The results of this study indicated first that patients report similar changes regardless of the kind of psychotherapy they have experienced. Neither are the changes reported by patients of one school more favorable than the others nor are there sectarian preferences in the kinds of changes. These are, of course, subjective impressions which might not be confirmed by the opinions of relatives, of the therapists responsible for the treatment, by independent observers or by objective measures if such existed. The findings may, in fact, reveal nothing more than that these patients had started treatments with similar expectations. Nevertheless, a tenable conclusion is that therapists of various schools are not working toward dissimilar goals for their patients. Although different means may be employed—as will be seen later—the ends to be achieved in psychotherapy appear to be essentially the same.

A second finding was that patients associated with various schools differed significantly in their selection of the therapeutic factors which they felt accounted for the changes. Whether patients felt greatly benefited or not, patients within any one school tended to report similar factors as being responsible.

The data show that the psychoanalytic group differs significantly from the other two groups in the weight given favorable techniques, while the nondirective group differs from the other two groups in the emphasis put on therapeutic atmosphere.

In a sense, these results lend validity to the description of the respective psychotherapeutic procedures by authorities (1, 2, 4, 8) of the three schools. The psychoanalytic school unquestionably uses the greatest variety of techniques, hence an analysand would be obliged to make many more decisions between technique and atmosphere items than, for example, the nondirective client. Conversely, the clients of the nondirective school, which has as one of its main objectives the creation of an atmosphere favorable to self-exploration, would be expected to regard as the most efficacious factor that which its exponents sought to create —a benign, accepting, friendly atmosphere. Both with respect to technique and atmosphere the Adlerians fall between the two extreme groups. From the analysis of individual items one sees even more clearly that clients do react to features of treatment which have been presumed to differentiate one therapeutic procedure from another. Thus, the psychoanalytic group as compared with the nondirective and Adlerian groups, emphasized the importance of the interpretation of transference and of free association. In comparison with the Adlerian group, the psychoanalytic subjects emphasized the freedom of communication and the passivity of the therapist.

The items on which the nondirective subjects scored significantly higher than the other groups seem to center about freedom from constraint and self-determination in the course of treatment. While in one sense this seems to contradict the impression of the psychoanalytic subjects that they were granted the widest possible latitude, it is doubtful whether any contradiction exists. Hypothetically the reconciliation might be along the following lines. The psychoanalytic client is encouraged to express uncritically whatever comes to mind during the therapy hour, but at the same time the therapist is silent the greater share of the time. In contrast, the nondirective counselor while permitting his client to say what he pleases, gives additional support by reflections to whatever associational trend is followed. One might readily assume that the nondirective client has much more evidence that he is on the right track, since the counselor shows interest in and responds (albeit neutrally) to whatever the client offers. The analysand, on the other hand, is frequently left to his own devices without any external standard against which to judge the appropriateness or usefulness of his communications. Thus, a paradoxical situation arises. The nondirective client feels quite free despite the fact that by responding frequently the counselor introduces a control over the associational trend. The analysand feels less free because, in the absence of responses from the analyst, he must cast around for material which will stimulate the therapist to respond in a manner which will give some guidance to subsequent associations.

The Adlerian subjects reflected in their placement of items the directive and educative features of the procedures of that school. There are apparently certain concomitants to such procedures. For example, the Adlerians give significantly higher mean scores to statements which imply the withholding of negative self-reference in the interests of avoiding real or implied criticism by the therapist.

It is not unreasonable that persons treated in schools with differing techniques should reflect these, as well as differing notions as to the atmosphere that should be created, in accounting for the changes experienced. These differences were implied in certain of Fiedler's (3) findings, as well as in the data discussed above. It is interesting that such differences as were presumed to exist can, in part, be demonstrated experimentally. More important, however, is the broad area of agreement among the subjects of the three schools. Of the 120 statements only 20 significantly differentiated one school from another. Hence it is of interest to approach the individual items from the opposite point of view and ask on which of the items all the schools showed close agreement.

With respect to favorable technique there appear to be two foci of agreement. Most prominent is that of assisting the patient by asking questions which have the effect of clarifying feelings or attitudes. Secondarily, there is the technique of expressing for the client straightforwardly feelings which the client approaches hesitantly and hazily.

Techniques which all groups agreed were negatively related to change include direct and highly specific advice concerning important decisions, an emphasis on past history in contrast to present difficulties, demands by therapist that the patient achieve certain changes within a specific time limit, and dismissal of symptoms as "imaginary." Suggestions and other types of guidance with a light touch, while placed on the "not applicable" side of the scale, were so close to the mean of the total distribution as to indicate no consistent belief on the part of all patients that such techniques were negatively related to the change they experienced.

On the side of favorable atmosphere agreement centers about feelings of trust, of being understood, and of independence in reaching solutions to problems. Conversely, indications of distance or lack of interest or overly sympathetic attitudes were atmospheres seen as counter to favorable change. In addition, the fear that the therapist would be judgmental was a center of agreement on the negative side of the scale.

When the items were analyzed in terms of their applicability for each school represented, one sees a clear indication that both the Adlerian and nondirective subjects are much more concerned with the therapist as a person in his own right possessing personal characteristics which have a bearing on the therapeutic relationship. Both the Adlerian and nondirective subjects seem much more aware of the interpersonal and social aspects of the therapeutic relationship and hence are more conscious of the question of trust, of telling or not telling about some aspect of their life history, and of being understood. The psychoanalytic subjects, on the other hand, when they refer to atmosphere, are more concerned with the acceptability of expressing strong affect or of "telling the therapist off."

In closing this part of the discussion it should be added that there is no greater agreement among the subjects as to atmospheres related to change than there is with respect to techniques. This finding, again, is not at odds with those of Fiedler (3) who found that differences existed between the experts of the three schools in terms of emotional distance and status.

Despite the influence of the schools of psychotherapy on patients' reports of factors responsible for change, there was a strong underlying trend related to the degree of favorable change experienced by patients. Those patients who reported great benefit from psychotherapy consistently chose similar factors in the treatment process as having been responsible. The patients who reported little benefit were likewise similar to one another in their reports but different from the much improved group.

Several inferences might be drawn from this third finding. It is, for example, possible that while patients were responding consciously to aspects of treatment which differentiate the practices of the three schools, they were also reacting, perhaps less consciously to interpersonal aptitudes and skills which all therapists have in common but in variable degrees.

Various schools of psychotherapy, after all, are differentiated on the basis of theories of personality and by the weight given certain therapeutic techniques. The medium through which theoretical material is utilized is the therapist-patient relationship. While this relationship may be circumscribed by theoretical and technical considerations and often by rules of thumb laid down by teachers associated with various schools, the personality of the therapist can never be more than partially obscured. It is not possible to be one personality outside one's office and a totally different personality when one is with a patient. It is a truism that a person whose interpersonal behavior is broadly maladaptive cannot be consistently successful as a psychotherapist, yet this simple observation is often diluted by token acceptance.

The third finding suggests that patients in this study looked beyond the differences in learned techniques and responded to the personal characteristics of the individual therapists. The descriptions of the therapy of patients greatly benefited had much in common irrespective of school affiliation—as did the descriptions of therapy by the less benefited. The second and third findings taken together imply that theoretical background and techniques per se are less important than the characteristics of the person who employs them.

All of the findings together lend weight to attempts to reconcile the many "schools of convictions," as J. McV. Hunt* has described the schools of psychotherapy, and to make combined and intensive investigations of the attributes of a salutary treatment relationship and of the individual therapists who are consistently able to sustain such a relationship.

SUMMARY AND CONCLUSIONS

Twenty-four subjects, of whom eight had been treated in each of three schools of psychotherapy—psychoanalytic, nondirective, and Adlerian— were asked to describe with prepared statements changes resulting from therapy and the factors in the therapeutic experience related to the changes.

The following conclusions seem merited on the basis of the results: (1) there are no differences in the changes reported attributable to the school membership of the therapist; (2) there are significant differences between subjects of various schools in the report of factors responsible for changes. These differences are in accord with differences appearing in authoritative descriptions of the techniques and attitudes favored by the three schools represented; (3) irrespective of school affiliation, subjects showing similar changes tend to report similar factors as having been responsible. The principal implication of the study is that some factor (or factors) common to all schools is the therapeutic agent rather than particular features of the theory and practice of any one school. If one accepts the scientific precept that identical effects have common antecedents, then those interested in psychotherapy as a science should be working toward the goal of developing *a psychotherapy* rather than a variety of psychotherapies.

* From his presidential address before the Division of Personality & Social Psychology of the APA in Chicago, September 1, 1951.

REFERENCES

1. ADLER, ALFRED: *The Practice & Theory of Individual Psychology.* Trans. P. Rodin. (2nd Ed.) London: Kegan, Paul & Co. Ltd., 1946.

2. ALEXANDER, FRANZ and FRENCH, THOMAS: *Psychoanalytic Therapy.* New York: Ronald Press, 1946.

3. FIEDLER, FRED E.:   A comparison of therapeutic relationships in psychoanalytic, nondirective & Adlerian therapy. *J. of Consult. Psychol.,* 1950, *14,* 434–445.

4. ROGERS, CARL R.:   *Counseling & Psychotherapy.* New York: Houghton Mifflin Co., 1952.

5. ROSENZWEIG, SAUL: A Dynamic Interpretation of Psychotherapy Oriented toward Research. *Psychiatry,* 1938, *1,* 521–526.

6. ――――――: Areas of Agreement in Psychotherapy. 1940 Section Meeting. *Amer. J. Ortho. Psychiat.,* 1940, *10,* 703–704.

7. SHOBEN, EDWARD J., JR.:   Psychotherapy as a problem in learning theory. *Psychol. Bull.,* 1949, *46,* 366–392.

8. THOMPSON, CLARA: *Psychoanalysis: Evolution & Development.* New York: Hermitage House, 1950.

Reviewed in the VA and published with the approval of the Chief Medical Director. The statements and conclusions published by the author are his own and do not necessarily reflect the opinions or policy of the VA.—This paper contains the major findings and conclusions of the writer's doctoral dissertation. The writer wishes to express his gratitude to Drs. James G. Miller, Hedda Bolgar, and Donald W. Fiske of the University of Chicago for their guidance in the formulation of the research project and in the preparation of the dissertation manuscript.

40

Gert Heilbrunn, M.D.

Results with Psychoanalytic Therapy
and Professional Commitment

DEFINITION OF CONCEPTS

Of 173 patients whom I have treated with psychoanalytic psychotherapy in the course of the last seventeen years, 77 or 45% were considered improved. However, there are at least three points in this opening statement which require considerable elucidation and which seem to challenge the significance of the quoted figures. The three items in question pertain to (1) the personal pronoun "I" with its implications as to the personality of the therapist, (2) the concept of psychoanalytic psychotherapy, and (3) the criteria of improvement.

(1) The Personality of the Therapist

The curriculum of my psychoanalytic life began in 1942 at the Chicago Psychoanalytical Institute. It has since included membership in the American Psychoanalytic Association, several publications in the field, and some modest executive and academic assignments. Several of my colleagues may question my dedication to psychoanalysis. I do not. I know that I am not exclusively devoted to psychoanalysis as a way of life. I belong to that group of psychiatrists who consider psychoanalysis as a supreme investigative and research tool, but who retain critical reservations about its therapeutic efficacy in general and its applicability to certain diagnostic categories in particular. I mention this skeptical attitude because it may have prevailed even before I had found the unfavorable results in several diagnostic entities.

(2) The Concept of Psychoanalytic Psychotherapy

The employ of the word "psychotherapy" committed its adjective "psychoanalytic" to a clinical cause which had to define its goal in more

Reprinted by permission of the publisher and the author from *American Journal of Psychotherapy*, 1966, 20, 89–99.

precise than generally educational or emotional benefits, or both. The application of the treatment varied in total duration and number of weekly sessions. The varying treatment lengths and densities obtained in many instances from the patient's economic, local, and occupational circumstances, in others from my initial and admittedly speculative prescription and finally from the termination of therapy. Termination was indicated when the therapeutic goals had been reached, or when continuation of therapy seemed to add nothing to partial improvement or complete failure. In some cases termination was dictated by outer circumstances and in a few by the patient. It seemed most proper academically to differentiate three treatment classifications:

(1) "Psychoanalysis" was predicated on a minimum of three weekly sessions for a total exceeding 300 therapeutic hours. I counted thirty-seven patients who had been in analysis for an average of 527 hours, most of them at a rate of four or five hours per week.

(2) "Extended psychoanalytic therapy" comprised fifty-four patients with a 100- to 300-hour treatment span, an average total of 208 hours and a frequency of from two to three weekly sessions. Four patients whose total number of treatment hours had well passed the 300 mark were assigned to this group because they rarely had more than two therapeutic sessions per week.

(3) "Brief psychoanalytic psychotherapy" included seventy-five patients. They had received from one to three therapeutic sessions per week for a total average of 51 hours, which was calculated from a 20- to 100-hour treatment span. More than eighty patients below a 20-hour total were excluded from this statistical evaluation because the "relatively large number of drop-outs—many times for bona fide, unavoidable reasons—would unfairly distort the efficacy of a method before its proper deployment" (1).

(3) Criteria of Improvement

In addition to the chronologic trichotomy and its statistical framework, the concept of psychoanalytic psychotherapy was determined by technical adaptations in response to the demand of varying treatment goals. The realization of these goals defined the criteria of improvement. One would assume that orthodox psychoanalysis aimed at a structural change of the personality, that extended psychoanalytic therapy reached this goal less often than analysis and that brief psychotherapy had to be content with a mere removal of symptoms. However, the results did not always substantiate these neat, academic postulates. Not always did improvement after analysis or extended therapy meet each of Knight's criteria of "symptomatic improvement, increased productiveness, improved adjustment and pleasure in sex, improved interpersonal relationships and ability to handle ordinary psychologic conflicts and reasonable reality stresses" (2); nor did success with brief psychotherapy always consist of symptom relief only.

I am unable at this time to explain why one patient benefited from the tedious 500- to 600-hour analysis of his resistances only partially, while another conquered similar difficulties in one-third or one-fourth of that time. I had originally rated symptoms and structural improvements on separate, quantifying scales but chose for statistical convenience to contrast an all inclusive "improved" with a categorical "unimproved." Patients whose slight improvement was just a shade above a negative result were listed within the unimproved group. The clinical evaluations pertained to the time of termination. I conducted no organized follow-up studies, but collected posttherapeutic, direct, or indirect information about 71 of the 173 patients. In nearly all cases did the katamnestic evaluation confirm the original one. However, the data were obtained through clinical interview from the eleven patients only, whereas those of the other sixty were based on casual or indirect information, or both.

STATISTICAL EVALUATION

For gross statistical purposes the clinical diagnoses were limited to five major divisions and complied with the spirit and nomenclature of the American Psychiatric Association's *Manual of Mental Disorders* (3). They comprised (1) psychotic reactions, (2) personality pattern disturbances, (3) sociopathic personality disturbances (including perversions, homosexuality, and addictions), (4) psychoneuroses, and (5) personality trait disturbances. (I took the liberty for simplicity's sake to include three cases of psychophysiologic disorders in the fifth category.) When these diagnostic divisions were correlated with their appropriate improvement rates under the three different treatment spans, we were confronted with the results indicated in Tables 40–1, 40–2, and 40–3.

Group A totaled thirty-seven patients. The treatment type was classic psychoanalysis. Of five schizophrenic and three schizoid patients none improved. Their average length of treatment had been 705 hours. Of seven patients with the diagnosis "sociopathic personality disorder," 14% improved.

The greatest interest was perhaps focused on the "personality trait disturbances," or to use the former terminology, the character neuroses, for whom psychoanalysis was considered the treatment of choice. Eleven patients (57%) had improved after an average of 500 hours. Curiously enough there was only one patient classified as psychoneurotic. Since this patient improved, the ensuing improvement rate was 100%. It is obvious that the all-or-none result which obtains from the percentage calculation of one single case may be rather misleading. For this reason and to annul possible faulty diagnostic crossings, I computed two different subtotals. The first added the psychoneuroses to the personality trait disturbances. It read: eleven of twenty-two patients (59%) im-

TABLE 40-1

Group A: Psychoanalysis
(Treatment Duration Exceeding 300 Hours)

Diagnosis	Number of Patients	Average Number of Treatment Hours	Percent Improvement
1—Psychotic Disorders	5	633	0
2—Personality Pattern Disturbances	3	825	0
1 plus 2	8	705	0
3—Sociopathic Personality Disturbances	7	408	14
4—Psychoneurotic Disorders	1	314	100
5—Personality Trait Disturbances	21	500	57
4 plus 5	22	492	59
3 plus 4 plus 5	29	472	47
TOTAL	37	527	38

TABLE 40-2

Group B: Extended Psychoanalytic Therapy
(Treatment Span 100-300 Hours)

Diagnosis	Number of Patients	Average Number of Treatment Hours	Percent Improvement
1—Psychotic Disorders	6	195	0
2—Personality Pattern Disturbances	1	418	0
1 plus 2	7	227	0
3—Sociopathic Personality Disturbances	8	184	25
4—Psychoneurotic Disorders	8	171	38
5—Personality Trait Disturbances	31	219	58
4 plus 5	39	209	54
3 plus 4 plus 5	47	205	49
TOTAL	54	208	43

TABLE 40-3

Group C: Brief Psychoanalytic Therapy
(Treatment Span 20-100 Hours)

Diagnosis	Number of Patients	Average Number of Treatment Hours	Percent Improvement
1—Psychotic Disorders	2	55	0
2—Personality Pattern Disturbances	4	51	0
1 plus 2	6	52	0
3—Sociopathic Personality Disturbances	15	46	13
4—Psychoneurotic Disorders	17	57	70
5—Personality Trait Disturbances	37	50	54
4 plus 5	54	52	59
3 plus 4 plus 5	69	50	49
TOTAL	75	51	45

proved. The second combined the psychoneuroses, the personality trait disturbances, and the sociopathic personality disorders for a total of twenty-nine patients of whom fourteen (49%) improved. This figure was, in my opinion, particularly meaningful because it reflected the prognosis for an average, unselected group of nonpsychotic analytic patients. It was a great surprise to find nearly the identical improvement rates for the comparable subtotals in the extended and brief treatment groups (see Tables). Each charted a 49% improvement rate for their groups of forty-seven and sixty-nine patients respectively for the combined psychoneuroses, sociopathic, and personality trait disorders.

It was noteworthy that the personality trait disturbances alone showed also nearly identical responses in all three divisions. The readings were 57, 58, and 54. A marked difference existed, however, in the improvement rates of the psychoneuroses. It was only 38% for group B, but 70% for the brief psychotherapy column. These contrasting readings as well as the steeply declining total number of patients so diagnosed from seventeen in group C, to eight in group B, to one in group A suggest that the psychoneurotic patient has a good chance to get well quickly. It seems doubtful that the unimproved patients could have reversed the unfavorable outcome with continued treatment in view of the marked drop to the 38% level in group B. A similar paradox existed in the treatment of the sociopathic groups. The best results, 25%, were achieved with extended psychotherapy, while only 14% responded favorably to psychoanalysis. *One must remember, however, that these figures indicate chiefly group prognoses and cannot be applied to the individual patient.*

An exception from this injunction seems to exist for the psychotic patients and those with a disturbed personality pattern, based on the uniformly negative results in a total of twenty-one patients regardless of duration, technique, and intensity of treatment. A personal prognosis, fortunately a good one, may be ventured in still another diagnostic category, namely that of "adolescent maladjustment." It might be mentioned in passing—the group is not represented in the Tables—that of seven patients 68% improved in an average of forty-four hours. One patient left therapy upon his parents' and against his physician's advice. He probably spoiled his adjustment and my statistics. According to my experience I would feel justified to expect salutary results with practically all of these patients in fewer than 100 therapeutic hours, but would urge them not to terminate prematurely since none of six patients improved who had left therapy before the twentieth hour.

In summary, the results indicate a rather hopeless outlook for the ultimate improvement of patients with psychotic reactions and personality pattern disturbances. This does not invalidate continuous psychotherapy as a tool for the alleviation of anxiety and other superimposed neurotic symptoms in these conditions.

Patients with the diagnosis of sociopathic personality fared somewhat better, provided they remained in therapy for more than 100 hours. None of the male homosexuals improved, in contrast to the more favorable prognosis for female homosexuality.

Brief psychotherapy was so successful with maladjusted adolescents and psychoneurotics that none of the adolescents and only a few of the neurotics had to remain in therapy past the 100-hour mark.

The prognosis for the patients with personality trait disturbances as well as the joined group of the psychoneuroses, sociopathic, and personality trait disorders were strikingly similar with brief, extended, or orthodox psychoanalytic therapy. Approximately one-half of the patients improved in each category, leaving us with the practical, but as yet unsolved task to convert general academic data into individual specifications.

EPICRITIC CONCLUSIONS

Reflection on this statistical venture evoked ambivalent feelings and heretic thought. In an apologetic mood I blamed my uneven therapeutic talents for the consistent therapeutic failure with all schizophrenics, schizoid personalities, and male homosexuals. I pondered inconclusively about the possibility of improvement due to fortuitous circumstance (4) or due to spontaneous maturation within the lapse of years spent in analysis. Naturally, I was suspicious of the subjectivity of my evaluations, in quiet sympathy with many of my colleagues who escaped the statistical summons of the American Psychoanalytic Association in 1952 through the argument of lack of conformity of diagnosis, severity of illness, and criteria of improvement (5). I puzzled a good deal over the possible mechanisms underlying good and bad results, particularly among the patients with character neuroses. The ordinary statistical elements of sex, age, marital status, socioeconomic conditions, and diagnostic subdivisions contributed nothing, nor did psychodynamic and psychoeconomic assessments. Which factors were responsible for the different improvement speeds? Invoking the patient's varying abilities to utilize the therapeutic process did no more than beg the question.

If, then, these statistics do not allow for treatment prediction in a given case, what gains accrue to us from the group prognoses?

(1) Classic psychoanalysis does not emerge as the general treatment of choice, since it shares equal percentages with the briefer methods at best and undue expenditure of money, time, and energy at worst. *However, it will prove of value especially in the character neuroses, after the "psychotherapies" have failed.*

(2) One can enter upon quantitative and qualitative comparisons with nonanalytic methods and spontaneous improvement rates. Such academic exercise appears to lead to strange conclusions. To quote only

from a few incisive reports, we have Eysenck's 64% improvement fig
which he computed from nineteen studies of approximately 7,300 ad
patients, including those with neuroses, character disorders, and psychopathic states treated with eclectic psychotherapeutic techniques (6).
Then there are the impressive results published by Wolpe and his followers: 90% positive results with methods based on learning theory;
average duration of treatment twenty-five to thirty sessions; standards
of evaluation: explicit compliance with Knight's criteria (7–11).

When we are finally apprised by several sources that from 40 to
100% of neurotic (6, 4, 12–14) and 40% of schizophrenic patients
recuperate spontaneously (15), it would seem that my psychotherapeutic
efforts were a decided hindrance to more than one-third of my patients.
It may be held as redeeming circumstance that with a few exceptions
my patients had been ill in excess of the time postulated for spontaneous recovery, thus allowing for a definite causal relationship between treatment and improvement. To add sadness to mounting irony
and confusion, our traditional, proud assertion linking lengthy therapy
with structural reorientation is seriously challenged by the following
sobering disclosures: Pfeffer observed the presence of unresolved,
neurotic residues in all of nine patients who had completed successful
psychoanalysis several years prior to reexamination (16) and Helene
Deutsch summarized her similar postanalytic experience in two patients
(one of whom she had portrayed as one of her best therapeutic results)
with this gloomy comment: "We do not eliminate the original sources
of neurosis; we only help to achieve better ability to change neurotic
frustrations into valid compensations" (17). In essence, these two
authors seem to bear out Freud's terse statement, which must have been
based on like disappointments: "We have no means of predicting what
will happen later to a patient who has been cured" (18).

(3) The disparity of findings and the divergence of opinions should
certainly dispel the belief in psychotherapeutic monopolies, as they are
dictated by financial, professional, academic, or ideologic commitments.
Novel approaches should be welcomed and judged fairly, according to
their therapeutic or research value, even at the risk that the claim for
psychogeneity of several mental and emotional disorders will have to
undergo corrective restriction. In order not to pit our hopes against those
of our patients, it is high time that we switch from our role of medicine-
men to that of men-of-medicine. The aggregate of recent neurochemical
and neurobiologic data make this long overdue conversion very rewarding. The review of the literature provides fascinating reading. There is
the Bucy-Klüver syndrome of hypersexuality, hyperplagia, and placidity
in amygdalectomized monkeys and humans (19, 20) with its implications to the phenomenon of repression (21); there are the electrical
stimulation experiments through implanted electrodes in the brains of
animals and humans (22–26), which disclosed multiple appetitive and
aversive foci as possible structural correlates for the pleasure-pain
principle (20) and, to mention another, there are the protocols by
Penfield, charting manifestations of the patient's unconscious and in-

duced hallucinations (27) upon electrical stimulus of the temporal cortex (28).

Ethology (29) and genetics (30–32) yield axioms of nature which relegate to nurture a complementary but not exclusive role. Neurochemistry, through the psychoactive drugs, has found immediate, practical application. However, our chief interest at this point focuses past the temporary interference with mere symptoms upon the site and mode of the drug action, and thus hopefully upon the anatomy of the emotions. The sophisticated methods of quantitative histochemistry, implantation of micro-cannulae into specific cerebral areas, electron miscroscopy, x-ray diffraction, radioactive labeling, and others may in the not so distant future give us unequivocal information about certain depressions, components of the obsessive-compulsive syndrome and, most important, schizophrenia. Recent investigation into the physiologic nature of memory may perhaps enable us to define psychotherapy in terms of ribonucleic acid coding. Hyden (33) advanced the hypothesis which was subsequently supported by McConnell's work with planarians (34), that learning and memory were connected with an alteration of the ribonucleic acid in the neurons. Based on the evidence that ribonucleic acid was associated with protein synthesis, Hyden suggested that electrical neuronal impulses are translated into long-lasting, biochemical codes which can be used and interpreted repeatedly under varying conditions. The modulated frequency of neuronal impulses changes the ionic equilibrium of the cell plasma and causes substitution of one base for another at a specific site in the RNA molecule. This newly formed molecule determines the sequence of structural elements as well as evoking complementary molecules. The degree of variation in protein structure has been estimated at about 10^{15}, which according to Hyden is the probable number of engrammed impressions during a human lifetime. The storage and availability of coded protein molecules as fragments of memory add new chemical emphasis to the psychologically and empirically known significance of early life experiences.

We may speculate that pain and pleasure centers add their frequencies to the messages of the percepts determining their pleasant or unpleasant character and consequently their later avoidance or repetition analogous to electrical self-stimulation. The quantity of stimulation either by intensity or repetition of the stimulus evokes engramming in proportionate amounts. When, for example, threatening percepts of the superego variety charge certain instinctual drives with impulses from the pain area, their motor expression is inhibited or repressed. In successful psychotherapy these electrically muffled percepts are superseded by nonthreatening percepts which through their electrical association with pleasure centers reverse the former damping charge: repression is lifted. Beneficial coding, that is, repetition of a formerly traumatic event under more auspicious circumstances, may be achieved through dramatic reenactment, directives, or verbalization. The latter is particularly well-suited to fathom and correct the noxious percepts through the positively charged impressions imparted by interpretations and the transference. The plasticity of the individual, his propensity toward molecular accommodation seems to differ from person-to-person and to decline with advancing age. Hence, in general the better psychotherapeutic outlook for a young than an old person.

These advances and the meager results in certain diagnostic categories should caution us against imperialistic "psychofication" of disorders with rather questionable psychogenesis. The eventual replacement of certain psychopathologic by neurochemical profiles might induce many a medical psychotherapist to extend his interest to neuromedical parameters and potentiate the unique forces of psychotherapy by chemical and electronic expedients.

SUMMARY

The present evaluation comprised 173 private patients. Thirty-seven were treated with the traditional analytic technique, exceeding a total of 300 hours at a rate of at least three weekly sessions. "Extended psychoanalytic psychotherapy" included fifty-four patients during a 100- to 300-hour treatment span at a frequency of from two to three weekly sessions. Eighty-two patients received "brief psychoanalytic therapy," that is, one to three therapeutic hours per week for a total of from 20 to 100 sessions.

The results were uniformly negative for the patients with psychotic reactions and personality pattern disturbances. Patients with the diagnosis of sociopathic personality fared somewhat better, provided that they remained in therapy for more than 100 hours. None of the male homosexuals improved, in contrast to the more favorable prognosis for homosexual women. Brief psychotherapy was so successful with maladjusted adolescents and psychoneurotics that none of the adolescents and only a few of the psychoneurotics had to remain in therapy past the 100-hour mark.

The prognoses for the patients with personality trait disturbances as well as the joined group of those with psychoneuroses, sociopathic, and personality trait disorders were strikingly similar, with brief, extended, or orthodox psychoanalytic therapy. Approximately one-half of the patients improved in each category, leaving us with the practical, but as yet unsolved task to convert group forecasts into individual prognoses.

In the epicrisis I pondered over the criteria of improvement and discussed comparisons with nonanalytic techniques, cautioned against imperialistic "psychofication" of disorders with questionable psychogenesis, and advocated the amalgamation of psychodynamic and psychotherapeutic concepts with neurobiologic data and RNA coding.

REFERENCES

1. HEILBRUNN, G.   Results with Psychoanalytic Therapy. *Am. J. Psychother.*, 17: 427, 1963.
2. KNIGHT, R. P.   Evaluation of the Results of Psychoanalytic Therapy. *Am. J. Psychiat.*, 98: 434, 1941.
3. AMERICAN PSYCHIATRIC ASSOCIATION.   *Diagnostic and Statistical Manual of Mental Disorders,* Washington, D. C. Committee on Nomenclature and Statistics, American Psychiatric Association, Mental Hospital Service, 1952.
4. STEVENSON, T.   Processes of "Spontaneous" Recovery from the Psychoneuroses. *Am. J. Psychiat.*, 117: 1057, 1961.
5. BRODY, M. W.   Prognosis and Results of Psychoanalysis. In *Psychosomatic Medicine.* Nodine, J. H. and Moyer, J. H., Eds. Lea & Febiger, Philadelphia, 1962.
6. EYSENCK, H. J.   The Effects of Psychotherapy. In *Handbook of Abnormal Psychology.* Eysenck, H. J., Ed. Basic Books, New York, 1961.
7. WOLPE, J.   The Prognosis in Unpsychoanalyzed Recovery from Neurosis. *Am. J. Psychiat.*, 118: 35, 1961.
8. WOLPE, J.   Learning Versus Lesions as the Basis of Neurotic Behavior. *Am. J. Psychiat.*, 112: 923, 1956.
9. STEVENSON, J.   Direct Instigation of Behavioral Changes in Psychotherapy. *A. M. A. Gen. Arch. Psychiat.*, 1: 99, 1959.
10. STEVENSON, J. and WOLPE, J.   Recovery from Sexual Deviations Through Overcoming Nonsexual Neurotic Responses. *Am. J. Psychiat.*, 116: 737, 1960.
11. WOLPE, J.   Reciprocal Inhibition as the Main Basis of Psychotherapeutic Effects. *A. M. A. Arch. Neur. Psychiat.*, 72: 205, 1954.
12. LANDIS, C.   Quoted in The Effects of Psychotherapy. In *Handbook of Abnormal Psychology.* Eysenck, H. J., Ed. Basic Books, New York, 1961.
13. DENKER, P. G.   Quote ibidem.
14. HASTING, D. W.   Follow-up Results in Psychiatric Illness. *Am. J. Psychiat.*, 114: 1057, 1959.
15. NOYES, A. P. and KOLB, L. C.   *Modern Clinical Psychiatry.* W. B. Saunders, Philadelphia, 1959.
16. PFEFFER, A. Z.   A Procedure for Evaluating the Results of Psychoanalysis. *J. Am. Psychoanal. Ass.*, 7: 418, 1959.
17. DEUTSCH, H.   Psychoanalytic Therapy in the Light of Follow-up. *Am. J. Psychoanal. Ass.*, 7: 445, 1959.
18. FREUD, S.   Analysis Terminable and Interminable. In *Collected Papers,* Vol. 5, Hogarth Press, London, 1950.
19. KLÜVER, H.   "The Temporal Lobe Syndrome." Produced by Bilateral Ablations. In *Neurological Basis of Behavior.* Ciba Foundation Symposium, Little, Brown & Co., Boston, 1958.
20. TERZIAN, H. and DALLEORE, G.   Syndrome of Klüver and Bucy Reproduced in Man by Bilateral Removal of the Temporal Lobes. *Neurology,* 5: 373, 1955.
21. HEILBRUNN, G.   The Neurobiologic Aspect of Three Psychoanalytic Concepts. *Compreh., Psychiat.*, 2: 261, 1961.
22. OLDS, J.   Selective Effects of Drives and Drugs on "Reward" Systems of the Brain. In *Neurological Basis of Behavior.* Ciba Foundation Symposium, Little, Brown & Co., Boston, 1958.
23. DELGADO, J. M. R. and HAMLIN, N.   Spontaneous and Evoked Electrical Seizures in Animals and Humans. In *Electrical Studies on the Unanesthetized Brain.* Ramey, E. R. and O'Doherty, D. S., Eds. Paul B. Hoeber, New York, 1960.
24. HEATH, R. G. and MICKLE, W. H.   Evaluation of Seven Years' Experience with Depth Electrode Studies in Human Patients. See reference 23.
25. SEM-JACOBSEN, C. W. and TORKILDSEN, A.   Depth Recording and Electrical Stimulation in the Human Brain. See reference 23.

26. LILLY, J. C. The Psychophysiological Basis for Two Kinds of Instincts. *J. Am. Psychoanal. Ass.*, 8: 659, 1960.

27. PENFIELD, W. and ROBERT, L. *Speech and Brain Mechanism.* Princeton University Press, Princeton, N.J., 1959.

28. PENFIELD, W. and JASPER, H. H. The Role of the Temporal Cortex in Recall of Past Experience and Interpretation of the Present. In *Neurological Basis of Behavior.* Ciba Foundation Symposium, Little, Brown & Company, Boston, 1958.

29. MASSERMAN, J. H. Ethology, Comparative Biodynamics and Psychoanalytic Research. In *Theories of the Mind.* Scher, E., Ed. Free Press of Glencoe, New York, 1962.

30. RAINER, J. D. The Concept of Mind in the Framework of Genetics. See reference 29.

31. SHIELDS, J. *Monozygotic Twins Brought up Apart and Brought up Together.* Oxford University Press, New York, 1962.

32. HAM, G. C. Genes and the Psyche: Perspective in Human Development and Behavior. *Am. J. Psychiat.*, 119: 828, 1963.

33. HYDEN, H. In Sourkes, T. L., *Biochemistry of Mental Disease.* Paul B. Hoeber, New York, 1962.

34. McCONNELL, J. V. Memory Transfer Through Cannibalism in Planarians. *J. Neuropsyhiat.*, 3: 542, 1962.

Presented at the Second National Meeting of the Association for the Advancement of Psychotherapy, St. Louis, Mo., May 5, 1963.

41

R. *Bruce Sloane, M.D., Fred R. Staples, Ph.D.,
Allan H. Cristol, M.D., Neil J. Yorkston, MD.,
& Katherine Whipple*

Short-Term Analytically Oriented
Psychotherapy Versus Behavior Therapy

Behavioral techniques are coming to be widely accepted in the treatment of monophobias, sexual impotence, and other "unitary" psychiatric problems; this acceptance is supported by a good deal of research. Gelder and associates (1, 2) showed that patients suffering from severe phobias tend to improve more quickly with behavioral than with psychoanalytically oriented or group therapy. However, in their studies this initial advantage was not maintained over time. Moreover, their research and that of others (3) have been criticized for failing to use experienced therapists for either modality.

Paul's study (4), which is often cited in support of behavior therapy, showed one technique, desensitization, to be clearly superior in treating unitary phobias among college students recruited as subjects; this superiority was maintained at follow-up (5). However, it is unlikely that the nature of these subjects' problems and their motivation for improvement are comparable to those of patients who spontaneously seek treatment. Similar criticisms as well as the use of inexperienced therapists apply in Di Loreto's comparative study of students with anxiety (3). In this study, desensitization clearly worked best, but this was because it was applicable to both introverts and extroverts.

Phobic patients, especially monophobic patients, are much rarer than patients with anxiety neuroses and personality disorders. There have been very few controlled evaluations of behavior therapy with patients with anxiety neuroses and personality disorders. The tendency has been to assume that only a "deeper" therapy could produce a lasting effect for these patients by attacking the underlying causes of general psychiatric problems.

Our aim in this study was to compare the relative effectiveness of behavior therapy and more traditional analytically oriented therapy conducted by experienced therapists with patients with anxiety neuroses and personality disorders. We also compared both therapies with the effect of an initial assessment interview plus the mere promise and expectation of help.

METHOD

Patients

Patients who applied for treatment at a university psychiatric out-patient clinic were initially seen by one of three experienced psychiatric interviewers (assessors). Patients who were below the age of eighteen or over the age of forty-five, who seemed too mildly ill, or who were too seriously disturbed to risk waiting four months were excluded from the study. Also excluded were those who were psychotic, mentally retarded, organically brain damaged, or primarily in need of drug therapy. All others who wanted to have psychotherapy rather than drugs or some other treatment and for whom the assessor considered this to be the treatment of choice were accepted into the study. Twenty-nine applicants did not meet the criteria and were referred elsewhere or treated outside the study.

The ninety-four patients who were accepted were predominantly in their early twenties, women (60%), and white (only 7% were black). They had completed an average of fourteen years of education (about two years of college or other post-secondary-school training). Over half of the patients were students, and about half were self-supporting. Roughly two-thirds suffered from psychoneuroses (usually anxiety) and one-third from personality disorders. The most frequent specific symptoms were, in decreasing order, generalized anxiety, interpersonal difficulties, especially with the opposite sex; low self-esteem; generalized worry; and bodily complaints.

Psychological Tests

Mill Hill Vocabulary Scale. The mean intelligence quotient of the whole sample on this scale was ninety-nine.

Minnesota Multiphasic Personality Inventory (MMPI). The overall means on this test showed a considerable degree of pathology in these patients. Four of the nine subscale mean scores (for depression, psychopathic deviate, psychasthenia, and schizophrenia) were within the abnormal range (above seventy). The overall mean of the eight clinical scales was also in the abnormal range. Only eight patients scored normally on all scales.

Eysenck Personality Inventory. The mean scores of the patients on this scale showed them to be introverted and neurotic at the eighty-sixth percentile of neuroticism.

California Psychological Inventory. The patients as a group showed lowered but not abnormal self-control, sociability, and socialization on this scale.

Assessment

One of three experienced psychiatrists saw each patient at the initial interview. These psychiatrists were not connected with the treatment. The patient and interviewer together drew up a list of three target symptoms—the major specific symptoms that had led the patient to seek treatment. Both the psychiatrist and the patient rated each target symptom on a five-point scale of severity (6, 7). To judge the patient's general level of functioning, the Structured and Scaled Interview To Assess Maladjustment (SSIAM) (8, 9) was used. The SSIAM rates the patient's level of adjustment on eleven-point scales for ten items in each of the following five areas: work; social and leisure; sexual; and relationships with spouse, children, and family of origin.

These two measures, the list of target symptoms and the SSIAM, provided the main indices of change. In addition, a global impressionistic rating of overall improvement was made. Other measures taken will be reported separately.

Treatment

After interviewing and testing, the patients were randomly assigned in the following manner. Thirty-one were assigned to behavior therapy, thirty to psychotherapy, and thirty-three to the waiting list. Within this random assignment, patients were matched within the three groups in terms of sex and severity of neurosis as assessed by the Eysenck Personality Inventory.

The Therapists

Of the three therapists in each group, one had more than twenty years of experience, one had ten to twelve years of experience, and one had six or more years of experience. One was a Ph.D. psychologist and the other five were M.D.s. Two of the psychotherapists were psychoanalysts and a third was in personal analysis with a training analyst. All of the behavior therapists were formally trained. By using experienced therapists, we hoped to avoid the twin pit-falls of exposing a patient to an ineffective treatment (because a technique probably does not attain its full potential in the hands of a beginning therapist) and of biasing our results in favor of behavior therapy (where it is possible that less experience is required to attain a minimal level of competence than in psychotherapy) (10, 11). Each therapist treated at least ten patients.

A list of stipulative definitions of each therapy was drawn up. This is presented in abbreviated form in Appendix 1. This list outlined which procedures were common to both therapies and which were allowable only within one or the other modality. The therapists approved these definitions and felt that they would not restrict them in their respective treatments. Tranquilizers were discouraged; they were used very rarely in either treatment group.

Each behavior therapist used a variety of behavioral techniques, including systematic desensitization, assertive training, and avoidance conditioning, which he tailored to the needs of each individual patient. Similarly, the psychotherapists used various analytically oriented techniques of short-term insight therapy.

Analyses of the two therapies using a variety of rating scales and other questionnaire measures will be reported in detail elsewhere (12). These data verify that the two groups of therapists were using quite different techniques, had formed different types of relationships with their patients, and were in fact doing in therapy very much what they said they did.

Behavior therapy and psychotherapy patients received four months of usually weekly hour-long therapy (an average of 13.2 and 14.2 sessions, respectively). Fees were paid through the outpatient clinic according to its usual sliding scale.

Waiting List

The control patients were told that they would be placed in treatment but that because there were currently no openings in the clinic there would be a waiting period of no more than four months. During this waiting period they were contacted by telephone every few weeks by a research assistant, who asked how they were getting along and assured them that they had not been forgotten and would be placed in treatment as soon as there was a vacancy. They were also told that if there was a crisis they could call on the psychiatrist who interviewed them initially or the emergency unit of the department at any time. They thus received a moderate amount of nonspecific therapy that aroused hope, expectation of help, and the relief afforded by an initial interview.

Follow-Up

The patients were reinterviewed and reassessed by the original interviewers after four months and after one year. These assessors were blind as to type of therapy in most cases, but a few patients inadvertently gave clues to their therapist's identity.

The assessor rated the target symptoms as before on an absolute severity scale and on a comparative rating scale. He also made a rating of overall improvement. Both patient and assessor rated work, social, sexual, and overall adjustment. The SSIAM was administered again.

A comparison of outcome ratings did not reveal bias by an assessor toward any group. Symptomatic self-assessments by the patients correlated well with the assessor ratings ($r = .66$ by Pearson product-moment correlation).

Two years after the initial assessment, a research assistant contacted as many patients as possible to rate target symptom severity and take SSIAM measures.

RESULTS

Four-Month Follow-Up

At four months all three groups had significantly improved on their three target symptoms (See Table 41–1), but the psychotherapy and behavior therapy groups improved equally well and significantly more than those on the waiting list (See Table 41–2).

Patients treated by behavior therapy improved significantly on both work adjustment and social adjustment (See Table 41–3). Psychotherapy patients showed marginally significant improvement on work and no significant improvement in social functioning. Patients placed on the waiting list had significantly improved in social adjustment and marginally in work adjustment. However, analyses of variance indicated that the amount of improvement shown by the three groups was not significantly different either for work ($F = 1.46$, $p > .10$) or social adjustment ($F = .55$, $p > .10$).

On a rating scale of overall improvement, 93% of the behavior therapy patients in contrast to 77% of the psychotherapy and waiting list patients were considered either improved or recovered ($x^2 = 3.93$, $p < .05$). Thus all treatments (including placement on the waiting list) were highly successful, but behavior therapy was significantly more successful in terms of the traditional global measure of improvement.

The amount of improvement was independent of the sex of the patient, the amount of experience of the therapist, and the severity of the neurosis, except that the anxiety of women, especially those with high neuroticism scores, improved more than that of men.

A few patients whose initially reported symptoms had not improved in four months reported additional symptoms that were either new or had been too trivial to report at the initial interview. However, no patient in any group whose original problems had substantially improved reported new symptoms. Thus there was no evidence of symptom substitution.

TABLE 41-1

*Interviewer Ratings of Severity of Three Target Symptoms for Ninety-two Patients at Initial Interview and Follow-Up**

Group	Rating at Initial Interview		Rating at Four Months			Rating at One Year		
	Mean	SD	Mean	SD	Significance**	Mean	SD	Significance**
Behavior therapy*								
Total group (N = 29)	8.79	1.36	4.52	1.89	$p < .001$	3.83	2.59	$p < .001$
Patients who obtained no further therapy after four months (N = 14)	8.85	1.66	4.85	1.99	$p < .001$	4.14	2.30	$p < .001$
Psychotherapy								
Total group (N = 30)	9.13	1.65	5.27	2.70	$p < .001$	4.90	3.54	$p < .001$
Patients who obtained no further therapy after four months (N = 21)	9.14	1.71	4.90	2.32	$p < .001$	4.24	3.18	$p < .001$
Waiting list								
Total group (N = 33)	8.82	2.01	6.45	2.84	$p < .001$	5.45	2.95	$p < .001$
Patients who obtained no therapy after four months (N = 14)	8.43	1.76	5.57	2.38	$p < .001$	5.29	2.77	$p < .01$

*The scores represent the sum of the severities of the three target symptoms, each rated on a 5-point scale (4 = severe, 3 = moderate, 2 = mild, 1 = doubtful or trivial, and 0 = absent).

**Represents change from initial interview (by two-tailed t tests).

***The numbers represent the number of patients who had complete ratings on all three assessments.

TABLE 41-2

Univariate and Multivariate F *Values for Comparisons*
Among Treatment Groups and Control Group
on Changes in Target Symptoms at Four-Month Follow-Up

Groups Compared	Univariate F Values			Multivariate F Value
	Symptom 1	Symptom 2	Symptom 3	
Behavior therapy versus waiting list	9.0148*	8.0513*	9.5708*	4.9292*
Psychotherapy versus waiting list	12.1725*	6.7628**	4.6018***	4.5742**
Behavior therapy versus psychotherapy	.2374	.0563	.9027	.5184

*$p < .005$;
**$p < .01$.
***$p < .05$.

One-Year Follow-Up

One year after the initial interview all three groups of patients had significantly improved symptomatically since their initial assessment (See Table 41–1). The behavior therapy patients had improved significantly more on their target symptoms ($p < .05$) than the waiting list patients ($t = 2.18$, $p < .05$), but the psychotherapy patients had not. These data excluded two behavior therapy patients whom it was impossible to interview. (They were informally known to have improved.)

Both treated groups were significantly improved on work and social adjustment at the end of one year, but the control group was no longer significantly improved on work adjustment (See Table 41–3); there were no significant intergroup differences in amount of adjustment improvement.

However, after four months on the waiting list, fourteen of the control patients no longer felt that they required therapy; those who did were assigned to senior residents, most of whom practiced analytically oriented insight therapy. In addition, many of those who had received treatment wanted and received small amounts of additional therapy, in most cases with their original therapists, between the four-month and one-year interviews. Thus fifteen behavior therapy patients averaged a further 10.1 sessions and nine psychotherapy patients averaged 19.3 sessions.

The varying amount and type of therapy between four months and one year tended to make comparisons between the original groups less valid than comparisons with those who received no treatment after four months. These latter patients, who did not differ from their total groups in any pretreatment or change measures, showed significant and equal

TABLE 41-3

Mean Scores on SSIAM Factors for Treatment Groups and Control Group at Initial Interview and Follow-Up

Group	Score Initial Interview		Score at Four Months				Score at One Year			
	Work	Social Adjustment	Work	Significance	Social Adjustment	Significance	Work	Significance	Social Adjustment	Significance
Behavior therapy*										
Total group (N = 29)	4.02	3.31	2.98	$p < .001$**	2.71	$p < .05$**	2.59	$p < .001$**	2.27	$p < .001$**
Patients who obtained no further therapy after four months (N = 14)	3.98	3.56	2.79	$p < .05$**	2.64	$p < .05$**	2.54	$p < .05$**	2.73	$p < .05$***
Psychotherapy										
Total group (N = 30)	3.42	3.10	2.85	$p < .05$***	2.72	n.s.	2.15	$p < .001$**	2.12	$p < .001$**
Patients who obtained no further therapy after four months (N = 21)	3.07	3.15	2.67	n.s.	2.48	$p < .05$**	2.14	$p < .05$**	1.92	$p < .001$**
Waiting list*										
Total group (N = 30)	3.49	3.52	2.81	$p < .05$***	2.78	$p < .01$**	2.85	n.s.	2.77	$p < .05$**
Patients who obtained no therapy after four months (N = 11)	4.04	3.78	2.57	$p < .05$**	2.64	$p < .05$**	2.80	$p < .05$***	2.38	$p < .05$***

*The numbers represent the number of patients who had complete ratings on all three assessments.
**By two-tailed t tests.
***By one-tailed t test only.

symptomatic, social, and work improvement at one year (See Table 41–1 and 41–3).

Two-Year Follow-Up

Two years after the initial interview, sixty-one patients were interviewed by a research assistant. All groups had either maintained their status or continued to improve in all areas. Unfortunately, the psychotherapy patients who could be reassessed at two years proved to be those who had already shown the most improvement at one year. Because of this sample bias, a between-group comparison with the behavior therapy and waiting list patients, who were representative of their original samples, was not feasible.

DISCUSSION

There was very little difference between the two active treatment groups in amount of improvement, although it is tempting to argue that behavior therapy was somewhat more effective than psychotherapy. On a global measure of improvement, behavior therapy proved significantly better at four months than either psychotherapy or being on a waiting list. Moreover, behavior therapy patients had significantly improved on all three specific measures at four months, while psychotherapy patients had not improved in social adjustment.

At one year, patients originally treated by behavior therapy but not those originally treated by psychotherapy showed greater improvement than waiting list patients in reduction of the severity of target symptoms. The conclusion that behavior therapy is therefore more effective is tempered by the finding of no significant difference between groups in the amount of improvement in social adjustment and the fact that the one-year comparison of the two groups was confounded by treatment after four months. We conclude that there is no clear evidence for the superiority of behavior therapy over psychotherapy.

However, behavior therapy is clearly a generally useful treatment. Both active treatments were found effective in treating specific symptoms and in improving the patient's reported ability to cope with life. Our data do not support the view that although behavior therapy may have a short-term or limited value in dealing with specific symptoms, only deeper and more analytic treatment can produce general change in the patient by treating the underlying causes of symptoms as well as the symptoms themselves.

CONCLUSIONS

Behavior therapy produced significantly more overall improvement at four months than psychotherapy. However, this is a very general subjective measure and there was no significant difference between psychotherapy and behavior therapy on any other measure at any other time.

At four months both treated groups had improved significantly more than the waiting list group on target symptoms but not in general adjustment. This is impressive in view of the great improvement shown by patients receiving the minimal treatment of placement on a waiting list.

All groups improved in general adjustment, but at four months this improvement was clearly significant only for the behavior therapy and control groups.

At one year, behavior therapy patients but not psychotherapy patients showed significantly more symptomatic improvement than did control patients. However, this result may be confounded by the fact that differing amounts of further treatment were given after the four-month study period. There were no differences between those who received no further treatment after four months.

All groups maintained or continued their improvement between four months, one year, and two years regardless of whether or not further treatment was received during this period.

REFERENCES

1. GELDER, M. G. and MARKS, I. M.:   Severe agoraphobia: a controlled prospective trial of behavior therapy. *Br. J. Psychiatry* 112:304–319, 1966.

2. GELDER, M. G.,   MARKS, I. M. and WOLFF, H. H.:   Desensitization and psychotherapy in the treatment of phobic states: a controlled inquiry. *Br. J. Psychiatry* 113:53–73, 1967.

3. DI LORETO, A. O.:   *Comparative Psychotherapy: An Experimental Analysis.* Chicago, Aldine-Atherton, 1971.

4. PAUL, G. L.:   *Insight vs. Desensitization in Psychotherapy.* Stanford, Calif., Stanford University Press, 1966.

5. PAUL, G. L.:   Insight vs. desentization in psychotherapy two years after termination. *J. Consult. Psychol.* 31:333–348, 1967.

6. SLOANE, R. B., CRISTOL, A. H., PEPERNIK, M. C. et al.:   Role preparation and expectation of improvement in psychotherapy. *J. Nerv. Ment. Dis.* 150:18–26, 1970.

7. HOEHN-SARIC, R., FRANK, J. D., IMBER, S. D., et al.:   Systematic preparation of patients for psychotherapy: I. Effects on therapy behavior and outcome. *J. Psychiatr. Res.* 2:267–281, 1964.

8. GURLAND, B. J., YORKSTON, N. J., STONE, A. R., et al.:   The structured

and scaled interview to assess maladjustment (SSIAM): I. Description, rationale, and development. *Arch. Gen. Psychiatry* 27:259–263, 1972.

9. GURLAND, B. J., YORKSTON, N. J., GOLDBERG, K., et al.: The structured and scaled interview to assess maladjustment (SSIAM): II. Factor analysis, reliability, and validity. *Arch. Gen. Psychiatry* 27:264–269, 1972.

10. HARTLAGE, L. C.: Subprofessional therapists' use of reinforcement versus traditional psychotherapeutic techniques with schizophrenics. *J. Consult. Clin. Psychol.* 34:181–183, 1970.

11. PATTERSON, V., LEVENE, H., and BREGER, L.: Treatment and training outcomes with two time-limited therapies. *Arch. Gen. Psychiatry* 25:161–167, 1971.

12. SLOANE, R. B., STAPLES, F. R., CRISTOL, A. H., et al.: *Psychotherapy vs. Behavior Therapy.* Commonwealth Fund Publication. Cambridge, Mass., Harvard University Press, 1975.

APPENDIX I

Techniques Characteristic of Behavior Therapy and Psychotherapy

CONTRASTING ELEMENTS

Specific advice is given frequently by behavior therapist; given infrequently by psychotherapist.

Transference interpretation is avoided by behavior therapist; may be given by psychotherapist.

Interpretation of resistance is not used by behavior therapist; used by psychotherapist.

Report of dreams: behavior therapist shows polite lack of interest; psychotherapist may use in treatment.

Relaxation training is directly undertaken by behavior therapist; occurs only as an indirect consequence of a relaxed atmosphere in psychotherapy.

Desensitization is directly undertaken by behavior therapist; occurs only as an indirect consequence of discussing problems in a relaxed atmosphere in psychotherapy.

Practical retraining is directly undertaken by behavior therapist; not emphasized by psychotherapist.

Assertive training is directly undertaken and encouraged in everyday life by behavior therapist; only indirectly encouraged in everday life by psychotherapist, but assertive or aggressive speech permitted in psychotherapy session.

Report of symptoms: interest is shown by behavior therapist, who may explain them biologically; discouraged by psychotherapist, who may explain them symbolically.

Childhood memories: behavior therapist usually takes history as such; psychotherapist usually looks for further memories.

Aversion (e.g., electric shock) may be used by behavior therapist; not used by psychotherapist.

Role training may be used by behavior therapist; not used by psychotherapist.

Repetition of motor habits may be used by behavior therapist; not used by psychotherapist.

ELEMENTS IN COMMON

Both therapists may take a biographical psychiatric history; formulate the patient's problems; attempt to reconstruct possible original causes of the disorder; look for continuing causes of the difficulty; aim to produce a change that benefits the patient, such as reducing subjective complaints or behavior that distrubs the patient or others; correct misconceptions; elucidate objectives; and attempt to change others, e.g., family, employer, doctor.

Based on a paper read at a New Research session at the 125th annual meeting of the American Psychiatric Association, Dallas, Tex., May 1–5, 1972. This work was supported by grant MH–15493 from the National Institute of Mental Health.

The authors would like to thank Drs. Herbert Freed, Arnold A. Lazarus, Michael Serber, Jay Urban, Raul H. Vispo, and Joseph Wolpe for their help in the completion of this study. They would also like to thank Ms. Olga Aigner and Ms. Diana Horvitz for their help as research assistants.

NAME INDEX

SUBJECT INDEX